MW01252798

PSYCHOLOGY OF DECISION MAKING IN EDUCATION, BEHAVIOR AND HIGH RISK SITUATIONS

1611-01

PSYCHOLOGY OF DECISION MAKING IN EDUCATION, BEHAVIOR AND HIGH RISK SITUATIONS

JEANINE A. ELSWORTH

EDITOR

GUELPH HUMBER LIBRARY
205 Humber College Blvd
Toronto, ON   M9W 5L7

Nova Science Publishers, Inc.

New York

Copyright © 2007 by Nova Science Publishers, Inc.

All rights reserved. No part of this book may be reproduced, stored in a retrieval system or transmitted in any form or by any means: electronic, electrostatic, magnetic, tape, mechanical photocopying, recording or otherwise without the written permission of the Publisher.

For permission to use material from this book please contact us:
Telephone 631-231-7269; Fax 631-231-8175
Web Site: http://www.novapublishers.com

NOTICE TO THE READER

The Publisher has taken reasonable care in the preparation of this book, but makes no expressed or implied warranty of any kind and assumes no responsibility for any errors or omissions. No liability is assumed for incidental or consequential damages in connection with or arising out of information contained in this book. The Publisher shall not be liable for any special, consequential, or exemplary damages resulting, in whole or in part, from the readers' use of, or reliance upon, this material.

Independent verification should be sought for any data, advice or recommendations contained in this book. In addition, no responsibility is assumed by the publisher for any injury and/or damage to persons or property arising from any methods, products, instructions, ideas or otherwise contained in this publication.

This publication is designed to provide accurate and authoritative information with regard to the subject matter covered herein. It is sold with the clear understanding that the Publisher is not engaged in rendering legal or any other professional services. If legal or any other expert assistance is required, the services of a competent person should be sought. FROM A DECLARATION OF PARTICIPANTS JOINTLY ADOPTED BY A COMMITTEE OF THE AMERICAN BAR ASSOCIATION AND A COMMITTEE OF PUBLISHERS.

LIBRARY OF CONGRESS CATALOGING-IN-PUBLICATION DATA
Psychology of decision making in education, behavior, and high risk situations / Jeanine A. Elsworth (editor).
    p. cm.
Includes bibliographical references and index.
ISBN-13: 978-1-60021-933-7 (hardcover)
ISBN-10: 1-60021-933-0 (hardcover)
1. Decision making. 2. Risk-taking (Psychology) 3. Education. I. Elsworth, Jeanine A.

BF448.P97 2007
153.8'3--dc22
            2007027835

Published by Nova Science Publishers, Inc. ✦ New York

CONTENTS

PREFACE

In a fast-moving world, the necessity of making decisions, and preferably good ones, has become even more difficult. One reason is the variety and number of choices perhaps available which often are not presented or understood. Alternatives are often unclear and complex paths to them confusing and misleading. Thus the process of decision making itself requires analysis on an ongoing basis. Decision making is often made based on cultural factors whereas the best alternative might be quite different. The subject touches ethics aspects as well as psychological considerations. This new book presents important research on the psychology of decision making related to education, behavior and high risk situations.

Expert Commentary - The phenomena and facts of decision-making are closely related to our daily life, and the what, how and why of our psychological responses during the course of this process have fascinated psychologists throughout academic history. This commentary suggests the potential of qualitative approaches to research into the psychology of decision-making, and proposes a 6Rs framework to ensure good practice in the preparation and implementation of these studies. Finally, existing research should be recognized, and future researchers should be encouraged to consider the ability of qualitative inquiry to enrich our understanding of decision-making and other areas of psychology.

Chapter 1 - This chapter demonstrates how biases produced by verbal comparisons (Choplin & Hummel, 2002) might produce a variety of phenomena in the psychology of judgment and decision making. The biases produced by verbal comparisons cause people to overestimate the importance of small differences and underestimate the importance of large differences. Simulations will demonstrate that overestimating the importance of small differences and underestimating the importance of large differences from a reference point (default value, status quo, etc.) would produce s-shaped evaluation functions. Simulations will also demonstrate that overestimating the importance of small differences and underestimating the importance of large differences from other contextual stimuli would produce distribution-density effects (often called frequency effects). Because large differences are underestimated, when the variance in people's unbiased estimates is large as in anchoring effects, these biases will often look like assimilation effects. Biases produced by verbalized social comparisons would also overestimate the importance of small differences and underestimate the importance of large differences so that moderate downward comparisons will produce higher evaluations of the self than will extreme downward comparisons and moderate upward comparisons will produce lower evaluations of the self than will extreme upward comparisons. Comparison strategies might also help explain decoy effects such as asymmetric dominance effects and phantom decoy effects. Testable and falsifiable assumptions of this model are described thereby laying a foundation for future empirical research.

Chapter 2 – Education systems must develop the ability to change in order to cope with the goals set by society. The education system today needs to prove its effectiveness. Today's society demands that education systems prove that their methods and modes of operation are effective in achieving the goals of education as formulated by the society. These demands, of meeting standards set by the society, require that the education system develop instruments of evaluation and measurement, that it formulate more accurate methods for collecting and analyzing data and that it develop methods for reaching conclusions.

For this purpose the education system must undergo a process of change. Do we know how to generate a change in the education system? Are there mechanisms that can be used to generate change? Does education research afford us with tools to cope with these demands? Do the information and data supplied by education research join the body of knowledge that comprises an instrument for navigating in and improving the education system? Is education research identical to research in the other sciences in the ways in which it collects data and formulates theories, or does education research have unique goals, research methods and ways of reaching conclusions? If so, we must formulate the goals and determine the extent to which these goals are indeed achieved by education research. It is possible that the research approach in the field of education requires change. This requires the consolidation of a method which will enable the systematic achievement of this change.

Three terms which should be considered when referring to the process of consolidating a unique research approach in the field of education are:

1. Conceptualization: To what extent are the concepts which we use in the education research process indeed identical concepts?
2. Collecting and handling scientific knowledge: How can scientific knowledge be accumulated? How should the knowledge be handled and how should conclusions be reached?
3. Rules for constructing a body of knowledge: Can a body of knowledge be constructed? It may be appropriate to carry this out only for defined and limited sections in the field of education, whereas for others we will agree that they have no rules or that other rules apply to them .

It may be assumed that there exist factors in the education system which accelerate processes of change and others which decelerate these processes: Do we know which factors affect the process of change within the education system? What are the mechanisms which enable effective change? Can these changes be measured and evaluated?

Chapter 3 - Two studies were conducted to: (1) identify the motives underlying dangerous driving among young males, and (2) evaluate the hypothesized structural relations (both direct and indirect) between the personality construct of sensation seeking, perception of danger, and the identified motives in representing the way risky driving decisions are made. In study 1, exploratory factor analysis ($N = 200$) yielded a three-factor structure representing three major motives for risky driving – *driving fast/risk taking, confidence in one's driving skills, disrespect for traffic laws*. Confirmatory factor analysis ($N = 264$) confirmed and further clarified this factor structure in representing the motives underlying young males' driving behavior. In study 2, path analysis ($N = 384$) provided overall support for the 'fit' of the hypothesized model for dangerous driving. The implications of the findings with regard to the development of effective intervention strategies for dangerous driving among young males are discussed.

Chapter 4 - When making decisions between different options, we often consider two basic properties of these options, how risky they are and when they will occur. For example, we may choose to gamble or to wait for a larger reward. Decisions under risk refer to decisions among known probabilistic options, inter-temporal decisions refer to choices between options that will be realized at known future timepoints. Risky and inter-temporal decisions have been captured theoretically primarily by ecology and microeconomics but findings from behavioral economics, psychology and neuroscience often contradicted theoretical predictions. As a consequence, a wealth of more descriptive Models has emerged to explain the findings. A subset of these models has stressed the Similarities between risky and inter-temporal decisions. In this chapter the authors review both core theoretical approaches and empirical findings. The authors discuss possible explanations for discrepancies and identify key behavioral experiments.

Chapter 5 - This chapter describes a quantitative and qualitative needs assessment of a potential social service resource telephone program component among high risk youth who received the Project Towards No Drug Abuse (TND) classroom-based program (approximately 1-year earlier). Information was obtained to determine whether the targeted youth would be interested and receptive, or even need the information available from such a program. Results supported youths' overwhelming receptiveness of a social service referral program. The vast majority of respondents indicated a strong desire for resource and referral information on vocational, educational, recreational, transportation, and mental health and drug counseling. Participants' responses will be used to better structure and tailor our booster program. Further research is needed to investigate the effectiveness of the provision of social service resource information on drug use among emerging adults.

Chapter 6 - Decision-making under uncertainty is to be expected in natural environments. The greatest source of uncertainty comes from the passage of time, because time—and the environmental variability it allows to proceed—discounts the reliability of information on which decisions are based. Information is most reliable if it can be acted on immediately, but as time passes, an average of past values of the alternatives is the best estimate of current value, since this subjective process matches the objective tendency of biological variables to regress to their means. The most optimal strategy, therefore, would be to flexibly shift from tracking the most recent outcomes to averaging across them. A model, the temporal weighting rule (TWR), accomplishes this transition. The output of TWR is a dynamic average whose rate matches the rate of environmental change. The authors review empirical studies showing the wide range of species that make dynamic foraging decisions consistent with TWR, the special predictions the model makes and their accuracy, its ecological relevance, and the memory mechanisms it appears to rely on. The authors conclude that this quantitative model and its accompanying decision rule, or something very similar to it, solve the one of the commonest problems animals face in their variable environments. TWR minimizes decision error made under uncertainty.

Chapter 7 - Mountaineers can be viewed as "edgeworkers" who carefully manage risks in a voluntary activity that has the potential for serious injury or death. The authors maintain that the act of managing risks contributes to a sense of "flow" or transcendence that is a major psychological motivation for mountaineers. The authors also maintain that decisions associated with engaging in mountaineering as an activity, choices of particular types of mountaineering, locations, specific mountains, etc., and decisions associated with the act of mountaineering itself are conducted, implicitly or explicitly, within a rational multi-objective risk management framework. There are numerous risk-risk, risk-benefit, and benefit-cost tradeoffs throughout this risk management hierarchy. Furthermore, the risk management process is dynamic on a number of different levels. This rational process must be conducted within a context of uncertainty and fear, balanced with the sense of flow, and survival is sometimes at stake. Based on a review of the peer-reviewed, mountaineering association, and popular mountaineering literature, interviews with mountaineers and professional guides, and personal experience, the authors were unable to find any explicit exploration of dynamic hierarchical multi-objective risk management in voluntary, recreational risky activities. The psychology of decision-making in this context is also largely unexplored. Thus, the authors have developed a qualitative framework, based on Hammond, Raiffa, and Keeney's PrOACT framework, that helps elucidate and inform the decision-making processes associated with mountaineering. This approach may help mountaineers and society understand the psychology and tradeoffs associated with this activity, and may be useful for risk management of other types of risky recreational activities.

Chapter 8 - Results from many studies suggest that people violate the principles of rational choice in both the domain of gain and that of loss. People usually treat probabilities non-linearly by overweighting low and underweighting moderate and large probabilities. The violations of rational choice in human decision-making were disregarded by the normative point of view (von Neumann & Morgenstern's (1947) Expected Utility theory, EUT) until Allais (1953) and Kahneman and Tversky (Kahneman & Tversky, 1979; Tversky & Kahneman, 1981, 1986, 1992) developed a descriptive theoretical approach. In this chapter the authors investigate what might affect decision-makers' preferences with respect to described real-world protective prospects. People's precautionary ('protective') decision-making in the face of risk implies that they may judge and weight the probability of risky events in characteristic ways that deviate from both normative EUT and psychological descriptive theory of decision-making tested with abstract gambles. The following theoretical frameworks contribute to an explanation of protective decision-making: (a) experience-based decision-making models - past and immediate experience affect decision-makers' preferences (Dougherty et al., 1999; Frisch, 1993; Hertwig, Barron, Weber & Erev, 2004; Stewart, Chater & Brown, 2006; Tversky & Koehler, 1994) - and (b) accessibility of information (Higgins, 1996; Kahneman, 2003; Koriat & Levy-Sadot, 2001) - not all available observations of risks are equally accessible in memory.

Chapter 9 - Human and non-human animals essentially face the same problem: how to find the best long-term option within an environment that contains uncertainty for relevant items. Against this background the Iowa Gambling Task is a biologically relevant task to study such decision-making processes. The authors have recently developed an animal analogue of this task in rodents. An interesting cross-species finding in this task is that performance differences exist between males and females: while males tend to focus exclusively on long-term goals, females tend to balance short- and long-term interests, in other words males shift from exploration to exploitation, while females remain exploratory. In this chapter the authors try to answer the question what may underlie these differences between males and females, focussing thereby on humans. First, the authors discuss a neurobehavioural model for the Iowa Gambling Task. Subsequently, the authors look at the contribution of the menstrual cycle using both data from the literature and an experiment that the authors conducted. The authors conclude that the menstrual cycle is not a decisive factor for these differences to occur. Finally, the authors discuss the possibility that differences in choice behaviour may be due to differences in the general dynamics of neurotransmitter systems. Based on recent experiments the authors conclude that differences in brain serotonergic and dopaminergic activity may contribute to the observed behavioural differences.

Chapter 10 - Seeing in a box is a direct way of knowing what is in the box. There is evidence that 4-year-olds engage with the idea that equally reliable knowledge can also be gained indirectly, via inference. For example, if you see that there is one cup to each saucer, the cups can be put away out of sight, and just by counting the saucers you can infer the number of the uncounted cups. But sometimes it is possible to make an inferential mistake. The authors review recent evidence of young children's decisions on whether people know things via inference, and add new evidence to test a claim about a false inference test. That test involved asking children to judge another's knowledge through inference when the other was misled to input the wrong premises into her calculation. The finding that children performed better in the false inference task compared to the true inference task, together with their explicit verbal justifications, attests to children's theoretical understudying of inference. The authors suggest that that is the growth point for the next round of research.

Chapter 11 - The research attention paid to career decision making among Mainland Chinese adolescents and college students is of recent origin (e.g., Creed & Wong, 2006; Hampton, 2005). Such attention is mainly due to major changes in two salient policy areas by the government of the People's Republic of China (PRC). Firstly, the labor distribution system has been changed from a planned to a market economic system in which employers and graduates are free to choose each other. Before the middle of the 20th century in the PRC, college graduates had to accept the jobs assigned by the government. The freedom of selection by both employers and fresh employees has stimulated Chinese graduates to consider how to choose a suitable career for their own sake. Secondly, higher education in the PRC is undergoing a radical transformation from an elite to a mass system. The increasing intake of the youth into college had led to the sharp competition in the labor market, which in turn has produced the employment pressure among college graduates. The number of college graduates pouring into the labor market each year has increased from 1.15 million in 2001 to 4.2 million in 2006 (China Ministry of Education, 2005). Meanwhile, graduate school admission has become a top priority for the majority of undergraduates: 0.714 million senior undergraduates sat for the national entrance examination for a Master's Degree in January, 2007. Although the need for career and other counseling services in the Mainland is continually increasing (Zhang, Hu, & Pope, 2002), it is obvious that the antecedents of adaptive career decision making among Chinese postgraduates still remain unclear.

Chapter 12 - Choosing an appropriate mate is one of the most important decisions that any animal has to make. The traditional view in non-human systems is that animals are largely slaves to their genes and an individual's mate choice is handed down from their parents. However, in recent years it has become clear that many animals show active decision making in who to mate with and that females may copy mate preferences from other females in the population. In other words, females' mating decisions are affected by the current fashion in their population. Here, the authors explore whether "mate choice copying" occurs in a model monogamous mating system—the zebra finch. Females were given the opportunity to observe another female courting a particular type of male (the authors manipulated male appearance by placing small colored leg bands on each bird). In preference tests, our focal females significantly shifted their mate preferences towards the type of male that they had observed as being courted by other females. Therefore, female finches do seem to copy mate preferences, implying that there is social inheritance of information that fundamentally affects mating decisions. This is one of the first demonstrations of mate choice copying in any monogamous system and implies that many other birds may also use social information to affect their mating decisions. The authors need to rethink evolutionary models of mate choice and sexual selection incorporating this form of social decision making process.

Chapter 13 - The Monty Hall Dilemma (MHD) is a notorious brain-teaser where people have to decide whether switching to another option in a game is advantageous. Most adults erroneously believe that chances of winning remain equal or that they should stick to their original choice. The present study tested the impact of cognitive development on MHD reasoning to examine possible differences in the nature of the erroneous intuitions. Twelve to seventeen year old high school students were presented the MHD and selected one of three responses (switch, stick, or chances equal). Results showed that whereas maturation decreased adherence to the erroneous "stick with your first pick" belief, the "chances are equal" belief became more dominant with increasing age. Consistent with predictions, children who selected the latter response also scored better on a syllogistic reasoning task. Results further showed that twelve year old eighth graders selected the correct switching response more frequently than senior high school students. Implications for popular reasoning and decision making theories are discussed.

In: Psychology of Decision Making in Education
Editor: Jeanine A. Elsworth, pp. 1-5

ISBN: 978-1-60021-933-7
© 2006 Nova Science Publishers, Inc.

Expert Commentary A

NEW DIRECTIONS IN THE PSYCHOLOGY OF DECISION MAKING

Liqing Zhang[*]
Peking University

The psychology of decision making has been gaining more attention than before. It is growing rapidly. Three main perspectives of the psychology of decision making include the standpoint of cognitive psychology, the influence of social psychology and the viewpoint of neuropsychology. The present commentary reviews briefly these three major approaches to the psychology of decision making, points out their contributions and limitations, and suggests new directions.

The approach of cognitive psychology has produced a flourish of research and gained much attention from other fields, such as economics, political science, and management. From the viewpoint of cognitive psychology, decision making is considered an outcome of information processing. Early work addresses how people compare and weigh different dimensions of a choice set and then select the optimal (or best) outcome. Later research demonstrates that people may not be able to process all the relevant information related to a choice due to their limited cognitive resources. They may also be unwilling to process all the information related to a decision. For instance, people do not think and compare an extensive list of foods for breakfast, they may just pick a satisfactory option. Thus, people may stop their search for information when they encounter a satisfying option (Simon, 1957). Additionally, people may rely on heuristics and other rules of thumb in decision making. The application of heuristics reserves cognitive resources and adapts to its social environment in many situations (Gigerenzer & Goldstein, 1996). However, the application of heuristics also generates significant costs and produces decision errors (Tversky & Kahneman, 1974).

Another important contribution of the cognitive approach is the prospect theory (Kahneman & Tversky, 1979; Tversky & Kahneman, 2000). Prospect theory includes three major propositions. First, people perceive loss and gain differently. The pleasure people

[*] Correspondence to: Liqing Zhang, Department of Psychology, Peking University, 5 Yi-He-Yuan Avenue, Beijing, P. R. China, 100871. Email: liqingzhang@pku.edu.cn.

derive from a certain amount of gain is much less than the pain people derive from the same amount of loss. Second, whether an outcome is perceived as a gain or a loss depends on how the outcome is framed based on a reference point. The reference point may be determined by one's wealth, income, allowance, past experiences, future expectation or social comparison. Third, people are usually risk averse in the domain of gain and are risk seeking in the domain of loss. The prospect theory has been applied to different fields of decision making, such as marketing and management. A recent development of this standpoint is to apply prospect theory into new real life decisions through field experiments. Another development is to address limitations of the prospect theory. Researchers identify situations in which people are risk seeking in the domains of gain. For instance, if they had to choose between a sure gain of a penny and a 0.01% probability of attaining $100, most people may be willing to take the risk.

The major limitation of the perspective of cognitive psychology is that it neglects some important human motivations. Thus, practitioners often argue that these findings are different from the decision process in everyday life. Research on social psychology and decision making may have the potential to fill in the gap on motivations and choices.

The contribution of the approach of social psychology includes research on how fairness, emotion and self-control influence choices. First, people take fairness into consideration in their choices. Fairness puts a crucial constraint on profit maximization. For instance, restaurants usually do not raise their prices during popular hours, such as evenings on weekends because they worry that consumer may view such an opportunistic behavior to be unfair. Second, emotions influence choices. Research suggests that not only do emotions elicited by the choice situation impact judgment and decision making, but incidental emotions generated by sources irrelevant to the choice situation also influence the decision. Research has contributed to the field by examining the diverse effects of positive and negative emotions on choice. Recent research suggests that some emotions may have their specific effects. For instance, even though both anger and fear are negative emotions, anger leads to risk seeking, while fear produces risk aversion (Lerner & Keltner, 2001). A next step of the research on emotions and choices may address whether these specific emotions differ on systematic dimensions, such as arousal-calm, approach-avoidance, and examine how these different dimensions of emotions influences choices. Third, self-control influences an important aspect of decision making, intertemporal choices, which involve tradeoffs between costs and benefits at different times (Loewenstein, Read, & Baumeister, 2003). People often need to exert their self-control in stifling their immediate desire for short-term gain so as to achieve long-term benefits. For instance, dieters have to resist the temptation of tasty desserts in order to keep their body fit. People may override their desire for luxuries and save money for their children's education.

One major question that remains in the research on motivation and decision making is whether motivation influences decisions directly or motivation shapes behaviors through biased information processing. Encouraging progress has been made on how emotion shapes choices. Some research suggests that people ignore the probability of winning when they are under intense emotions (Loewenstein, Weber, Hsee, & Welch, 2001). The other research has focused on how emotion influences the perception of information (Schwarz, 1990). The theoretical model on how emotion or motivation shapes behavior deserves more attention (Baumeister, Vohs, DeWall, & Zhang 2007; Zajonc, 1980).

The study on neuropsychology and decision making is an emerging topic (Eshel, Nelson, Blair, Pine, & Ernst, 2007). The advantage of meuropsychology is that it provides an objective measure of mental processes. However, this approach is constrained by the fact that the structure and function of the human brain is still a mystery. This approach has contributed more to confirming available theories using a new method than to construct new theories.

The psychology of decision making includes three major approaches –cognitive, social, and neurological perspectives, each has contributed to the field and gains much attention in the scientific disciplines beyond psychology. The crucial question is what the next step of the psychology of decision making is. The progress of a general theory may be needed. In the past decades, research on psychology and decision making has benefited from inspiring theories, such as prospect theory. In the recent thirty years, research has progressed more in generating middle-level theories than constructing integrative theories. The impressive middle-level theories, elaborated experimental techniques, and abundant empirical findings have accumulated building blocks for new theories. The emergence of new integrative theories may contribute greatly to the further development of this field.

What perspectives have the potential to integrate the previous findings and provide general theories? First, a better understanding of the attention process may offer an integrative theory on the psychology of decision making. Attention is an operational phase of information processing. Recent research suggests that attention is related to the platform of all sorts of cognitive activities—working memory (Engle, Tuholski, Laughlin, & Conway, 1999). Since the resource of attention is limited, attention may explain application of heuristics in decision making. The limited resource of attention may also explain bounded rationality.

Second, an understanding of the impact of self-esteem on choices may facilitate the formation of an integrative theory on motivation and decision making. People are motivated to defend, maintain and enhance their self-esteem (Baumeister, 1988; Greenwald, 1980; Steele, 1988; Taylor & Brown, 1988). In social psychology, a large amount of research has documented the importance of self-esteem in shaping goals, emotion and cognition. Self-esteem may affect why people care about fairness, when and why people experience intense emotions, and how they choose options that are important to their identity. Recent research has started to explore how self-esteem influences individual choices and interpersonal negotiations (Larrick, 1992; Zhang & Baumeister, 2006; Zhang, 2004; Zhang, 2007). Future research should construct a theory on the role of self-esteem in decision making.

Researchers may find other viewpoints in constructing integrative theories. The science, psychology of decision making, may have a bright future if a few new breakthrough theories are proposed.

AUTHOR NOTE

I want to thank Huiling Yu for her comments on an earlier draft of this paper.

REFERENCES

Baumeister, R. F. (1998). The self. In. G. T. Gilbert, S. T. Fiske, & G. Lindzey (Eds.), *The Handbook of Social Psychology(Vol.1, 4th Ed., pp.680-740);*. New York, NY: Oxford University Press.

Baumeister, R. F., Vohs, K. D., DeWall, C. N., & Zhang, L. (2007). How emotion shapes behavior: Feedback, anticipation, and reflection, rather than direct causation? *Personality and Social Psychology Review, 11, 167-203.*

Engle, R. W., Tuholski, S. W.., Laughlin, J. E. & Conway, A. R. A (1999). Working memory, short-term memory, and general fluid intelligence: A latent-variable approach. Journal of Experimental Psychology: General, 128(3), 309-331

Eshel, N., Nelson, E. E., Blair, R. J., Pine, D. S., & Ernst, M. (2007). Neural substrates of choice selection in adults and adolescents: Development of the ventrolateral prefrontal and anterior cingulate cortices. Neuropsychologia, 45, 1270-1279.

Gigerenzer, G., & Goldstein, D. G. (1996). Reasoning the fast and frugal way: Models of bounded rationality. *Psychological Review*, 103, 650-669.

Greenwald, A. G. (1980). The totalitarian ego: Fabrication and revision of personal history. *American Psychologist, 35,* 603-618.

Kahneman, D., & Tversky, A. (1979). Prospect theory: An analysis of decisions under risk. *Econometrica, 47,* 263-291.

Kahneman, D., & Tversky, A. (2000). Choices, values, and frames. New York, NY, US Cambridge University Press.

Larrick, R. P. (1993). Motivational factors in decision theories: The role of self-protection. *Psychological Bulletin*, 113, 440-450.

Lerner, J. S., & Keltner, D. (2001). Fear, anger, and risk. *Journal of Personality and Social Psychology,* 81, 146-159.

Loewenstein, G.., Read, D., & Baumeister, R. (2003).*Time and decision: Economic and psychological perspectives on intertemporal choice.* New York, NY, US : Russell Sage Foundation.

Loewenstein, G. F., Weber, E. U., Hsee, C. K., & Welch, N. (2001). Risk as feelings. *Psychological Bulletin, 127,* 267-286.

Schwarz, N., (1990). Feelings as information: Informational and motivational functions of affective states. In E. T. Higgins, & R. M. Sorrentino (Eds.) *Handbook of motivation and cognition: Foundations of social behavior*, (Vol. 2., pp. 527-561) New York, NY, US : Guilford Press.

Simon, H. A. (1957). *Models of man; social and rational.* Oxford, England Wiley.

Steele, C. M. (1988). The psychology of self-affirmation: Sustaining the integrity of the self.(In L. Berkowitz (Ed.), *Advances in experimental social psychology* (Vol. 21, pp. 261—302). New York: Academic Press.

Taylor, S. E., & Brown, J. D. (1988). Illusion and well-being: A social psychological perspective on mental health. *Psychological Bulletin, 103,* 193-210.

Tversky, A., & Kahneman, D. (1974). Judgment under uncertainty: Heuristics and biases. *Science*, 185, 1124-1131.

Zajonc, R. B. (1980). Feeling and thinking: Preferences need no inference. *American Psychologist, 35,* 151-175.

Zhang, L., & Baumeister, R. F. (2006). Your money or your self-esteem: Threatened egotism promotes costly entrapment in losing endeavors. *Personality and Social Psychology Bulletin, 32*, 881-893.

Zhang, L. (2004). Self-esteem boost reduces responders' rejections in the ultimatum bargaining game. *Dissertation.* Case Western Reserve University.

Zhang, L. (2007). An exchange theory on money and self-esteem. *Working paper.* Peking University.

In: Psychology of Decision Making in Education
Editor: Jeanine A. Elsworth, pp. 7-10

ISBN: 978-1-60021-933-7
© 2006 Nova Science Publishers, Inc.

Expert Commentary B

PSYCHOLOGY OF DECISION-MAKING: 6RS FOR QUALITATIVE RESEARCH METHODOLOGICAL DEVELOPMENT

Zenobia C. Y. Chan[1,*]

RN, Master of Primary Health Care, Assistant Professor
Centre for Health Education and Health Promotion
School of Public Health,Faculty of Medicine
[1]The Chinese University of Hong Kong, Hong Kong

ABSTRACT

The phenomena and facts of decision-making are closely related to our daily life, and the what, how and why of our psychological responses during the course of this process have fascinated psychologists throughout academic history. This commentary suggests the potential of qualitative approaches to research into the psychology of decision-making, and proposes a 6Rs framework to ensure good practice in the preparation and implementation of these studies. Finally, existing research should be recognized, and future researchers should be encouraged to consider the ability of qualitative inquiry to enrich our understanding of decision-making and other areas of psychology. (97 Words)

COMMENTARY

Decision-making occurs in, and affects, our daily life in many ways: it allows us to choose the most appropriate actions or strategies for a particular event or task in order to attain the best outcome; it allows us to be flexible in an ever-changing world, reacting quickly to both routine and specific life matters in a timely manner; and it allows us to enhance our chances of success and minimize our chances of failure by doing things in a smart and correct manner as much as possible. In light of the importance of this process, many disciplines have

[*] Correspondence to: [1]The Chinese University of Hong Kong, Hong KongE-mail: zehippo@yahoo.com

put great effort into contributing to our knowledge of it and making it more transparent. Psychology is one of the most active and committed of these disciplines, making a continuous effort to explore this significant research area: humans' psychological responses toward decision-making in various cultures, when faced with various life events.

This commentary has two main objectives: to state the importance of adopting qualitative research approaches when studying the psychology of decision-making related issues; and to suggest a "6Rs framework" for quality psychological research which can reveal the what, why and how of participants' experience with decision-making in their individual contextual circumstances. Naturalistic and interpretive approaches can offer new insight into this process.

Stealing is prohibited and protecting everyone's property is stressed in this civilized world. The same is true in academic realms, where acknowledgement of any ideas, theories, research contributions and research methods suggested by any inventors, authors, scholars and researchers is a pivotal means for us to express respect and recognition of original claims and discoveries in advancing knowledge to benefit human welfare. However, in qualitative research in psychology, it seems that the importance of accreditation of our colleagues' ideas on the development and modification of an approach to exploring social facts, human behaviors or experiences in relation to health issues has not been well supported, and it may be time for an in-depth and constructive discussion. It is understandable why qualitative inquiry and its methods are perceived as secondary to quantitative research, due to the politics of methodological development. Applying standards and rigor to all aspects of research, including collection and analysis of data and publication of results, in the realm of the psychology of decision-making, are the issues I wish to draw to our readers' attention, by using some thought-provoking ideas from Dr. Morse's editorial in Qualitative Health Research (Vol. 16, 1) titled "The Politics of Developing Research Methods."

When qualitative researchers set out to develop research methods, political considerations should be discussed, including:

(A) Who is the inventor or moderator of this research method?
(B) Where has this research method been mentioned in an extensive and relevant literature review?
(C) Where was this research method adopted?
(D) In what context and setting was this research method conducted?
(E) What advantages and disadvantages of this research method have been documented?
(F) What of interest about the process and outcome of this research method has been noted?

As a concrete action plan to answering these questions, I suggest the "6Rs:"

- The first R - Reference others' work. This is the primary step to crediting and honoring our colleagues' contributions. Originality has been stressed as a top priority of scholarship. This is not only a matter of hard work; it is a matter of wisdom, intuition, creativity, passion for knowledge, and sensitivity in human encounters. Therefore, when someone is going to suggest, adopt or modify a research method, they should review the related literature thoroughly and properly reference others' ideas that have affected their conceptualization and implementation of such methods. I think only when their research methods are so innovative and have truly never before been mentioned or employed, can the creator be rightfully proud of developing such methods. Otherwise, it is shameful to call the method their own creation.

- The second R - Reflexivity is a crucial mental process for every researcher throughout the entire research process. They should reflect on their own assumptions, biases, knowledge base and interpretations which might affect the development of research methods. We must check in with our hearts and minds to determine whether the research method really has been developed by ourselves without any inspiration or input from other people or not.

- The third R – Replication is another issue for handling the politics of development of research methods. The research results might not be the same when conducted by other researchers due to the subjectivity of analyzing and interpreting data, but the clear and systematic documentation of each research method and process can ensure replication when the same research method is employed by other researchers in other settings. So, justification for using one or more research methods should be provided. A detailed description of how to implement the research process should be offered as well.

- The fourth R – Remarks. This is a significant role for an editor or reviewer when a colleague submits a paper for peer review. Critical and frank reading can help spot any research methods that have not been referenced, if these methods are known to the editor or reviewer from their own previous experience but perhaps not to the writer of the paper. Some researchers do not have certain knowledge about their suggested research methods, and may end up claiming the methods for their own unintentionally.

- The fifth R – Reproach must be applied to anyone who does not reference other researchers' methods properly. Whether someone's use of another's method without giving due credit was intentional or not, there is no excuse for tolerating any attempt to claim a method as one's own when it is not. The worst case -- consciously using another's ideas without quoting the author – is a grave offence.

- The sixth R - Registration of one's proposed research methods. Registration systems or organizations could be developed to record qualitative research methods in an international data base. Registering research methods can provide comprehensive information about who, when, where, what and how such methods were developed. It also admits the importance of research ethics not for the participants' benefit only, but for all qualitative researchers. It allows us to learn about who they are, what their research methods are, where they adopted their research methods, who their participants were and how the research methods have been implemented. As such, I sincerely call for an international inquiry to consider how we can register our methods and categorize them both historically and by health topic.

The 6Rs is a framework proposed for researchers or scholars who are interested in using a qualitative approach to research into the psychology of decision-making. The key issue of the politics of research method development should be revisited. I deeply believe that the simple pursuit of being published is inadequate. It is time for us to remember the importance of integrity as academics, researchers and scholars and that we should be true to ourselves about the origins of the research methods stated in our studies – just as we teach our children that honesty is one of the primary responsibilities of every human being. Integrity and the 6Rs offer a guide that can help us remain aware of the politics of the development of research methods, and one that will hopefully safeguard both originality and ethics.

REFERENCES

Morse, J. M. (2006). Editorial –. The Politics of Developing Research Methods. *Qualitative Health Research, 16(1)*, 3-4.

In: Psychology of Decision Making in Education
Editor: Jeanine A. Elsworth, pp. 11-40

ISBN: 978-1-60021-933-7
© 2006 Nova Science Publishers, Inc.

Chapter 1

TOWARD A COMPARISON-INDUCED DISTORTION THEORY OF JUDGMENT AND DECISION MAKING

Jessica M. Choplin[*]
DePaul University

ABSTRACT

This chapter demonstrates how biases produced by verbal comparisons (Choplin & Hummel, 2002) might produce a variety of phenomena in the psychology of judgment and decision making. The biases produced by verbal comparisons cause people to overestimate the importance of small differences and underestimate the importance of large differences. Simulations will demonstrate that overestimating the importance of small differences and underestimating the importance of large differences from a reference point (default value, status quo, etc.) would produce s-shaped evaluation functions. Simulations will also demonstrate that overestimating the importance of small differences and underestimating the importance of large differences from other contextual stimuli would produce distribution-density effects (often called frequency effects). Because large differences are underestimated, when the variance in people's unbiased estimates is large as in anchoring effects, these biases will often look like assimilation effects. Biases produced by verbalized social comparisons would also overestimate the importance of small differences and underestimate the importance of large differences so that moderate downward comparisons will produce higher evaluations of the self than will extreme downward comparisons and moderate upward comparisons will produce lower evaluations of the self than will extreme upward comparisons. Comparison strategies might also help explain decoy effects such as asymmetric dominance effects and phantom decoy effects. Testable and falsifiable assumptions of this model are described thereby laying a foundation for future empirical research.

[*] Research supported by a grant from the National Science Foundation (NSF-0621664) awarded to Jessica M. Choplin. Correspondence to: Jessica M. Choplin; Department of Psychology; DePaul University; 2219 North Kenmore Avenue; Chicago, IL 60614-3504; jchoplin@depaul.edu

INTRODUCTION

Hedonic and other types of attribute evaluations have wide ranging implications for decision-making and the consequences of those decisions for well-being. Evaluations of price and other consumer-product attributes affect the decisions people make as consumers and, in turn, how satisfied they are with the products they buy (e.g., Choplin & Hummel, 2002; Choplin & Hummel, 2005; Huber, Payne, & Puto, 1982; Wedell & Pettibone, 1996). Evaluations of people's own personal attributes—often informed by social comparisons (e.g., Festinger, 1954; Lavine, Sweeney, & Wagner, 1999; Morse & Gergen, 1970; Mussweiler, 2003; Wedell & Parducci, 2000)—affect how people see themselves on any personal attribute one might imagine. Evaluations of food intake (taste, calories, portion size, Riskey, Parducci, & Beauchamp, 1979; Schifferstein & Frijters, 1992; Wansink, 2004) affect people's dietary decisions and all of the consequences of those decisions. People's subjective evaluations of their own well-being (i.e., how happy they see themselves, Kahneman, 1999; Parducci, 1995; Schwarz & Strack, 1999) often affect actual well-being.

In this chapter, I present an introduction to a model of attribute evaluation, comprehension, memory, and estimation wherein verbal, language-expressible comparisons of attribute values systematically bias how people evaluate, comprehend, remember, and estimate the compared attribute values (comparison-induced distortion theory, CID theory, Choplin & Hummel, 2002, 2005). Judging one product to be more expensive than a second product, for example, might bias people's judgments of how affordable those products are. I will present simulation data that suggests that comparison-induced biases might create a variety of phenomena in the psychology of judgment and decision making and provide key insights into yet other phenomena. My goal in this chapter is merely to introduce readers to the basic tenants of CID theory. I will use simulation data to demonstrate that biases produced by verbal comparisons are sufficient to explain these phenomena and to describe some key novel predictions that can be tested in future research. It is not my focus in this basic introduction to argue that it is necessary to appeal to comparison-induced biases to explain these phenomena nor is it my focus to argue that CID theory provides a better account of these phenomena than other theories provide. Arguments and empirical results demonstrating that CID theory provides a better account than other accounts are presented elsewhere (Choplin & Hummel, 2005, and in papers currently in process or preparation, and ongoing empirical research). Furthermore, the fact that CID theory can account for such a large variety of phenomena (a larger variety of phenomena than any of its competitors) is itself strong evidence in its favor.

COMPARISON-INDUCED DISTORTION THEORY

Comparison-induced distortion theory (CID theory, Choplin & Hummel, 2002) is a theory of attribute evaluation in which language-expressible magnitude comparisons (e.g., "I am older than Susan is") systematically bias how people evaluate, comprehend, remember, and estimate attribute values. The basic idea behind CID theory is that language-expressible magnitude comparisons suggest quantitative values. For example, to investigate the meanings of English age comparisons Rusiecki (1985) gave his participants sentences such as "Mary is older than Jane" and "Martin's wife is older than Ken's wife" and asked them to report the ages they imagined. Rusiecki found considerable agreement in the values imagined by his participants. In response to the comparison "Mary is older than Jane" participants imagined Mary to be 20.2 years old on average and Jane to be 17.9 years old on average. In response to the comparison "Martin's wife is older than Ken's wife" participants imagined Martin's wife to be 37.2 years old on average and Ken's wife to be 33.0 years old on average.

Of particular interest to the current discussion, the age differences imagined by Rusiecki's (1985) participants were remarkably similar. Regardless of the ages they imagined, participants imagined a difference between the ages of approximately 2 to 5 years (slightly larger for larger values; more on this topic below)—not 1 month or 30 years. Inspired by these results, Rusiecki argued that comparisons suggest quantitative differences between compared values. I will henceforth call these quantitative differences "comparison-suggested differences," because they are the differences suggested by comparisons. In the case of age comparisons, Rusiecki's results demonstrate that comparison-suggested differences are approximately 2 to 5 years. For ease of discussion I will operationally define the difference suggested by age comparisons to be 3.5 years in the discussion that follows. Please note, however, that the actual size of the difference likely depends upon many factors as I discuss below and that empirical measurements of the comparison-suggested difference will have to be cognizant of these factors.

Choplin and Hummel (2002) proposed that language-expressible magnitude comparisons (like those investigated by Rusiecki, 1985) might bias evaluations toward the quantitative values suggested by comparisons. For example, if the actual age difference between two people were 1.5 years (i.e., less than the comparison-suggested difference of 3.5 years), then a comparison might bias evaluations of their ages apart—toward a difference of 3.5 years. The younger person might be evaluated younger than she or he would have been evaluated otherwise and the older person might be evaluated older than she or he would have been evaluated otherwise. If the actual age difference between two people were 5.5 years (i.e., more than 3.5 years), then a comparison might bias evaluations of their ages together—again toward a difference of 3.5 years. The younger person might be evaluated older and the older person might be evaluated younger.

Formally, the comparison-suggested value of the smaller of two compared values (E_S; E for Expected) and the comparison-suggested value of the larger of two compared values (E_L) can be calculated from Equations 1a and 1b respectively:

$$E_S = S_L - D \qquad (1a) \qquad\qquad E_L = S_S + D \qquad (1b)$$

where S_L and S_S (S for Stimulus values) are the values of the larger and smaller values unbiased by comparisons respectively and D is a parameter representing the comparison-suggested difference (Choplin & Hummel, 2005). Participants probably do not calculate these comparison-suggested values on the fly. Rather, these values likely come from their memory of previous times in which they judged one value to be larger or smaller than another value (e.g., memory of the age of previous people they had judged to be older than 33.0 years old).

In the tradition of previous judgment models (Anderson, 1965; Huttenlocher, Hedges, & Vevea, 2000), CID theory is a weighted average model in that represented values are assumed to be a weighted mean of values unbiased by comparisons and comparison-suggested values:

$$R_S = wE_S + (1-w)S_S \qquad \text{(2a)} \qquad\qquad R_L = wE_L + (1-w)S_L \qquad \text{(2b)}$$

where w is the relative weights of the two values, is bound between 0 and 1, and is constrained so as to prevent impossible values (e.g., negative years or sizes of geometric figures) from being represented. For example, assuming a comparison-suggested difference, D, of 3.5 years (an oversimplification used here for demonstration purposes only; see discussion below on measuring comparison-suggested differences), a comparison between a 22-year old and a 28-year old would bias evaluations of their ages toward each other. If the weight given to comparison-suggested values were 0.2 (I use this value for demonstration purposes only; to model real data this value would be found by fitting the model to empirical data), then the represented age of the 22-year old would be 22.5 years and the represented age of the 28-year old would be 27.5 years. That is, the 22-year old would be evaluated, i.e., treated, half a year older and the 28-year old would be evaluated half a year younger.

Analogous to previous weighted-average judgment models that weight information from various sources (e.g., Huttenlocher et al., 2000), Parameter w represents the degree to which people rely upon comparisons to evaluate attribute values. If people have an accurate understanding of how large or small or good or bad attribute values are and they are completely certain of their own understanding, then they will have little need to use comparison information to evaluate attribute values and Parameter w would take a low value. By contrast, if they do not have an accurate understanding and need to evaluate attribute values relative to other contextual attribute values, then they will need to rely upon comparison information and Parameter w would take a high value. In cases where people need to recall attribute values from memory, if they remember exact values, they will have little need to rely upon comparison information to aid their recall and Parameter w would take a low value. If they do not remember exact values, they might use verbal comparison information to aid their recall and Parameter w would take a high value. Many cognitive processes could potentially produce this averaging and like other weighted-average models CID theory does not need to commit itself to any one specific cognitive process.

Sometimes people might hesitate to describe one value as larger (or smaller) than another value even if it is larger (or smaller). It might seem odd, for example, to describe a person who is 28 years and 4 months old as "older" than a person who is 28 years and 2 months old. People might prefer to describe these ages as "approximately the same" or "similar." These comparisons suggest that there is little to no difference between the compared values and so biases in evaluation created by these comparisons can be modeled by setting parameter D in Equations 1a and 1b to zero. If Parameter w in Equations 2a and 2b were set to .2, the comparison "a 28 year and 4 month old person is approximately the same age as a 28 year and 2 month old person" would bias the evaluation of 28 years and 4 months to be about 12 days younger and the evaluation of 28 years and 2 months to be about 12 days older.

The decision to describe a given difference as "approximately the same" or "similar" can be modeled stochastically using Shepard's (1987) law of generalization. That is, the probability of describing a difference between two stimuli (i.e., S_L and S_S) as approximately the same or similar can be modeled as:

$$p("\,same"\,|\,S_L - S_S\,) = e^{-c(S_L - S_S)} \qquad (3)$$

where c is a sensitivity parameter.

Equations 1a through 3 employ three parameters (D, w, and c). Note that although the theory uses these three parameters, Parameters D and c can usually be measured empirically so these two parameters will generally not be free. The ability to measure Parameters D and c empirically leaves only Parameter w as a free parameter in CID theory—the same number of free parameters as some of its competitors such as adaptation-level theory (AL theory, Helson, 1964) and range-frequency theory (RF theory, Parducci, 1965, 1995) and fewer free parameters than other competitors (Frederick & Loewenstein, 1999; Stevens, 1961). Parameter D in Equations 1a and 1b can be measured by asking a control group of participants about the types of differences they imagine in response to a comparison (as Rusiecki, 1985, did) or by looking at real-world differences under the assumption that participants have been exposed to these differences and that their experiences with these differences have shaped their understanding of the differences implied by these comparisons. Parameter c in Equation 3 which reflects the probability that people will judge values to be "approximately the same" can be measured by asking a control group of participants whether or not they would describe a given difference as "approximately the same." I discuss the ways one might measure these values in the next sections.

MEASURING COMPARISON-SUGGESTED DIFFERENCES

As described above, comparison-suggested differences (Parameter D in Equations 1a and 1b) and values (E_S and E_L in Equations 1a and 1b) can be measured empirically by asking control groups of participants to imagine that one value is more than, less than, larger than, smaller than, better than, worse than, etc. another value and then ask them about the differences they imagine. My students, colleagues, and I have measured comparison-suggested differences in this manner many times.

For example, in one study my students and I measured comparison-suggested differences and values in personal attributes (grade point average, height, weight, income, dates per month, and commute to campus) by asking a control group of participants about the differences they imagined. In particular, we described a fictional DePaul University undergraduate student (Jennifer for women; Brad for men; the personal attributes of these two people were collected from yet another control group of participants who imagined the average female or male undergraduate DePaul University student) and asked the control group to imagine the personal attributes of another DePaul University undergraduate student (Michelle for women; Michael for men). Michelle was better on every personal attribute than Jennifer (higher grade point average, taller, weighed less, earned more, went out on dates more often, and lived closer to campus); and Michael was better on every personal attribute than Brad (higher grade point average, taller, more muscular and so weighed more, earned more, went out on dates more often, and lived closer to campus). Jennifer and Brad's personal attributes as well as the median imagined personal attributes of Michelle and Michael are presented in Table 1. The median imagined personal attributes of Michelle and Michael represent comparison-suggested values. Comparison-suggested differences were calculated from these comparison-suggested values. Perhaps unsurprisingly the attributes of average female and male undergraduate DePaul University students imagined by these pretest participants fit gender stereotypes. The average female student imagined by women (Jennifer) earned a higher grade point average, was shorter, weighed less, earned much less money (65¢ on the dollar), went out on more dates, and lived closer to campus than did the average male student imagined by men (Brad). We will use these values later in the chapter when we discuss social comparisons.

Table 1. Values and Differences Suggested by Comparisons to Michelle and Brad

	Jennifer's personal attributes (collected in another pretest)	Michelle's median imagined personal attributes (comparison-suggested values)	Comparison-suggested differences
g.p.a.	3.17	3.5	0.33
Height	64 inches	66 inches	2 inches
Weight	134 pounds	125 pounds	9 pounds
Income	$7,868.00	$9,000.00	$1,132.00
Dates	3.1	5	1.9
Commute	9.2 miles	5 miles	4.2 miles
	Brad's personal attributes (collected in another pretest)	Michael's median imagined personal attributes	
g.p.a.	3.1	3.38	0.28
Height	70 inches	72 inches	2 inches
Weight	173 pounds	190 pounds	17 pounds
Income	$12,084.00	$15,000	$2,916.00
Dates	2.45	4	1.55
Commute	18.9 miles	10 miles	8.9 miles

The sizes of comparison-suggested differences depend upon many factors. For one, the size of the comparison-suggested difference often depends upon the size of the base of the comparison. For example, Choplin and Hummel (2005) studied comparison-induced distortions in judgments of line length. To measure comparison-suggested values and differences in judgments of line length, John Hummel and I showed a control group of participants lines of various lengths (each control participant only saw one line) and then asked them to imagine a line that was longer or shorter than that line and draw it. Looking first at participants who drew longer lines than the lines they saw: Of those who viewed a line that was 10.0 mm long, the median redrawn longer line was 36.3mm (a difference of 26.3mm). Of those who viewed a 14.0 mm-line, the median redrawn line was 42.5mm (a difference of 28.5mm). Of those who viewed a 22.0 mm-line, the median redrawn line was 53.0 mm (a difference of 31.0 mm); and of those who viewed a 30.0 mm-line, the median redrawn line was 60.0 mm (a difference of 30.0 mm). Next looking at participants who drew shorter lines than the lines they saw: Of those who viewed a line that was 34.0 mm long, the median redrawn shorter line was 18.0 mm (a difference of 16.0 mm). Of those who viewed a 30.0 mm-line, the median redrawn line was 15.0 mm (a difference of 15.0 mm). Of those who viewed a 22.0 mm-line, the median redrawn line was 9.0 mm (a difference of 13.0 mm); and of those who viewed a 14.0 mm-line, the median redrawn line was 6.0 mm (a difference of

8.0 mm). In this case, the sizes of the comparison-suggested differences depended upon the size of the base of the comparison such that as a general trend comparison-suggested differences were larger when the base of the comparison was larger.

Comparison-suggested differences might not always be larger when the base of the comparison is larger. Rather, the size of the comparison-suggested difference might depend upon the distribution of values out in the world. The comparison "a man taller than 5'8"," for example, might suggest a larger difference than would the comparison "a woman taller than 5'8"," because the distribution of men's heights is larger than the distribution of women's heights. Also if people have some idea of the amount of variance in a category, comparison-suggested differences might be larger when variance is larger. The variance in the high school g.p.a.s of all high school graduates, for example, might be larger than the variance in the high school g.p.a.s of DePaul University undergraduate students, because DePaul University undergraduate students are a self-selecting group and the self-selection process involves high school g.p.a. among other factors. Comparison-suggested differences would then likely be larger if one were comparing the high school g.p.a.s of two high school graduates than if one were comparing the high school g.p.a.s of two DePaul University undergraduate students.

Furthermore, not all ways of wording comparisons will suggest the same quantitative difference. Wording a comparison "slightly larger," for example, will suggest a smaller quantitative difference than will wording it "larger;" and wording a comparison "much larger" will suggest a larger quantitative difference than will wording it "larger." The fact that alternative ways of wording comparisons will suggest smaller or larger quantitative differences gives us a method of isolating the evaluation biases created by verbal comparisons from the evaluation biases produced by some other factors. Once a researcher has measured the quantitative differences suggested by alternative ways of wording verbal comparisons among control participants, an experimenter will be able to manipulate the quantitative differences suggested to experimental participants by manipulating how a comparison is worded while keeping all other factors constant. Once all other factors have been held constant, any observed effects would have to be due to the verbal comparisons that were used. Note that special care would be needed to hold emotional factors constant as emotional factors could also potentially be affected by different ways of wording comparisons. Emotional factors might be held constant by testing for the effects of alternative ways of wording comparisons on dimensions that have no hedonic consequences such as line length or size of geometric shapes.

MEASURING LIKELIHOOD OF JUDGING TWO VALUES THE SAME

The likelihood that people will describe two values as approximately the same can be modeled using Shepard's (1987) law of generalization (shown in Equation 3). The law of generalization has one parameter (Parameter c). A value for Parameter c can be measured empirically by asking control groups of participants how they would describe differences (e.g., as "same"—or perhaps "approximately the same" or "same ballpark"—versus "different," "larger than," or "smaller than"), fitting Equation 3 to these results using a root mean squared error (RMSE) criterion, and thereby finding the best-fit value for Parameter c.

Empirically measuring the value of Parameter c for control participants allows CID theory to make a priori predictions about how experimental participants will evaluate attributes.

My students and I measured the likelihood that people will judge values to be the same and found the best-fitting value for Parameter c as described above in an experiment in which they judged whether prices for an all-you-can-eat lunch were the same as or different than $6.53. In particular, participants imagined that they worked for a summer camp that had been charging $6.53 for an all-you-can-eat lunch. For some of the participants, the camp was considering raising the price and they were asked whether they would consider each of the prices $6.62, $6.71, $6.80, $6.89, $6.98, $7.07, and $7.16 to be the same as or different than $6.53. Half of these participants simply judged whether the prices were "the same as" or "different than" $6.53. The other half of these participants judged whether the prices were in "the same ballpark as" or "a completely different ballpark than" $6.53. For other participants the camp was considering lowering the price and they were asked whether they would consider each of the prices $6.44, $6.35, $6.26, $6.17, $6.08, $5.99, and $5.90 to be the same as or different than $6.53. The proportions of participants describing each price as the same as $6.53 are plotted in Figure 1. Shepard's (1987) law of generalization (Equation 3) was fit to the results using a root mean squared error criterion. Best-fits are also plotted in Figure 1. In the condition wherein participants simply judged whether the prices were "the same as" or "different than" $6.53, the best-fitting value for Parameter c for raising prices was 3.33 (RMSE = 0.05) and the best-fitting value for lowering prices was 2.46 (RMSE = 0.12). In the condition wherein participants s judged whether the prices were in "the same ballpark as" or "a completely different ballpark than" $6.53, the best-fitting value for Parameter c for raising prices was 1.77 (RMSE = 0.09) and the best-fitting value for lowering prices was 1.58 (RMSE = 0.09).

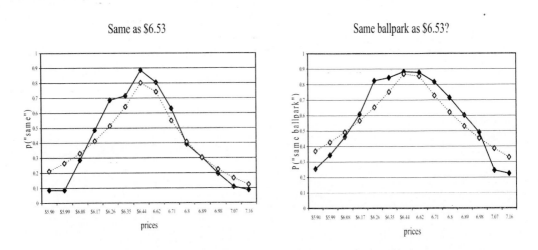

Figure 1. Probabililty of describing prices as the same as $6.53. Black diamonds represent the proportion of participants who described each price as the same as $6.53. White diamonds represent the best-fitting values when Equation 3 was fit to participants' responses.

Once comparison-suggested differences (Parameter D in Equations 1a and 1b) and likelihood of judging two values approximately the same (Parameter c in Equation 3) have been empirically measured, only the weighting of the information provided by comparisons (Parameter w in Equation 2a and 2b) will remain as a free parameter. Additionally, as described below CID theory will only be able to explain certain phenomena, if Parameters D and c take certain values. If CID theory is to explain these phenomena, then, it will have to predict that these parameters will take these values and these predictions can then be empirically verified (or else the CID theory account of these phenomena would be empirically falsified).

Quantitative modeling (discussed shortly) demonstrates that biases in evaluation created by verbal comparisons might play a key role in a number of well-known phenomena in the psychology of judgment and decision making. In particular, biases in evaluation created by verbal comparisons might play a key role in producing s-shaped evaluation functions, distribution-density effects, anchoring effects, social comparisons, and decoy effects. Although I will not be pitting CID theory against alternative theories here in this chapter, note that to compete with CID theory any alternative theory would have to provide a more parsimonious account of all of these phenomena combined, not just a more parsimonious account of one phenomenon. The fact that CID theory can account for such a large variety of phenomena is itself strong evidence in favor of CID theory. The remainder of this chapter will describe the role that biases produced by verbal comparisons might play in these phenomena. To lay the ground work for future empirical research, empirically testable predictions of the CID theory account of these phenomena will also be described.

S-SHAPED EVALUATION FUNCTIONS

Previous research has found considerable evidence that evaluations often follow s-shaped functions (see Figure 2, Frederick & Loewenstein, 1999; Kahneman & Tversky, 1979). Following Helson's (1964) AL theory, these evaluation functions predict that evaluations are made relative to a single reference point (RP), i.e., the point at which people consider values "normal" or "average." This function differs from Helson's original formalization of AL theory, however, in that it has an s-shape. Evaluations are concave (downward) for positive changes from the RP and convex (concave upward) for negative changes from the RP. Helson assumed that evaluations are linearly transformed around the RP.

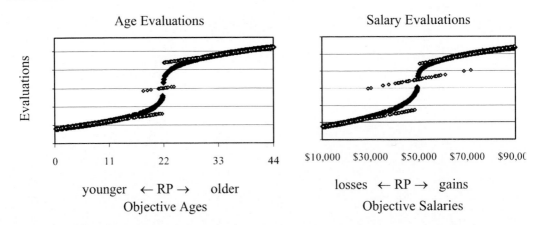

Figure 2. Evaluations made relative to reference points (RPs; 22 years and $50,000). Evaluation functions are generally s-shaped. They are formalized here using Stevens' (1961) Power Law (black s-shaped functions) and CID theory (speckled lines).

To see that evaluations are often s-shaped, consider how evaluations of age change over one's lifespan. As a child (e.g., the RP might be 6 years), all adults—and even teenagers—seem old. The portion of the curve representing adults and teenagers (i.e., the upper portion of the s-shape) is relatively flat. As a young adult of 22 years (i.e., the RP is 22 years; see Figure 2 Age Evaluations), children all seem young, mature adults all seem old, and the difference between 18-year olds and 25-year olds is huge. The portion of the curve representing children (i.e., the lower portion of the s-shape) and the portion of the curve representing mature adults (i.e., the upper portion of the s-shape) are both relatively flat, but the portion of the curve representing the difference between 18-year olds (just to the left of the RP) and 25-year olds (just to the right of the RP) is the steepest portion of the curve. As an adult of retirement age (e.g., the RP might be 65 years), the differences between children, teenagers, and young adults all seem insignificant, young parents appear to be kids having kids, and the lower portion of curve representing these ages is relatively flat.

Since this s-shape is generally thought to reflect the psychophysical law that sensitivity to differences decreases at greater magnitudes, it is often formalized as plotted in Figure 2 solid black lines using Stevens' (1961) Power Law (Kahneman & Tversky, 1979):

$$Evaluation(X) = \begin{cases} a_{more}(X-RP)^{b_{more}} ,if\ X>RP \\ -a_{less}(RP-X)^{b_{less}} ,otherwise \end{cases} \tag{4}$$

where X is the value being evaluated, RP is the reference point, a_{more} scales sensitivity to positive differences from adaptation, a_{less} scales sensitivity to negative differences from adaptation, b_{more} scales the curvature of the portion of the function representing positive differences, and b_{less} scales the curvature of the portion of the function representing negative differences. To produce s-shaped evaluation functions like those in Figure 2, the parameters b_{more} and b_{less} will take values greater than zero and less than one. They will be equal to one, if evaluations are linear (see Briesch, Krishnamurthi, Mazumdar, & Raj, 1997). They will be greater than 1 only in rare cases (e.g., perhaps evaluations of electric shocks, Stevens, 1962).

CID theory provides an alternative way of formalizing the s-shaped evaluation function than does Stevens' Law. The top-most lines in Figure 2 represent biases created by more-than comparisons simulated using Equations 1a through 2b. For example, the comparison "a 35-year old is older than a 22-year old" would produce the evaluation of the 35-year old shown in Figure 2 Age Evaluations. The middle lines represent biases created by approximately-the-same comparisons. The likelihood that people will describe values as approximately the same to the RP is simulated using Equation 3 and the biases produced by these approximately-the-same comparisons are simulated using Equations 1a through 2b with Parameter D set at 0 (since the comparison-suggested difference of describing two values as approximately the same would be zero difference). Unlike Stevens' Law, CID theory can capture indifference around the RP (Kalyanaram & Little, 1994), if people judge a wider range of values as "approximately the same as" the RP. The bottom lines represent biases created by less-than comparisons.

Continuous s-shaped evaluation functions similar to the Stevens' Law evaluation function would be produced by averaging across the three types of comparisons. When values are very close to the RP almost all participants will describe differences as the same, but the tendency to do so usually tapers off quickly for values that are farther from the RP (see Figure 1). It tapers off at a rate that usually produces a function that, once biases from all three types of comparisons are averaged together, is very similar to (but not identical to) the function produced by Stevens' Law.

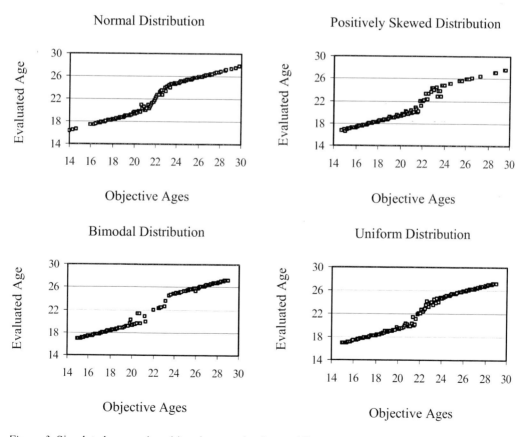

Figure 3. Simulated comparison-biased age evaluations—All ages are compared to 22 years.

To demonstrate what the evaluation function looks like when evaluations for less than, approximately the same, and more than comparisons are averaged together, I again simulated age evaluations from the perspective of a 22-year old who compares all ages to her or his own age (see Figure 3). Five hundred ages were randomly drawn from each of a normal, a positively skewed, a bimodal, and a uniform distribution. For demonstration purposes only, Parameter D in Equations 1a and 1b was set to 3.5 years, Parameter c in Equation 3 was set to 1.5 (before modeling empirical data, these two values would have to be empirically measured), and Parameter w in Equations 2a and 2b was set to .5 (to model empirical data, this value would be found by fitting this free parameter to data).

At c set to 1.5, the age 22 years and 3 months was judged to be the same age as 22 years 69% of the time. The comparison "22 years and 3 months is approximately the same age as 22 years" biased the evaluation of 22 years and 3 months to be approximately 22 years and 1.5 months. The other 31% of the time 22 years and 3 months was judged older than 22 years. The comparison "22 years and 3 months is older than 22 years" biased the evaluation of 22 years and 3 months to be approximately 23 years and 10.5 months. Averaging across these two types of comparisons, 22 years and 3 months was evaluated as approximately 22 years and 4.3 months. An actual difference of 3 months was then evaluated as if it were (treated as if it were) 4.3 months. This extra sensitivity close to the RP can be seen in Figure 3 by the steeper slope around 22 years (the immediate region around the RP is not always steep, sometimes there is a region in which values are judged to be the same, see Kalyanaram & Little, 1994). Sensitivity quickly decreased for values that were farther away from the RP. An age of 24 years was evaluated as if it were 24 years and 10 months and an age of 26 years was evaluated as if it were 25 years and 10 months making a difference of 2 years seem like 1 year.

Notice also from Figure 3 that CID theory predicts that evaluations will be s-shaped and unaffected by the type of distribution from which values are drawn, if all values are verbally compared to a central RP and compared to no other contextual values. Simulation results presented in the next section demonstrate that evaluation functions will depend upon the type of distribution from which values are drawn, if values are compared to other contextual values.

A well-known phenomenon associated with s-shaped evaluation functions is that people's aversion to losses is often greater than their affinity for gains (Kahneman & Tversky, 1979). Consider evaluations of income (Figure 2 Salary Evaluations). For someone who earns $50,000 a year, the subjective difference between $40,000 and $50,000 (a difference that represents a loss) is large, likely larger than the subjective difference between $50,000 and $60,000. Reflecting this fact, the evaluation function for values to the left of the RP in Figure 2 Salary Evaluations is steeper than the evaluation function for values to the right of the RP. This pattern would reverse, if large values represented loss (e.g., being charged more).

Previous research has shown that loss aversion is due to affective factors. These affective factors might affect how people use language to describe differences. For example, the comparison words they use to describe losses (e.g., loss, less, deficit, shortfall, or shortage) might suggest larger differences than do the comparison words they use to describe gains (e.g., gain, more, surplus, or excess). They also might be less likely to describe losses as approximately the same as RP values than to describe gains as approximately the same as RP values. If loss aversion causes people to use their language in either of these ways, then the biases produced by verbal comparisons would not only be s-shaped, but would also reflect the fact that people are loss averse. This model of the s-shaped evaluation function assumes that verbal comparisons mediate the effects of affective factors on evaluations. That is, this model assumes that affective factors play a role in evaluations by changing comparison words; verbalized comparisons in turn bias evaluations.

The speckled lines in Figure 2 Salary Evaluations demonstrate the point that biases produced by verbal comparisons would reflect loss aversion by plotting what the comparison-biased evaluation function would look like, if—because of loss aversion—comparison-suggested differences (parameter D in Equation 1) were larger for losses than for gains. As seen in Figure 2 Salary Evaluations, biases produced by verbal comparisons nicely capture the asymmetry in the evaluation function caused by loss aversion. To mathematically demonstrate this point, comparisons to an RP were simulated with Parameter D set higher for losses than for gains. Sensitivity to losses and gains was assessed by fitting Equation 4 to the simulation results using a minimized root mean squared error criterion. Demonstrating increased sensitivity to losses, the best-fitting value for Parameter a in Equation 4 was greater for losses than for gains.

Not plotted in Figure 2, a tendency to avoid describing losses as "approximately the same" (Parameter c) would also nicely capture the asymmetry in evaluations of losses and gains. To investigate the effects of asymmetries in Parameter c on sensitivity to losses and gains, comparisons to an RP were simulated with Parameter c set higher for losses than for gains. Again, sensitivity to losses and gains was assessed by fitting Equation 4 to the simulation results using a minimized root mean squared error criterion; and again the best-fitting value for Parameter a in Equation 4 was greater for losses than for gains.

Importantly, once Parameters D and c are measured empirically as described above, the CID theory account of the s-shaped evaluation function has fewer free parameters than does Steven's Law. The Steven's Law account has 4 free parameters (a_{more}, a_{less}, b_{more}, and b_{less}), while the CID theory account only has one (w, or two, if w takes different values for losses than for gains). Not only can Parameters D and c be measured empirically, but also to explain some phenomena CID theory will have to predict that Parameters D and c will take certain values. These predictions can then be tested empirically. These parameters, therefore, represent testable predictions of the model rather than free parameters. For example, the CID theory account of the s-shaped evaluation function predicts that either comparison-suggested differences will be larger for losses than for gains or people will be less likely to describe losses as "approximately the same" than to describe gains that way, or both. If people do neither of these things, then CID theory would be unable to capture loss aversion or explain the s-shaped evaluation function.

Of course, finding the predicted correlations between how people use language and biases in their judgments and choice behavior would not in itself establish that these biases are caused by verbal comparisons (as CID theory maintains) as both could be caused by third variables (i.e., affective factors, psychophysical factors, or both) or the causal direction could be reversed. To establish, that verbal comparisons cause biases in judgment, one can manipulate these parameters. Parameter D might be manipulated, for example, by tagging the adjectives "slightly" or "much" on to comparisons; Parameter c might be manipulated by describing sameness as "same," "approximately the same," or "in the same ballpark." To control for affective factors, one might study evaluations of non-hedonic dimensions such as line lengths or sizes of geometric shapes.

Previous research has found that evaluation functions are not always s-shaped. Rather, evaluation functions will often depend upon the distribution of contextual attribute values. Typically, for example, (if the range of values is held constant) an attribute value that is drawn from a positively skewed distribution will be judged larger than the same attribute value that is drawn from a negatively skewed distribution (Birnbaum, 1974; Hagerty, 2000; Haubensak, 1992; Niedrich, Sharma, & Wedell, 2001; Parducci, 1965, 1995; Riskey et al., 1979; Stewart, Chater, & Brown, 2006). I will discuss these distribution-density effects and how CID theory might explain them in the next section.

DISTRIBUTION-DENSITY EFFECTS

Niedrich, Sharma, and Wedell (2001) described models of evaluation—like Helson's (1964) adaptation-level theory and the model formalized in Equation 4 as prototype models. An alternative to these models is suggested by the view that values might be compared to other exemplars that are drawn from the distribution. That is, instead of being compared to a central prototypical example, a to-be-evaluated attribute value might instead be compared to large values sometimes, small values sometimes, and frequent values most commonly of all (i.e., most commonly compared to central values in a normally skewed distribution, large values in a negatively skewed distribution, and small values in a positively skewed distribution). The most successful exemplar model of evaluation in the literature is Parducci's (1965; 1995) range-frequency theory (RF theory) in which evaluations are affected by two types of information: the range score of x in distribution k (R_{xk}) and the frequency score (percentile rank) of x in distribution k (F_{xk}). The range score is calculated as shown in Equation 5:

$$R_{xk} = \frac{X - Min_k}{Max_k - Min_k} \tag{5}$$

where Max_k is the largest value in distribution k and Min_k is the smallest value in distribution k (see also Janiszewski & Lichtenstein, 1999; Volkmann, 1951). The frequency score represents the percentile rank of value x among all values in distribution k as shown in Equation 6:

$$F_{xk} = \frac{Rank_{xk} - 1}{N_k - 1} \tag{6}$$

where $Rank_{xk}$ is the rank of value x in distribution k and N_k is the number of exemplars in distrbution k. It is these frequency scores that create distribution-density effects. Category rating evaluations of x are assumed to be a linear function of the range-frequency compromise score of x ($RFscore_x$) calculated as a weighted average of R_{xk} and F_{xk} as shown in Equation 7:

$$RFscore_x = wR_{xk} + (1 - w)F_{xk} \tag{7}$$

where w is a weighting parameter.

RF theory predicts s-shaped evaluation functions for any distribution that is dense at the center of the distribution and becomes sparse toward the tails on each side (e.g., normal distributions; see Figure 4, top left). It predicts s-shaped evaluation functions in these cases, however, not because people are less sensitive to differences at greater distances from the RP (i.e., not because of Stevens', 1961, Law), but rather because the density or frequency of exemplars in the distribution produces frequency scores (i.e., F_{xk}; Equation 6) that are s-shaped. The middle portion of the curve is steep, because values are dense at the center of the distribution. The slopes of the lower and upper portions of the s-shaped curve are shallow, because values are sparse at the tails of the distribution.

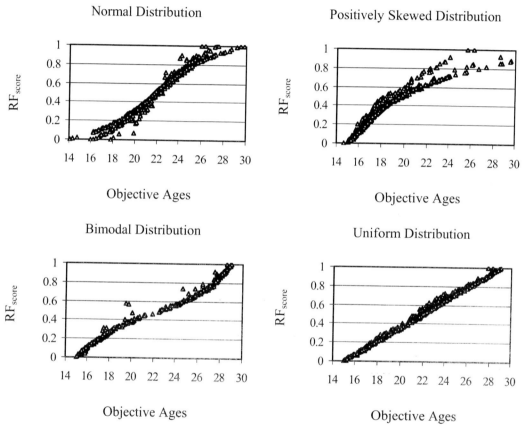

Figure 4: Age evaluation functions predicted by range-frequency (RF) theory. Evaluations follow range-frequency compromise scores (R-F Scores) and produce s-shaped evaluation functions for normal distributions, but not for skewed, bimodal or uniform distributions.

Unlike prototype models of evaluation, RF theory does not predict s-shaped evaluation functions for skewed (Figure 4; upper right), bimodal (Figure 4; lower left; the bimodal distributions in the simulations and proposed experiments below are normal distributions with the tails flipped in giving the end points the greatest density), or uniform (Figure 4; lower right) distributions. Rather, RF theory predicts that evaluation functions will be concave (downward) for positively skewed distributions, because the dense region at the lower end of positively skewed distributions produces larger frequency scores than would have been produced otherwise. It predicts that evaluation functions will be convex (concave upward) for negatively skewed distributions, because the sparse region at the lower end of negatively skewed distributions produces smaller frequency scores than would have been produced otherwise. Evaluation functions ought to flatten somewhat at the center of bimodal distributions because frequency at the center of bimodal distributions is sparse. Evaluations ought to be linear for uniform distributions because frequency is uniformly distributed.

Consistent with both prototype models and RF theory, Niedrich et al. (2001) found that evaluations of prices were s-shaped for normal distributions. But contrary to the predictions of prototype models[†], evaluations of prices in skewed and bimodal distributions were exactly as RF theory predicted they ought to have been. That is, evaluation functions were concave (concave downward) for positively skewed distributions and convex (concave upward) for negatively skewed distributions. Unlike normal distributions, the evaluation functions for bimodal distributions flattened in the sparse middle region. These results are consistent with previous research that has found distribution-density effects on evaluations (Birnbaum, 1974; Mellers & Birnbaum, 1982; Parducci, 1965, 1995; Riskey et al., 1979; Sokolov, Pavlova, & Ehrenstein, 2000; Wedell, Parducci, & Roman, 1989).

Although these results support RF theory, this theory is not able to account for several important findings. Most notably, consistent with CID theory and inconsistent with RF theory, in some cases people seem to have explicit RPs in mind (Holyoak & Mah, 1982). When evaluating body size, for example, people sometimes have a very particular body-size ideal in mind (Irving, 1990; Phelps et al., 1993; Richins, 1991). Unlike CID theory, RF theory also has no explanation for why evaluation functions are often steeper for changes that represent losses than for changes that represent gains (Kahneman & Tversky, 1979; but see Stewart et al., 2006).

Like prototype models of evaluation, CID theory predicts that whenever people verbally compare values to prototypical RPs, comparison-induced biases will generally produce s-shaped evaluation functions regardless of the type of distribution from which values are drawn (see Figure 3). Like RF theory, CID theory predicts that whenever people compare values to other exemplars drawn from the distribution evaluation functions will depend upon distribution density. Like RF theory, CID theory predicts s-shaped evaluation functions for normal distributions, but not skewed, bimodal, or uniform distributions when values are compared to other exemplars drawn from the distribution. Unlike RF theory, CID theory provides a natural account of how greater aversion to losses than affinity for gains could produce asymmetries in sensitivity to losses and gains.

To understand how comparisons to other exemplars in the distribution could create distribution-density effects, consider the positively skewed distribution of ages presented in Figure 5. Filled-in arrows represent biases created by comparisons between values that are closer together than the comparison-suggested difference and that are, therefore, biased apart. Outlined arrows represent biases created by comparisons between values that are farther apart than the comparison-suggested difference and that are, therefore, biased together. Values in dense regions (i.e., 18 – 22 years in Figure 5) are more likely to be closer than the comparison-suggested difference biasing evaluations apart. Values in sparse regions (i.e., 23 – 28 years) are more likely to be farther apart than the comparison-suggested difference

---

[†] A model utilizing Equation 4 in which the RP is always updated to be the value presented on the most recent trial or trials (Frederick & Loewenstein, 1999) would also produce distribution-density effects as described here.

biasing evaluations together. This difference in the effects of comparisons within dense versus sparse regions allows comparisons to create density effects.

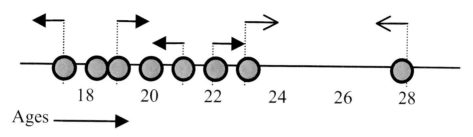

Ages

Figure 5: Comparison-induced biases in a positively skewed distribution of ages.

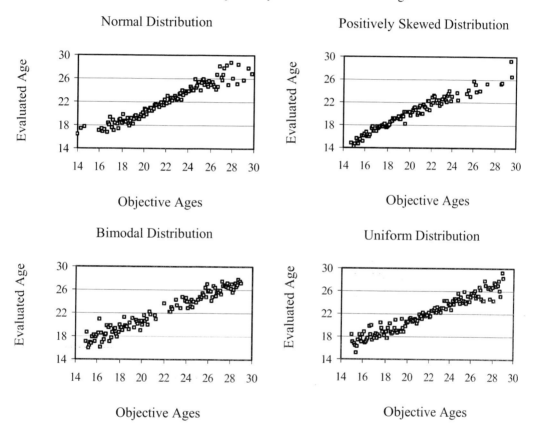

Figure 6. Simulated comparison-biased age evaluations. All values compared to contextual values.

To demonstrate how biases produced by verbal comparisons could produce distribution density-effects, five hundred ages were randomly drawn from each of a normal, a positively skewed, a bimodal, and a uniform distribution. As in the simulation presented in Figure 3, Parameter D in Equations 1a and 1b was set to 3.5 years, Parameter c in Equation 3 was set to 1.5 (these values were chosen for demonstration purposes only; before modeling empirical data, these two values would have to be empirically measured), and Parameter w in Equations 2a and 2b was set to .5 (this value was also chosen for demonstration purposes only; to model empirical data, this value would be found by fitting this free parameter to data). Each of the

500 values was compared to one other randomly drawn value. The results are presented in Figure 6 and they demonstrate that, like RF theory, CID theory predicts s-shaped evaluation functions for normal distributions (upper left), but not skewed (upper right), bimodal (lower left), or uniform (lower right) distributions when values are compared to other exemplar values in the distribution.

Before I conclude the discussion of distribution-density effects, please note that CID theory does not predict that evaluations will always be affected by distribution density. As demonstrated above, CID theory predicts that evaluation functions will be s-shaped whenever people compare all values to one RP and compared them to no other values. In addition, CID theory predicts no biases, if people do not compare values or Parameter w in Equation 2 is very small.

ANCHORING EFFECTS

In the anchoring effect paradigm, participants compare an unknown value to an arbitrary value called the anchor and then estimate the unknown value (but see Wilson, Houston, Brekke, & Etling, 1996, for a slightly different anchoring effect paradigm). Participants might, for example, be asked whether the length of the Mississippi River is longer or shorter than 3,000 miles and then estimate the length of the Mississippi River. Previous research has consistently found that estimates are biased toward the anchor. In our example, estimates of the length of the Mississippi River would be biased toward 3,000 miles.

CID theory offers one key insight into these anchoring effects, namely that estimates will usually be biased toward comparison-suggested values rather than toward anchor values per se (see Wilson et al., 1996, for a possible exception). This insight should be commonsensical. It bears to reason that if people think that the Mississippi River is shorter than 3,000 miles, then their estimates will not be biased toward 3,000 miles per se, but rather their estimates would be biased toward whatever value they think of as "less than 3,000 miles." That is, their estimates would be biased toward a comparison-suggested difference less than 3,000 miles. Before I describe simulations demonstrating the role that comparison-induced biases might play in creating anchoring effects, it is important to note that CID theory's possible contribution to our understanding of anchoring effects is orthogonal to the contributions offered by previous models of anchoring effects. Following previous models (Anderson, 1965; Huttenlocher et al., 2000), CID theory is a weighted average model of attribute evaluation. Like those previous models, it does not specify the mechanism underlying this weighted averaging. Comparisons could create anchoring effects by changing search strategies (Tversky & Kahneman, 1974), bringing to mind different diagnostic attributes (Strack & Mussweiler, 1997), priming values (Wilson et al., 1996), or changing conversational norms (Schwarz, 1990). Regardless of the particular mechanism that creates this weighted-average biasing, CID theory predicts a slightly different pattern of estimation than the pattern predicted by previous models. CID theory might thereby contribute key insights to our understanding of anchoring effect phenomena, but would not replace these previous models.

As described above, CID theory predicts that comparisons will bias estimates toward comparison-suggested values. If comparison-suggested values are closer to anchor values than are unbiased estimates, then comparisons will bias estimates toward anchor values. In particular, CID theory predicts biases toward anchor values whenever unbiased estimates are farther than a comparison-suggested difference away from the anchor or people judge the unknown value to be approximately the same as the anchor in which case the comparison-suggested value would be the anchor value. Previous research on anchoring effects has typically found such biases toward anchor values. By contrast, however, if comparison-suggested values are farther away from anchor values than are unbiased estimates, then comparisons will bias estimates away from anchor values. In typical anchoring effect scenarios such biases away from anchor values are rare for two reasons. First, because comparison-suggested differences are small relative to the range of people's estimates, most unbiased estimates will be more than a comparison-suggested difference away from the anchor. Most estimates will then be biased toward the anchor value leaving only a few estimates that would not be. Second, many people whose unbiased estimates are less than a comparison-suggested difference away from the anchor will judge the unknown value to be approximately the same as the anchor. These estimates will also be biased toward the anchor. Only in those rare cases in which unbiased estimates are less than a comparison-suggested difference away from the anchor and those unbiased estimates are judged to be different from the anchor (i.e., more or less than the anchor) will estimates be biased away from the anchor.

Even though the vast majority of values are biased toward the anchor value and this result is consistent with both CID theory and alternative theories, CID theory nevertheless makes novel predictions regarding the magnitude of the predicted biases toward the anchor value. In particular, CID theory predicts large biases toward the anchor among unbiased estimates at the extremes, smaller biases toward the anchor for unbiased estimates closer to the comparison-suggested difference away from the anchor, and large biases toward the anchor again as more and more participants start to describe the unknown value as "approximately the same" as the anchor.

To demonstrate how comparison-induced distortions could create anchoring effects, 500 values between 500 and 3100 were randomly drawn from a normal distribution to represent simulated unbiased estimates of the length of the Mississippi River. A histogram of the results is presented in the top panel of Figure 7. I then simulated comparison-biased estimates by comparing all 500 values to an anchor of 2,900 miles. For demonstration purposes only, the comparison-suggested difference (Parameter D in Equation 1) was set at 300 miles. To model real data, one would have to measure this value by asking a control group of participants about the length they imagine when they hear about a river that is shorter than 2,900 miles as described in the measuring comparison-suggested differences section above. Also for demonstration purposes only Parameter c in Equation 3 was set at 0.0002. Again to model real data, one would have to measure this value by asking control groups of participants whether they would describe a variety of values as the same as or less than the anchor value, fit Equation 3 to their responses, and find the best-fitting value for Parameter c. With Parameter c set at 0.0002, 18.6% of values were judged to be approximately the same as the anchor value of 2,900 miles. Parameter w in Equation 2 was set at 0.5. To model real data, Equations 1a through 3 would be fit to the data using the empirically measured values for Parameters D and c to find the best-fitting value for Parameter w. The results are presented in the middle panel of Figure 7. Notice that values were biased toward the anchor value of 2,900 miles. Only 2.2% of values were biased away from the anchor value. I also simulated

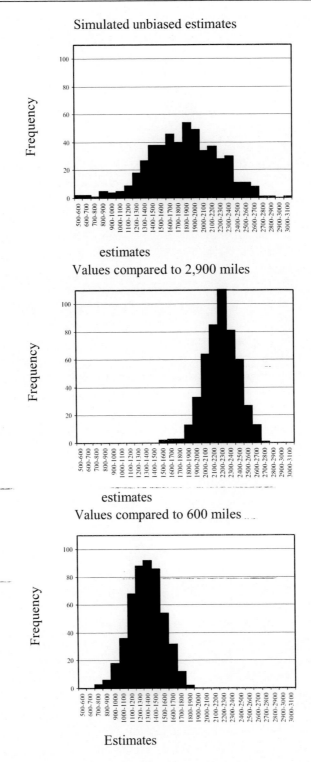

Figure 7. Simulated comparison-induced anchoring effects. The top panel presents a simulated unbiased distribution of estimates of the length of the Mississippi River. The middle panel presents what the distribution would look like, if all values were compared to 2,900 miles. The bottom panel presents what the distribution would look like, if all values were compared to 600 miles

comparison-biased estimates by comparing all 500 values to an anchor of 600 miles. All parameter were given the same values. With Parameter c set at 0.0002, 20.8% of values were judged to be approximately the same as the anchor value. The results are presented in the bottom panel of Figure 7. Notice that values are biased toward the anchor value of 600 miles. Only 2.0% of values were biased away from the anchor value. Note that these results do not depend upon the particular parameter values I used here for demonstration purposes only. The same basic pattern of results is observed no matter what values these parameters take.

Social Comparisons

Festinger (1954) suggested that people evaluate their own personal-attribute values by comparing their attribute values to the attribute values of their peers. For example, people might evaluate their income, their intelligence, their appearance, their body size, and so forth by comparing themselves to their friends and others who are similar to them. Verbal comparisons of these personal attribute values are likely to produce the same biases as other verbal comparisons. That is, if actual differences are the same size as comparison-suggested differences, then there will be no biases in evaluation. If actual differences are smaller than comparison-suggested differences, then people will overreact to the difference. That is, evaluations will be biased toward the larger comparison-suggested difference. The smaller value will be evaluated smaller than it would have been evaluated otherwise and the larger value will be evaluated larger than it would have been evaluated otherwise. If actual differences are larger than comparison-suggested differences, then people will under react to the difference. That is, evaluations will again be biased toward the comparison-suggested difference, but this time the comparison-suggested difference will be smaller. The smaller value will then be evaluated larger than it would have been otherwise and the larger value will be evaluated smaller than it would have been otherwise. The overall effect of these biases would be such that moderate downward comparisons would produce higher evaluations of the self than would extreme downward comparisons and moderate upward comparisons would produce lower evaluations of the self than would extreme upward comparisons.

Consider, for example, Jennifer and Michelle, the two fictional DePaul University undergraduate students described in Table 1. If Jennifer whose income was $7,868.00 were to compare her income to Michelle's income of $9,000.00, then there would be no biases. The $1,132.00 difference in their salaries would be exactly the same size as the $1,132.00 comparison-suggested difference so reliance on comparison information would create no biases (recall that these were the incomes imagined by actual DePaul University undergraduate women for full-time female students working part time jobs to help pay for school expenses, notice how much larger the incomes imagined by DePaul University undergraduate men were for full-time male students). However, if Michelle had an income of $8,000.00, instead of $9,000.00, and Jennifer were to describe her $7,868.00 income as less than Michelle's $8,000.00 income or Michelle's $8,000.00 as more than her $7,868.00 income (a difference of $132.00), then Jennifer would likely overreact to the difference (unless she were to describe these salaries as "approximately the same" in which case she would under react to the difference), because her evaluations would be biased toward the larger $1,132.00 comparison-suggested difference. Her income would be evaluated smaller than it would have been otherwise and Michelle's income would be evaluated larger than it would have been otherwise. By contrast, if Michelle had an income of $10,000, instead of $9,000.00, and Jennifer were to describe her $7,868.00 income as less than Michelle's $10,000 income (a difference of $2,132.00), then Jennifer would likely under react to the difference. Once again her evaluations would be biased toward the $1,132.00 comparison-suggested difference, but this time the $1,132.00 comparison-suggested difference will be smaller than the $2,132.00 actual difference. Her $7,868.00 income would then be evaluated larger than it would have been evaluated otherwise and Michelle's $10,000.00 income would be evaluated smaller than it would have been evaluated otherwise.

Simulated biases created when Jennifer compares her own and other people's salaries are presented in Figure 8. Jennifer's comparison-biased evaluations of other people's salaries (Figure 8 left panel) would follow an s-shaped evaluation function. This function is almost identical to the evaluation function shown in Figure 2 Salary Evaluations. The only difference would be that her reference point (RP) would be her own $7,868.00 income, rather than the RP of $50,000.00 shown in Figure 2 Salary Evaluations. Like Figure 2 Salary Evaluations, all other incomes would be evaluated relative to her RP. The top line represents evaluations of other people's salaries when she describes their salaries as more than her own $7,868 salary. The middle line represents evaluations of other people's salaries when she describes their salaries as approximately the same as her own salary. The bottom line represents evaluations of other people's salaries when she describes their salaries as less than her own salary. The Stevens' (1961) Law formalization of the evaluation function (Kahneman & Tversky, 1979) is also plotted. CID theory predicts a continuous function similar to Stevens' Law when evaluations from less than, approximately the same, and more than comparisons are averaged together (see Figure 3).

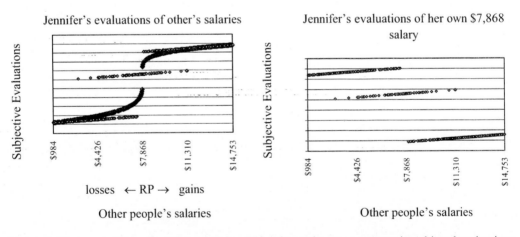

Figure 8. Biases created by social comparisons. The left panel presents comparison-biased evaluations of other people's salaries. The right panel presents comparison-biased evaluations of Jennifer's own salary. The middle lines in both panels represent biases created when Jennifer describes her salary as approximately the same as other people's salaries. The right most lines (top line on the left panel; bottom line on the right panel) represent biases created when Jennifer describes other people's salaries as more than her salary or her salary as less than other people's salaries. The left most lines (bottom line on the left panel; top line on the right panel) represent biases created when Jennifer describes other people's salaries as less than her salary or her salary as more than other people's salaries.

Jennifer's comparison-biased evaluations of her own salary are plotted in Figure 8 right panel. The top line represents evaluations of her own $7,868 salary when she describes it as more than other people's salaries. The middle line represents evaluations of her salary when she describes it as approximately the same as other people's salaries. The bottom line represents evaluations of her salary when she describes it as less than their salaries. Notice the unique predictions of this CID theory account of social comparisons. This account predicts that comparisons to salaries that are moderately lower than her own salary will cause her to evaluate her salary higher than comparisons to salaries that are much lower than her own salary. Likewise, comparisons to salaries that are moderately higher than her own salary will cause her to evaluate her salary lower than comparisons to salaries that are much higher than her own salary. This pattern of biases might not be observable using category rating measures of evaluation (but see Qian & Brown, 2005), but has been observed in my laboratory using recall of values from memory as the dependent measure.

DECOY EFFECTS

Consumers typically have to pick one option among several alternatives. If they are purchasing an airline ticket, they typically have several flight options to choose from and they have to pick one. If they are renting an apartment, they typically have to decide which of several apartments to rent. If they are purchasing pickles, they typically have to decide which of several brands, flavors, and jar sizes to purchase. These options typically vary along multiple attributes and choices between them often involve trade-off between desirable attribute values. One flight option might leave later in the morning allowing the consumer to sleep later but arrive at the destination later and have a longer layover. One apartment might have a shorter commute to work but cost more in rent. To study how people choose among multi-attribute alternatives such as these, researchers have studied the effects of decoys on choice. Decoys are options inserted into a choice set that people typically do not choose. Despite the fact that people do not choose these decoy options, they affect which of the remaining options people chose.

I will discuss two such decoy effects in this section: the asymmetric dominance effect and the phantom decoy effect. Both effects start with two options that typically vary along two dimensions (e.g., two apartment options that vary in rent and the length of the commute between the apartment and work). One option is better on one dimension, but the other option is better on the other dimension. For example, one apartment might have a shorter commute but cost more in rent than the other apartment. In Figure 9, apartment option 1 has a better commute time (25 minutes compared to 45 minutes for option 2), but apartment option 2 costs less in rent ($575 per month compared to $700 per month). Researchers try to set these values so that people are indifferent between these options. If the options in Figure 9 were set right (the correct values would differ across different groups and would need to be pre-tested), the value of the shorter commute from one apartment would be exactly equal to the extra rent one would pay for that apartment so that if those two options were the only ones presented people would be indifferent between these alternatives. This indifference is represented in Figure 9 by the indifference curve.

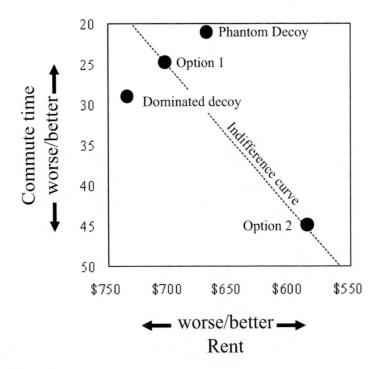

Figure 9. Decoy effects. Options 1 and 2 are designed to be equally attractive (because the benefit of the better value on one dimension is exactly equal to the detriment of the worse value on the other dimension) and so they lie on the indifference curve. Adding a dominated decoy to the option set causes people to choose the option that is similar to the dominated decoy (an effect called the asymmetric dominance effect). Adding a phantom decoy to the option set and marking it unavailable also causes people to choose the option that is similar to the phantom decoy (an effect called the phantom decoy effect).

In the asymmetric dominance effect (Huber et al., 1982), researchers place a dominated decoy in the option set (see Figure 9). This dominated decoy is similar to but worse than one of the other options so that no one would actually choose it. The dominated decoy in Figure 9, for example, is similar to option 1, but it has a longer commute and costs more in rent so that no one would actually choose it if option 1 were available. Nevertheless, its inclusion into the choice set affects the choices people make such that people will be more likely to choose the option that is similar to and better than the dominated decoy. That is, the inclusion of the dominated decoy in the choice set changes people's preferences so that they are no longer indifferent between option 1 and option 2, pushing option 1 above the indifference curve, pulling the indifference curve down, or both.

In the phantom decoy effect (Highhouse, 1996; Pratkanis & Farquhar, 1992), researchers place a phantom decoy in the option set (see Figure 9). This dominating decoy is similar to but better than one of the other options. The phantom decoy in Figure 9, for example, is similar to option 1, but it has a shorter commute and costs less in rent. If this option were available, almost everyone would choose it; but it is marked unavailable, sold out, discontinued, etc. so that it cannot be chosen. Nevertheless, its inclusion into the choice set affects the choices people make such that people will be more likely to choose the option that is similar to the dominating decoy despite the fact that it is not as good as the dominating decoy. The inclusion of the phantom decoy then, like the inclusion of the dominated decoy in the asymmetric dominance effect, changes people's preferences so that they are no longer indifferent between option 1 and option 2. The inclusion of the phantom decoy pulls option 1 above the indifference curve, pushes the indifference curve down, or both.

Choplin and Hummel (2002) argued that CID theory could explain the asymmetric dominance effect; and Choplin and Hummel (2005) discovered a one dimensional analogue of the asymmetric dominance effect and argued that unlike other models in the literature CID theory could account for this one dimensional effect. The basic idea underlying the CID theory account of the asymmetric dominance effect is that verbal comparisons (e.g., better, closer, less expensive, worse, farther, more expensive) between the option that is similar to the dominated decoy (option 1 in Figure 9) and the dominated decoy bias the evaluation of the option that is similar to the dominated decoy. Because the differences between the dominated decoy and the option that is similar to the dominated decoy are typically quite small (i.e., typically smaller than comparison-suggested differences), comparisons bias evaluations apart making the option appear better (and the dominated decoy worse) than it otherwise would and so people choose the dominating option. To simulate these predictions, I modeled the asymmetric dominance effect scenario presented in Figure 9. The choice set included apartment option 1 with a commute of 45 minutes and rent of $575.00 per month, apartment option 2 with a commute of 25 minutes and rent of $700.00 per month, and the dominated decoy with a commute of 29 minutes and rent of $750.00 per month. To model the effects of comparisons on evaluations, I set the comparison-suggested difference (Parameter D in Equation 1) for commute times at 8 minutes (any value larger than 4 minutes would create essentially the same pattern of bias) and the comparison-suggested difference for rent at $100.00 (any value larger than $50.00 would create essentially the same pattern of bias). With these values for Parameter D, CID theory predicts an asymmetric dominance effect as long as Parameter c in Equation 3 takes a value greater than 0.173 for commute times (the probability of describing a 4-minute difference in commute times as "approximately the same" is less than 50.0%) and Parameter c takes a value greater than 0.014 for rents (the probability of describing a $50.00 difference in rent as "approximately the same" is less than 50.0%). These predictions hold regardless of what value the weighting parameter (Parameter w in Equation 2) takes as long as that value is greater than 0.0.

Given this CID theory explanation of the asymmetric dominance effect it might appear at first that CID theory would be unable to account for phantom decoy effects (Highhouse, 1996; Pratkanis & Farquhar, 1992). Since the differences between phantom decoys and the items they dominate are also typically quite small (i.e., they also are typically smaller than comparison-suggested differences), comparison between phantom decoys and options should make the option that is similar to the phantom decoy appear worse. Why then would people choose the similar option?

CID theory could simultaneously account for both the asymmetric dominance effect and the phantom decoy effect only if the unavailability of the phantom decoy were to make people more likely to describe the difference as "approximately the same." Recent empirical results in my laboratory have found evidence that people are more likely to describe options as "approximately the same as" unavailable options than to describe them as "approximately the same as" available options. To simulate these predictions, I modeled the phantom decoy effect scenario presented in Figure 9. As in the simulation of the asymmetric dominance effect described above, the choice set included apartment option 1 with a commute of 45 minutes and rent of $575.00 per month and apartment option 2 with a commute of 25 minutes and rent of $700.00 per month. Instead of the dominated decoy with a commute of 29 minutes and rent of $750.00 per month, however, the phantom decoy with a commute of 21 minutes and a rent of $650.00 was placed in the set, but was not available. To model the effects of comparisons on evaluations, I used the same values for Parameter D described in the simulation of the asymmetric dominance effect above. With these values, CID theory predicts a phantom decoy effect as long as Parameter c in Equation 3 takes a value less than 0.173 for commute times (the probability of describing a 4-minute difference in commute times as "approximately the same" is greater than 50.0%) and Parameter c takes a value less than 0.014 for rents (the probability of describing a $50.00 difference in rent as "approximately the same" is greater than 50.0%). Again, these predictions hold regardless of what value the weighting parameter (Parameter w in Equation 2) takes as long as that value is greater than 0.0. If people were not more likely to describe decoys as "approximately the same" as options when decoys were marked unavailable than when they were not, CID theory would not be able to simultaneously account for both asymmetric dominance effects (Huber et al., 1982) and phantom decoy effects (Highhouse, 1996; Pratkanis & Farquhar, 1992) at the same time.

CONCLUSION

Simulation results demonstrated that biases created by verbal comparisons are capable of explaining or providing insights into a variety of phenomena in the psychology of judgment and decision making. In particular, simulation results demonstrated that biases created by verbal comparisons might help explain or provide insights into s-shaped evaluation functions (Frederick & Loewenstein, 1999; Kahneman & Tversky, 1979), distribution-density effects (Birnbaum, 1974; Niedrich et al., 2001; Parducci, 1965, 1995; Riskey et al., 1979), anchoring effects (Tversky & Kahneman, 1974), social comparisons (Festinger, 1954), and decoy effects such as the asymmetric dominance effect (Huber et al., 1982) and the phantom decoy effect (Highhouse, 1996; Pratkanis & Farquhar, 1992). Because verbal comparisons are ubiquitous whenever people decide between alternatives, future research may find that biases created by verbal comparisons might help explain or provide insights into other decision-making phenomena as well.

Simulation results demonstrated that biases created by verbal comparisons might help explain why evaluation functions are s-shaped (Frederick & Loewenstein, 1999; Kahneman & Tversky, 1979) when people compare to-be-evaluated values to a standard or reference point value. Consistent with previous research on s-shaped evaluation functions, comparisons to a standard or reference point would cause people to over emphasize the importance of small differences and under emphasize the importance of large differences. In addition, some people might describe small differences as "approximately the same." Describing small differences as "approximately the same" would cause people to under emphasize the importance of small differences. A continuous, monotonic function would be created by averaging across the different types of comparisons people make (i.e., less than, approximately the same, and more than comparisons). This continuous function would be concave downward for positive changes from the reference point and convex (concave upward) for negative changes from the reference point. Affective factors cause people to be loss averse (disliking losses more than they like gains). Biases created by verbal comparisons might mediate some of these loss aversion effects, if affective factors cause people to use different comparison words to describe losses than to describe gains, and these comparisons, in turn, affect evaluations.

Simulation results also demonstrated that reliance on information from verbal comparisons might help explain distribution-density effects (Birnbaum, 1974; Niedrich et al., 2001; Parducci, 1965, 1995; Riskey et al., 1979), if people compare to-be-evaluated attribute values to other values drawn from the distribution (i.e., compare them to smaller values sometimes, larger values sometimes, and frequent values—middle values in normal distributions, small values in positively skewed distributions, or large values in negatively skewed distributions—most frequently of all). Because these comparisons would also cause people to over emphasize the importance of small differences and under emphasize the importance of large differences, comparisons to these other values would cause the evaluation function to be s-shaped for values drawn from a normal distribution, concave downward for values drawn from positively skewed distributions, convex (or concave upward) for values drawn from negatively skewed distributions, inverted s-shaped for values drawn from bimodal distributions, and linear for values drawn from uniform distributions.

Simulation results demonstrated that considering the effects of verbal comparisons on estimates might provide insights into anchoring effects. In particular, if estimates are biased by verbal comparisons then when a participant notes that the unknown value is more than (or less than) the anchor value estimates will not be biased toward the anchor value per se, but rather estimates will be biased toward the comparison-suggested value more than (or less than) the anchor value. This CID theory insight into anchoring phenomena is orthogonal to the insights provided by most current accounts of anchoring effects (Schwarz, 1990; Strack & Mussweiler, 1997; Tversky & Kahneman, 1974; Wilson et al., 1996), but is important in its own right.

Biases produced by verbal social comparisons might also provide insights into social comparison phenomena. In particular, simulation results demonstrate that moderate downward comparisons will produce higher evaluations of the self than will extreme downward comparisons and moderate upward comparisons will produce lower evaluations of the self than will extreme upward comparisons.

Because consumers typically compare alternatives whenever they make a choice, biases produced by reliance on verbal comparisons might help explain some consumer decision-making phenomena. In particular, biases produced by verbal comparisons might help explain the effects of decoys on consumer choice. Choplin and Hummel (2002) demonstrated that biases produced by verbal comparisons might explain the asymmetric dominance effect (Huber et al., 1982) and Choplin and Hummel (2005) demonstrated a one-dimensional version of the asymmetric dominance effect and argued that CID theory provided the best account of this phenomenon. Simulation results presented here demonstrated that biases produced by verbal comparisons would be able to simultaneously account for both the asymmetric dominance effect and the phantom decoy effect only if the unavailability of the phantom decoy makes people more likely to describe other options as "approximately the same" as the decoy.

The simulation results presented here demonstrate that the CID theory account of these phenomena is feasible and that biases produced by verbal comparisons are either sufficient to explain phenomena or else provide important insights into phenomena. These simulation results have not shown that biases produced by verbal comparisons are necessary to explain these phenomena nor have they shown that CID theory provides a better account of these phenomena than alternative theories. Arguments that CID theory provides a better explanation of these phenomena than other theories are presented elsewhere.

Importantly, however, the fact that CID theory can account for such a large variety of phenomena is itself evidence in favor of CID theory. Far too often, researchers develop theories to account for one phenomenon or class of phenomena, rather than proposing theories that generalize across a wide variety of phenomena. CID theory follows Helson's (1964) adaptation-level theory and Parducci's (1965; 1995) range-frequency theory in proposing an account of attribute evaluation that generalizes across a wide variety of phenomena. Biases in evaluation produced by verbal comparisons are predicted whenever people compare alternatives. Since such comparisons are ubiquitous, this influence is likely to be pervasive.

REFERENCES

Anderson, N. H. (1965). Averaging versus adding as a stimulus-combination rule in impression formation. *Journal of Experimental Psychology, 70*, 394-400.

Birnbaum, M. H. (1974). Using contextual effects to derive psychophysical scales. *Perception & Psychophysics, 15*, 89-96.

Briesch, R. A., Krishnamurthi, L., Mazumdar, T., & Raj, S. P. (1997). A comparative analysis of reference price models. *Journal of Consumer Research, 24*, 202-214.

Choplin, J. M., & Hummel, J. E. (2002). Magnitude comparisons distort mental representations of magnitude. *Journal of Experimental Psychology: General, 131*, 270-286.

Choplin, J. M., & Hummel, J. E. (2005). Comparison-induced decoy effects. *Memory & Cognition, 33*, 332-343.

Festinger, L. (1954). A theory of social comparison processes. *Human Relations, 7*, 117-140.

Frederick, S., & Loewenstein, G. (1999). Hedonic Adaptation. In D. Kahneman, E. Diener & N. Schwarz (Eds.), *Well-being: The foundations of hedonic psychology* (pp. 302-329). New York: NY: Russell Sage.

Hagerty, M. R. (2000). Social comparisons of income in one's community: Evidence from national surveys of income and happiness. *Journal of Personality and Social Psychology, 78*, 764-771.

Haubensak, G. (1992). The consistency model: A process model for absolute judgments. *Journal of Experimental Psychology: Human Perception and Performance, 18*, 303-309.

Helson, H. (1964). *Adaptation-level theory*. New York: Harper & Row.

Highhouse, S. (1996). Context-dependent selection: The effects of decoy and phantom job candidates. *Organizational Behavior and Human Decision Processes, 65*, 68-76.

Holyoak, K. J., & Mah, W. A. (1982). Cognitive reference points in judgments of symbolic magnitude. *Cognitive Psychology, 14*, 328-352.

Huber, J., Payne, J. W., & Puto, C. (1982). Adding asymmetrically dominated alternatives: Violations of regularity and the similarity hypothesis. *Journal of Consumer Research, 9*, 90-98.

Huttenlocher, J., Hedges, L. V., & Vevea, J. L. (2000). Why do categories affect stimulus judgment? *Journal of Experimental Psychology: General, 129*(2), 220-241.

Irving, L. M. (1990). Mirror images: Effects of the standard of beauty on the self- and body-esteem of women exhibiting varying levels of bulimic symptoms. *Journal of Social and Clinical Psychology, 9*, 230-242.

Janiszewski, C., & Lichtenstein, D. R. (1999). A Range Theory Account of Price Perception. *Journal of Consumer Research, 25*(25), 353-368.

Kahneman, D. (1999). Objective happiness. In D. Kahneman, E. Diener & N. Schwarz (Eds.), *Well-being: The foundations of hedonic psychology*. New York, NY: Russell Sage.

Kahneman, D., & Tversky, A. (1979). Prospect theory: An analysis of decision under risk. *Econometrica, 47*, 263-291.

Kalyanaram, G., & Little, J. D. C. (1994). An empirical analysis of latitude of price acceptance in consumer package goods. *Journal of Consumer Research, 21*, 408-418.

Lavine, H., Sweeney, D., & Wagner, S. H. (1999). Dipicting women as sex objects in television advertising: Effects on body dissatisfaction. *Personality and Social Psychology Bulletin, 25*, 1049-1058.

Mellers, B. A., & Birnbaum, M. H. (1982). Loci of contextual effects in judgment. *Journal of Experimental Psychology: Human Perception and Performance, 8*, 582-601.

Morse, S., & Gergen, K. J. (1970). Social comparison, self-consistency, and the concept of self. *Journal of Personality and Social Psychology, 16*, 148-156.

Mussweiler, T. (2003). Comparison processes in social judgment: Mechanisms and consequences. *Psychological Review, 110*, 472-489.

Niedrich, R. W., Sharma, S., & Wedell, D. H. (2001). Reference price and price perceptions: A comparison of alternative models. *Journal of Consumer Research, 28*(3), 339-354.

Parducci, A. (1965). Category judgments: A range-frequency model. *Psychological Review, 72*, 407-418.

Parducci, A. (1995). *Happiness, pleasure and judgment: The contextual theory and its applications*. Mahwah, NJ: Lawrence Erlbaum.

Phelps, L., Johnston, L. S., Jimenez, D. P., Wilczenski, F. L., Andrea, R. K., & Healy, R. W. (1993). Figure preference, body dissatisfaction, and body distortion in adolescence. *Journal of Adolescent Research, 8*, 297-310.

Pratkanis, A. R., & Farquhar, P. H. (1992). A brief history of research on phantom alternatives: Evidence for seven empirical generalizations about phantoms. *Basic and Applied Social Psychology, 13*, 103-122.

Qian, J., & Brown, G. D. A. (2005). *Similarity-based sampling: Testing a model of price psychophysics*. Paper presented at the Twenty-seventh annual conference of the cognitive science society, Stresa, Italy.

Richins, M. L. (1991). Social Comparison and the Idealized Images of Advertising. *Journal of Consumer Research, 18*, 71-83.

Riskey, D. R., Parducci, A., & Beauchamp, G. K. (1979). Effects of context in judgments of sweetness and pleasantness. *Perception & Psychophysics, 26*, 171-176.

Rusiecki, J. (1985). *Adjectives and Comparison in English*. New York: Longman.

Schifferstein, H. N. J., & Frijters, J. E. R. (1992). Contextual and sequential effects on judgments of sweetness intensity. *Perception & Psychophysics, 52*, 243-255.

Schwarz, N. (1990). Assessing frequency reports of mundane behaviors: Contributions of cognitive psychology to questionnaire construction. In C. Hendrick & M. Clark, S.

(Eds.), *Research Methods in Personality and Social Psychology (Review of Personality and Social Psychology, vol. 11)* (pp. 98-119). Beverly Hills, CA: Sage.

Schwarz, N., & Strack, F. (1999). Reports of subjective well-being: Judgmental processes and their methodological implications. In D. Kahneman, E. Diener & N. Schwarz (Eds.), *Well-being: The foundations of hedonic psychology*. New York, NY: Russell Sage.

Shepard, R. N. (1987). Toward a universal law of generalization for psychological science. *Science, 237*, 1317-1323.

Sokolov, A., Pavlova, M., & Ehrenstein, W. H. (2000). Primacy and frequency effects in absolute judgments of visual velocity. *Perception & Psychophysics, 62*, 998-1007.

Stevens, S. S. (1961). To honor Fechner and repeal his law. *Science, 133*, 80-86.

Stevens, S. S. (1962). The surprising simplicity of sensory metrics. *American Psychologist, 17*, 29-39.

Stewart, N., Chater, N., & Brown, G. D. A. (2006). Decision by sampling. *Cognitive Psychology, 53*, 1-26.

Strack, F., & Mussweiler, T. (1997). Explaining the enigmatic anchoring effect: mechanisms of selective accessibility. *Journal of Personality and Social Psychology, 73*, 437-446.

Tversky, A., & Kahneman, D. (1974). Judgment under uncertainty: Heuristics and biases. *Science, 185*, 1124-1130.

Volkmann, J. (1951). Scales of judgment and their implications for social psychology. In J. H. Roherer & M. Sherif (Eds.), *Social psychology at the crossroads* (pp. 279-294). New York: Harper & Row.

Wansink, B. (2004). Environmental factors that increase the food intake and consumption volume of unknowing consumers. *Annual Review of Nutrition, 24*, 455-479.

Wedell, D. H., & Parducci, A. (2000). Social Comparison: Lessons from basic research on judgment. In J. Suls & L. Wheeler (Eds.), *Handbook of social comparison: Theory and research* (pp. 223-252). New York: Plenum.

Wedell, D. H., Parducci, A., & Roman, D. (1989). Student perceptions of fair grading: A range-frequency analysis. *American Journal of Psychology, 102*(233-248).

Wedell, D. H., & Pettibone, J. C. (1996). Using judgments to understand decoy effects in choice. *Organizational Behavior and Human Decision Processes, 67*, 326-344.

Wilson, T. D., Houston, C. E., Brekke, N., & Etling, K. M. (1996). A new look at anchoring effects: Basic anchoring and its antecedents. *Journal of Experimental Psychology: General, 125*, 387-402.

In: Psychology of Decision Making in Education
Editor: Jeanine A. Elsworth, pp. 41-71

ISBN: 978-1-60021-933-7
© 2006 Nova Science Publishers, Inc.

Chapter 2

ANALYSIS AND DECISION-MAKING MODELS IN THE PROCESS OF THE ASSIMILATION OF CHANGE AND INNOVATION IN LEARNING SYSTEMS

Baruch Offir

Bar-Ilan University , School of Education, Israel

Research has shown that a relation exists between the level of learning in the schools and universities and a country's strength. A relation also exists between education and the level and quality of life. Education today is a significant factor for ensuring society's normal existence, development and prosperity. However, major cities can afford the student the opportunity to acquire knowledge more than cities found in the periphery. A gap therefore exists between the level of learning in the major cities and the level of learning in the peripheral settlements. Students with high learning abilities who live in the cities can participate in university courses and other learning centers, whereas students with learning abilities who live in the periphery do not have a framework which can afford them knowledge in accordance with their talents and abilities.

This reality was the basis for our research on the integration of technological systems for the advancement of students in the periphery towards academic studies. Our research aims to investigate how technological systems can be used to advance populations of students who live in distant areas, to afford them the opportunity to learn academic courses and to be university students while still learning in high school.

A proper combination of this means during the learning process requires a change in the teaching method. This process of change is very complex, since it must take numerous educational and pedagogical factors which are involved in the process into account. It must recognize the teachers' and students' personal attitudes, must evaluate the student's level, analyze the sociological processes taking place in the classroom, formulate an appropriate teaching method, recognize the teacher's position and status in the classroom, etc. Proper activation of technological systems in order to reduce gaps between populations is a very complex system and its successful implementation depends on the understanding and control of numerous diverse and complex parameters.

The function of the education system today is indeed complex. It must educate towards values and mold each student's behavior, afford the student the ability to crystallize his viewpoint and attitude while concomitantly leading him towards achievements and affording him the tools with which he will be able to learn and acquire a profession so that he will be able to earn a living for himself and his family and will be able to contribute to the society in which he lives. These goals are not identical, and are sometimes not compatible, since the strict and demanding educational framework which accurately evaluates and judges the student's achievements is not necessarily the same educational framework which is soft, encouraging, educating and guiding.

The education system is not static. History shows that its goals, methods of operation and structure have changed during different periods of history, according to sociological influences and society's goals . The goals of education have undergone changes according to the particular period, from a framework whose function was to watch over the children and thus enable the parents to join the workforce, to a framework which affords the student knowledge and skills in order to enable him to become integrated in society and contribute to his environment.

Education systems must develop the ability to change in order to cope with the goals set by society. The education system today needs to prove its effectiveness. Today's society demands that education systems prove that their methods and modes of operation are effective in achieving the goals of education as formulated by the society. These demands, of meeting standards set by the society, require that the education system develop instruments of evaluation and measurement, that it formulate more accurate methods for collecting and analyzing data and that it develop methods for reaching conclusions.

These processes will comprise the basis for a change in the methods of learning, for improvement in existing teaching approaches, for the construction of appropriate tests for evaluation, while affording more accurate and effective instruments for guiding the education system towards the effective achievement of its goals, as currently takes place in other fields such as medicine, engineering, agriculture and economics.

For this purpose the education system must undergo a process of change. Do we know how to generate a change in the education system? Are there mechanisms that can be used to generate change? Does education research afford us with tools to cope with these demands? Do the information and data supplied by education research join the body of knowledge that comprises an instrument for navigating in and improving the education system? Is education research identical to research in the other sciences in the ways in which it collects data and formulates theories, or does education research have unique goals, research methods and ways of reaching conclusions? If so, we must formulate the goals and determine the extent to which these goals are indeed achieved by education research. It is possible that the research approach in the field of education requires change. This requires the consolidation of a method which will enable the systematic achievement of this change.

Three terms which should be considered when referring to the process of consolidating a unique research approach in the field of education are:

1. Conceptualization: To what extent are the concepts which we use in the education research process indeed identical concepts?

2. Collecting and handling scientific knowledge: How can scientific knowledge be accumulated? How should the knowledge be handled and how should conclusions be reached?

3. Rules for constructing a body of knowledge: Can a body of knowledge be constructed? It may be appropriate to carry this out only for defined and limited sections in the field of education, whereas for others we will agree that they have no rules or that other rules apply to them .

It may be assumed that there exist factors in the education system which accelerate processes of change and others which decelerate these processes: Do we know which factors affect the process of change within the education system? What are the mechanisms which enable effective change? Can these changes be measured and evaluated?

EVALUATING A PROCESS OF CHANGE

We have carried out research on the integration of technological systems in the education system for the past three decades. However, our interest did not focus on the technological systems and their integration in the education system. Rather, we examined processes of change within the education system. The advanced technological systems comprised a tool by whose means we created a research situation that enabled examination of the mechanisms which characterize and accompany processes of change. For example, integration of computers in schools in the 1970's or systems for transmission of information via broadband lines on the internet today, require changes in the education system. The researches we performed monitored these attempts and tried to assess and measure the various variables related to this process and thus to contribute to a better understanding of the process of change: What factors affect this process? How does it occur in the education system? What variables slow the process of change?

A better understanding of the processes of change will make it possible to guide and direct these processes. It will enable assessment of their effectiveness and measurement of the change's contribution to the achievement of the education system's goals.

In this chapter we will deal with the integration of technological systems in the learning process. Integration of technological systems in the learning system is a change. Research on the various variables involved in this change will enable a better understanding of how the process of change takes place in the education system. It will also elucidate the factors and rules that affect this process.

Integration of a technological system must enable the education system to achieve its goal of educating and imparting knowledge to the student. It must therefore take into account the abilities, feelings, attitudes, wishes, personalities and worldviews of all factors involved in the process of change. Integration of technological systems in teaching and education requires making a change. A longitudinal research which will accompany the process of the integration of these systems in teaching and education may therefore afford measurement and evaluation tools and a better understanding of the process of change.

Our occupation with the subject of integrating technological systems is only the framework and research field through which we wish to study and understand processes, mechanisms and variables accompanying the process of change in the education system in order to consolidate ways in which to generate a change in the field of education and learning. The results of the investigations afford tools for generating and guiding change within the education system.

Any change in education which tries to become integrated in the school encounters a teacher who is found in the classroom. The teacher is therefore a most significant factor for the success or failure of the introduction of change into the learning process . The presence of a flesh and blood teacher is essential in some fields of the education system, where the teacher has no substitute. It will be more complicated and less justified to integrate technological systems in these fields. However, there are other fields in the learning process in which it will be easier to integrate technological systems. Technological systems can be used to relieve the teacher of some of his responsibility, especially in the transmission of knowledge. This will enable the teacher to invest more time and to concentrate on the promotion of processes in which his presence comprises an advantage, fields in which he cannot be substituted.

An accepted and consolidated process for analyzing education systems will assist us in evaluating and quantifying various variables that take part in the process of integrating a new technology system. The integration of a technology system in learning necessitates a determination of which measurable components of the learning process can be most easily transferred to the technology system and which subjective non-measurable components should be left to the teacher. We thus wish to design a map of the optimal division of roles between the teacher's contribution, the student's activity and the help afforded by the technology system and other variables in order to achieve a more effective teaching system.

According to this approach we will not measure whole learning systems. Rather, we will divide the super-goal of the system into secondary goals. Some of these goals can be accurately measured and evaluated while others cannot be measured. The Firm Effects Model statistical method enables division between the general investment and a goal-directed investment. In the analysis of a learning system we will also separate between the general learning goals and secondary learning goals which can be measured at different levels. The resultant evaluation is then composed of a measurement of different goals. Some of the secondary goals can be measured accurately, some can be measured less accurately and some can only be evaluated subjectively.

Integrating computers in the school is a process of change which depends on several factors, such as: the learning method, the teacher's role in the classroom, the student's contribution. Research which is directed towards reaching conclusions and understanding processes of change in the school can monitor the processes of integrating computers in the school.

Although many predicted that the integration of computers in teaching will lead to a revolution in the learning system, the appearance of computers within the learning framework did not lead to the expected change. This raised the following questions: Why was this process not realized? Why it did not generate a revolution in teaching? Indeed, expectations were high whereas the changes that took place were negligible.

The process of integrating computers in teaching in the 1980's comprised a research field for our team. It comprised a framework in which to investigate and understand the variables related to the process of change and to elucidate the reason why the expected change did not take place. (Offir , 1987 ; 1993 Offir etal 1998 ;1990a ; 1990b ;1995 ;1999 , Katz & Offir 1988; 1990a; 1990b ; 19911 ;1993;1994)

Since the 1990's we have focused on the subject of distance learning. Examination and evaluation of distance learning processes also serve as a framework for understanding processes of change and renewal in the school. Our research on distance learning attempts to assess those factors which promote change and those which interfere and prevent change.

Understanding the variables involved in the assimilation of distance learning systems, which are based on the results of field experiments, may contribute to a more in-depth understanding of the process of change within the teaching and learning frameworks. Evaluating the attitudes of the teachers and the students, the teacher's personality, examining the teaching methods, achievements and other variables and their integration within a comprehensive theory will help us understand the process of integrating advanced technologies in the school. Their integration and evaluation will afford a better understanding of the process of change.

The subject of the process of change, from the 1980's to the 1990's, was the computer and its integration in the teaching process. Since the 1990's, the subject of the process of change has become the distance learning system. Researches dealing in the integration of computers in teaching as well as those dealing in distance learning aim at affording a better description and understanding of the processes of generating a change in the school . We need language. We need concepts that are as accurate as possible, which can be used to produce meaningful information in order to describe and evaluate a process and reach conclusions. The desired direction of development cannot be described without concepts, and research hypotheses cannot be hypothesized or proven. Progress cannot take place without a pool of concepts.

Concepts are formulated by asking questions that are as accurate as possible and affording answers to these questions. Concepts accumulate during generations of ongoing research. One research is the continuation of a previous research. Every research helps make the concept more accurate and differentiates it from other similar concepts.

Scientific research helps us differentiate between concepts which appear similar and defines the differences between similar concepts. A collection of concepts and elucidation of the connections between them affords a body of information which is essential for describing processes in any scientific field. A body of information is effective only when it is constructed of clear and defined concepts, with clear relations between them.

We must assess and measure the change in order to monitor and describe a change. This will enable the production of information on this change. Terms and concepts are necessary in order to define essential elements that comprise the process of change. Thus, scientific research deals in the definition of concepts and their classification. It affords tools for quantifying concepts. This process has been ongoing in scientific research for decades.

Concepts which are defined and clear to everyone are an essential condition in the processes of analyzing and understanding a process. The defined concept has a measurable quantitative value, and can be integrated in the process. Its intensity can be calculated and its effect can be evaluated. Defined concepts enable the achievement of results. They enable evaluation of the effectiveness of a process. Above all, concepts are tools which can be used to explain the past, analyze the present and predict the future. Science defines concepts and thus enables calculations, formulations of hypotheses as well as conclusions pertaining to the effectiveness of the process.

When we deal in learning, the task is much more complex. Not all concepts that are related to the learning process can be defined accurately and measured. The concepts brilliance, creativity, thinking ability and conclusion ability are concepts which are related to learning but are difficult to quantify. In contradistinction, concepts such as "achievement" can be defined, and can be used to judge the success of the process. They can be calculated and quantified more accurately. Measuring and quantifying is even more difficult when discussing and investigating changes in behavior.

Learning and educational theories contain measurable concepts as well as concepts which are difficult to measure. Reaching conclusions will be enabled when the definition of the concepts is more accurate. It will be possible when a larger number of concepts in the process are defined and a more accurate connection between concepts is found.

The need for conceptualization exists in all fields of science. It is, therefore, an essential condition for the development of an education and learning system, as it is essential for the development of any information system. The field of learning, of behavior, has indeed remained a field in which is it difficult to consolidate a paradigm, compared to the natural sciences or even compared to economics, where the result is usually measured by an economic profit. Three main reasons for this are:

The sample size: The sample in the natural sciences is very large. A researcher who bases his conclusions on a milliliter of material actually has a sample with an immense number of molecules. For example, a milliliter of water contains 3.3×10^{22} molecules. The researcher controls this immense sample, and learns from a sample with a large number of items. In contradistinction, the sample in the behavioral sciences is small and limited.

The research population: The research samples in the natural sciences are identical. An experiment can be performed on a chemical substance. This experiment can be repeated and will yield an identical result. The equation in the natural sciences presents the bottom line of the process. In contradistinction, in the behavioral sciences the individual student is also taken into consideration. Understanding the individual is a necessary and essential condition for understanding processes in the behavioral sciences.

The research and measurement tools: The research and measurement tools in the natural sciences are identical during all experimental and information collection processes. The research tools collect objective and measurable data (such as temperature, pressure, etc.). The situation is different in behavior research, where the concepts are subjective. The measurement tools are not identical and the collected data can be manipulated such that their conclusions are not identical.

Theories in the behavioral sciences which referred to the concept "learning" referred to the level of behavior that can be shaped, directed, behavior that can be controlled and evaluated and whose results could be measured. The behaviorist theory, when using the concept "learning", refers to a level of behavior that has rules, learning that can be directed and guided, learning that can be evaluated and judged. However, there exist additional levels of learning, such as discovery, invention, conclusion, etc.

(Offir 2000b; 2003a ; 2006 ; Offir etal 2000b; 2005 ; 2002 ;2007 ; 2003b ;2000c ; 2004)

THE OCCURRENCE OF LEARNING

Attempts to understand the learning process have been made for centuries, beginning already with Aristotle, Socrates and Plato and on through the philosophical approaches of Hume, Luke and Kant.

How does learning occur? The answer to this question may be obtained by observing man in nature. In ancient times man was a nomad, migrating from place to place in order to find food for his family and livestock. Man then discovered, by asking the right questions and answering them, that there is no need to migrate. He discovered that he could grow his food near his home. He learned to grow wheat in the correct season, he learned to transport water in a canal in order to water this wheat, how to reap the wheat, grind it and bake bread. Man learned to control nature and direct it to his needs. The ability to ask questions, the ability to relate to his environment, the ability to investigate and reach conclusions converted man from a nomad into a wheat grower.

The entire process began when for the first time, by chance, water fell on a pile of wheat grains. The wheat germinated and man was not indifferent to this event. He asked questions: What factors led to the germination of the wheat? Can we ourselves promote the germination of the wheat? Can I grow a field of wheat?

A natural environment is a stimulus-rich environment. Stimuli arouse questions. An environment which supplies the student with questions at the appropriate level is an essential condition for learning. Curiosity, alertness, asking the right questions, logical thinking, an environment that stimulates the asking of questions, trial and error, these are the conditions that enable learning.

This approach emphasizes the importance of the interaction between the student and the learning environment. A student who is naturally curious tries to afford meaning to everything he sees. Knowledge and understanding are processes that are related to the student's tendency to afford meaning, to understand his surroundings. This is learning. The natural environment in which man lives is rich in stimuli and encourages asking questions and answering them. An environment that arouses curiosity is the most suitable environment for learning. Based on this viewpoint, efforts are made to create a learning environment in the classroom which is as natural as possible, an environment that stimulates the asking of questions.

The modern constructivist theory adopted this approach. The constructivist theory believes that knowledge is constructed by the student and is not transmitted by the teacher. Jerome Bruner calls this process "meaning making". This is a process of affording meaning which is the fundament of the constructivist theory. Development of thinking is carried out by thinking. Learning does not occur without understanding. Knowledge is acquired by power of the student as a result of contact with the learning material. Each student's interpretation of the learning material will comprise a stimulus according to his knowledge from the past and according to his intellectual abilities. Learning is the product of activity, response and referral to the material at the student's disposal. Every person has different wishes and therefore a different and complex behavior. Every person needs to be treated uniquely.

The constructivist theory claims that there is limited room for a system of rules in the learning process, the education process and the change in behavior. Every child and every person learns in a method that is unique to him. He learns from the environment, from a collection of stimuli which is appropriate for his ability, his perception and his knowledge. The contact and the relations with the environment, the thinking, the person's ability to cope with the learning material, are essential conditions for the occurrence of learning. Therefore, learning will occur in the classroom only if we supply the student with an environment rich in stimuli which are suitable and significant for his level, interest and knowledge.

Thus, the student does not learn from his teacher. The student learns from the actual thinking process. The student thinks about what he does, what he believes, what others are doing. Thinking is aroused by action, by creating contact. A different action creates different thinking. A different thinking requires use of memory, remembering prior knowledge, reading, learning, experiencing. We learn from experience, from cases, events and activities, from processes in which we were involved. The interpretation of our experience is influenced by what we know. Knowledge is created by thinking and is not transmitted by teaching. Knowledge is acquired by the student's activity and is influenced by his prior knowledge and experience.

Knowledge is influenced and explained by the environment in which it is acquired. The explanation takes place in the student's mind. Problems, questions, deliberations or agreement, striving to acquire knowledge, the student's personality, motivation, all these are intervening variables and influence the knowledge acquisition process. The learning process is, therefore, an individual process. The student acquires knowledge by contact with a rich environment which is meaningful to his prior knowledge. The student acquires knowledge by thinking. The constructivist approach distances itself from any attempt to direct and consolidate regularity in learning.

According to this approach the student must be supplied with a stimulus-rich environment. The learning process must be left to different influences – external influences from the environment or internal influences created by the student's thinking process. These influences are different in every individual and every student absorbs, collects and sorts the meanings which are suitable for him through his contact with the environment.

Direct contact with the environment is the basis for learning according to the constructivist approach. The open school tries to implement this approach. The role of the teacher in the open school is to allow learning to occur by light, careful and positive intervention which will enable the interaction between the student and the environment to take place and develop. The teacher promotes and creates a close and warm atmosphere and turns the student's attention to information which is meaningful to the learning process.

This approach distances itself from any attempt to formulate learning programs and strategies, except for the obligation to supply the appropriate conditions and environment and information which will enable and promote the existence of the learning process. Therefore the teacher's role also changes. It is less fixed and defined. It depends on the teacher's personality and considerations and on the student's feelings. Any action by the teacher is intended to meet the student's thinking and needs.

The constructivist approach aims to create an environment similar to the natural environment in which man discovered how to grow wheat. An education system that affords the student a learning environment which is compatible with his level and with the interest he exhibits in the learning subject, an open learning environment, a learning environment which enables the student to raise questions and find solutions to these questions by himself using a trial and error method, is a more effective method. However, this method is also more expensive, and requires more resources and manpower. A system which enables constant and free interaction with the teacher, with the learning environment and with the knowledge sources is a necessary condition for the realization of the constructivist approach. This is the way for ideal learning, learning which has its own rate and development stage. A learning system in which every student is afforded an environment which is challenging and suitable for him is very expensive, requires many resources that will enable each student to learn at his own rate.

The constructivist approach is based on a theory that claims that the motive driving the learning process is the person himself – the knowledge and interest, the talent and the student's motivation. A learning method according to the constructivist approach will supply every student with the means for expressing his ability. This should be achieved without pressure, without direction and without competition. Every individual will be judged against himself, and not against his friends' achievements. Every student will invest according to his ability, and the environment will stimulate him to express his latent potential.

The student's development is smooth and continuous and takes place one stage after the other, i.e. a continuous growth of knowledge. This method does not claim to understand and control the laws of learning and the process of the acquisition of knowledge by the student. The environment supplies the learning needs and learning takes place.

The constructivist approach comprised the basis for the evolution of teaching methods: active learning, experiential learning and self-regulated learning. These learning processes enable the student to cope with data taken from the situation with which he is faced and creates an interaction with the knowledge he accumulated in prior experiences. The person acquires knowledge via problem solving and shaping. Learning occurs by doing, where the student and the teacher are active. This is learning which involves the students in doing and in thinking about what they are doing. The students are encouraged to experience things and understand them beyond the basic facts. They are encouraged to analyze the ideas and carry out synthesis while working. This led to the development of curricula adapted to the student's fields of interest. The major characteristics of these curricula are:

- The student is involved in doing.
- Less emphasis is placed on transmitting information and more on the development of the student's skills and abilities.
- The student creates a connection between activities by discussion, writing and presenting.
- Emphasis is on the student. The student is afforded the possibility of researching the approaches and values he chooses.

Learning is not effective if it does not include the acquisition of knowledge while developing skills, experience and doing. Learning is a skill that includes training, instruction, trial and correction of errors while learning. These curricula emphasize the acknowledgement of the variance of the individual and his development as a student. An interpersonal relation evolves, which emphasizes the importance of democracy as an existential need in the individual's worldview. The goal is to achieve a balance between the needs of the individual and care for the society. The needs of the individual are expressed in the development of the ability to learn, the development of moral judgment, the development of personal abilities and the development of tools that will enable the individual to act and learn autonomously. The needs of the society are expressed in the development of tolerance, cooperation, social skills and improved interpersonal communication. The principles of learning are:

- Emphasizing human and warm relations between those participating in the learning and emphasizing the student's activity in directing independent learning.
- Developing a flexible curriculum which is adapted to the student.
- Developing and organizing materials and resources in the learning environment which stimulate learning and investigation.
- Using alternative teaching and a diversity of social designs for developing learning experiences.

Meaningful learning occurs via methods which develop activity that combines learning tasks, learning and education experiences that promote in-depth learning. Experience in social roles is very important in the moral and spiritual development of those experiencing the process.

These approaches are based on the assumption that meaningful learning occurs via the manner of experiencing or the personal experience or the teamwork. These teaching methods are based on maximal activity by the student. The teacher's role is to direct and organize the learning experience. It includes affective and psychomotor components which are integrated into a complete whole. This type of learning is suitable for the development of high levels of thinking and problem solving.

In his book *The Third Way*, Anthony Giddens analyzes the trends existing today in the Western World. Today the state passes as much authority and responsibility as possible to its citizens. In order to serve this goal, the education system must educate citizens who will be able to take their fate into their own hands. The goal of the education system is therefore to develop the student's ability, so that he will be able to fulfill his needs. Give the people the ability to solve their problems. Do not supply them with the solutions themselves! The education system thus needs to afford the student with the means and the ability by which he will be able to become integrated in society and will be able to earn a living for himself and his family.

According to this approach we can define the goals of learning, analyze the way and stages by which we will achieve these goals and finally judge the extent to which the goals were achieved. Giddens' approach is based on the assumption that we can direct, guide and lead the students towards goals that we shall define.

A similarity exists between the behaviorist approach and the approach of Hobbes, Luke and Hume. Their approach assumes that man is born a *tabula rasa* (clean slate) and all information reaches him from experiences and that the experience can be measured and directed and influenced. In contradistinction, the philosopher Immanuel Kant claims that a process of thinking can be found behind behavior. The individual's behavior is influenced and directed by the events that take place in his internal world, in his awareness and in his thought. These occurrences are not always understood and are not given to simple evaluation and measurement.

These are two approaches to learning with two methods for activating them. The policy makers must decide which method to use. This is an almost impossible task. It is difficult to use both methods. They are not always complementary and are sometimes even contradictory.

The constructivist approach will dictate freedom in the classroom, an open learning system, a stimulating learning environment, inquiry and experience. On the other hand, the behaviorist approach will demand discipline, presentation of goals, measurements, evaluation, judgment of the teacher and his achievements, constant evaluation of the student, giving grades, giving prizes and encouraging excellence, control of the learning process and making changes in it according to the students' performances.

Which approach will the education system choose? Do we have the tools to decide which method is preferable? Will we afford the teacher or the education system a tool by which they can make decisions in the field of teaching? When should one method be used and not the other? Can the accumulation of knowledge through research in the field of curricula help us improve the manner of collecting information, analyzing and making decisions?

JUDGING AND EVALUATING LEARNING PROCESSES

The school system must therefore judge itself. It must evaluate the education and teaching methods. An objective and clear scale which will enable the assessment of processes must be formulated using a systematic and reliable method that will enable measurement, evaluation, control and conclusions.

A system of concepts is required in order to succeed in measuring a process and reaching conclusions about the process. The chances of evaluating and reaching conclusions about a process improve when the process contains more defined and measurable concepts.

The learning process is a complex process. Not all variables that participate in this process are measurable. Not every variable in the field of learning and teaching can be evaluated objectively. Some variables are subjective and cannot be measured. Nonetheless, when discussing these fields we should strive to as clear and accurate a definition as possible of as many variables of the variables which take part in the process as possible.

Data collection, defining concepts and their accuracy is identical in all sciences. This process is essential for increasing knowledge in the field. The concepts become more accurate as more information is supplied by research. This process enables the development of knowledge.

In order to guide a learning process we must define different methods of teaching and the differences between them as well as which goals can be achieved by each method. A series of researches which we carried out during the 1980's helped us differentiate between different methods of activating technological systems in teaching.

The teaching methods are a factor that should be taken into account during the process of planning an effective curriculum (Offir, 2003b; 2004; 2005). A method of learning by computer may be considered along a spectrum. The "traditional method" is at one end of the spectrum and the "open method" is at the other end. The traditional method provides the student with information. The computer directs the student according to his particular level and in response to his answers. The learning processes and stages are well-defined and documented and all possible correct answers are known. In contradistinction, the open method enables the student to operate independently. The student can use different methods and applications in different subjects according to his interests, inclinations and abilities. The computer serves as an information store, and a broad variety of information can be presented to the student.

The concepts of open and traditional methods can be regarded as being derived from the definition of the open and traditional classroom. There is no consistent way of defining open classrooms. Amabile (1983) cites several definitions or views. Openness can be viewed as "a style of teaching involving flexibility of space, student choice of activity, richness in learning materials, integration of curriculum areas, and more individual or small-group instruction", or one can emphasize the open classroom atmosphere as being conducive to developing curiosity, exploration and self-directed learning. This is in contrast to the traditional classrooms which are characterized by authoritative teaching, examinations, grading, large group instruction and strict adherence to curricula. We adopted Blitz's (1973) definition of the open classroom. This definition includes several fundamental characteristics:

- The open classroom stresses the need to be actively engaged with the environment as a means for achieving meaningful learning.
- The open classroom is tailored to individual interests and activities, and learning must therefore take place at an individual pace and style.
- The open classroom content is relevant to the student's environment, the environment is important in structuring learning.
- The open classroom is designed to be used according to the individual student's particular pace and learning style.
- The open classroom strives to achieve learning which is exciting and enjoyable.
- The open classroom promotes learning which is diagnostic, guiding and stimulating, rather than authoritative.

However, as Blitz points out, additional elements exist which may vary greatly, in addition to the above-mentioned basic characteristics. These elements depend on the teacher's particular philosophy and personality as well as on the teaching facilities.

Research supports the prediction that the open classroom contributes to creativity to a greater extent than the traditional classroom. Amabile (1983), in a review of studies performed on open classrooms and creativity, reports that most of the evidence supports the open classroom:

- The open classroom leads to a consistent and maintained superiority among children.
- Children in the open classroom achieve higher scores on creativity tests.
- The open classroom contributes to higher scores in open-ended tests.

The open method follows the same guidelines as the open classroom. The most frequent activities in the traditional classroom are group reading and mathematics drills. In contradistinction, the most frequent activities in the open classroom are creative writing, group projects and independent reading. The traditional method thus typically consists of drills and practice, whereas the open method usually includes tools for supporting creative writing and exploration.

The open method may include other elements, such as fewer or no constraints on performance, team effort, etc. The open classroom may be designed as such, or may be used in a special way as a standard tool. A database may be introduced as a useful tool in the technological world, and the student can learn to use this database, collect and analyze data (which are traditional applications of the tool). Alternately, the database may be used as a tool for exploration.

According to Schank and Farell (1990), the fastest way to change a traditional classroom into an open classroom is via computer technology. For example, the biggest obstacle to proposing and introducing new and original ideas is the fear of failure. The computer creates an environment which allows for failure and encourages originality. The student asks questions, formulates a hypothesis and examines the hypothesis using a computer simulation or database. The student can make as many mistakes as necessary in order to find the answer, without fear of embarrassment.

Previous research has shown that different variables influence the computer's effectiveness. It is assumed that the presence of certain factors will improve the effectiveness of the open classroom, whereas the presence of others will improve the effectiveness of the traditional classroom. The student's level of creativity should apparently be taken into consideration when using either the open or the traditional method (Crawford, 1988).

We carried out a research with a sample of 140 high school students aged 16 from two socio-economic statuses. Different methods were used as an integral part of their learning process. The different methods were divided according to their degree of openness. The open method was at one end of the scale and the traditional method was at the other end. Two research instruments were used in this study. The first was a 15-item questionnaire designed to examine the students' computer-related attitudes. The items form a general factor, i.e. computer-related attitudes, which explained at least 10% of the variance. The second instrument was the "Torrance Test" for measuring the "level of creativity". Socio-economic information about each participating student was also collected. Statistical analysis of the data did not indicate any significant differences between the "flexibility" and "originality" scores received by students from a low socio-economic status and those from a high status. However, significant differences were found in the scores obtained by the two groups in "fluency". Students from the high socio-economic group received higher scores than those from the low socio-economic status.

Significant differences were also found between the attitudes of these two groups of students towards the methods of using computers in the learning process. The students from the low socio-economic status preferred to work with word processors. In contradistinction, students from the high socio-economic status expressed no preference. The open method was preferred by students with high scores in "originality", whereas the traditional method was preferred by students with low scores in "originality". Thus, differences were found between the creativity level of students from a low and high socio-economic status. Furthermore, the students' level of creativity influenced their attitudes towards different teaching methods in the classroom.

Significant differences were found between three aspects of creativity: "fluency", "flexibility" and "originality". The level of originality was found to be significantly related to the type of computer method preferred by the students. The open method was preferred by students with a high level of originality, whereas the traditional method was preferred by students with a low level of originality. This correlation was found in both groups, i.e. those with a low and those with a high socio-economic status. Significant differences were also found in the level of fluency of students with a low and a high socio-economic status, with those with a low status exhibiting a lower level of fluency.

The computer stores information in a databank and a wide variety of information may be presented to the student for analysis or for searching for information. The student needs to perform the difficult task of assessing the information and reaching conclusions. It may be concluded that the level of originality is significantly related to the student's attitude towards using technology during the process of learning. As the level of originality increases, so does the preference for an open method of learning. This conclusion is also supported for the level of fluency.

This connection between the level of originality and the preference for an open method of teaching is found only when the level of fluency is high. When this level is low, the influence of originality is not related to the preference for an open teaching method. When the level of originality is low, the influence of other factors, such as the student's attitude towards the subject matter, increases. The research results prove that the concept "open method" is not similar to the concept "traditional method".

Any method proves its effectiveness in different populations in order to achieve different goals. Each method has a different definition. This research helped us define concepts and understand the difference between them. As we define more concepts, we will have more tools to construct a model that will help us make decisions in the process of activating technological systems.

The introduction of instructional technology into the classroom has not always met with success. Technology itself is obviously just another tool with the potential to revolutionize the education system. However, a revolution in education will occur only if the correct educational steps and decisions are taken in order to ensure the successful introduction of technology into the learning and instruction process. Thus, decision making is a major variable that must be taken into account when deciding on the introduction of any instructional technology methodology into the education framework (Offir, 1993; 2000b).

THE TEACHER'S ROLE IN INSTRUCTIONAL TECHNOLOGY

The method for operating instructional technology depends mainly on the goal of learning. Instructional technology can contribute towards achieving the learning goal only when the teacher is not essential for learning. Decision making on the part of the teacher demands a clear definition of the different aims of learning and the different methods of operating a technological system in learning.

In the first phase of defining the goal of learning, different psychology theories, such as Bloom's (1956) taxonomy of the cognitive domain, can be used. The lowest cognitive level is knowledge. The students must remember and recall information. The highest level is evaluation. The students must be able to assess the value of a method for attaining a particular purpose.

Guilford (1959) presented a model for representing separate mental abilities which collectively form a map of structure, of intelligence. His theory can also be used for defining the method of teaching. One aspect of his model, called operations, is particularly relevant to the present discussion. Guilford suggested that retrieval of information from storage in memory basically involves two kinds of operations, divergent production and convergent production. When divergence is high, or the level on Bloom's scale is high (for example, evaluation), the role of instructional technology is minimal since it cannot fully cope with this task given the present state of the art in software. The teacher must take the dominant role in teaching such a subject. However, when the subject matter is low in divergence (convergent) or is mainly a transfer of knowledge, instructional technology can replace the teacher to a higher extent. The teacher's role becomes less effective.

The accuracy of the goal definition increases as more information is collected by the system. Instructional technology can be operated by different methods for establishing different levels of teacher-student interactions. These levels have been found to affect the student's needs for the teacher's presence. These findings directed us in our effort to try and define different methods for operating instructional technology.

OPERATING INSTRUCTIONAL TECHNOLOGY

The teacher is an important factor in the introduction of instructional technology into the schools. Instructional technology will be used in a school if the teacher considers it to be a more effective method for achieving the aim of teaching. Two extreme methods can be found on the continuum of instructional technology methods. These extremes are the two extremes mentioned above, i.e. the open and the traditional method.

With the traditional method, the material and process of learning are well-defined. All possible answers are known and the aim of the method is solely to transfer information. The "teaching machine", for example, is a traditional method. In contradistinction, the "open method" aims to develop the student's way of thinking and his ability to analyze material, to draw conclusions and present original ideas. The teacher makes a different contribution to the process of learning in these two extreme methods of teaching. In the traditional method the teacher transfers knowledge, i.e. delivers information to the student. This task can be accomplished by lectures, books or other sources of information. In the open method the teacher asks the students open questions, discusses ideas and encourages the students to present their own original conclusions. The teacher's presence in the classroom is more important in the open method. This method of learning is suitable for achieving the aim of "evaluation".

The method of operating instructional technology should be directed by the goals of teaching. In the traditional method, when the aim of learning is mainly the transfer of information, instructional technology can control the learning process. In this situation the student can even obtain information at home via the Internet, television, satellite, book or fax. The effectiveness of the teacher-student interaction in this case is less critical.

In the open method, instructional technology should be operated so that it leaves the teacher in the classroom with enough space for expressing himself. The teacher-student interaction is important in this method. The student should have the opportunity to express his or her ideas and comments, whether the teacher is in the instructional technology studio or in the classroom.

The different systems for operating instructional technology can be classified according to the level of interaction which they enable, with each possessing advantages and disadvantages. Videoconferencing enables full interaction between the teacher and the student. Both can see and hear each other. Learning by satellite enables limited teacher-student interactions. The students can see the teacher, but the teacher cannot see the students. The students can ask and answer questions mainly in writing. Television and fax enable unidirectional delivery of information. Therefore, the aim of learning will affect the method of learning. The method of learning will affect the type of instructional technology that will be used and this technology will affect the level and quality of the teacher-student interaction.

We found that the teacher-student interaction is an important factor affecting the level of learning. The interaction is important mainly in the open method. However, the instructional technology system is limited in constructing a teacher-student interaction. It may be concluded that when the importance of the teacher-student interaction increases, the importance of the teacher's presence in the classroom also increases.

We have constructed a model for analyzing the messages in instructional technology. The validity and reliability of our research tool for analyzing interactions was developed as an integral part of operating our instructional technology system (Offir & Lev, 2000). During the past twenty years our research has directed us towards developing a model for decision making, i.e. where, when and how to use different instructional technology means for achieving defined aims of education (Katz & Offir, 1990; Offir, 1988; Offir & Katz, 1990a,b,c).

The teacher must be taken into account when generating a change in the learning and teaching system. The model which was consolidated enables the analysis of the goals of the learning process which will be achieved by the teacher and those which will be achieved by technological systems: Which teaching method is suitable for achieving a defined measurable and objective aim? Which teaching method is suitable for achieving a less defined and subjective aim?

According to this model, the teacher will concentrate mainly on imparting ability, developing thinking and tasks that involve individual attention. The technological systems will be operated mainly in order to impart information to the student. A combination and integration between technological systems and a flesh and blood teacher will lead to an improvement in the learning and teaching framework and will thus increase their effectiveness.

Research Process for Evaluating the Integration of Technologies in Learning

The process of integrating technological systems in teaching and learning thus requires a unique research strategy which includes four stages, as presented in the following diagram:

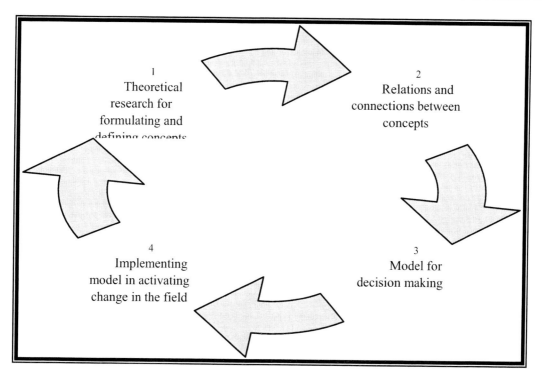

1
Theoretical
research for
formulating and
defining concepts

2
Relations and
connections between
concepts

4
Implementing
model in activating
change in the field

3
Model for
decision making

The concepts which we use for discussing and making decisions in the field of the "integration of technological systems in learning" are concepts that were created and formulated in various disciplines: psychology, sociology, curricula, business administration, economics, etc. Some of these concepts will be found to be relevant to the research and will be able to help in the process of assimilating and evaluating technological systems in learning. Other concepts will be found unsuitable for the assimilation and evaluation process. The theoretical research must locate the concepts relevant to the field. It affords tools for formulating and defining the goal which we wish to achieve with the learning process.

Defining the concepts and determining their use in the process of assimilating and evaluating technologies is the first stage, i.e. the theoretical research for formulating and defining concepts, some of which will be found relevant to the assimilation process. Some innovative technological systems will be found appropriate, and some will be found unsuitable.

The second stage of the research will deal in defining relations and connections between the concepts. For example, the research methods were defined on a continuum, where the "open method" is at one end and the "traditional method" is at the other end. Determining the methods on this continuum enables reference to methods found between these two extremes, i.e. an open method which also contains fixed objective elements, for example a simulation or model. The concept of "goal" in the second stage of our research can be found to have a relation and connection to different types of "goals". Different theories can be used in order to define the goals, as defined in the previous section.

The third stage will deal in the presentation of a model which will demonstrate complex relations between the various concepts and the relations between the teaching method and the goal which we are planning to achieve. The model will present the relation between the teaching method, the goal, and the teacher's contribution to the teaching process. The model that is constructed in the third stage is three-dimensional and presents relations between various variables.

The validity of the model which is constructed in the third stage will be examined in the fourth stage of the process, i.e. the implementation stage. This is the stage in which we activate the project in the field, make decisions according to the model which we designed and examine the model's effectiveness in improving the discussion and the decision making process. The model's effectiveness is examined by the extent of its contribution to improving the achievement of the project's aims.

STAGES OF RESEARCH AND IMPLEMENTATION IN THE FIELD OF INSTRUCTIONAL TECHNOLOGY

Thus, the first stage of research is theoretical and attempts to understand the relations and effects between diverse variables. A major part of this research will we found to be non-relevant, i.e. no relations will be found between the variables. However, some variables with significant relations and effects will be found. These variables will comprise the basis for continuing research.

In our research the teacher was found to comprise a significant factor in the process of change. We therefore asked: Does a relation exist between any of the teacher's characteristics, personality or abilities and his willingness to carry out a change in his teaching habits? We carried out investigations in an attempt to discover significant relations between the teacher's willingness to assimilate change and his personality traits. The teacher's personality trait as a risk-taker was found to be significant. The teacher's risk-taker trait can predict his willingness to cope with change.

In the next stage of our research we tried to understand the relation between the level of the teacher's willingness to take risks (risk-taker) and his attitudes towards the use of technological systems in his teaching process. An investigation was carried out with the aim of examining the relations between the concepts and their contribution to the consolidation of a model that will help in the decision making process (Offir, 1990). Two questionnaires were designed especially for this study:

1.   Risk-taking questionnaire: This questionnaire was comprised of 12 items and was intended for assessing the subjects' risk-taking level. A principal components analysis with VARIMAX rotation, designed to rotate the initial factors such that each item loads high on one factor but almost zero on others, yielded one significant factor comprising six questionnaire items (this factor had an eigenvalue greater than 1.0, indicating that it consisted of homogeneous content and explained at least 10% of the variance). A higher score in this aspect of the factor indicated that the subject indulged more in high level risk-taking behavior. The second aspect of the factor included these 6 risk-taking experiences where the subjects were asked to predict the number and levels of risk-taking behavior which they thought they would undertake in the future. A higher score on this aspect indicated a higher number and level of future risks

chosen. The compound risk-taking score was based on the cumulative score achieved on both of the risk-taking aspects.

2. Attitude to computers questionnaire: This questionnaire contained one significant factor (eigenvalue greater than 1.0 and explaining at least 10% of the variance) and was comprised of 13 items. The subjects were asked to state their computer-related attitudes on a scale from 1 (low level attitude) to 5 (high level attitude). The final score was based on a summation of the answers to all 13 items.

The subjects were divided into three levels of risk-taking according to their responses in the risk-taking questionnaire. Analysis of variance performed for the risk-taking attitude towards computer variables indicated the existence of a significant difference between the three risk-taking level groups. A *post hoc* Scheffe test, designed to examine the significance of inter-group differences resulting from the significant main effects was performed. The results indicated that high level risk-takers have a significantly more positive attitude towards computers than medium level risk-takers, who in turn have a significantly more positive attitude towards computers than low level risk-takers.

These results can help us make a decision regarding the suitable method for carrying out a change in the education system. Instructional technology is generally accepted by teachers as being an innovation in the field of education and instruction (Katz & Offir, 1988). When technology is introduced into the classroom, the teachers must carry out changes in their instructional and teaching methods in order to effectively accommodate instructional technology in the instructional process. However, any institutional, curriculum or instructional change is only as effective as the teaching staff's ability to implement the change effectively. The effectiveness of any staff development policy can only be considered in light of the manner in which the teachers respond to this policy. Understanding the teachers' behaviors and attitudes is therefore a prerequisite for the implementation of any reform in the teaching and instruction methods.

The relation between change and personality variables is well-known in society in general and in education in particular. When society feels that a fundamental change is necessary, it calls upon innovative leaders to initiate the necessary change. This is also the case in education (Duke, 1987). Technology is a new instructional aid and only those teachers whose personalities are comfortable with innovative teaching methods will respond positively to technology and will make a firm decision to use instructional technology in the classroom (Glasman & Nevo, 1988).

The results of our investigation clearly demonstrate that a positive attitude towards using technology in the classroom is significantly related to the personality trait of risk-taking. High level risk-takers are apparently more likely to be capable of making the transition to using instructional technology than are medium or low level risk-takers. The risk-taking trait appears to be necessary for the adoption of a new and innovative instructional and teaching method and can be used to predict successful introduction of novelty into the classroom. In contradistinction, low level risk-takers appear to reflect traditionalism in the teachers' perceptions of teaching methods. This impairs their ability to accept novel teaching methods in the classroom. These results confirm findings that certain personality traits are necessary for the successful implementation of novel situations in the classroom (Katz, 1984).

When use of instructional technology in the classroom is universally perceived as successful, all teachers (low, medium and high level risk-takers) will agree to implement this technology within their instructional activities. However, if instructional technology is perceived as only about 50% successful, then the low level risk-takers will agree to implement it in only about 10% of their teaching activities. Medium level risk-takers will use this technology in 50% of their instruction, whereas the high level risk-takers will use instructional technology in 80% of their teaching.

These results indicate that schools which are intent on introducing instructional technology into their classrooms should do so only with teachers who are classified as high level risk-takers. After instructional technology is demonstrated as being useful in teaching by these risk-taking teachers, it can be introduced into the classrooms of medium and low level risk-takers. These teachers will then be more inclined to accept instructional technology as a new, but not threatening, teaching method.

Further research should be carried out in order to examine whether the findings of this research are unique to the field of instructional technology.

With the development of the computer in the 1980's, many believed that the computer would become integrated in the teaching process and would comprise an effective tool. Some even predicted that it would replace the teacher. Many believed that the change in the education system would result from a flooding of the school with computers. The model which we consolidated as a result of our researches indicates and directs towards a different method for integrating technological systems in education:

1. The system must take the teacher's needs and wishes into account.
2. The teacher's personality is an important factor in his willingness to cope with new systems in teaching.
3. Success in using instructional technology systems in the past influences the teacher's attitudes towards the change.

A teacher who experienced more successful and tangible success in integrating instructional technology systems in the past will have less resistance to the integration of such systems in the classroom.

The model therefore guides us to the decision to integrate instructional technology systems in slow steps. If we wish to succeed, instructional technology should at first be introduced into a limited number of schools. Concentrating the efforts to a limited number of schools will increase the chances for success. Evidence of success will enable the introduction of more technological systems into the education process. Integration of technological systems in additional schools will be carried out only in places where the chances for success are high. Acting according to this model will lead to greater assurance of success. This method is contradictory to the method that was customary in the past, i.e. "flooding the school with technology" and stems from the research which we carried out and which is based on research results and models that were consolidated in order to make decisions based on these models.

Assimilating Distance Learning as an Environment for Investigating the Generation of Changes in the Education System

We have been investigating distance learning systems since the 1990's. Activation of a distance learning system within the framework of the classroom is a change and an innovation which evoke responses by the teachers who must cope with this change.

Distance learning today is similar to the integration of computers in the teaching of the 1980's. Both are innovative systems which are supposed to become integrated within the teaching system and are under the authority and influence of the teacher. It is therefore natural that the teacher's attitudes and willingness to cooperate with this process of change are important and dominant variables that must be taken into account in the decision making process when deciding on the most suitable method for integrating technological systems in education.

Our research on distance learning, similarly to our research on the integration of computers in teaching, focuses on the investigation, measurement, assessment and becoming familiar with the process of change generated in the learning systems. It aims to elucidate factors which influence the teacher's place, role and status in the classroom. The evaluation and research process of distance learning systems indicated the importance of the concept "interaction", since in distance learning contact between the teacher and the student is not face to face. Rather, learning is carried out at a distance. The teacher is found in a distant location and the issue of contact with the student is significant, dominant and important.

Teacher-student interactions have always been regarded as a crucial variable for determining learning and attitudinal outcomes in distance learning environments. Many of the recent studies reviewed by Liaw and Huang (2000) are based on the "interaction quality hypothesis" (Trentin, 2000). These studies assume the existence of a direct correlation between the quality of the teacher-student interaction and positive learning outcomes. However, the term "quality" is not always defined. Furthermore, the "interaction quality hypothesis" is not always supported when empirically examining the nature of the relationship that exists between specific types of teacher-student interactions and learning outcomes.

Our interaction research therefore focused on the development and validation of instruments that can be used to analyze the content of verbal and nonverbal teacher-student interactions (Offir & Lev, 1999; 2000). These instruments enabled a comparison of teacher-student interaction patterns in conventional as opposed to distance learning environments. These interaction patterns were used to elucidate how interaction patterns change across contents, using content analysis for establishing empirical links between different types of interactions and student attitudinal outcomes (Offir, Lev & Barth, 2002).

A content analysis instrument which was developed and validated in our studies (Offir & Lev, 2000) was used in order to calculate the frequencies and ratios of different teacher-student interaction categories. This instrument was based on Henri's (1992) content analysis framework, which was subsequently modified by Oliver and McLoughlin (1996). The instrument's coding scheme contained the following categories:

- Social interaction: Teachers interact with students in order to create social relations and support affective-motivational aspects of the learning process.

- Procedural interaction: Statements containing information about administrative and technical issues related to the lesson or course.
- Expository interaction: Statements which present knowledge content.
- Explanatory interaction: Teachers use the students' reactions to explain content.
- Cognitive task engagement: Teachers present a question or learning task which requires the students to engage in information processing.

Data generated by interaction content analysis was used online to supply the teacher with formative evaluation and data-based recommendations regarding his interaction management. After each lesson, the teacher received a "map" which reflected his use of interactions during the lesson. This objective feedback helped the teacher identify the specific interactions which should be increased or decreased during the next lesson. Ongoing research on the teacher's interactions enabled us to feed information directly "back into the loop" in order to help the teacher make more effective use of interactions.

However, when the number of students in the project increased, it became apparent that the question "effective for whom?" needed further investigation. We had a situation in which students with similar levels of ability (as indicated by their teachers' recommendations) and motivation (self-selection) were producing very diverse learning outcomes. We realized that instead of asking which interaction patterns were effective, we should establish the types of interaction that worked effectively for specific students. We would have to establish what works for which types of students and why. Only then could we use interaction analysis in order to help us design and deliver an effective distance learning program. We began to track the students' performance and learning outcomes in each lesson, so as to understand the diversity in learning outcomes. Multiple criteria were used to collect data on each student's learning outcomes.

As we shall see, when educational research moves from the laboratory to the field, it becomes almost impossible to isolate and control the numerous variables involved. Researchers who focus on content analysis can adopt a systematic and integrative approach in order to examine how person, process or product variables interrelate in a distance learning environment. Online data collection on the students' performance, combined with analysis of the teacher's interactions during each lesson, enable researchers to identify patterns of teacher interactions that support effective learning. Significant correlations between types of interaction patterns and positive learning outcomes can be immediately "fed back into the loop" in order to help teachers manage their interactions more effectively. The objective "map" generated by content analysis helps teachers understand which specific interactions they should increase or decrease. Use of content analysis as a formative evaluation tool, as opposed to summative evaluation at the end of the course, helps both researchers and practitioners maximize the potential of the distance learning environment.

Examination of the data indicated that the category "teacher's explanatory interactions" should be re-divided into the following three sub-categories:

- Learning assistance interactions: The teacher's explanatory interactions which are designed to facilitate the students' comprehension and retention of content. This sub-category contains the teacher's use of advance organizers, overviews and summaries, explicit definition of the lesson's objective and structure, emphasis on the relevance of the target content and other teaching strategies designed to gain and maintain the student's attention. This sub-category was subsequently defined as a category in order to enable the user to differentiate between expository statements which present content and statements which facilitate students' information-processing (Offir & Barth, 2002).

- Superficial teacher feedback: The teacher's responses which do not contain an informative explanation of why the student's answer or comment is incorrect. Teachers' responses such as: "Incorrect, anyone else?" and "You are in the right direction, try again", can be included in this category.
- In-depth teacher feedback: In-depth explanatory feedback in response to students' questions and comments. Statements in this sub-category supply students with a detailed explanation of why their comments or answers are correct or incorrect. Teacher statements such as: "Your argument leaves out data relating to ..." or "You are assuming that a correlation necessarily implies causality", can be included in this category.

After the category of explanatory interactions was sub-divided, a significant positive correlation was found between the teachers' social interactions and learning assistance interactions. A larger correlation was found at the end of the teaching process than at the beginning.

One of the main aims of interaction content analysis research is to systematically observe and categorize types of teacher-student interactions in order to illuminate interaction patterns that might otherwise be overlooked (Stubbs & Delamont, 1986). Interaction content analysis helps researchers "tease apart" the essential elements of the interaction and investigate which interactions correlate with positive learning and attitudinal outcomes. Empirical examination of interaction patterns which exhibit a significant correlation with positive outcomes facilitates data-based decisions on the quality of the interaction and enables researchers to supply teachers with an effective formative evaluation.

For example, as the course progressed, the correlation between social interactions and learning assistance interactions increased. No such correlation was found at the beginning of the course, whereas later it became significant. The correlation increased even further during the last part of the learning process (Offir 2003a; 2006; 2007). However, no correlations were found between the other categories of teacher interactions. The increased correlation between social interactions and learning assistance interactions was accompanied by a concomitant increase in the percentage of students who confirmed that they understood the content of the unit.

The category of social interactions included all non-content related teacher statements that support motivational-affective aspects of the learning process. This category includes instructors' attempts to increase student confidence and mediate a feeling of competence. For example, statements such as: "Come on guys, this just looks complicated – when you begin using it you will see that you have already mastered much more complicated material", may be classified in this category. When teacher-related findings were correlated with student-related findings, a correlation of $r=.9582$ was found between the percentage of students who thought they understood the content of the unit and the teacher's social interactions. Furthermore, a correlation of $r=.8357$ was found between the percentage of students who indicated that they thought they understood the content of the unit and the teacher's learning assistance interactions. The significant increase in the number of students who confirmed that they understood the content when the teacher's learning assistance interactions were correlated with the teacher's social interactions emphasizes three basic assumptions on which this study was based:

1. Non-intellective factors play a key role in determining the extent to which talented students realize their learning potential. The significance of a cluster of non-intellective factors was identified by Terman and Oden (1959) in their thirty year follow-up study of high IQ persons. Their study clearly indicates that traits such as persistence, integration towards goals, self-confidence and freedom from inferiority complexes differentiated between achieving and non-achieving persons. Feuerstein and Tannenbaum (1993) also examined the relationship between non-intellective dispositions and underachievement among highly talented students.

2. Students with a high learning potential who live in peripheral areas must be taught non-intellective dispositions together with the subject content. Acquisition of content alone, without these enabling dispositions, will not necessarily empower these students to maximize their full potential. High school students' participation in a university course within the framework of their own school creates a challenging but supportive learning environment that also focuses on the acquisition of enabling dispositions. In our project, one of the main functions of the on-site facilitator is to identify and prevent potential obstacles to effective learning. These obstacles have been reviewed by Tzuriel (1991). They include rapid loss of persistence in the face of failure, interpretation of errors as indicative of insufficient ability and expectation of future failure.

3. In a conventional learning environment, effective instructors constantly use verbal and nonverbal messages in order to encourage and reassure their students that they are capable of learning the material. In a distance learning environment, the students do not have access to the teacher's nonverbal expressions and gestures. According to Cookson and Chang (1995), distance learning instructors must compensate for the loss of this visual dimension. Our findings regarding concomitant improvements in students' self-evaluations of content comprehension when the teacher's social interactions correlate with learning assistance interactions reinforce this position.

This field project was designed to identify and enrich students whose psychometric scores and school grades did not reflect their high levels of learning potential. The student sample therefore did not contain the full range of ability levels. The findings regarding the correlation between types of teacher interactions and students' evaluation of content comprehension reinforce our previous findings (Offir & Lev, 2000). However, our conclusions remain limited to samples consisting of students with relatively high ability levels. Furthermore, our findings regarding the impact of teacher interactions remain limited to students' subjective feelings and attitudes towards content comprehension. Future research should focus on clarifying when and under what conditions the teachers' interactions significantly affect the students' objective scores.

Our findings regarding the use of objective feedback to modify teaching behaviors reflect previous research on feedback and behavior modifiability as reviewed by Mory (1996). Thus, our future research will focus on teacher-related variables which affect the modifiability of teacher interactions. Further research is also necessary in order to establish the extent to which teacher interactions influence student outcomes when the content's difficulty level is increased. We hope to include additional courses in future studies in order to investigate how teacher interactions affect student outcomes in a distance learning environment across subject-content areas and across varying levels of student ability.

In the first stage of our research we always try to define and examine concepts. This is how we defined the concept of interaction. The research helped us differentiate between different types of teacher-student interactions. Definition of the different types of interaction enabled investigation of the differences between the interactions that exist in a distance learning environment and interactions which exist in the traditional classroom. This will enable us to assess which interactions should be left to the teacher in the classroom and which interactions can be operated in a distance learning environment. The results of the research will help in the process of training teachers. The teacher in the classroom will fulfill the same tasks and will help achieve those goals of the curriculum which are difficult or impossible to achieve via distance learning systems. Defining the concepts helps us understand a model for operating a distance learning system as an auxiliary aid and will help the teacher's activity in the teaching and learning processes. The results of this investigation direct us to those interactions which are beneficial in different teaching situations.

CONCLUSIONS

The education system must achieve two main goals. One is to shape the student's behavior, to impart habits, to shape his attitudes, to increase his willingness to integrate in the society in which he lives and to contribute from his abilities and skills, to develop the student's thinking and motivation and to educate him to become an independent learner. The other goal is to impart as much knowledge as possible to the student. Some of these goals can be achieved by individual education and direction. When our goal is to transmit knowledge we will ask: What are the efforts? What is the investment which we are willing to make and which it is correct to invest in order to reach a defined achievement? In such systems the investment will be measurable and the products quantifiable.

When we activate a distance learning system we turn to a large population of students. Hundreds of students who are dispersed over the entire country can participate in a distance learning lesson. Here we will measure: What is the investment, the input? To what achievements have we led the students? What is the profit gained from activating the distance learning system, i.e. the output?

When referring to large populations of students, the considerations systems are not measurable. In such cases we refer to the mean achievements of the population. Decision making models are therefore models that measure and characterize quantitative products.

The overall goals of learning cannot be achieved solely by measurable and objective processes. There exist subjective variables such as the teacher's contribution, education to moral behavior, attitudes, thinking and learning ability, motivation and interest. These concepts are not measurable and cannot be judged in terms of objective measures. The cooperation, integration between the distance learning system and a flesh and blood teacher are parameters which must be taken into account when constructing and designing an education and teaching system. The quantitative concepts cannot be used solely to appropriately and accurately describe the learning process, and neither can the qualitative concepts.

Our research began with an attempt to define concepts taken from the field of the social sciences (psychology, sociology). Our aim was to quantify and define these concepts as accurately as possible. These concepts comprise basic elements for a model which helps us in decision making and deliberations processes.

The learning process can be described on a continuum which begins at a particular point and ends when the learning goals have been achieved. Parts of this continuum can be described using objective concepts. Parts of this continuum can be quantified. However, such a model does not afford an accurate picture since some of its parts cannot be defined in objective terms. This fact does not absolve us of attempting to consolidate models and trying and make them as accurate as possible. The most accurate picture is described using objective concepts. However, where objective concepts are limited, subjective concepts will be added in order to understand and describe the picture. This combination of objective and subjective concepts will present the true picture. Accurate mathematical models cannot describe and explain the decision making process. This process includes objective evaluation along with subjective concepts. In our research we use psychological, i.e. subjective, concepts and try to define them as accurately as possible. We then try to use these concepts in order to predict processes.

This chapter detailed three fields which have developed during the years of this ongoing research. The first field enables definition of the method of operating technological systems according to the teaching goals. Different teaching goals were achieved using different methods (Offir, 1995; 2000). The second field helps determine a method for the assimilation of innovative systems within the education system. This method indicated that the preferable method for activating a "change" is to first activate it within a limited environment where it can be controlled and where its non-failure can be ensured. Success of this change reduces resistance to the change to a minimum and enables its growth and expansion (Offir, 1990). The third field in which our research concentrates is the field of teacher-student interactions. First we invested an effort in an attempt to define various teacher-student interactions. Then we attempted to examine which interactions are suitable for face to face teaching in the classroom and which interactions can be completed by distance learning (Offir, 1999; 2000c; 2002; 2003a, 2003b; 2004; 2005; 2006; 2007).

The results of this research help define the division of roles in the teaching process between the teacher and the technological system. It defines which teaching goals will be achieved by a flesh and blood teacher and which will be achieved by the technological system. The research process in these fields began with an attempt to define concepts and variables which are relevant to the learning process via technological systems. We then tried to find connections and influences between these variables and to present a model which will comprise a basis for analysis and decision making processes in this field.

There is general agreement that the field of learning and education is a most important field in modern society. Few will disagree with the assumption that a relation exists between the level of learning and the effectiveness of the education systems and the strength of the society in which we live. Shaping the behavior of tomorrow's citizens is carried out within today's schools. However, the learning and education systems must undergo a process of change in order to achieve these goals.

The fields of business administration, economics and sciences have models for collecting and classifying information. These models are directed towards and aid in the analysis of processes and making decisions. However, in spite of the great importance of the field of learning and education, this field has not adopted and assimilated these ways of thinking, discussion and analysis: How are changes generated in the learning systems? What are the mechanisms which promote change? What are the dominant variables in the process of consolidating models for evaluation and measurement of change in learning systems? These are subjects that have been investigated by our research team for approximately twenty-five years.

In contradistinction to economic and business systems, judgment and evaluation in the field of education and learning are mainly intuitive. Analysis of research data demonstrated that the integration of computerized systems within the school framework is a process of change. However, this process of change is not identical to processes of change in economical systems and therefore cannot use the same models.

A change in the field of learning systems must take many data that belong to the field of education and learning into account, including attitudes and the teachers' and students' ability and personality, psychological and sociological processes that accompany a process of change, the teaching method, the learning goals as well as cost versus effectiveness (Offir, 1999). However, these concepts are not accurate and it is difficult and complex to quantify them. The researches that were carried out and published by our research team deal in this issue. The complexity of the issue increases because economic models as a sole means are not effective. Nonetheless, knowledge on learning and education is also not sufficiently quantified to comprise a basis for analysis and decision making. We must find a method that will use an accurate quantitative model but will at the same time leave some room for subjective considerations.

These conclusions were reached by our team already in the 1980's, in light of the fact that computers were not generating the expected revolution in the education system. Since the 1980's the team has investigated and published articles dealing in the issue of the integration of technological systems in learning. The aim of these researches is to consolidate models for the assimilation of change in learning and education systems.

Computers and distance learning systems are only means which bring the change to the learning frameworks. Integration of these systems within learning systems creates a situation of change. Evaluation and research on the processes of assimilation of innovative technologies enables evaluation research and elucidates the process of change in learning systems.

The research method which was used is the "ongoing research". The experimental fields in which data are collected are the schools that decided to join the research and assimilate a change. The collected data comprise the basis for decisions for improving methods of operating the project in the following stages of its development. As the project progresses, the decision making model becomes more accurate and effective. The research process thus aspires to:

- Formulate a definition that is as accurate as possible of psychological and sociological concepts that appear to be relevant to the evaluation of the process of assimilation of innovative systems in teaching, according to the literature.
- Examine connections between variables and the accuracy of their definition by researches carried out within the framework of the project in the schools.
- Find relations between the variables. Relations and connections between the variables may help present a holistic model which will contribute to the decision making process.
- Confirm the model, i.e. examine the accuracy of the model in the decision making process.

The teaching and learning system cannot waive the teacher's contribution, the personal human contact between the student and the teacher. The research results indicate that the teacher's contribution is not fixed and changes according to the learning goals. The model defines those goals for which the teacher can use teaching means.

The research team is interested mainly in increasing the effectiveness of the teaching and learning system. The teacher is mainly a mediator. His contribution is mainly in those complex fields of education, development of thinking ability, crystallization of attitudes and moral behaviors in which the teacher's contribution as having a personal-human approach is critical. There is no technological system that can exchange the teacher and which can replace the personal human teacher-student contact. The fact that technological systems fulfill some of the teacher's functions (such as the transmission of information) enables the teacher in the classroom to pay greater attention to individual education in small groups. This enables the teacher to contribute from his ability and uniqueness as a person and as a teacher. With this approach the level of teaching and the transmission of information is carried out in a more professional and strict manner.

The process of the confirmation of the objectivity of the model is a process that has been taking place for years. It is based on the relation between the investment and the product. The model is more effective when the investment is smaller and the product is greater. Our aspiration is, of course, to make a small investment and achieve a high output. Investment when implementing a model in an educational learning environment is measured by concepts which have a varying value in terms of being quantifiable. For example, the investment includes the type of teacher involved in operating the system, the effort invested by the teacher, the teacher's willingness and ability, etc. On the other hand, the products include, for example, the student's motivation, his willingness to contribute to the environment in which he lives, his ability, his skill, the knowledge he acquired and the achievements he attained.

REFERENCES

Amabile, T.M. (1983). *The Social Psychology of Creativity*. New York: Springer Verlag.

Blitz, B. (1973). *The Open Classroom: Making it Work*. Boston: Allyn and Bacon.

Bloom, B.S. (1956). *Taxonomy of Educational Objectives, Handbook 1: Cognitive Domain*. New York: Longman.

Cookson, P.S. & Chang, Y. (1995). The multidimensional audio conferencing classification system. *American Journal of Distance Education*, 9 (3), 18-35.

Crawford, R. (1988). Computer and curriculum in 1999 computers in education. In: F. Lovis & E.D. Tagg (eds.) *Proceedings of the IFIP TC3, European Conference on Computers in Education*, pp. 645-650.

Duke, D.L. (1987). *School Leadership and Instructional Improvement*. New York: Random House, pp. 40-47.

Feuerstein, R. & Tannenbaum, A.J. (1993). Mediating the learning experiences of gifted underachievers. In: B. Wallace & H.B. Adams (eds.) *Worldwide Perspective on the Gifted Disadvantaged*. Natal: AB Academic Publishers.

Giddens, A. (1999). *The Third Way: The Renewal of Social Democracy*. Melden MA: Polity Press.

Glasman, S.L. & Nevo, D. (1988). *Evaluation in Decision Making*. Boston: Kluwer Academic Publishers, pp. 71-112.

Guildford, J.P. (1959). Three faces of intelligence. *American Psychologist*, 14, 469-479.

Henri, F. (1992). Computer conferencing and content analysis. In: A.R. Kaye (ed.) *Collaborative Learning through Computer Conferencing: The Najaden Papers*. New York: Springer, pp. 115-136.

Katz, Y.J. & Offir, B. (1988). Computer oriented attitudes as a function of age in an elementary school population. *Computers in Education*. Elsevier Science Publishers, pp. 371-373.

Katz, Y.J. & Offir, B. (1990a). Computer assisted instruction and students' social orientations. *Proceedings of the 5th Jerusalem Conference on Information Technology*. Los Alamitos CA IEEE: Computer Society Press, pp. 660-664.

Katz, Y.J. & Offir, B. (1990b). Learning and teaching with computers: psychological and counseling considerations. *Educational Counseling*, 1 (2), 124-130.

Katz, Y.J. & Offir, B. (1991). The relationship between personality and computer related attitudes of Israeli teachers. *Education and Computing*, 7, 249-252.

Katz, Y.J. & Offir, B. (1993). Computer assisted learning and cognitive abilities: hardware and software planning implications. In: A. Knierzinger & M. Moser (eds.) *Informatics and Changes in Learning*. Linz, Austria: IST Press, pp. 11-13 (section I).

Katz, Y.J. & Offir, B. (1994). Computer games as motivators for successful computer end-use. In: J. Wright & D. Benzie (eds.) *Exploring a New Partnership: Children Teachers and Technology*. Amsterdam: Elsevier Science Publishers, pp. 81-87.

Liaw, S. & Huang, H. (2000). Enhancing interactivity in Web-based instruction: a review of the literature. *Educational Technology*, 40, 41-45.

Mory, E.M. (1996). Feedback research. In: D.H. Jonassen (ed.) *Handbook of Research for Educational Communications and Technology*. New York: Simon and Schuster Macmillan, pp. 919-956.

Offir, B. & Cohen-Fridel, S. (1998). Psychological factors in conducting an interactive distance learning system. *Teleteaching*, Edited by the Austrian Computer Society, pp. 779-787.

Offir, B. & Katz, Y.J. (1990a). Learning-curve as a model for analyzing the cost-effectiveness of a training system. *Education and Computing*, 6 (1-2), 161-164.

Offir, B. & Katz, Y.J. (1990b). Computer oriented attitudes as a function of risk-taking among Israeli elementary school teachers. *Journal of Computer Assisted Learning*, 6, 168-173.

Offir, B. & Katz, Y.J. (1995). The teacher as initiator of change: fact or fiction. *Curriculum and Teaching*, 10 (1), 63-66.

Offir, B. & Lev, J. (1999). Teacher-learner interaction in the process of operating D.L. (distance learning) system. *Educational Media International*, 36 (2), 132-138.

Offir, B. & Lev, J. (2000a). Constructing an aid for evaluating teacher-learner interaction in distance learning. *Educational Media International*, 37 (2), 91-98.

Offir, B. (1987). Application of psychology theory in computer-based instruction. *Educational Technology*, XXII (4) , 47-49.

Offir, B. (1993). C.A.I. as a factor in changing the self image of pre-school children. *Computer in Education*, Pedagogical and Psychological Implications, UNESCO Publishers, pp. 68-74.

Offir, B. (2000b). Map for decision making in operating distance learning – research results. *Educational Media International*, 37 (1), 8-15.

Offir, B. (2003a). Analyzing of teacher-students interaction. *Proceedings of the Fourth International Conference on Teacher Education – Teacher Education as a Social Mission – A Key to the Future*. Achva College of Education, Mofet Institute.

Offir, B. (2006). Influence of a distance learning environment on university students' attribution of success and failure factors. *Computers in Education Journal*, 16 (1), 82-94.

Offir, B., Barth, I., Lev, J. & Shteinbok, A. (2005). Can interaction content analysis research contribute to distance learning. *Educational Media International*, 42 (2), 161-171.

Offir, B., Bezalel-Rosenblatt, R. & Barth, I. (2007). Introverts, extroverts, and achievement in a distance learning environment. *The American Journal of Distance Education*, 21 (1).

Offir, B., Golub, M.R. & Cohen-Fridel, S. (1993). Attitude towards courseware as a function of high schools' creative level. *Information and Changes in Learning*, Elsevier Science Publishers, 7, 211-218.

Offir, B., Katz, Y.J. & Schmida, M. (1991). Do universities educate towards a change in teacher attitudes? The case of computer attitudes. *Education and Computing*, 7, 289-292.

Offir, B., Lev, J., Harpaz, Y. & Barth, I. (2002). Using interaction content analysis instruments to access distance education. Special issue of the journal *Computer in Schools*, 18 (2/3), 27-42.

Offir, B., Lev, J., Lev, Y., Barth, I. & Shteinbok, A. (2003b). Teacher-student interactions and learning outcomes in a distance environment. *Internet and Higher Education*, 6 (1), 65-75.

Offir, B., Lev, Y. & Lev, Y. (2000c). Matrix for analyzing verbal and non-verbal teacher-learner interactions in distance learning. In: D. Benzie & D. Passey (eds.) *Educational uses of Information and Communication Technology*. Publishing House of the Electronics Industry, pp. 319-326.

Offir, B., Lev. Y., Lev, Y., Barth, I. & Shteinbok, A. (2004). An integrated analysis of verbal and nonverbal interaction in conventional and distance learning environments. *Journal of Educational Computing Research*, 31 (2), 101-118.

Oliver, R. & McLoughlin, C. (1996). An investigation of the nature and form of interaction in live interactive television. *ERIC Document* Number 396738.

Schank, R.C. & Farell, R. (1990). *Creativity in Education: New Standard for Teaching with Computers*. New Haven: Yale University.

Stubbs , E & Delamont , S . (1986) *Explorations in classroom Observation* , in . P. Croll (ED) Systematic classroom Observation (London . The falmer Press) .

Terman, L.M. & Oden, M.H. (1959). *Genetic Studies of Genius: The Gifted Group at Mid-life*. Stanford CA: Stanford University Press.

Trentin, G. (2000). The quality-interactivity relationship in distance education. *Educational Technology*, January/February, 17-27.

Tzuriel, D. (1991). Cognitive modifiability, mediated learning experience and affective-motivational processes: a transactional approach. In: R. Feuerstein, P.S. Klein & A.J. Tannenbaum (eds.) *Mediated Learning Experience: Theoretical, psychological and Learning Implications*. London: Freund Publishing House.

In: Psychology of Decision Making in Education
Editor: Jeanine A. Elsworth, pp. 73-97

ISBN: 978-1-60021-933-7
© 2006 Nova Science Publishers, Inc.

Chapter 3

Driving Dangerously: Motives Underlying Young Men's Decision to Engage in Risky Driving

Robert Ho[1], and Rita Yong Gee*

[1]School of Psychology and Sociology, Central Queensland University
Rockhampton, QLD 4702, Australia

Abstract

Two studies were conducted to: (1) identify the motives underlying dangerous driving among young males, and (2) evaluate the hypothesized structural relations (both direct and indirect) between the personality construct of sensation seeking, perception of danger, and the identified motives in representing the way risky driving decisions are made. In study 1, exploratory factor analysis ($N = 200$) yielded a three-factor structure representing three major motives for risky driving – *driving fast/risk taking, confidence in one's driving skills, disrespect for traffic laws*. Confirmatory factor analysis ($N = 264$) confirmed and further clarified this factor structure in representing the motives underlying young males' driving behavior. In study 2, path analysis ($N = 384$) provided overall support for the 'fit' of the hypothesized model for dangerous driving. The implications of the findings with regard to the development of effective intervention strategies for dangerous driving among young males are discussed.

* Correspondence to: [1]School of Psychology and Sociology, Central Queensland University, Rockhampton, QLD 4702, Australia, Telephone No:+61+7-49 30 9105, Fax No:+61+7-49+30 6460, Email:r.ho@cqu.edu.au

INTRODUCTION

The recently published *World Report on Road Traffic Injury Prevention* (Peden, 2004) identified road traffic injuries as a major cause of morbidity and mortality worldwide, with an estimated 1.2 million people killed in road traffic crashes each year and as many as 50 million injured or disabled. Projections indicate that these figures will increase by about 65% over the next 20 years unless there is new commitment to prevention. More specifically, without appropriate action, by 2020, road traffic injuries are predicted to be the third leading contributor to the global burden of disease and injury (Murray & Lopez, 1996). Such statistics are no less appalling in Australia, where deaths due to transportation-related crashes now rank eighth among the ten leading causes of death (Australian Bureau of Statistics, 2003).

While motor vehicle crashes result from a variety of factors, studies examining demographic factors relating to traffic fatalities show that age and gender are major predictors of involvement in accidents. Road trauma is most likely to be the leading cause of death for young people in industrialized countries, with young drivers being injured or killed more often than older drivers (Arnett, 1990; Evans, 1991; Lourens, 1992; Levy, 1990). In terms of gender differences, research findings have consistently shown that males are significantly over-represented in road crashes compared to females. Death rates for road injury in Australia are around three times higher for males than females and this differential has been consistent for the last decade or more (Australian Transport Safety Bureau, 2004; Kreisfeld, Newson, and Harrison, 2004).

While age and gender have been identified as important predictors of involvement in road accidents, their interactive effect clearly points to young male drivers as a high risk group in regard to accident involvement. While males made up 72% of motor vehicle traffic deaths in Australia in 2002, males in the 15-29 year age range accounted for 29% of such fatalities in the same period. Statistics show that within the young driver group, males have a higher risk of being involved in a road crash leading to injury or death due to risky driving (Groeger & Brown, 1989), aggressive driving (Simon & Corbett, 1996), and excessive speed (Federal Office of Road Safety, 1997a). These causal factors suggest that the high crash rates among young male drivers may not be due simply to their relative inexperience as drivers or possible exposure to particularly hazardous driving conditions, but rather that there is something problematic about the judgments or decisions that they make when driving (Harré, 2000). In particular, the plethora of research evidence suggests that it is the propensity to take risks by young male drivers that explains their tendency to be involved in dangerous driving practices (DiBlasio, 1986; Evans, 1991; Hurrelmann, 1990).

A considerable body of literature has examined the underlying factors that may contribute to risky driving by young males. These factors include personality, attitude, risk acceptance, overconfidence, and mood.

Personality

Of particular importance is the link between the personality trait of *sensation seeking* and risk taking behavior which is often cited as a characteristic of young male drivers that explains their higher crash risk. Sensation seeking is defined as the need for varied, novel and complex sensations and experiences and the willingness to take physical, social, legal, and financial risks for the sake of such experiences (Zuckerman, 1994). In his review and synthesis of the literature relating to sensation seeking and risky driving, Jonah (1997) reported that (1) sensation seeking is higher in males than females and is highest in the 16 to 19 year age group, and (2) risky driving behaviors such as speeding, impulsivity, driving under the influence of alcohol, and failure to wear set belts all correlated highly with thrill seeking and boredom susceptibility. Together, these findings suggest that young male drivers who rate highly on sensation seeking tend to drive dangerously.

Attitude

Driving safely or dangerously is a choice a driver makes. Young drivers have been shown in a number of studies to have different attitudes toward safe driving compared to older drivers. For example, while older drivers have been found to drive with the aim of getting from point A to point B, young male drivers tend to drive for recreational purposes as it provides them with a sense of freedom and control over their lives (Zimbardo, Keough, & Boyd, 1997). Their attitudes toward law enforcement and in particular, traffic laws also differ from other groups. Young male drivers expect less negative outcomes as a result of committing traffic offences, perceive such offences as socially acceptable, and experience less self-control when conducting such behavior (Parker, Manstead, Stradling, Reason, & Baxter, 1992). This display of non-compliance with law enforcement, lack of self-control, and perceived social acceptability, appears also to be related to their attitudes toward speed and a desire for danger. Speeding has been found to be three times more common among male drivers who had a high number of traffic offences compared to other drivers with no violations. This desire for danger appears to reflect their lower perception of risk, as well as a higher evaluation of their driving ability compared to older drivers (Donovan, Marlatt, & Salzberg, 1983).

Risk Acceptance

Risk acceptance is the individual's level of perceived risk, or risk threshold in which they are willing to accept and consequently act upon. This level of risk acceptance provides a number of explanations as to why an individual engages in dangerous driving, such as continuing to speed when a pedestrian walks onto the road. First, such behavior may reflect their poor risk perception and/or their overconfidence, resulting in the driver misjudging the distance to the pedestrian and the time to brake effectively. Second, the behavior may reflect poor driving skills, which may not allow the driver enough time to respond and slow down. Finally, a high level of risk acceptance, combined with overconfidence in their driving ability may motivate the young driver to accept risks in order to minimize time delays (Deery, 1999).

Overconfidence/Optimism Bias

A number of studies have demonstrated higher levels of confidence in young drivers compared to older drivers (Dejoy, 1992; Guerin, 1994; Guppy, 1993). However, this bias appears to be particularly strong in young male drivers who have consistently been found to perceive themselves as at less risk of having an accident than their peers of the same age and sex (Bragg & Finn, 1982; Matthews & Moran, 1986). McKenna, Stanier, and Lewis (1991) also reported that individuals tend to exhibit either a positive self-judgment and/or negative other-judgment. They found that when drivers rated their driving skill on a 1 to 10 scale, ranging from very poor to very good, they tended to rate the skill of other drivers as average, while rating themselves as above average. These findings suggest that while drivers do not have a negative view of others, they do see themselves as better than the average driver.

Mood

There is evidence to suggest that mood factors such as a high intensity of anger and aggression, emotional instability and impulsiveness, and emotionally involved driving are more characteristic of drivers (both adolescent and adult) who have a history of crashes than those who have not. In particular, the evidence suggests that younger drivers who have less control of their risk taking impulses were more likely to drive for emotional release (Arnett, Offer, & Fine, 1997; Dukes, Clayton, Jenkins, Miller, & Rodgers, 2001). Grey, Triggs, and Haworth (1989) found that young male drivers scored significantly higher on measures of impulsivity and were more likely to use their motor vehicles to express impulses. Lajunen and Parker (2001) found that younger drivers tend to engage in aggressive risk- taking driving more than do older drivers. They proposed that this might be due to the fact that younger drivers are more prone to being annoyed and react accordingly through more violent acts than older drivers do.

It is clear from the above review that considérable work has already been done in identifying the background factors that predispose some young male drivers to engage risky driving choices. While there is clearly much value in this approach, the mere identification of such factors however, does not provide a framework for understanding the judgments made by this group of drivers in different driving situations and the psychological processes that underlie these judgments. That is, the mere identification of these factors and the measurement of their relationship with the incidence of accidents say very little about how young drivers think and why they think the way they do. In order to gain a better understanding of the decision-making process that underlies their driving practices, theoretical models are needed to move the level of discourse from identification towards an explanation of the decision making process. Such models can be employed to integrate the diverse empirical findings that already exist as well as to guide research on both the motives and the subjective processes involved in risky driving choices.

The present study was designed to achieve two aims. First, the study was designed to examine the motives underlying dangerous driving among young males. Although a number of factors have been identified that may predispose some young male drivers to engage in risky driving, a review of the literature showed that there are presently no assessment tools that tap into the motives for dangerous driving. Although there are a number of measures such as Zuckerman's (1994) Sensation Seeking Scale, which measures sensation-seeking and risk taking behaviors, and the Driver Anger Scale, which measures a driver's level of anger in a variety of driving situations (Deffenbacher, Oetting, & Lynch, 1994), these scales are essentially unidimensional and each identifies only one major facet of driving practices. As there is no one parsimonious motive for young males to drive dangerously, it would be advantageous to have available a multidimensional measurement tool that can reliably tap into different motives simultaneously. The second aim of the study was to investigate the association between the personality construct of sensation seeking, perception of danger, and the identified motives in influencing young male drivers' decision to engage in risky driving. Such investigation is important because the decision-making process underlying risky driving choices (which may involve sensation seeking, danger perception and specific motives to some degree) is likely to serve as a cognitive mechanism that links sensation seeking, the perception of danger and specific motives to actual risky-driving practices. The present study reports on two studies that were designed and conducted to achieve the above two aims.

STUDY 1: DEVELOPMENT OF THE MOTIVES FOR DANGEROUS DRIVING SCALE

The primary aim of study 1 was to develop a comprehensive, multidimensional instrument that can tap into the motives for risky driving. It is hoped that the development of such a tool can serve firstly, to identify the motives underlying dangerous driving by young males and secondly, to contribute to the development of a theoretical model that can aid understanding of the psychological processes underlying such motives in dangerous driving.

Step 1

A focus group consisting of 15 males between the ages of 18 to 28 years and who held a current driver's license were involved in this stage of the study. The participants, who volunteered for the study, were recruited from a university campus in the Brisbane metropolitan area in Queensland, Australia. At the initial stage of this study, the participants took part in a group discussion of the types of dangerous behaviors young males engage in while driving. After approximately 15 minutes of discussion, the participants were asked to write down on a piece of paper as many reasons as they could think of as to why young males engage in these types of dangerous driving behavior. A total of 94 reasons for driving dangerously were generated and recorded.

The 94 responses were initially grouped together by two judges on the basis of similarity of phrasing. For example, "they get excited about driving fast" was grouped with "speed excites them". A third independent judge resolved any disparities. This reduced the number of responses to 72. The responses were then content-analyzed, based on an arbitrary frequency criterion in which responses listed at least four times were grouped. For example, based on the frequency criterion, responses reflecting motives toward speed were grouped together. This further reduced the number of responses to 54.

A subsequent content analysis (on the basis of similarity of meaning) was carried out on these responses. From the analysis, four thematic categories of responses were identified as motives for dangerous driving. These categories were labeled 'risk-taking', 'mood', 'attitude', and 'skill'. Finally, in order to reduce the number of responses to a more manageable unit, a proportionate number of statements were written by the authors to reflect the meaning-content of each of the 4 categories. A total of 40 statements were written (10 statements for each category/motive) and these were included in a questionnaire for final scale construction and item analysis.

Step 2: Exploratory Factor Analysis (EFA)

Participants and Procedure
A total of 200 male participants from the Brisbane metropolitan area, Australia volunteered to fill the in the study's questionnaire. Their ages ranged from 18 to 24 years, with a mean age of 21 years. The participants held a current driver's license for an average of two years and three months. The majority of the participants (47%) was employed at the time of the study, and had a mean income ranging from $10,001 to $20,000 per year.

Materials
Participants responded to a questionnaire consisting of two sections. Section 1 consisted of the 40 statements written to reflect the 4 categories/motives for dangerous driving identified in step 1 of the study. Each statement was to be rated on a 6-point Likert scale with high scores indicating strong endorsement of the driving motives: 1=strongly disagree, 2=moderately disagree, 3=barely disagree, 4=barely agree, 5=moderately agree, 6=strongly agree. Section 2 was designed to elicit demographic information relating to the participant's age, level of education, personal income, employment status, and how long they have held a driver's license.

Results
Participants' responses to the 40-item questionnaire were subjected to a principal components analysis, followed by oblique rotation. Inspection of the results revealed that seven factors had eigen-values greater than 1.00. However, examination of the items that loaded on these seven factors indicated that only three factors were interpretable, as well as containing the fewest number of cross-correlated items. In conjunction with results obtained from the scree-plot, these findings suggested a three factor solution. These three factors accounted for 41.12, 7.53, and 5.01% of the total variance respectively, for a combined total of 53.67%. Since the factor correlation matrix showed that the factors were correlated (0.29 to 0.35), oblique rotation, limited to three factors was then conducted.

From the obtained pattern matrix, a total of 29 items were retained, using the criteria of selecting items with factor structure coefficients greater than or equal to 0.33 and no significant cross-correlations. The use of the 0.33 value as a criterion for selecting items is based on the logic that squaring the correlation coefficient (0.33^2) yields approximately 10% of the variance explained. Of the 29 items, 15 correlated with Factor 1, eight correlated with Factor 2, and six correlated with Factor 3. Examination of the items that correlated with these three factors indicated that Factor 1 consisted of items that reflected a desire to drive fast and/or to take risks while driving (e.g., driving fast calms me down; I often overtake on the solid line on my side of the lane). Factor 2 consisted of items that reflected confidence in one's driving skills (e.g., I am a skillful driver and am always in control of my driving; my driving skills allow me to negotiate traffic hazards safely). Factor 3 comprised of items that reflected a negative attitude (disrespect) toward traffic laws (e.g., the present traffic laws are too harsh; it is okay to violate traffic laws).

In order to maximize the internal consistency of the derived factor solution, the items representing each of the three factors were item analyzed. Two criteria were used to eliminate items from these factors. First, an item was eliminated if the inclusion of that item resulted in a substantial lowering of Cronbach's Alpha (Walsh & Betz, 1985). Second, an item was considered to have an acceptable level of internal consistency if its corrected item-total (IT) correlation was equal to or greater than 0.33 (Hair, Anderson, Tatham, & Black, 1997). Examination of the Cronbach's Alphas for the three factors and their items' IT correlations showed that all items were acceptable based on the above two criteria. As such, all 29 items were retained to represent their respective factors. Table 1 presents the three-factor multidimensional Motives for Dangerous Driving Scale (MDDS), together with the factor loadings and corrected item-total correlations for the 29 items.

Table 1. Factor Loadings and Corrected Item-Total (IT) Correlations for the Motives for Dangerous Driving Scale

	Factor loadings	IT correlations
Factor 1: Driving fast/risk taking		
Driving fast calms me down (m34)*	0.77	0.79
I like to drive close behind slower drivers (m8)	0.74	0.80
I often sound my horn or make obscene gestures at other drivers if they cut in front of me (m7)	0.73	0.62
I often overtake on the solid line on my side of the lane (m25)	0.72	0.63
When driving at night, it is okay to drive through red lights or stop signs as long as I am careful (m33)	0.71	0.72
I have no problems exceeding the speed limit because I know I am a good driver (m31)	0.67	0.82
Driving fast is one way of showing my friends that I am a skillful driver (m15)	0.66	0.80

Table 1. Continued

Factor loadings IT correlations

	Factor loadings	IT correlations
I often pull out into oncoming traffic (m39)	0.64	0.68
I like to "race" other cars at the traffic lights (m32)	0.61	0.71
I try my best not to violate traffic laws (m38*[1])	0.56	0.50
Playing loud music in the car makes me drive faster (m9)	0.55	0.70
I often like to change lanes even in heavy traffic (m6)	0.52	0.73
I take out my frustrations by driving fast (m2)	0.49	0.73
I tend to drive fast so I can get to my destination sooner (m13)	0.45	0.79
I often drive through traffic lights when the light is amber (m26)	0.42	0.58

Cronbach coefficient = 0.94

Factor 2: Confidence in one's driving skills

I react quickly when faced with unexpected traffic hazards (m40)	0.81	0.66
I am fluent in changing lanes in heavy traffic (m37)	0.75	0.79
I am a skillful driver and am always in control of my driving (m4)	0.60	0.62
My driving skills allow me to negotiate traffic hazards safely (m21)	0.60	0.62
I am able to judge accurately the speed of an oncoming car (m36)	0.57	0.64
I am a more skillful driver than most other drivers on the road (m24)	0.57	0.67
I often pay attention to other road users (m27)	0.48	0.34
I can easily re-gain control of my car if it skids in wet weather (m29)	0.42	0.50

Cronbach coefficient = 0.86

Table 1. Continued

Factor loadings IT correlations

Factor 3: Disrespect for traffic laws

It is okay to drink and drive as long as I know I am in control of my car (m18)	0.77	0.54
It is highly unlikely that my driving will ever cause an accident (m30)	0.69	0.40
The present traffic laws are too harsh (m28)	0.62	0.54
Exceeding the speed limit by 10 km per hour is no big deal (m11)	0.59	0.71
It is okay to violate traffic laws (m3)	0.55	0.67
I would rather drive a car that is powerful than one that is comfortable (m10)	0.53	0.67

Cronbach coefficient = 0.82

* Order of items in questionnaire: 1= strongly disagree; 6=strongly agree
*[1] Reverse-scored

Step 3: Confirmatory Factor Analysis

Confirmatory factor analysis (CFA) was carried out to evaluate the adequacy of the factor structure identified in the exploratory factor analysis. CFA, unlike exploratory factor analysis, allows the researcher to explicitly posit an *a priori* model (e.g., on the basis of the factors identified through exploratory factor analysis) and to assess the fit of this model to the observed data. Based on the factor structure identified through exploratory factor analysis, a three-factor model representing the three motives for dangerous driving was posited. For this measurement model, the three latent constructs of 'driving fast/risk taking', 'confidence in one's driving skills', and 'disrespect for traffic laws' were represented by 15, 8, and 6 indicator items respectively (generated from EFA in step 2). While it can be argued that a greater number of indicators per latent construct will represent that latent construct to a higher degree than fewer indicators, in practice however, too many indicators make it difficult if not impossible to fit a model to data (Bentler, 1980). Based on Hair et al.'s (1997) suggestion that three is the preferred minimum number of indicators to represent a construct, it was decided to limit the number of indicators to three for each of the model's latent construct. This was achieved by using item parcels to represent the original number of items for each latent construct.

Item parcels. This technique involves summing responses to individual items and then using scores on these summed parcels in the latent variable analysis. For example, on the basis of a reliability analysis of the 15 items representing the latent driving motive of 'driving fast/risk taking', the items were divided into three parcels, and the items in each parcel were then summed to form three measured variables to operationalize the latent construct.

Adapting the procedure described by Russell, Kahn, Spoth, and Altmaier (1998), the development of these item parcels involved the following steps:

1. A reliability analysis on the 15 items assessing 'driving fast/risk taking' was conducted.
2. The items were rank-ordered on the basis of their corrected item-total (I-T) correlation coefficients.
3. Items were assigned to parcels in a way that equated the average I-T coefficient of each parcel of items with the factor.

Specifically, items ranked 1, 2, 7, 14 and 15 were assigned to parcel 1; items ranked 3, 4, 8, 12, and 13 were assigned to parcel 2; and items ranked 5, 6, 9, 10, and 11 were assigned to parcel 3. This procedure ensured that the resulting item parcels reflected the underlying latent driving motive of 'driving fast/risk taking' to an equal degree.

Figure 1 presents the three-factor measurement model representing the three motives for driving dangerously (driving fast/risk taking; confidence in one's driving skills; disrespect for traffic laws). Each latent driving motive was represented by three computed indicator variables (item parcels). For this model, all factor loadings were freed, indicators were allowed to correlate with only one factor, and the three factors were allowed to correlate (equivalent to oblique rotation).

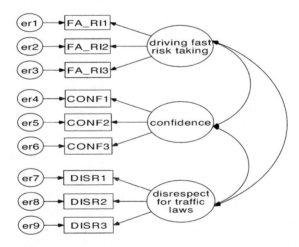

Figure 1. Confirmatory Factor Analysis Model for Dangerous Driving Motives.

Participants and Procedure

The sample consisted of 264 male participants recruited from the Rockhampton and Brisbane metropolitan areas, Australia by the researcher and fourth year psychology students from Central Queensland University. None of these participants were part of the exploratory factor analysis stage of the study. Their ages ranged from 18 to 28 years, with a mean age of 21 years. The participants held a current driver's license for an average of four years. The majority of the participants (48%) was employed at the time of the study, and had a mean income ranging from $10,001 to $30,000 per year.

Materials

Participants responded to a questionnaire consisting of four sections. Section 1 consisted of 5 items written to tap the participant's age, level of education, personal income, employment status, and how long they have held a driver's license.

Section 2 consisted of the 29-item Motives for Dangerous Driving Scale (MDDS), representing the three identified motives of driving fast/risk taking, confidence in one's driving skills, and disrespect for traffic laws. The items were to be rated on 6-point Likert scales with high scores indicating strong endorsement of the driving motives.

Section 3 consisted of Zuckerman's (1994) Sensation Seeking Scale (SSS) (Form V). The 40 forced choice items on this scale require participants to choose between a statement which reflects a desire for sensation ("I like wild and uninhibited parties") and one that reflects a more cautious predilection (I prefer quiet parties with good conversation"). The forced choice items were to be scored with '0' and '1' responses, with high scores indicating high sensation seeking. It is important to note that none of the items refer to driving behavior. The SSS yields four sub-scales: Thrill and Adventure Seeking (TAS), Experience Seeking ES), Disinhibition (DIS) and Boredom Susceptibility (BS). The four subscales, when summed together, provide and overall index of the sensation seeking trait.

Section 4 consisted of the 19-item Danger Assessment Questionnaire (Franken, Gibson, & Rowland, 1992). This measurement tool measures the extent to which a variety of activities are considered to be dangerous. Each item was to be rated on a 6-point Likert scale from 1 (not at all dangerous) to 6 (very dangerous), with high scores indicating strong endorsement of that activity as being dangerous.

Results

The purpose of this phase of the study was to evaluate the posited *a priori* model of dangerous driving motives (Figure 1). A χ^2 goodness-of-fit test (via the statistical program AMOS 5.0; SPSS, Inc. 1997) was employed to test the null hypothesis that the sample covariance matrix was obtained from a population that has the proposed model structure. Table 2 presents the goodness-of-fit indices for this model.

Table 2. χ^2 Goodness-of-Fit Value, Normed Fit Index (NFI), Incremental Fit Index (IFI), Tucker-Lewis Index (TLI), Comparative Fit Index (CFI), and Root Mean Square Error of Approximation (RMSEA)

Model	χ^2 (N=264)	df	p	NFI	IFI	TLI	CFI	RMSEA
Null Model	1883.87	36	<.001	0.00	0.00	0.00	0.00	0.37
Three-factor Model	110.92	24	<.001	0.94	0.95	0.93	0.95	0.07

Although the overall chi-square value was significant, χ^2 (df = 24, N = 264) = 110.92, p <.001, the incremental fit indices ((NFI, IFI, TLI, CFI) are all above 0.90 (range: 0.93 – 0.95). These fit indices indicated that the model provided a good fit relative to a null or independence model (i.e., the posited model represented over 90% improvement in fit over the null or independence model), and support the hypothesized structure of the posited three-factor model for dangerous driving. The RMSEA value of 0.07 is also within the range suggested by Browne and Cudeck (1993) and indicates that the model fits the population covariance matrix reasonably well.

While the above fit indices can be used to evaluate the adequacy of fit in CFA, it must be noted that this is only one aspect of model evaluation. As pointed out by Marsh and his colleagues (e.g. Marsh, 1996; Marsh & Balla, 1994; Marsh, Hau, & Wen, 2004), model evaluation should be based on a subjective combination of substantive or theoretical issues, inspection of parameter estimates, goodness-of-fit, and interpretability. Table 3 presents the standardized regression weights, residuals, and explained variances for the three-factor model.

Table 3. Standardized Regression Weights, Residual Variances, and Explained Variances for the Dangerous Driving Motives Indicator Variables

Parameter	Standardised Regression Weights	Residual Variances	Explained Variances
Driving fast-risk taking → FA_RI1	0.83	0.32	0.68
Driving fast-risk taking → FA_RI2	0.84	0.29	0.71
Driving fast-risk taking → FA_RI3	0.95	0.11	0.89
Confidence → CONF1	0.77	0.41	0.59
Confidence → CONF2	0.75	0.43	0.57
Confidence → CONF3	0.80	0.37	0.63
Disrespect for traffic laws → DISR1	0.68	0.54	0.46
Disrespect for traffic laws → DISR2	0.65	0.58	0.42
Disrespect for traffic laws → DISR3	0.81	0.34	0.66

The standardized regression coefficients (factor loadings) for the measurement indicators were all positive and significant by the critical ratio test, $p<.001$. Standardized loadings ranged from 0.65 to 0.95 (M = 0.78). These values indicated that the indicator variables hypothesized to represent their respective latent driving motives did so in a reliable manner.

The percentage of residual (unexplained) variances for the 9 indicator variables ranged from 11% (i.e. 89% of the variance explained) (FA_RI3) to 58% (i.e. 42% of the variance explained) (DISR2).

While CFA has confirmed the fit of the three-factor model, an evaluation of the factor correlations yielded by EFA, CFA, and the raw scale scores would be useful in identifying the extent of the overlap between the factors. Table 4 presents these factor correlations.

Table 4. Factor Correlations Generated from Exploratory Factor Analysis, Confirmatory Factor Analysis, and Raw Scale Scores

	Driving fast-Risk taking	Confidence	Disrespect for traffic laws
Driving fast-Risk taking			
Confidence	0.21a 0.56b 0.49c		
Disrespect for Traffic laws	0.33a 0.78b 0.63c	0.31a 0.58b 0.47c	

a Exploratory factor analysis
b Confirmatory factor analysis
c Scale scores

The results indicated that the three factors were moderately correlated (range: 0.21 – 0.78; M = 0.48) and suggest some overlapping between the three motives for dangerous driving. These correlations are not unexpected given that all three motives reflect reasons to engage in risky driving. Indeed, the correlations between these motives suggest that they are jointly implicated, either directly or indirectly, in the decision-making process of young males when they get behind the steering wheels of their cars.

Step 4: Test of Convergent Validity

Convergent validity refers to the degree the developed scale is correlated with other concepts in a theoretically based model. That is, theoretically supported relationships from prior research or accepted principles are identified and then the scale is assessed as to whether it has corresponding relationships. High correlations indicate that such relationships, based on theory and/or prior research, do exist. Test of convergent validity for the developed Motives for Dangerous Driving Scale (MDDS) was demonstrated by correlating the summated scales for the three identified motives of driving fast/risk taking, confidence in one's driving skills, and disrespect for traffic laws with the summated scores obtained from the Sensation Seeking Scale (Zuckerman, 1994) and the Danger Assessment Questionnaire (Franken et al., 1992). It is hypothesized that the three identified motives of driving fast/risk taking, confidence in one's driving skills, and disrespect for traffic laws will be (1) positively correlated with sensation seeking, and (2) negatively correlated with perception of danger.

Results

The items representing the three motives for dangerous driving were summed across their respective factors and their means computed. Similarly, the 40 forced choice items on the sensation seeking scale and the 19 items on the Danger Assessment Questionnaire were summed across their respective scales and their means computed. Pearson's product-moment correlation analysis was then conducted to investigate the direction and strength of the relationships between the three driving motives and sensation seeking and perception of danger. The results of this analysis are presented in Table 5.

Table 5. Correlations Between the Driving Motives of Driving Fast/Risk Taking, Confidence in One's Driving Skills, and Disrespect for Traffic Laws with Sensation Seeking and the Perception Of Danger

	Driving fast/ Risk taking	Confidence	Disrespect traffic laws	Sensation seeking	Perception of danger
Driving fast/ Risk taking					
Confidence	.49***				
Disrespect Traffic laws	.63***	.47***			
Sensation Seeking	.60***	.40***	.59***		
Perception Of danger	-.58***	-.33***	-.44***	-.47***	

*** $p < .001$

The results indicated that all three motives for dangerous driving were highly and significantly correlated with sensation seeking and perception of danger ($p < .001$). More specifically, the three identified motives of driving fast/risk taking, confidence in one's driving skills, and disrespect for traffic laws were found to be significantly and positively related to sensation seeking and significantly and negatively related to the perception of danger. Thus, the stronger the participants' desire to drive fast/take risks, the stronger their confidence in their driving skills, and the greater their disrespect for traffic laws, the stronger is their need for sensation seeking and the lower their perception of danger. These findings are in line with the study's hypotheses and offer support for the developed Motives for Dangerous Driving Scale's convergent validity.

Discussion

The substantive purpose of study 1 was to identify motives underlying the dangerous driving behaviors of young males. Initial exploratory factor analysis of responses derived from qualitative analysis identified a three-factor structure representing three major reasons for risky driving. Reliability analysis indicated good internal consistency for all three factors. Confirmatory factor analysis confirmed and further clarified the adequacy of this factor structure in representing the motives underlying young males' driving behavior. Finally, correlation analysis offered support for the developed Motives for Dangerous Driving Scale's convergent validity. Together, these findings suggest that the decision by young males to engage in risky driving is a joint function of their desire to drive fast and to take risks, an inflated sense of confidence in their driving ability, and a negative attitude (disrespect) toward traffic laws. While these findings point to the motives underlying the decision to engage in dangerous driving, what is still unclear is what roles these motives play in influencing the decision-making process. That is, do they operate directly and/or indirectly, being mediated by other motives, in influencing the way young male drivers think? And what other factors may interact with these motives in influencing their decision-making process? These questions were investigated in study 2.

STUDY 2: MOTIVATIONAL MODEL FOR DANGEROUS DRIVING

In order to understand how young drivers think and why they think the way they do when driving, this study posits a motivational model that integrates the identified motives for risky driving with the personality characteristics of sensation seeking and risk/danger perception - two characteristics that have been shown to be strongly related to the propensity to take risks by young males. Figure 2 presents the motivational model for dangerous driving, representing the structural relations hypothesized to exist between the personality characteristic of sensation seeking and risk/danger perception, and the endogenous driving motives (driving fast/risk taking, confidence in one's driving skills, and disrespect for traffic laws) identified in study 1. The model is fully specified.

Relations Between Sensation Seeking, Perception of Danger and Driving Fast/Risk Taking

Several studies have noted that high sensation seekers perceive less risk (i.e. lower perception of danger) in various driving situations and that danger perception and risky driving are negatively correlated (Arnett, 1990; Yu & Williford, 1993). This suggests that danger perception may mediate the relationship between sensation seeking and risky driving. High sensation seekers may not perceive certain driving behaviors as dangerous because they feel that they can speed, follow closely, or drive after drinking and still drive safely as a result of their perceived superior driving skills. Alternatively, high sensation seekers may not only perceive less risk in such activities, they may judge these risks to be desirable. That is, they may initially perceive their behavior as being risky but accept the risk in order to experience the thrill of engaging in it. As pointed out by Jonah (1997), once high sensation seekers have experienced risky driving behavior which has not resulted in negative consequences, they may lower their perceived level of risk, and engage in the behavior more often in the future.

Relations Between Overconfidence, Risk/Danger Perception, and Driving Fast/Risk Taking

When young drivers have reduced risk/danger perception, they underestimate the level of risk in a situation. The considerable evidence that young drivers may tend toward reduced risk/danger perception points to two major reasons. First, there is the tendency for young male drivers, compared to older drivers, to underestimate the risks involved in driving. Past studies that have investigated differences between younger and older drivers in their perception of how risky they consider various driving situations or behaviors to be, have generally found younger drivers to perceive less risk in dangerous situations than older drivers (Bragg & Finn, 1982; Matthews & Moran, 1986; Tränkle, Gelau, & Metker, 1990). Second, young driver crashes are often attributed to overconfidence or excessive optimism about driving skills. The existence of an optimism bias, in which subjects believe they are more skilled and safer in comparison to their peers, has been found in all age groups of drivers (Forsyth, 1992; Guerin, 1994; Guppy, 1993). However, this bias appears to be particularly strong in young male drivers who have consistently been found to perceive themselves as at less risk of having an accident than their peers of the same age and sex (Bragg & Finn, 1982; Finn & Bragg, 1986; Matthews & Moran, 1986).

Relations Between Sensation Seeking, Attitudes Toward Traffic Laws, and Driving Fast/Risk Taking

Young male drivers may recognize that violations of traffic laws increase their risk of a crash, and judge this undesirable, but are prepared to accept this risk because they consider it necessary to achieve another aim. This acceptance of traffic law violations appears to be particularly true for high sensation seekers. Horvath and Zuckerman's (1993) examination of their Risk Appraisal Scale found that high sensation seekers scored higher than low sensation seekers on the Crime factor and Minor Violations factor (which included involvement in collisions as a result of running red lights or speeding). Moreover, they found that perceived personal risk of engaging in risky driving was negatively correlated with both sensation seeking and the Minor Violations scale, such that high sensation seekers believed their risk was lower than that of low sensation seekers, and that people who perceived less risk were more likely to engage in risky driving behaviors.

Based on the above rationale underlying the posited model for dangerous driving (Figure 2), it is hypothesized that the structural relation between sensation seeking and the decision to drive fast/take risk is both direct and indirect, being mediated by risk/danger perception and the driving motives of confidence and attitudes (disrespect) toward traffic laws. The hypothesized direct relationship reflects the argument that the personality characteristic of sensation seeking is a significant indicator of overall driving intention, and operates directly to influence young male drivers' decision to engage in risky driving. The hypothesized indirect relationships suggest that at least part of the hypothesized direct relationship may be mediated by risk/danger perception and the driving motives of confidence and attitudes toward traffic laws. Thus, young male drivers' level of sensation seeking relates directly to the way they evaluate the risk/danger associated with their risky driving, their level of confidence in their driving abilities, and their attitude toward traffic laws. These responses, in turn, are related to their decision to engage in speeding and risky driving in general.

PARTICIPANTS AND PROCEDURE

The participants were recruited from the Brisbane and Rockhampton metropolitan areas. The sample consisted of 384 males aged between18 to 24 years with a mean age of 21 years and who held a current driver's license for an average of two years and three months. The majority of the participants (46%) was employed at the time of the study, and had a mean income ranging from $10,001 to $20,000 per year. None of these participants took part in the exploratory and confirmatory factor analysis stages of the study.

MATERIALS

Participants responded to the same questionnaire that was employed for the confirmatory factor analysis stage in study 1. That is, the questionnaire consisted of four sections, with section 1 designed to tap the participants' demographic characteristics. Section 2 consisted of the 29-item Motives for Dangerous Driving Scale (MDDS). Section 3 consisted of Zuckerman's (1994) Sensation Seeking Scale (SSS) (Form V), and section 4 consisted of the 19-item Danger Assessment Questionnaire (Franken, Gibson, & Rowland, 1992).

RESULTS

Structural equation modeling was employed to test the path model presented in Figure 2. The model incorporates the three previously identified motives underlying dangerous driving behaviors of young males, together with the two latent constructs of sensation seeking and risk/danger perception. The latter two latent constructs were operationalized by three indicator *item parcels* each (the procedure for deriving these item parcels was described in the earlier CFA section). The fit of the path model posited to represent the direct and indirect structural relationships between sensation seeking and the decision to drive fast/take risk was tested using the statistical program AMOS 5.0 (SPSS, Inc., 1997). This program analyzed the covariance matrix generated from the model's measurement variables.

Table 6 presents the goodness-of-fit indices for this model. Although the overall chi-square value was significant, χ^2 (df = 101, N = 384) = 388.43, p <.001, the incremental fit indices (NFI, IFI, TLI, CFI) are all above 0.90 (range: 0.90 – 0.93). These fit indices indicated that the model provided a good fit relative to a null or independence model (i.e. the posited model represented over 90% improvement in fit over the null or independence model), and support the hypothesized structure of the posited path model for dangerous driving. The RMSEA value of 0.08, while within the range suggested by Browne and Cudeck (1993), suggests that the posited model represents reasonable errors of approximation in the population.

Table 6. χ^2 Goodness-of-Fit Value, Normed Fit Index (NFI), Incremental Fit Index (IFI), Tucker-Lewis Index (TLI), Comparative Fit Index (CFI), and Root Mean Square Error of Approximation (RMSEA)

Model	$\chi 2$ (N=384)	df	p	NFI	IFI	TLI	CFI	RMSEA
Null Model	4026.10	136	<.001	0.00	0.00	0.00	0.00	0.27
Path model	388.43	101	<.001	0.90	0.93	0.90	0.93	0.08

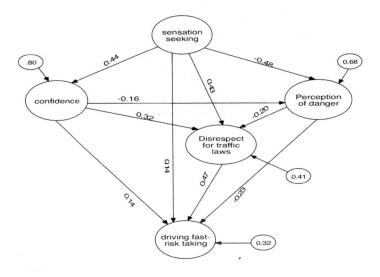

Figure 3. Path Model for Dangerous Driving with Significant Standardized Path Coefficients.

The model's standardized path coefficients are shown in Figure 3. All path coefficients are statistically significant (i.e. $p < .05$). As shown in Figure 3, sensation seeking was found to be associated directly and indirectly with the motive to drive fast/take risk. Specifically, for the young male respondents, the higher their sensation seeking scores, the stronger was their motive to engage in speeding and risky driving ($\beta = 0.14$). High sensation seeking also increased their level of confidence in their driving abilities ($\beta = 0.44$) and decreased their perception of danger ($\beta = -0.48$), which subsequently increased their motive to drive fast/take risk ($\beta = 0.14$ and $\beta = -0.23$ respectively). Increase in their level of confidence also increased their level of disrespect for traffic laws ($\beta = 0.32$) and decreased their perception of danger ($\beta = -0.16$). Disrespecting traffic laws in turn, increased their motive to engage in speeding and risky driving ($\beta = 0.47$).

Figure 3 also reports the standardized residual for each endogenous variable in the model. These coefficients provide an estimate of the proportion of variance in each endogenous variable not predicted by the model. Alternatively, subtracting these values from 1.00 indicates the proportion of variance predicted by the model. These coefficients indicated that the posited model accounted for 20% of the variance in respondents' confidence, 32% of the variance in their perception of danger, 59% of the variance in their attitude toward traffic laws, and 68% of the variance in their motive to drive fast and to take risk.

DISCUSSION

The finding of a direct relationship between sensation seeking and the motive to drive fast/take risk fits well with past studies that have linked sensation seeking to a range of risky driving practices including speeding, racing with another vehicle, and illegal passes (Arnett, 1996; Jonah, 1997). While young male drivers are highly aware that such activities are dangerous, the growing body of literature is consistent in showing that they are willing to take the physical and social risks for the sake of such experiences (Arnett, 1992a; McMillen, Smith, & Wells-Parker, 1989; Yu & Williford, 1993). Young males have also been found to score more highly than other groups with regard to "lethality", a related concept that includes an orientation toward danger and violence, bravery and adventure, and thrill seeking and fast driving (Thorsen & Powell, 1987). Together, these findings suggest that the young male sensation seeker feels at risk but judges this to be desirable, with the challenge posed by the risk of driving dangerously overwhelming the fear of the risk and the desire to be cautious.

The findings that sensation seeking is associated with an increase in driving confidence and a decrease in the perception of danger are also in line with past studies that have shown that young driver crashes are often attributed to overconfidence or excessive optimism about driving skills and reduced risk/danger perception. While it has been well established that most drivers consider themselves above average in terms of skill (e.g., Sivac, Soler, & Tränkle, 1989; Svenson, 1981), a number of studies have demonstrated higher levels of confidence in young drivers compared to older drivers, particularly for young males (e.g., Dejoy, 1992). Other studies have argued that the problem for young drivers is underestimation of the risks involved in driving rather than a tendency to over-rate their ability to cope with these situations (e.g., Tränkle, Gelau, & Metker, 1990). The research of Dejoy (1992) demonstrated that the problem seems to be related to both aspects, with young males being characterized by an exaggerated view of their own driving competency and lower perceptions of risk in hazardous on-road situations. When adolescent drivers possess both an inflated sense of their own driving ability and a reduced risk perception, they underestimate the level of risk in a situation, and ultimately strengthening their motivation to drive dangerously and to take risks.

For the young male drivers in the present study, their level of sensation seeking was found to be associated with an increase in negative attitudes (disrespect) toward traffic laws. This finding is supported by social norms relating to both gender and age. For example, women (who tend to score lower on sensation seeking) evaluate traffic violations more seriously than do men (Agostinelli & Miller, 1994; Moyano, 1997), whereas men are more angered than are women by the presence of police (Deffenbacher, Oetting, & Lynch, 1994). Furthermore, research by Rienzi, McMillin, Dickson, and Crauthers (1996) found that adolescents considered drink-driving to be more acceptable for boys than for girls. With regard to age, findings from past studies showed that, young drivers, compared with older drivers, give a lower evaluation of the risk involved in the commission of traffic violations (Dejoy, 1992; Finn & Bragg, 1986; Tränkle et al., 1990). These findings are consistent with those obtained from the present study and suggest that men and younger drivers not only have a higher disrespect for traffic laws, but also expect less negative outcomes as a result of committing traffic violations, perceive more social approval of such behaviors, and experience less control over such behaviors, compared to women and older drivers (Parker et al., 1992).

GENERAL DISCUSSION

The development of the multidimensional Motives for Dangerous Driving Scale (MDDS: in study 1) represents an important contribution to the identification, measurement and ultimately, the understanding of the motives underlying the dynamics of risk-taking behaviors among young male drivers. Such an understanding provides the basis for developing tools and strategies that can be employed to predict at-risk drivers as well as to evaluate and guide responses to them. For example, as young males over-represent crash statistics, it is imperative that driver-training and traffic-safety programs are effective at tapping into what motivates them to engage in high-risk driving practices. Through the development of both reliable and valid assessment tools, researchers and program planners may be able to focus on specific motives for dangerous driving practices. Given the ability of the MDDS to discriminate between motives for dangerous driving, the scale may be used as a screening tool for identifying possible at-risk individuals. By identifying sub-groups of high-risk drivers, interventions or training programs may be tailored specifically to that group.

The MDDS may also be useful in the evaluation of driver-safety programs, particularly where young male drivers may be required to enter court-ordered driver-safety programs as a result of traffic violations. The effectiveness of such programs can be evaluated by applying the MDDS prior to and at the completion of these programs and examining any changes in the 'sub-scales' scores. Similarly, the MDDS may also be utilized in the evaluation of traffic safety campaigns such as those that focus on peer intervention programs. These programs are aimed at motivating the young driver's peers to intervene when high-risk behaviors are likely in a given situation, such as drink-driving after a party.

The overall findings from study 1 and study 2 fit well with the growing body of literature that characterizes those at greatest driver risk as: high risk takers, sensation seeking, overconfident in their driving ability, low in danger perception, disrespectful of traffic laws, and male. In particular, past research has shown young male drivers' overconfidence in their driving ability to be primarily responsible for the way they assess risk and danger when driving. The relationship is clearly demonstrated in study 2 where path analysis showed that the young male drivers' confidence in their driving abilities lowered their perception of danger while increasing their negative attitude (disrespect) toward traffic laws as well as their willingness to drive fast and take risks. The problem of overconfidence may, paradoxically lie with the very driver training courses that have been and are still used to train novice drivers the skills to handle and to control their vehicle. While such skills are necessary to be able to even begin to drive, a by-product of such skill-based training is an overestimation of the young drivers' skills. A more effective training strategy may be one that moves the emphasis on training new drivers in basic driving skills to one that helps them to have some insight into their own limits as drivers. The rationale underlying "insight training" is that by making young drivers more aware of the limits to their ability to handle the driving situation, their overconfidence will be reduced (Gregersen, 1996).

A review of the dangerous driving literature will show that there has been more relevant research on risk seeking than on any other factors. Yet, it is probably the most difficult state to shift. This is largely because it is propped up with an entire social system of norms and media images that equate fast driving and 'skillful' maneuvers with masculinity, adulthood, and peer group approval (Harré, 2000). At the individual level, intervention strategies are unlikely to succeed if they fail to acknowledge the youthful imperative to increase social status by courting danger to demonstrate courage. As pointed out by Nell (2002), driving represents the most common form of sensation seeking in young men because "it bypasses the genetic endowments of strength and speed and makes the demonstration of courage available to all young men, including the slow and the weak" (p. 78). At the social level, risk taking is a highly prized social virtue. One only has to look to certain groups of people – soldiers, police, paramedics, firefighters – to see that risk taking is not only highly valued but is also entrenched in our social establishment where young men learn and exploit the value of risk taking.

In conclusion, the present study provides evidence in support of the two aims posited for this study. The development of the MDDS provides future researchers with an instrument that can act as a quick screening tool to evaluate driving behaviors in young males. Understanding how young male drivers think and why they think the way they do provides directions for the development of effective interventions, as well as the identification of high risk individuals and situations. While these findings contribute to the understanding of the decision-making process underlying risky driving choices, continued investigation of this area is crucial if effective intervention programs are to be developed that can effectively lower the high road injury rate of this group of drivers.

REFERENCES

Agostinelli, G., & Miller, W. (1994). Drinking and thinking: How does personaldrinking affect judgments of prevalence and risk? *Journal of Studies on Alcohol*, 55, 327-337.

Arnett, J. J. (1990). Drunk driving, sensation seeking, and egocentrism amongadolescents. *Personality and Individual Differences*, 11, 541-546.

Arnett, J. J. (1992a). Reckless behavior in adolescence: A developmental perspective. *Developmental Review*, 12, 339-373.

Arnett, J. J. (1996). Sensation seeking, aggressiveness and adolescent reckless behavior. *Personality and Individual Differences*, 20, 693-702.

Arnett, J. J., Offer, D., & Fine, M. A. (1997). Reckless driving in adolescence: 'state' and 'trait' factors. *Accident Analysis and Prevention*, 29, 57-63.

Australian Bureau of Statistics (2003). *Deaths*. ABS Catalogue No. 3302.0

Australian Transport Safety Bureau (2004). *Road fatalities Australia: monthly bulletin (June 2004)*. ACT.

Bentler, P. M. (1980). Comparative fit indexes in structural models. *Psychological Bulletin*, 107, 238-246.

Bragg, B. W., & Finn, P. (1982). *Young driver risk-taking research: Technical report of experimental study* (Report No. DOT HS-806-375). Washington, DC: U.S. Dept. of Transportation.

Browne, M. W., & Cudeck, R. (1993). Alternative ways of assessing model fit. In K. A.

Bollen & J .S. Long (Eds.), *Testing structural equation models* (pp. 445-455). Newbury Park, CA: Sage.

Deery, H. A. (1999). Hazard and risk perception among young novice drivers. *Journal of Safety Research*, 30, 225-236.

Deffenbacher, J. L., Oetting, E. R., & Lynch, R. S. (1994). Development of a driving anger scale. *Psychological Reports*, 74, 83-91.

Dejoy, D. M. (1992). An examination of gender differences in traffic accident risk perception. *Accident Analysis and Prevention,* 24(3). 237-246.

DiBlasio, F. A. (1986). Drinking adolescents on the roads. *Journal of Youth and Adolescence*, 15(2), 173-188.

Donovan, D. M., Marlatt, G. A., & Salzberg, P. M. (1983). Drinking behavior, personality factors and high-risk-driving. *Journal of Studies on Alcohol*, 44, 395-423.

Dukes, R. L., Clayton, S. L., Jenkins, L. T., Miller, T. L., & Rodgers, S. E. (2001).

Effects of aggressive driving and driver characteristics on road rage. *Social Science*, 38, 323-332.

Evans, L. (1991). *Traffic safety and the driver*. New York: Van-Nostrand Reinhold.

Federal Office of Road Safety (1997a). Young Driver Research Program – Mass crash data analyses: Overview of results from Australian and USA mass crash database analyses. CR 131 (11). Retrieved May 12, 2000 on http//www.general.monash.edu.au/muarc/rptsum/escr131.htm.

Finn, P., & Bragg, B. W. (1986). Perception of risk of an accident by young and older drivers. *Accident Analysis and Prevention,* 18(4), 289-298.

Forsyth, E. (1992). *Cohort study of learner and novice drivers, Part 2: Attitudes, opinions and the development of driving skills in the first 2 years*. TRL Report No: RR372. Crowthorne, England: Dept. of Transport.

Franken, R. E., Gibson, K. J., & Rowland, G. L. (1992). Sensation seeking and the tendency to view the world as threatening. *Personality and Individual Differences,* 13(1), 31-38.

Gregersen, N. P. (1996). Young drivers' overestimation of their own skill – An experiment on the relation between training strategy and skill. *Accident Analysis and Prevention*, 20(2), 243-250.

Grey, E. m., Triggs, T. J., & Haworth, N. L. (1989, March). Driver aggression: The role of personality, social characteristics, risk and motivation. *Transport and Communications*. Federal Office of Road Safety.

Groeger, J. A., & Brown, I. D. (1989). Assessing one's own and other's driving ability: influence of sex, age, and experience. *Accident Analysis and Prevention*, 21, 155-168.

Guerin, B. (1994). What do people think about the risks of driving? *Journal of Applied Psychology*, 24(11), 994-1021.

Guppy, A. (1993). Subjective probability of accident and apprehension in relation to self-other bias, age, and reported behavior. *Accident Analysis and Prevention*, 25(4), 375-382.

Hair, J. F., Anderson, R. E., Tatham, R. L., & Black, W. C. (1997). *Multivariate data analysis with readings* (4th ed.). Englewood Cliffs, NJ: Prentice-Hall.

Harré, N. (2000). Risk evaluation, driving, and adolescents: A typology. *Developmental Review*, 20, 206-226.

Horvath, P., & Zuckerman, M. (1993). Sensation seeking, risk appraisal, and risky behavior. *Personality and Individual Differences*, 14, 41-52.

Hurrelmann, K. (1990). Health promotion for adolescents: Preventive and corrective strategies against problem behaviour. *Journal of Adolescence*, 13, 231-250.

Jonah, B. A. (1997). Sensation seeking and risky driving: A review and synthesis of the literature. *Accident Analysis and Prevention*, 29(5), 651-665.

Kreisfeld, R., Newson, R., & Harrison, J. (2004). *Injury deaths, Australia 2002*. Australian Institute of Health and Welfare: Canberra.

Lajunen, T., & Parker, D. (2001). Are aggressive people aggressive drivers? A study of the relationship between self-reported general aggressiveness, driver anger and aggressive driving. *Accident Analysis and Prevention*, 33, 243-255.

Levy, D. M. (1990). Youth and traffic safety: the effects of driving age, experience and education. *Accident Analysis and Prevention*, 11, 125-127.

Lourens, P. F. (1992). Young drivers in the Hague. *International Journal of Adolescent Medicine and Health*, 5 (3-4), 257-267.

Marsh, H. W. (1996). Positive and negative global self-esteem: A substantively meaningful distinction or artifactors? *Journal of Personality and Social Psychology*, 70, 810-819.

Marsh, H. W., & Balla, J. (1994). Goodness of fit in confirmatory factor analysis: The effects of sample size and model parsimony. *Quality and Quantity*, 28, 185-217.

Marsh, H. W., Hau, K-T., & Wen, Z. (2004). In search of golden rules: Comment on hypothesis-testing approaches to setting cutoff values for fit indexes and dangers in overgeneralizing Hu and Bentler's (1999) findings. *Structural Equation Modeling*, 11(3), 320-341.

Matthews, M. L., & Moran, A. R. (1986). Age differences in male drivers perception of accident risk: The role of perceived driving ability. *Accident Analysis and Prevention*, 18(4), 299-313.

McKenna, F. P., Stanier, R. A., & Lewis, C. (1991). Factor underlying illusory self-assessment of driving skill in males and females. *Accident Analysis and Prevention*, 23, 45-52.

McMillen, D. L., Smith, S. M., & Wells-Parker, E. (1989). The effects of alcohol, expectancy and sensation seeking on driving risk-taking. *Addictive Behaviors*, 14, 477-483.

Moyano, D. E. (1997). Evaluation of traffic violation behaviors and the causal attribution of accidents in Chile. *Environment and Behavior*, 29, 264-282.

Murray, C. J. L., & Lopez, A. D. (1996). *The global burden of disease: A comprehensive assessment of mortality and disability from diseases, injuries, and risk factors in 1990 and projected to 2020*. Boston, MA, Harvard School of Public Health.

Nell, V. (2002). Why young men drive dangerously: Implications for injury prevention. *Current Directions in Psychological Science*, 11(2), 75-79.

Parker, D., Manstead, A. S. R., Stradling, S. G., Reason, J. T., & Baxter, J. T. (1992). Determinants of intention to commit driving violations. *Accident Analysis and Prevention*, 24, 117-134.

Peden, M. (2004). *The world report on road traffic injury prevention*. Geneva, World Health Organization.

Rienzi, B. M., McMillin, J. D., Dickson, C. J., & Crauthers, D. (1996). Gender differences regarding peer influence and attitude toward substance abuse. *Journal of Drug Education*, 26, 339-347.

Russell, D. W., Kahn, J. H., Spoth, R., & Altmaier, E. M. (1998). Analyzing data from experimental studies: A latent variable structural equation modelling approach. *Journal of Counseling Psychology*, 45 (1), 18-29.

Simon, F., & Corbett, C. (1996). Road traffic offending, stress, age, and accident history among male and female drivers. *Eregonomics*, 39, 757-780.

Sivac, M., Soler, J., & Trankle, U. (1989). Cross-cultural differences in driver self-assessment. *Accident Analysis and Prevention*, 21, 371-375.

SPSS Inc. (1997). *Statistical Package for the Social Sciences*. Chicago, U.S.A.

Svenson, O. (1981). Are we all less risky and more skillful than our fellow drivers? *Acta Psychologia*, 47, 143-148.

Thorsen, J. A., & Powell, F. C. (1987). Factor structure of a lethal behaviors scale. *Psychological Reports*, 61, 807-810.

Tränkle, U., Gelau, C., & Metker, T. (1990). Risk perception and age-specific accidents of young drivers. *Accident Analysis and Prevention*, 22(2), 119-125.

Walsh, W., & Betz, N. (1985). *Tests and assessments*. New Jersey: Prentice-Hall Inc.

Yu, J., & Williford, W. R. (1993). Alcohol and risk/sensation seeking: Specifying a causal model on high-risk driving. *Journal of Addictive Diseases*, 12(1), 79-96.

Zimbardo, P., Keough, K. A., & Boyd, J. N. (1997). Present time perspective as a predictor of risky driving. *Personality and Individual Differences*, 23, 1007-1023.

Zuckerman, M. (1994). *Behavioral expressions and biosocial bases of sensation seeking*. Cambridge University press, New York.

Driving fast/risk taking
FA_RI1
I have no problems exceeding the speed limit because I know I am a good driver
Driving fast is one way of showing my friends that I am a skillful driver
I often like to change lanes even in heavy traffic
I often drive through traffic lights when the light is amber
I try my best not to violate traffic laws
FA_RI2
I like to drive close behind slower drivers
Driving fast calms me down
When driving at night, it is okay to drive through red lights or stop signs as long as I am careful
I often overtake on the solid line on my side of the lane
I often sound my horn or make obscene gestures at other drivers if they cut in front of me
FA_RI3

I tend to drive fast so I can get to my   destination sooner
I take out my frustrations by driving fast
I like to "race" other cars at the traffic lights
Playing loud music in the car makes me drive faster
I often pull out into oncoming traffic

Confidence
CONF1
I am fluent in changing lanes in heavy traffic
I am a more skillful driver than most other drivers on the road
I often pay attention to other road users
CONF2
I can easily re-gain control of my car if it skids in wet weather
I am a skillful driver and am always in control of my driving
I react quickly when faced with unexpected traffic hazards
CONF3
I am able to judge accurately the speed of an oncoming car
My driving skills allow me to negotiate traffic hazards safely

Disrespect for traffic laws
DISR1
Exceeding the speed limit by 10 km per hour is no big deal
It is highly unlikely that my driving will ever cause an accident

DISR2
It is okay to violate traffic laws
The present traffic laws are too harsh

DISR3
I would rather drive a car that is powerful than one that is comfortable
It is okay to drink and drive as long as I know I am in control of my car

In: Psychology of Decision Making in Education
Editor: Jeanine A. Elsworth, pp. 99-123

ISBN: 978-1-60021-933-7
© 2006 Nova Science Publishers, Inc.

Chapter 4

COMPARING RISKY AND INTER-TEMPORAL DECISIONS: VIEWS FROM PSYCHOLOGY, ECOLOGY AND MICROECONOMICS

Tobias Kalenscher[1,] and Philippe N. Tobler[2,†]*

[1]Animal Physiology & Cognitive Neuroscience
Neurobiology Section of Swammerdam Institute for Life Sciences (Sils)
University of Amsterdam, Faculty of Science Kruislaan 320 1098 sm, Amsterdam
The Netherlands
[2]Department of Physiology, Development and Neuroscience
University of Cambridge Downing street Cambridge cb2 3dy United kingdom

ABSTRACT

When making decisions between different options, we often consider two basic properties of these options, how risky they are and when they will occur. For example, we may choose to gamble or to wait for a larger reward. Decisions under risk refer to decisions among known probabilistic options, inter-temporal decisions refer to choices between options that will be realized at known future timepoints. Risky and inter-temporal decisions have been captured theoretically primarily by ecology and microeconomics but findings from behavioral economics, psychology and neuroscience often contradicted theoretical predictions. As a consequence, a wealth of more descriptive Models has emerged to explain the findings. A subset of these models has stressed the Similarities between risky and inter-temporal decisions. In this chapter we review both

* Corrrespondence to: University of Amsterdam, Faculty of Science, Kruislaan 320 1098 sm, Amsterdam The Netherlands, Ph +31 (0)20 525 7658 Fax +31 (0)20 525 7709 Email t.kalenscher@uva.nl, Web http://home.medewerker.uva.nl/t.kalenscher/
† Correspondence to: [2]Department of Physiology, Development and Neuroscience, University of Cambridge Downing street Cambridge cb2 3dy United Kingdom, Ph +44 1223 339 544 Fax +44 1223 333 786 Email pnt21@cam.ac.uk

core theoretical approaches and empirical findings. We discuss possible explanations for discrepancies and identify key behavioral experiments.

MAIN TEXT

1. Introduction

When we make decisions, the outcomes of our choices rarely occur with certainty, and often we have to wait some time for the consequences to happen. For example, investing time and money into a good education makes more likely, but doesn't guarantee, a successful professional career and a high income; in other words, the outcome of your investment decision is probabilistic. Likewise, when paying the high tuition fees for your education, you invest resources now for benefits that are yet to come, because you will only be able to harvest the fruits of your labor once you finish your education in a couple of years. Choices between probabilistic outcomes are called 'risky decisions' and choices between outcomes That will be realized at different instants in the future are called 'inter-temporal decisions'. Both types of decisions have been extensively discussed in several scientific disciplines, Including biology, ecology, micro- and macroeconomics, psychology and cognitive neuroscience. In this chapter, we review some of the most influential theories on risky and inter-temporal decision making, and will outline the theoretical and empirical differences in the different approaches. We will then discuss to what degree attempts to unify the two research fields are and can be successful and identify key behavioral and neuroscientific experiments. We conclude with highlighting the importance of cooperation between the various disciplines in elucidating the effects of risk and time on choice.

2. Decisions Without Risk

Decisions between certain, immediate, but quantitatively different choice outcomes appear easy: you just compare which of the two outcomes results in the higher gain or the smaller loss, and choose accordingly. However, how do you compare two qualitatively different commodities, for example, apples and pears? In economics, this problem is solved by assuming that different commodities are translated into a common currency, the subjective value, or the utility of a prospect. Utility is a measure of relative satisfaction or gratification which allows to rank-order and therefore compare the different possible outcomes (montague And berns, 2002). Although frequently used in financial contexts (also in this chapter), utility does not exclusively refer to monetary gains (and losses), but also to more abstract benefits, Such as obtaining pleasure from engaging in a favorite recreational activity, or enjoying one's favorite food, or the like. Although embracing essentially the same solution, behavioral ecology has given a biological twist to the common currency problem. It replaces utility with fitness which, depending on the model, may correspond to e.g. rate of energy gained per unit of time spent foraging (charnov, 1976) or to reproductive success (hamilton, 1964). The utility of an outcome is not a linear function of its objective (e.g., monetary) Value, but a function of the current level of wealth (friedman and savage, 1948; bernoulli,

1954; kahneman and tversky, 1979; tobler et al., 2007a). More precisely, it has been argued That each additional unit in the utility function, the so-called marginal utility (mankiw, 2004), Is smaller than the previous unit, resulting in a progressive decrease in marginal utility with Increasing assets or energy reserves (friedman and savage, 1948; bernoulli, 1954; sibly and Mcfarland, 1976; kahneman and tversky, 1979; kacelnik, 1997; kacelnik and bateson, 1997; tobler et al., 2007a). As a consequence, the utility of a commodity is presumed to be a Decelerating concave function of this commodity (figure 1a). For example, winning $100 would be more valuable to you when you are poor than when you are a millionaire.

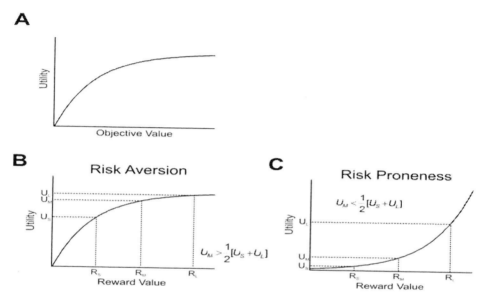

Figure 1. Utility functions. (a) utility as a function of the objective value of a commodity. The utility curve is a concave function of the current level of wealth because the Marginal utility, i.e., the utility increment with each additional unit, decreases with increasing level of wealth. (b) a concave utility function predicts risk aversion when choosing between a medium-sized, certain and a large and small risky reward. In a multi-choice situation, the average utility of the certain rewards exceeds the average utility of the risky rewards because the utility of the large reward is sublinearly larger compared to the utilities of the other rewards. (c) a convex function predicts risk proneness.

3. Decisions Under Risk

Risky decisions are decisions between probabilistic outcomes. The level of riskiness is equivalent to the spread from the mean (variance) of the risky outcomes. For example, a gamble that pays either $ 9 or 11 with 50% probability is less risky than a gamble that pays either $ 2 or 18 with 50 % probability (although both gambles have the same mean payoff of $ 10). This notion of risky decision making is important, as it differs from the common, folk-psychological conception of risky behavior, which frequently implies that a person engaging in risky choices is consciously willing to accept high losses ("the gambler who bets his house and family"). However, although the readiness to accept large losses may certainly play a role in biasing an individual's risk attitude, academic research of risky decision making focuses on the formal impact of outcome variance on choice.

Neither humans nor animals are risk-neutral (friedman and savage, 1948; kacelnik and bateson, 1996, 1997; bateson and kacelnik, 1998): when deciding between a certain and a risky option, one is often chosen more frequently than the other, even when the expected values of the respective options (their probabilities multiplied with their objective values) are identical. Most animals, including humans, are risk-averse, but show occasional risk-Proneness (friedman and savage, 1948; kacelnik and bateson, 1996, 1997; bateson and Kacelnik, 1998; glimcher, 2002; mccoy and platt, 2005a, 2005b; hayden and platt, 2007; Tobler et al., 2007b). Importantly, this suggests subjective differences in the valuation of the aame objective options. Utility theories have been put forward in order to capture subjective valuation with a particular focus on risk.

Economic Utility Theories

Utility theories assign numbers to preferences with both a descriptive and a normative purpose. Specially psychology is interested in explaining choice behavior and has thus focused on the descriptive aspect whereas economy and statistics, more so in the past, have put stronger weight on the normative aspect of characterizing consistent, coherent and optimal choice and ecology is interested in both descriptive and normative aspects. Utility theories all make basic assumptions (axioms) about the elements of the decision space and the preference relations of the decision maker with respect to these elements. From these axioms they deduce statements (theorems) for example about how the preference relations as observed from choices can be transformed into utility relations (numbers).

Von neumann and morgenstern (1944) axiomatized utility theory by requiring completeness, transitivity, continuity and (not explicitly stated but necessary) independence of preferences. Thereby they founded expected utility theory (eut), which provides the most prominent normative framework for the analysis of decisions under risk. The completeness axiom requires that the decision maker has preferences across options, transitivity that preferences are in a basic hierarchical order, continuity that for each option there is a better and worse one and independence that preferences do not change by adding common outcomes to all options. If these axioms are fulfilled then a number u (x) can be assigned to each x so that:

$$X = y \text{ if and only if } u(x) <= u(y). \tag{1}$$

The preference relation x = Y may be read as "alternative x is not preferred to alternative y", <= corresponds to the standard "smaller than or equal to" and u(x) and u(y) refer to the utilities of x and y. If this is true then utility function u preserves the ordering of = and allows translating utilities to preferences and vice versa.

As long as the axioms described above hold eut proposes that a decision whether to accept or reject a choice option should be made by multiplying the utility of all possible outcomes of the option with their probabilities, integrating across products, and choosing the option with the larger sum. Thus, the utility of a choice option with risky outcomes Corresponds to its expected utility. For example, if you consider that it is relatively likely to receive a high income following a good education, and that with the expected income you will be better than with your current situation, then you should decide to invest into a good education. In general, benefits represent positive utility values, costs negative values.

The shape of the utility curve can be related to people's risk attitudes. A risk neutral person has a linear utility curve, and for such a person the expected utility of a gamble is equivalent to the utility of the mean of the gamble. Convex utility curves correspond to risk-proneness, concave curves to risk aversion (figure 1b and 1c). To use a simple example, imagine a situation in which an agent chooses between a certain option, offering a medium-sized reward, and a risky option, offering a large and a small reward with a 50% chance each. The expected value of both options is identical. According to eut, the expected utility of a given choice option is the sum of the utilities of each possible outcome multiplied with their probability

$$E[u_{option}] = \sum p_{outcome} \cdot U_{outcome} \qquad (2)$$

The expected utility of the certain option would accordingly be computed as:

$$E[u_{certain}] = 1 \cdot U_{medium\text{-}reward} \qquad (3)$$

and the expected utility of the risky option would be computed as:

$$E[u_{risky}] = (0.5 \cdot U_{small\text{-}reward}) + (0.5 \cdot U_{lArgE\text{-}reward}) \qquad (4)$$

Due to the concavity of the utility function of risk averse agents, the utility of the large reward, ularge-reward, is sublinearly larger than the utilities of the medium or small rewards, umedium-reward and usmaller-reward. Thus, eurisky will be smaller than eucertain and agents will avoid the risky option (see figure 1b). Put in simpler words, an agent receives the large and small rewards with equal probability when choosing the risky option. Because the utility of the large reward is sublinearly smaller than the utilities of the other rewards, the mean utility of the large and small rewards (risky option) would be smaller than the utility of the gamble's expected value and thus the utility of the medium-sized certain option. As a consequence, the agent will avoid the risky option. Risk-proneness can be explained by assuming a convex, accelerating utility curve, in which the utility of the large reward is supralinearly larger than the utility of a medium or a small reward (figure 1c).

Violations of Preference Axioms

Empirical research showed violations of most of the normative axioms of eut. Reports of violations of the independence axiom appeared relatively soon after von neumann and morgenstern's seminal work (allais, 1953; ellsberg, 1961). As an example, consider the following two decisions (kahneman and tversky, 1979):

Decision 1)
A) \$ 2500, p = 0.33; \$ 0, p = 0.67 (read as: a 33% chance of winning \$ 2500 and a
     67% chance of winning nothing)
B) \$ 2400, p = 0.34; \$0, p = 0.66

Decision 2)
A) \$ 2500, p = 0.33; \$ 2400, p = 0.66; \$ 0, p = 0.01
B) \$ 2400, p = 1.0; \$ 0, p = 0.0

Most people choose a) in decision 1) and b) in decision 2). However this pattern of preference reversals violates the independence axiom because 2a and 2b result from adding ($ 2400, p = 0.66) to 1a and 1b and therefore either a) or b) should be chosen in both cases.

Also the transitivity axiom can be systematically violated such that decision makers show cyclic preferences (a=b, b=c, c=a; e.g. loomes et al., 1991; shafir, 1994; waite, 2001). For example (waite, 2001), blue jays prefer one raisin, 28 cm into a tube (option a) over two raisins, 42 cm into a tube (option b). They also prefer option b over three raisins 56 cm into a tube (option c) but when given the choice between options a and c, they do not prefer a. Humans also show systematic violations of transitivity in certain choice situations (tversky, 1969), for example, when the choice options are composed of several features that vary along different dimensions. Models of context-dependent choice such as regret theory (loomes and sugden, 1982) suggest that violations of the transitivity axiom arise from changes in utility because decision makers evaluate options not in isolation but consider also the outcomes of unchosen alternatives.

Kahneman and tversky (1979) have pointed out another problem of eut in that it does not account for differences in how decision problems are described (framed). As an example, consider the following two decisions (tversky and kahneman, 1986):

Decision 3)
A) $ 240, p = 1.0
B) $ 1000, p = 0.25; $0, p = 0.75

Decision 4)
A) $ -750, p = 1.0
B) $ -1000, p = 0.75; $ 0, p = 0.25

Most people choose 3a and 4b. However, the combination of 3a and 4b is dominated by (has a lower expected value than) the combination of 3b and 4a.

Findings of axiom violations have provoked different reactions. Some theorists have relaxed one or more of the axioms (e.g. machina, 1982; fishburn, 1982) others have given up on the project of axiomatising utility theory and proposed purely descriptive models. The most famous of these latter approaches is prospect theory (kahneman and tversky, 1979; 1992). Prospect theory suggests that the subjective value function is concave for gains and convex for losses and steeper for losses than gains (figure 2). This reflects the finding that decision makers are usually risk seeking for losses, risk averse for gains and reluctant to accept a fair bet on the toss of a coin (in fact, potential gains have to exceed potential losses by a factor of about 2 in order to achieve indifference). The different steepness for gains and losses introduces a "kink" in the value function which makes it difficult to treat mathematically and which has been termed "reference point". Although not formally defined, The reference point often corresponds to the status quo or the current wealth level. Moreover,

Decision weights modulate probabilities according to an inverted-s-shaped probability Weighting function. This reflects the finding that many decision makers overweigh small and underweigh large probabilities, at least when making hypothetical decisions. Insert figure 2 around here

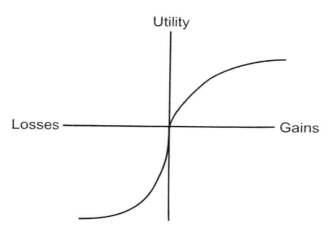

Figure 2. Utility function as proposed in kahneman and tversky's (1979) prospect Theory. The utility function is concave in the domain of gains, and convex in the domain of Losses, and steeper for losses than for gains. The crossing of the axes corresponds to the Reference point against which the prospects are contrasted, for example, the current level of Wealth.

Contribution from Behavioral Ecology Risk-sensitive forAging Theory

The importance of the utility function is to relate subjective to objective value. This is useful because subjective value is often not a linear function of objective value. However, what causes this non-linearity? Bernoulli (1954) suggested that wealth renders the utility function concave. Behavioral ecology suggests additional factors such as upper boundaries on how much energy can be stored and lower boundaries on how much energy is needed for survival can also introduce curvature or even "kinks" into the utility function. Consider for example birds foraging for the night. Because of their small body size and high metabolic rate they face the possibility of starving over night if they fail to accumulate enough resources during the day. As a consequence, a normally risk averse bird might become risk-prone towards the end of the day or at low temperatures, if its energy requirements for the night are not yet met (caraco et al., 1990). Thus, in addition to varying over individuals, risk attitudes vary also over situations and time.

Energy requirements change not only over the course of a single day but also over the year, for example in the pre-migratory period of migratory birds (Moore and Simm, 1986). In that period birds must acquire sufficient reserves for the migration and they behave in a risk-prone manner until they reach maximal body size. Conversely, birds that are not in the pre-migratory period or pre-migratory birds that have reached maximal body size avoid risky foraging options.

Risk-sensitive foraging theory considers decision optimality given reserve constraints. Stephens (1981) showed that it is optimal for birds on a negative energy budget to choose options with higher variance. Conversely, they should avoid risky options when the less risky options provide the birds with a mean rate of intake that exceeds the starvation threshold, i.e. they are on a positive energy budget. For example, a bird almost starved to death (negative energy budget) should avoid the certain option if the certain food amount is not sufficient to guarantee its survival (certain death), and the only chance to survive would be to obtain the large, risky reward (possible survival). On the other hand, a bird on a higher energy budget should be risk-averse if the certain option is sufficient to guarantee survival (certain survival), and the small food amount of the risky option would be insufficient for survival (possible death). Current models of risk-sensitive foraging incorporate the possibility of sequential choices and the costs of foraging (e.g. McNamara and Houston, 1986).

In addition, life-history trade-offs may have favoured the evolution of risk-attitude in a similar fashion (Wolf et al., 2007). Animals differ in behaviours that affect their future fitness, for example, in their exploration effort during foraging. Animals that put more emphasis on future than immediate fitness returns have higher expectations regarding their future reproductive success than others. Investment into the future only pays out if the animal survives until it is able to realize the upcoming opportunities. Because survival is thus important for the strategy to work out, evolution may have favoured the development of risk-aversion towards predators and aggressive conspecifics in individuals with high fitness/reproductive expectations who have more to lose, whereas individuals with low expectations who have little to lose should be less risk-averse.

In summary, the minimal energy requirement (and by extension the maximal reserves) and/or the life-history of an animal may provide an inflection point ("kink"), where the curvature of its utility function changes.

A Normative Framework for Inter-Temporal Decisions

The second type of decisions making discussed in this chapter concerns decisions between outcomes that can only be realized at different instants in the future: Inter-temporal decisions. Humans and non-human animals prefer immediate over delayed rewards (so-called temporal discounting): Provided that the costs for both options are identical, the preference for an immediate or a temporally remote expected outcome is a function of the value of the respective outcomes and their delays, i.e., the time until the outcomes can be realized (McDiarmid and Rilling, 1965; Rachlin and Green, 1972; Ainslie, 1975; Mazur, 1984, 1987, 1988; Grossbard and Mazur, 1986; Logue, 1988; Benzion et al., 1989; Green et al., 1994, 1997; Evenden and Ryan, 1996; Evenden, 1999; Frederick et al., 2002; Reynolds et al., 2002; Kalenscher et al., 2005, 2006a).

Inter-temporal decisions have been extensively studied in psychology and ecology, but were and still are also of great interest in economic models of choice. As with decisions under risk, many of the normative models in economics are based on several theoretical assumptions and theorems, including preference monotonicity, stationarity, and maximization of utility rate.

A fundamental assumption in rational choice theories is that preference orders should be consistent across time. Preference monotonicity and stationarity are directly related to this assumption. Monotonicity means that a prospect X1 that is preferred over another prospect X2 will also be assigned a higher utility than X2 as long as the utility function is monotonic. Monotonicity of time preference (Lancaster, 1963) holds that

$$X(t_1) \geq X(t_2), \text{ if, and only if, } t_2 \geq t_1 \qquad (1)$$

This means that commodity X, available at timepoint t_1, will be preferred over X, available at timepoint t_2, only when t_2 occurs later than t_1.

Stationarity is related to the axiom of monotonicity of time preference and posits that

$$\text{If } X(t) \sim Y(t+\tau) \text{ then } X(s) \sim X(s+\tau) \qquad (2)$$

This means that if an agent is indifferent (~) between commodity X, delivered at timepoint t, and commodity Y, delivered at timepoint $t+\tau$, he would still be indifferent when X was delivered at timepoint s and Y at timepoint $s+\tau$ (Strotz, 1955; Koopmans, 1960; Fishburn and Rubinstein, 1982). Indifference means that the utility of both options is identical, and thus the frequency of choosing A or B is about 50%. Thus, if both options were deferred by the same time interval, preference orders should be preserved. In other words, if you desire to receive $10 in 5 days as much as receiving $50 in 20 days, then you will still desire to receive $10 in 15 days as much as receiving $50 in 30 days, i.e., when both delays are prolonged by 10 days.

It was proposed that the discounting rate by which future commodities are delivered should be constant (Samuelson, 1937), for instance resulting in a linear or exponential discount function. Many theories, therefore, assumed exponential discounting (Lancaster, 1963; Fishburn and Rubinstein, 1982; Benzion et al., 1989; cf., Ainslie, 1975; Loewenstein, 1992; Fehr, 2002). Combining exponential discounting with stationarity yields (Lancaster, 1963):

$$(A,t) \sim Ae^{-k(t-t_0)} \tag{3}$$

This expression states that a reward with the amount A, delivered at timepoint t, is equally valuable (~) as a reward amount A at t_0 (i.e., now), exponentially discounted for the interval $t-t_0$, with t_0 referring to the present timepoint, and k being an individually different discount value. In other words, the utility of a future outcome can be expressed as an exponential function of the same outcome realized today.

Violation of Stationarity

As outlined above, stationarity predicts that the ranking of preferences between several future outcomes should be preserved when the choice outcomes are deferred by the same time interval. This has been investigated in an empirical study where human subjects chose between pairs of monetary rewards available after different delays (Green et al., 1994). Subjects preferred a small, short-delayed over a large, long-delayed reward, but their preference reversed away from the small towards the large reward when the delays to both rewards were advanced by the same time interval. Notably, the prolongation of the delays resulted in a preference reversal even though the difference in the delays remained identical (Green et al., 1994). This finding therefore represents a violation of stationarity. Numerous other studies with human subjects (Ainslie, 1975; Logue, 1988; Benzion et al., 1989; Loewenstein, 1992; Kirby and Herrnstein, 1995; Green et al., 1997; Frederick, Loewenstein and O'Donoghue, 2002; McClure et al., 2004; Rohde, 2005), pigeons (Chung and Herrnstein, 1967; Rachlin and Green, 1972; Ainslie, 1974; Green et al., 1981) and rats (Ito and Asaki, 1982; Bennett, 2002) replicated and confirmed these results (cf., Kalenscher and Pennartz, *in preparation*). Thus, human and non-human animals systematically violate the crucial assumption of inter-temporal consistency of choice. Note that many studies in the animal literature do not defer both choice outcomes equally, but only one outcome is increasingly delayed, whereas the delay to the other outcome remains constant (see e.g. figure 4A). Preference reversals in those cases do not challenge stationarity, as changes in valuations would be predicted for the increasingly delayed outcome, but not the constant outcome.

The fact that human and animal subjects prefer the small, short-term reward over the large, delayed reward when the receipt to the small reward is near, but not when it is in the relatively far future, suggests that short-term rewards are discounted more steeply than long-term rewards. Such asymmetric discounting poses a strong challenge for the postulation of exponential discounting (Lancaster, 1963). Accordingly, as theoretically suggested by Ainslie (1975), and later empirically shown by Mazur (Mazur, 1984, 1987, 1988; Grossbard and Mazur, 1986) and others (Rachlin et al., 1991; Myerson and Green, 1995; Green and Myerson, 1996; Rohde, 2005; Jones and Rachlin, 2006; Laibson, 1997), discounting curves can be better approximated with hyperbolic than exponential or other constant discount functions, as outlined in figure 3. Why do humans and other animals systematically violate such crucial laws in economics?

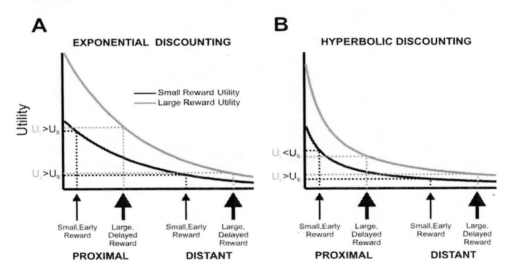

Figure 3. Exponential vs. Hyperbolic discounting of future events. (a) exponential Utility curve of a large, delayed (grey line) and small, short-term reward (black line). With Exponential discounting, stationarity holds because the utility of the large reward (ul) is always higher than the utility of the small reward (us). This is true when both rewards are temporally proximal, or when they are deferred by the same time interval into the future (distant rewards). (b) hyperbolic discounting can explain preference reversals and the violation of stationarity. Due to the steeper decay for short delays, the utility of the small, short-term reward is higher than the large, delayed reward for temporally proximal rewards, but the utility order reverses when both rewards are deferred into the future.

Why do we Discount the Future?

An assumption underlying most economic theories is utility maximization. This assumption is shared by many ecological theories of choice, namely the postulation that evolution favors choice mechanisms that maximize fitness levels, and minimize fitness losses. Applied to inter-temporal decision making, this means that the decision maker should act so as to maximize the utility rate, or in ecological terms, the energy intake rate per time unit (Stephens and Krebs, 1986). Rate maximization can explain why humans and animals sometimes prefer a less attractive, but temporally proximal outcome over a more attractive, but temporally remote outcome.

For example, we consider an inter-temporal choice task in which an animal has to choose between a small, always immediate reward and a large reward that is initially also delivered immediately, but that is delayed further as the experimental session progresses. Let's further assume that the large reward is 1.5 times as big as the small reward, and that the next choice opportunity always follows immediately after the animal has consumed its previous reward. The rate maximization hypothesis would predict that the animal should begin the session by preferring the large reward. However, the delay preceding the large reward gets longer and longer over the course of the session. So, at some point, the waiting time for the large reward, and thus the time until the next reward can be realized, will be more than twice as long as the delay preceding the small reward. Naturally, it would make sense now to prefer the small reward, as the hungry animal would be able to consume two small rewards in the same time that it would have to wait for only one large reward. Because two small rewards represent a larger food quantity than one large reward, the animal would maximize its energy intake per time unit by shifting its preference to the small reward once the delay preceding the large reward gets too long. In formal terms, optimal foraging theory assumes that organisms maximize, at least on the long run, the ratio of food intake and the time needed to obtain or consume the food, as described by the following quantity (Stephens and Krebs, 1986):

$$\max \frac{\sum_{i=1}^{\infty} G_i}{\sum_{i=1}^{\infty} t_i} \tag{4}$$

where G_i represents the net energy gain obtained from consuming the ith food item (here basically corresponding to its amount), and t_i represents the time between food item i and the previous food item i-1.

Animals do not (always) maximize intake rate

The above example implies that the next choice opportunity follows immediately after receipt of the reward. In many studies (Rachlin and Green, 1972; Ainslie, 1974; Grossbard and Mazur, 1986; Mazur, 1988; Evenden and Ryan, 1996; Cardinal et al., 2000; Isles et al., 2003, 2004; Winstanley et al., 2004, 2006; Kalenscher et al., 2005; Hwang et al., 2006; Louie and Glimcher, 2006), however, the inter-trial interval between reward and next choice was adjusted so that the total trial length was identical in all trials and independent of delay length and other factors. In such a scenario, the rate maximization hypothesis predicts that subjects should always choose the large reward, independent of the delay between response and reward, because only then would the animals maximize the total energy intake per trial, or per experimental session respectively. However, neither pigeons (Rachlin and Green, 1972; Ainslie, 1974; Grossbard and Mazur, 1986; Mazur, 1988; Kalenscher et al., 2005), nor rats (Evenden and Ryan, 1996; Cardinal et al., 2000; Winstanley et al., 2004, 2006; Roesch et al., 2006), mice (Isles et al., 2003, 2004), or monkeys (Hwang et al., 2006; Louie and Glimcher, 2006) show the predicted perseverance on the large reward alternative, but instead reverse their preference to the small, immediate reward once the large reward delay exceeds an individual threshold limit. This shows that the animals' choices depended on the waiting time preceding the rewards, but not on the ratios of reward amount and duration between the rewards, as would be predicted from rate maximization.

In fact, rate maximization models predict that amount and/or delay variations shouldn't play any role in the animals' decisions, because the choices should be only and exclusively directed towards maximizing the rate on the long-term. If, for example, an animal chooses between a fixed medium-term reward and or a variable-delay reward with either short or long delays (variable interval schedule), animals should always choose the option yielding the higher average reward rate. If the average reward rate is identical, animal should be indifferent between both options. However, contrary to this prediction, they usually prefer variable-interval over fixed schedules (Kacelnik and Bateson, 1996), indicating that delay variance does influence an animal's reward preference in addition to other factors, such as reward rate. This variance-proneness is interesting as animals are usually variance-averse if reward magnitude, and not delay, is variable, as explained above. Proneness to delay variance can be explained with hyperbolic discounting (see below).

In summary, animals do not make their choices according to the predictions of rate maximization models. They seem to employ rather short-sighted, waiting-time sensitive choice heuristics, and have a preference for delay variability.

Preference for delay variability

Hyperbolic discounting, as outlined in figure 3B, can explain the preference for variable over fixed interval schedules. Since, due to the hyperbolic decay, the utility of short-term rewards is disproportionally higher than the utility of medium-term or delayed rewards, but the difference in utility of medium-term and delayed rewards is negligible, the average expected utility of short-term and delayed rewards (variable interval schedules) will exceed the expected utility of fixed medium-term rewards. Hence, animals should prefer variable over fixed delays.

An alternative hypothesis, scalar expectancy theory (SET), can account for both variance aversion when reward magnitude is variable, and variance proneness when reward delay is variable. SET refers to the subjective time and magnitude representation which is normal around the actual means, but as a consequence of Weber's law, has a constant coefficient of variation (ratio of standard deviation to mean). Thus, the combination of an early and a late distribution results in a positively skewed integral, which explains preference for variation in delay (Reboreda and Kacelnik, 1991). Evidence for or against either SET or the hyperbolic discounting account is equivocal (Kacelnik an Bateson, 1997; Bateson and Kacelnik, 1998) and needs to be further tested in the future.

Ecological models of inter-temporal decisions: Ecological rationality

In addition to the unclear support, neither of these accounts can explain why animals developed delay sensitivity in the first place: Why does evolution favor choice heuristics that produce suboptimal results in many cases by over-emphasising the delay to the next reward (e.g., through hyperbolic discounting), and ignoring the long-term relevance of time/amount sequences? Obviously, animals may equate delay with collection risk, as outlined in greater detail below. If delays are mentally treated as risks, a risk-averse animal will naturally avoid long delays. However, this doesn't provide an acceptable answer because the question remains why evolution has favoured suboptimal decision rules, be they related to risk avoidance or delay aversion. The first answer that comes to mind is that short-sighted rules have higher fitness values than long-sighted rules because the animals' constitutions do not allow them to tolerate too long waiting periods. For example, animals with a high metabolism cannot afford to wait too long for a large amount of food, or, in other words, what is the use of high quality, high amount of food if the animal has starved to death while waiting for it? Thus, short-sighted rules may have a certain evolutionary advantage over long-sighted rules.

This would certainly hold if the waiting times were close to the animals' starvation thresholds. However, mice, rats, pigeons, monkeys or other animals used in inter-temporal choice experiments shift their preference away from the economically more advantageous reward even when the waiting time to the larger reward exceeds less than a few seconds, and not hours or days (cf., McDiarmid & Rilling, 1969). Certainly, all those animals would be able to survive longer waiting periods than just a few seconds without food, but nevertheless, they prefer the short-term option over the long-delayed option, even if the long-delayed reward is a multiple of the short-term reward. Such extremely myopic decision patterns are difficult to explain with a fitness advantage of faster available food items. Why does evolution favor such extremely myopic choice heuristics?

Bounded rationality or ecological models, such as the ecological rationality hypothesis (Stephens et al., 2004) claim that choice heuristics that fail to produce maximum fitness in artificial experimental settings do, in fact, perform well in more ecologically valid contexts. For example, Stephens and colleagues (2004) argued that a more ecologically valid choice context entails decisions about limited food resources. A typical decision would consist of whether to entirely exploit all food resources in a given food patch, or leave the food patch early before having consumed all resources, and search for a new patch. The difference between the patch situation and the standard inter-temporal choice task is that, in a standard inter-temporal choice task, an animal has a binary choice between a large, delayed or a small, immediate reward, whereas in the patch situation, it chooses whether to continue to stay in a given patch, or to leave and search for a new patch. Figure 4 illustrates an inter-temporal choice situation, often also referred to as a 'self-control' task (4A), and a patch situation (4B).

Put in more formalized terms, an animal consuming a reward in a food patch (the initial food amount, A_{Init}) has to decide whether to stay in the current patch and wait for further rewards until the patch is completely depleted, or whether to leave early and initiate a new travel time to the next patch. If it decides to leave, it has to travel for time t_{Travel} until the next patch is encountered where it receives a new initial reward amount A_{Init}. If it decides to stay, it obtains additional food rewards of amount A_{Stay} delivered after a certain waiting time t_{Stay} until the patch is depleted. It then has to leave the patch as well, and initiate a further travelling time t_{Travel} until it encounters a new patch and obtains reward amount A_{Init} in the new patch (see figure 4B).

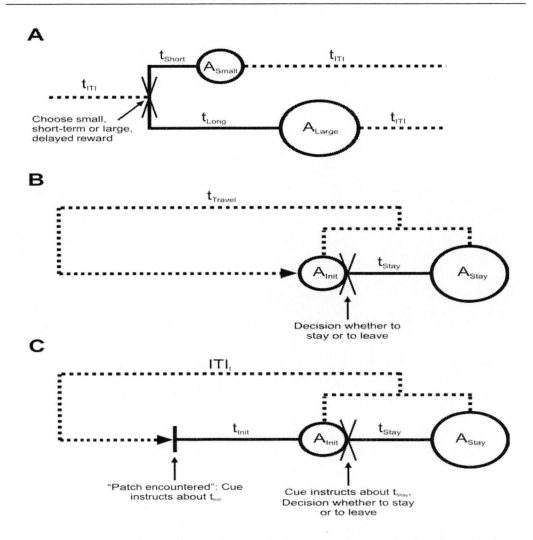

Figure 4. Inter-temporal choice and patch situation. (a) displays a schematic drawing of a standard inter-temporal choice task used in animal research, often also referred to as a 'Self-control' task. Following an inter-trial interval (titi), the animal makes a binary choice between a large and a small reward amount (alarge and asmall), delivered after a long or a short time delay (tlong and tshort). Reward consumption is followed by another iti until the next choice opportunity. The length of the iti, titi, is adjusted to compensate for differences in delay length and choice, so that every trial is of identical duration. (b) patch situation. An animal travels until it encounters a food patch, where it consumes an initial reward amount, ainit. After consumption, the animal has to decide whether to leave the patch and initiate travel time ttravel, until it finds the next patch, or whether to stay in the patch, wait time tstay for an additional food amount, astay, and then leave the patch and initiate the travel time ttravel to the next food patch. (c) patch situation as used in the experiment by stephens and Anderson (2001). The situation is equivalent to figure 1b, but includes an additional initial waiting time, tinit, preceding the initial reward ainit. In all panels, the cross of thin lines indicates the timepoint where the animal makes its decision.

Staying is more time-consuming ($t_{Stay}^{Total} = t_{Stay} + t_{Travel}$), but yields higher reward amounts ($A_{Stay}^{Total} = A_{Stay} + A_{Init}$), leaving is less time-consuming ($t_{Leave}^{Total} = t_{Travel}$) because the animal doesn't need to wait for the additional reward in the old patch, but it also misses out on that additional reward, and thus receives lower reward quantities ($A_{Leave}^{Total} = A_{Init}$). A far-sighted decision rule based on rate maximization would predict that the animal prefers to leave if it gained more rewards per time unit in the leave alternative than in the stay alternative, and it would stay in case it gained more rewards per time in the stay alternative than in the leave alternative. Assuming that travelling to a new patch takes always the same time, and that the yield in a new patch is always identical, an animal would leave if

$$\frac{A_{Init}}{t_{Travel}} > \frac{(A_{Add} + A_{Init})}{(t_{Stay} + t_{Travel})} \qquad (5)$$

and it would predict to stay in the opposite case.

A short-sighted, waiting-time sensitive rule, as observed in most experimental settings on inter-temporal decision-making, would predict that an animal considers only the delay until the next reward in its decision. That is, the rule would predict that an animal prefers to leave if

$$\frac{A_{Init}}{t_{Travel}} > \frac{A_{Add}}{t_{Stay}} \qquad (6)$$

and it would predict to stay in the opposite case. Because travel time, t_{Travel}, and initial reward amount, A_{Init}, are identical in the leave and the stay case, the long-term, rate-maximising rule in expression (5) is algebraically equivalent to the short-term, waiting-time-sensitive, impulsive rule in expression (6). Thus, in the above described patch situation, a short-sighted impulsive choice rule (expression 6) would approximate long-term rate maximization, consistent with predictions from optimal foraging theory.

If this theoretical line of argument was true, then the same short-sighted choice heuristic should produce rate maximization in the patch-situation, but not in the standard inter-temporal choice task. To test this prediction, Stephens and Anderson (2001) trained blue jays in a 'self-control' situation and a patch situation. The 'self-control' situation was essentially equivalent to the inter-temporal choice task sketched in figure 4A: Blue jays chose between a small, immediate or a large, delayed reward, A_{Small} and A_{Large}, delivered after t_{Short} and t_{Long}, by hopping on a perch on the left or right side in a training box. After reward delivery and consumption, they had to leave the perch, and an inter-trial interval (ITI, equivalent to travel time in figure 4B) was initiated, after which they could make their next choice. Instead of a binary choice between large and small rewards, the patch situation (figure 4C) consists of a sequence of choices between smaller rewards potentially summing up to a large reward: a cue instructed the animals about the delay t_{Init} to an initial reward of A_{Init} amount. By hopping on a randomly activated perch in the box, the initial reward was delivered after the indicated delay. Afterwards, the animals could choose whether to stay and wait for the additional reward by remaining on the perch (a second cue indicated the delay length t_{Stay} to the additional reward of amount A_{Stay}.), or whether to leave the perch, miss out on the additional reward, and initiate the ITI, and a new waiting time t_{Init} to the next small reward. Hence, the patch task resembled the situation illustrated in figure 4B, with the exception that there was an additional waiting time t_{Init} preceding the initial food reward A_{Init}. Moreover, in the patch situation, the travel time needed to leave the initial patch and move to the next one corresponds to the ITI of the standard inter-temporal choice task. Note that defined this way, the ITI becomes an integral part of the decision in the patch situation but not in the standard choice situation. This is because a short-term decision rule taking into account only the delay to the next reward would predict that, in the 'self-control' situation, animals consider the delays to the large and the small reward (t_{Short} versus t_{Long}), and that, in the patch situation, they consider the delays to the different rewards in the stay or leave cases (t_{Stay} vs. $t_{ITI} + t_{Init}$).

It is now possible to choose the task parameters so that the 'self-control' and the patch situation are economically equivalent: The sum of the two rewards in the patch situation equals the large reward amount in the 'self-control' situation, and the sum of the delays to the first and second rewards in the patch situation is equivalent to the delay preceding the large reward in the 'self-control' situation. This means that animals would receive the same amount of food within the same time when they chose to stay in the patch situation or when they chose the large, delayed reward in the 'self-control' situation

Because of this economical equivalence, the animals should always show identical preferences across both situations if their decision rule was purely economical, e.g., far-sighted. If, on the other hand, the animals indeed used a short-sighted decision rule, then they should show inconsistent choices under most circumstances, and should maximize their intake rate in the patch, but not in the 'self-control' situation. Such inconsistencies would arise because, first, the ITI is an integral part of the decision in the patch situation (remember that in the leave case, the total waiting time for the next reward would be $t_{Init}^{Leave} + ITI$), but not in the 'self-control' situation (the delay between choice and reward-delivery is not dependent on the ITI), and, second, because the large reward in the patch situation consists of a series of smaller rewards, and not of a one-shot delivery of one single large reward as in the 'self-control' situation.

In their study, Stephens and Anderson (2001) systematically varied the delays, amounts and ITIs, and tested the preference patterns of their blue jays. As predicted, they reported inconsistencies in choice between the two situations. In particular, they found that the blue jays were overall more ready to maximize their intake rate in the patch situation than in the 'self-control' situation. This supports the main notion of the ecological rationality hypothesis that one and the same short-sighted decision rule results in rate maximization in one, but not the other choice situation.

In summary, theoretical considerations and empirical evidence suggests that evolution may have favored the development of short-sighted choice heuristics because such rules produce long-term rate maximization in many natural situations, but not necessarily in artificial laboratory settings.

Ecological models of inter-temporal decisions: Feeding ecology

Although all animals have in common that they discount the future, the rate by which future events are discounted differs dramatically between species. Mice, for example, seem to tolerate waiting times up to only a few seconds (Isles et al., 2003, 2004), capuchin monkeys wait for several minutes (Ramseyer et al., 2006), and humans can wait for months or even years for a relatively attractive reward (Green et al., 1994, 1997). The ecological rationality hypothesis can explain why evolution has favored the development of impulsive decision rules, but it cannot readily account for these large inter-individual and inter-species differences in delay-tolerance.

Another theory, the feeding ecology hypothesis, aims to explain those differences. It departs from the comparison of discount rates between very similar monkey species: Cotton-top tamarins and common marmosets. These two new-world monkeys are similar in terms of social behavior, mating system, life span, life history, home range size, parental care, body size and weight, brain size and weight, and other factors (cf., Stevens et al., 2005a). However, despite those similarities, the animals show very different choice behavior when tested in an adjusting delay procedure. In an adjusting delay procedure (Mazur, 1987), animals choose between a small, short-term reward and a large, delayed reward. After large reward choices, the delay to its receipt is increased in the next trials, after small reward choices, the delay preceding the large reward is decreased. This procedure allows the measurement of indifference points, i.e., the delay length at which the large, delayed reward has equal value to the small, short-term reward. Stevens and colleagues (2005a) found that the marmosets waited considerably longer for a large reward than tamarins. However, when tested in a spatial version of the adjusting feature task, in which travelling distance, but not delay, to a large reward was varied, the pattern reversed: Whereas the tamarins preferred the large reward independent of the travel distance to the large reward, the marmosets preference for the large reward continuously decreased with increasing travel distance (Stevens et al., 2005b). Taken together, space and time affected the monkeys' decisions differentially: compared to tamarins, marmosets were more patient when waiting for a delayed reward, but discounted spatially distant rewards steeper than tamarins.

How come that the two monkeys have evolved so different discounting patterns? Because of their striking similarity in many aspects, differences in metabolism, physical condition, starvation threshold or the like can be ruled out as possible explanations. Stevens et al. (2005a, 2005b) point out that one of the main differences between the two New World monkeys is their diet: Although both species eat fruits, marmosets additionally feed on plant exudates, such as gum and sap, and tamarins feed on insects.

Feeding ecology plays a major role in shaping cognitive and neural functions (e.g., Clayton & Krebs, 1995; Basil et al., 1996; Emery & Clayton, 2001). Accordingly, the differences in foraging behavior between the tamarins and marmosets may prove to be the key evolutionary pressure for the differential development of the temporal and spatial discount rates: Marmosets feed on localized, immobile food sources that do not require far-distance travels. But feeding on gum and sap requires to scratch the bark of the tree and then wait for the sap to exude. For the marmosets, it is therefore essential to be patient (in time), but not necessarily mobile (in space) in order to get most of the slowly exudating sap. Conversely, for the insectivore tamarins, it is crucial to be constantly alert, and react quickly in order not to miss any passing-by insects. Moreover, they feed on dispersed food sources and have to cover rather large territories to find insects. Therefore, in contrast to marmosets, tamarins must be quick and impulsive, and willing to travel relatively far distances to find enough food to survive.

In summary, given the individual differences in foraging behavior, it may be more advantageous for the marmosets to be patient in time, but impulsive in space, and for the tamarins to be impulsive in time, but patient in space. The individual differences in foraging ecology may therefore explain the differential evolution of temporal and spatial discounting.

Commonalities and differences between risky and inter-temporal decisions

The preceding parts of this chapter have treated inter-temporal and risky decisions as separate. However, several authors argued that there might not be a real difference between delay and risk because each dimension can be expressed in terms of the other (Mischel, 1966; Stevenson, 1986; Rachlin et al., 1986, 1987, 1991; Mazur, 1989, 1995, 1997; Green and Myerson, 1996, 2004; Sozou, 1998; Hayden and Platt, 2007). A delayed reward might be less likely to occur (at least in natural situations) and therefore its expected value might be lower than that of earlier rewards. Moreover, as the state of the agent might change, the value of a later reward might also be more uncertain due to the unpredictability of the subject's own state, including its own survival. For example, our annual mortality risk is about 1% but was considerably higher in our evolutionary past. There is little use in waiting for a large, delayed reward if we will never experience the reward. Therefore a delayed reward may be equivalent to a risky reward and decision-makers may equate temporal distance with collection-risk (Kacelnik and Bateson, 1996; Sozou, 1998).

Theoretically, the proposal that delay and risk are processed similarly boils down to models that incorporate only either risk attitude or discounting as subjective weighting factors for utility but not both. For example, consider the following model (Mazur, 2007):

$$U = \Sigma P_i(A/1 + KD_i) \tag{7}$$

Here, utility is a function of objective probability (P) but subjective time discounting (K). A denotes reward amount and D delay. Conversely, the following model comprises three subjective weighting factors determining utility (Kheramin et al., 2003, adapted):

$$U = \Sigma(1/(1 + Q/q_i) \times 1/(1 + Kd_i) \times 1/(1 + H\theta_i)) \tag{8}$$

where q denotes reward amount, d reward delay and θ odds against reward ($\theta=[1/P_i]-1$). The subjective weighting factors Q, K and H denote subjective sensitivity to reward magnitude, delay and probability, respectively. H>1 corresponds to risk aversion, H<1 to risk seeking, Note, that this model treats probability and delay similarly by using a hyperbolic form for both.

Conversely, instead of treating delayed rewards as uncertain, it has also been proposed that risky rewards may be treated as variably delayed rewards (Rachlin et al., 1986; Mazur, 1989; Hayden and Platt, 2007). For example, take a gamble between two options with equal expected values, but where one option yields a medium-sized, certain reward and the other one yields either a large or a small reward with a 50% chance each. Animals are usually not risk-neutral in those types of tasks (Kacelnik and Bateson, 1996, 1997; Bateson and Kacelnik, 1998; McCoy and Platt, 2005b; Hayden and Platt, 2007). Macaques, for example, generally prefer the risky over the certain option (McCoy and Platt, 2005b; Hayden and Platt, 2007). To explain this risk-proneness, it has been argued that, if an animal consistently sticks with the risky option offering a 50% chance of a large pay-off, they will almost ce   rtainly   receive the large reward eventually: If not now, then on a future trial. Therefore, the risky option gives a practically guaranteed, though potentially delayed large pay-off. Thus, because probabilistic rewards may be treated as large and delayed rewards, they may recruit similar cognitive mechanisms (Rachlin et al., 1986; Mazur, 1989; Hayden and Platt, 2007).

The empirical evidence supporting commonalities of delay and risk sensitivity is equivocal (Mazur, 1989; Rachlin et al., 1986, 1991; Green and Myerson, 1996, 2004; Estle et al., 2006; Hayden and Platt, 2007). Commonalities are entertained by the occurrence of similar preference reversals when the delay or the probability of reward is increased for both options. Thus, violations of the independence axiom (Allais paradox) with probability are similar to violations of the stationarity axiom with delay (both described above). In other words, the utility of sooner and more probable rewards increases more than that of later and less probable rewards as reward immediacy and probability increase (reviewed in Green and Myerson, 2004). Accordingly, both probability and delay are amenable to hyperbolic discounting functions.

Conversely, there is considerable evidence that risk and delay are processed differentially. For example, humans discount smaller delayed rewards more steeply than larger delayed rewards but discount smaller probabilistic rewards less steeply than larger probabilistic rewards (Du et al., 2002; Estle et al., 2006). Inflation affects decisions involving delayed but not risky monetary rewards (Ostaszewski et al., 1998). Drug addiction appears to affect delay discounting more than risk processing (Reynolds et al., 2004) whereas problem gambling might have the opposite effect (Holt et al., 2003). Even culture appears to influence probability and delay differentially, with Japanese graduate students discounting probabilistic rewards more steeply and delayed rewards less steeply than Chinese students (Du et al., 2002). Further reinforcing the notion that delay differs from risk, earlier rewards may be preferred for several reasons over later rewards over and above to the later reward being riskier or the future subjective state more uncertain (Kacelnik and Bateson, 1996):

Earlier rewards can be put to use and earn compound interest (corresponding to offspring's offspring) before later rewards arrive.

Waiting for a delayed reward may prevent an agent from pursuing other courses of action. This might diminish the value of delayed rewards.

It might be easier to learn about action-reward and stimulus-reward contingencies with earlier rewards because at their arrival the mental representation of the causally relevant antecedents has decayed to a lesser degree compared with later rewards.

With long delays to the later reward and fixed intertrial duration, choosing earlier rewards can maximize the energy intake per unit time even if the later reward is larger than the earlier reward (as explained above on the chapter on rate maximization).

CONCLUSION

In the preceding sub-chapters, we have outlined a selection of different attempts from different disciplines to explain decisions under risk and inter-temporal choices. Broadly speaking, normative approaches, such as eut or optimal foraging (rate maximization), focus on how an animal should behave in order to meet formulated choice criteria, such as optimal decision-making, utility maximization or consistency of choice. Descriptive and empirical approaches, on the other hand, challenge many of the predictions and implications of normative models, and show that the normative analysis of decision making may not always be consistent with the empirical reality of choosing and acting. For example, humans do not always choose according to the predictions of eut, and, contrary to the prediction of optimal foraging theory, animals frequently fail to maximize their intake rate. Ecological models, such as the budget rule or the ecological rationality hypothesis, deal with the question why evolution favored the development of choice patterns that often violate the predictions of the normative approaches. In particular, they provide an analysis within an ecologically valid framework of the sense and non-sense of the way animals (and humans) make their decisions.

Last but not least, psychological approaches attempt to identify the choice-mediating Cognitive mechanisms, such as whether animals employ far-sighted vs. Myopic choice Heuristics.

We hope to have illustrated that these different approaches have strong limitations when isolated from each other. In particular, we believe that normative models have high explanatory power, but are of questionable validity if not substantiated with empirical results.

Empirical studies are of potentially higher validity per se, but it is difficult, if not impossible In many cases, to generalize single experimental results to a common framework of choice. They are therefore often of little use to answer the question how we generally make decisions

When presented outside a theoretical context. Moreover, although empirical studies can be used to identify the short-comings of theoretical models, such de-construction is only useful When followed by the formulation of a better theoretical model. In conclusion, neither normative, nor empirical, nor psychological approaches alone can produce useful results, but only the combination of all approaches yields fruitful outcomes.

ACKNOWLEDGEMENTS

We greatly appreciate the comments of Martin Kocher on an earlier version of the manuscript. TK is supported by a grant from senternovem (bsik-03053).

REFERENCES

Ainslie G (1974) Impulse control in pigeons. *J exp anal behav* 21:485-489.

Ainslie G (1975) Specious reward: a behavioral theory of impulsiveness and impulse control. *Psychol bull* 82:463-496.

Allais M (1953) Le comportement de l'homme rationnel devant le risque: critique des postulats et axiomes de l'école américaine. *Econometrica* 21:503-546.

Basil Ja, Kamil Ac, Balda Rp, Fite Kv (1996) Differences in hippocampal volume among food storing corvids. *Brain behav evol* 47:156-164.

Bateson M, Kacelnik A (1998) Risk-sensitive foraging: decision-making in variable environments. In: *cognitive ecology* (dukas r, ed), pp 297-341. Chicago, Illinois: University of chicago press.

Bennett Sm (2002) Preference reversal and the estimation of indifference points using a fast-adjusting delay procedure with rats. Dissertation, University of florida.

Benzion U, Rapoport A, Yagil J (1989) Discount rates inferred from decisions: an experimental study. *Management sci* 35:270-284.

Bernoulli D (1954) Exposition of a new theory on the measurement of risk. *Econometrica* 22:23-36.

Caraco T, Blanckenhorn WU, Gregory GM, Newman JA, Recer GM, Zwicker SM (1990) Risk-sensitivity: ambient temperature affects foraging choice. *Anim behav* 39:338-345.

Cardinal RN, Robbins TW, Everitt BJ (2000) The effects of d-amphetamine, chlordiazepoxide, alpha-flupenthixol and behavioural manipulations on choice of signalled and unsignalled delayed reinforcement in rats. *Psychopharmacology* (berl) 152:362-375.

Charnov EL (1976) Optimal foraging: the marginal value theorem. *Theor popul biol* 9:129-136.

Chung SH, Herrnstein RJ (1967) Choice and delay of reinforcement. *J exp anal Behav* 10:67-74.

Clayton NS, Krebs JR (1995) Memory in food-storing birds: from behaviour to brain. *Curr opin neurobiol* 5:149-154.

Du W, Green L, Myerson J (2002) Cross-cultural comparisons of discounting delayed and probabilistic rewards. *Psychol rec* 52:479-492.

Ellsberg D (1961) Risk, ambiguity, and the savage axioms. *Q j econ* 75:643-669.

Emery NJ, clayton NS (2001) effects of experience and social context on prospective caching strategies by scrub jays. *Nature* 414:443-446.

Estle SJ, green L, Myerson J, Holt DD (2006) Differential effects of amount on temporal and probability discounting of gains and losses. *Mem cognit* 34:914-928.

Evenden JL (1999) Varieties of impulsivity. *Psychopharmacology* (berl) 146:348-361.

Evenden JL, Ryan CN (1996) the pharmacology of impulsive behaviour in rats: the effects of drugs on response choice with varying delays of reinforcement. *Psychopharmacology* (berl) 128:161-170.

Fehr R (2002) The economics of impatience. *Nature* 415:269-272.

Fishburn PC (1982) Nontransitive measurable utility. *J math psychol* 26:31-67.

Fishburn PC, rubinstein A (1982) time preference. *Internat econ rev* 23:677-694.

Frederick S, Loewenstein G, O'donoghue T (2002) Time discounting and time preference: a critical review. *J econ lit* 40:351-401.

Friedman M, savage LJ (1948) The utility analysis of choices involving risk. *J polit Econ* 56:279-304.

Glimcher PW (2002) Decisions, decisions, decisions: choosing a biological science of choice. *Neuron* 36:323-332.

Glimcher PW, Rustichini a (2004) Neuroeconomics: the consilience of brain and decision. *Science* 306:447-452.

Green L, Fisher EB jr, Perlow S, Sherman l (1981) Preference reversal and self- control: choice as a function of reward amount and delay. *Behav anal lett* 1:43-51.

Green l, fristoe n, myerson j (1994) temporal discounting and preference reversals In choice between delayed outcomes. Psychonom bull rev 1:383-389.

Green L, Myerson J (1996) exponential versus hyperbolic discounting of delayed outcomes: risk and waiting time. *Amer zool* 36:496-505.

Green L, Myerson J (2004) a discounting framework for choice with delayed and probabilistic rewards. *Psychol bull* 130:769-792.

Green L, Myerson J, McFadden E (1997) Rate of temporal discounting decreases with amount of reward. *Mem cognit* 25:715-723.

Grossbard CL, Mazur JE (1986) A comparison of delays and ratio requirements in self-control choice. *J exp anal behav* 45:305-315.

Hamilton W D (1964) The genetical evolution of social behaviour. *J theor biol* 7:1- 52.

Hayden BY, Platt ML (2007) Temporal discounting predicts risk sensitivity in rhesus macaques. *Curr biol* 17:49-53.

Holt DD, Green L, Myerson J (2003) Is discounting impulsive? Evidence from temporal and probability discounting in gambling and nongambling college students. *Behav processes* 64:355-367.

Hwang J, Kim S, Lee D (2006) Neuronal signals related to delayed reward and its discounted value in the macaque dorsolateral prefrontal cortex. *Annual meeting of the Society for neuroscience, program no. 71.7.*

Isles AR, Humby T, Walters E, Wilkinson LS (2004) Common genetic effects on variation in impulsivity and activity in mice. *J neurosci* 24:6733-6740.

Isles AR, Humby T, Wilkinson LS (2003) Measuring impulsivity in mice using a novel operant delayed reinforcement task: effects of behavioural manipulations and d-Amphetamine. *Psychopharmacology (berl)* 170:376-382.

Ito M, Asaki K (1982) Choice behavior of rats in a concurrent-chains schedule: amount and delay of reinforcement. *J exp anal behav* 37:383-392.

Jones B, Rachlin H. (2006) Social discounting. *Psychol sci* 17, 283-286.

Kacelnik a (1997) Normative and descriptive models of decision making: time discounting and risk sensitivity. *Ciba found symp 208:51-67; discussion 67-70.*

Kacelnik A, Bateson M (1996) Risky theories - the effects of variance on foraging decisions. *Amer zool* 36:402-434.

Kacelnik Aa, Bateson M (1997) Risk-sensitivity: crossroads for theories of decision- making. *Trends cogn sci* 1:304-309.

Kahneman D, Tversky A (1979) Prospect theory: an analysis of decision under risk. *Econometrica* 47:263-291.

Kalenscher T, Ohmann T, Gunturkun O (2006) The neuroscience of impulsive and self-controlled decisions. *Int j psychophysiol* 62:203-211.

Kalenscher T, Windmann S, Diekamp B, Rose J, Güntürkün O, Colombo M (2005) Single units in the pigeon brain integrate reward amount and time-to-reward in an Impulsive choice task. *Curr biol* 15:594-602.

Kalenscher T, Pennartz CMA (2007) A bird in the hand is worth two in the future. *The Neuroeconomics of inter-temporal decision making.* In preparation.

Kheramin S, Body S, Ho M, Velazquez-Martinez DN, Bradshaw CM, Szabadi E, Deakin JF, Anderson IM (2003) Role of the orbital prefrontal cortex in choice between delayed and uncertain reinforcers: a quantitative analysis. *Behav processes* 64:239-250.

Kirby KN, Herrnstein RJ (1995) Preference reversals due to myopic discounting of delayed reward. *Psychol sci* 6:83-89.

Koopmans TC (1960) Stationary ordinal utility and impatience. *Econometrica* 28:287309.

Laibson DI (1997) Golden eggs and hyperbolic discounting. *Q j econ* 42: 861-871.

Lancaster K (1963) An axiomatic theory of consumer time preference. *Internat econ Rev* 4:221-231.

Loewenstein G (1992) The fall and rise of psychological explanations in the economics of intertemporal choice. In: *choice over time*, pp. 3-34. Eds G. Loewenstein, J. Elster. Russell sage foundation: New York.

Logue AW (1988) Research on self-control: an integrating framework.. *Behav brain Sci* 11:665-709.

Loomes G, Starmer C, sugden R (1991) Observing violations of transitivity by experimental methods. *Econometrica* 59:425-439.

Loomes G, Sugden R, (1982) Regret theory: an alternative theory of rational choice under uncertainty. *Econ j* 92:805-824.

Louie K, Glimcher PW (2006) Temporal discounting activity in monkey parietal neurons during intertemporal choice. *Annual meeting of the society for neuroscience,* Program no. 605.5.

Machina MJ (1982) "Expected utility" analysis without the independence axiom. *Econometrica* 50:277-323.

Mankiw, NG (2002) *Macroeconomics.* 5th Edition, Worth publishers: New York

Mazur JE (1984) Tests of an equivalence rule for fixed and variable reinforcer delays. *J exp psychol: anim behav process* 10:426-436.

Mazur JE (1988) Estimation of indifference points with an adjusting-delay procedure. *J exp anal behav* 49:37-47.

Mazur JE (1989) Theories of probabilistic reinforcement. *J exp anal behav* 51:87-99.

Mazur JE (1995) Conditioned reinforcement and choice with delayed and uncertain primary reinforcers. *J exp anal behav* 63:139-150.

Mazur JE (1997) Choice, delay, probability, and conditioned reinforcement. *Anim Learn behav* 25:131-147.

Mazur JE (2007) Species differences between rats and pigeons in choices with probabilistic and delayed reinforcers. *Behav processes* 75:220-224.

Mazur JE, Commons ML, Mazur JE, Nevin JA, Rachlin H (1987) An adjusting procedure for studying delayed reinforcement. In *Quantitavie Analyses of Behaviour: Foraging.* pp 55-73. Hillsdale, NJ: Erlbaum.

McClure SM, Laibson DI, Loewenstein G, Cohen JD (2004) Separate neural systems value immediate and delayed monetary rewards. *Science* 306:503-507.

McCoy AN, Platt ML (2005a) Expectations and outcomes: decision-making in the primate brain. *J comp physiol a neuroethol sens neural behav physiol* 191:201-211.

McCoy AN, Platt ML (2005b) Risk-sensitive neurons in macaque posterior cingulate cortex. *Nat neurosci* 8:1220-1227.

McDiarmid CG, Rilling ME (1965) reinforcement delay and reinforcement rate as determinants of schedule preference. *Psychon sci* 2:195-196.

McNamara JM, Houston AI (1986) The common currency for behavioral decisions. *Am nat* 127:358-378.

Mischel W (1966). Theory and research on the antecedents of self-imposed delay of reward. In ba maher (ed.), *progress in experimental personality research*: vol. 3 (pp. 85-132). New york: academic press.

Moore FR, Simm PA (1986) Risk-sensitive foraging by a migratory bird (dendroica coronata). *Experientia* 42:1054-1056.

Myerson J, Green L, (1995) discounting of delayed rewards: models of individual choice. *J exp anal behav* 64, 263-276.

Ostaszewski P, Green L, Myerson J (1998) Effects of inflation on the subjective value of delayed and probabilistic rewards. *Psychon bull rev* 5:324-333.

Powell K (2003) Economy of the mind. *Plos biol* 1:e77.

Rachlin h, castrogiovanni a, cross d (1987) probability and delay in commitment. J Exp anal behav 48:347-353.

Rachlin H, Green L (1972) Commitment, choice and self control. *J exp anal behav* 17:15-22.

Rachlin H, Logue AW, Gibbon J, Frankel M (1986) Cognition and behavior in studies of choice. *Psychol rev* 93:33-45.

Rachlin H, Raineri A, Cross D (1991) Subjective probability and delay. *J exp anal Behav* 55:233-244.

Ramseyer A, Pele M, Dufour V, Chauvin C, Thierry B (2006) Accepting loss: the temporal limits of reciprocity in brown capuchin monkeys. *Proc biol sci* 273:179-184.

Reboreda JC, Kacelnik A (1991) Risk sensitivity in starlings: variability in food amount and food delay. *Behav ecol* 2:301-308.

Reynolds B, De Wit H, Richards J (2002) Delay of gratification and delay discounting in rats. *Behav processes* 59:157-168.

Reynolds B, Richards JB, Horn K, Karraker K (2004) Delay discounting and probability discounting as related to cigarette smoking status in adults. *Behav Processes*, 65:35-42.

Rohde K (2005) The hyperbolic factor: a measure of decreasing impatience. *Research Memoranda 044*. Maastricht research school of economics of technology and Organization: Maastricht.

Samuelson PA (1937) A note on measurement of utility. *Rev econ stud* 4:155-161.

Shafir S (1994) Intransitivity of preferences in honey bees: support for 'comparative' evaluation of foraging options. *Anim behav* 48:55-67.

Sibly RM, McFarland DJ (1976) On the fitness of behaviour sequences. *Am nat* 110:601-617.

Sozou PD (1998) On hyperbolic discounting and uncertain hazard rates. *Proc r soc Lond b* 265:2015-2020.

Stephens DW (1981) The logic of risk-sensitive foraging preferences. *Anim behav* 29:628-629.

Stephens DW, Anderson D (2001) The adaptive value of preference for immediacy: when shortsighted rules have farsighted consequences. *Behav ecol* 12:330-339.

Stephens DW, Kerr B, Fernandez-Juricic E (2004) Impulsiveness without discounting: the ecological rationality hypothesis. *Proc r soc lond b biol sci* 271:2459-2465.

Stephens DW, Krebs JR (1986) Foraging theory. *Monographs in behavior and ecology*. Princeton. Princeton University press: New Jersey.

Stevens JR, Hallinan EV, Hauser M (2004) The ecology and evolution of patience in two new world monkeys. *Biol lett* 1:223-226.

Stevens JR, Rosati AG, Ross KR, Hauser MD (2005) Will travel for food: spatial discounting in two new world monkeys. *Curr biol* 15:1855-1860.

Stevenson MK (1986) A discounting model for decisions with delayed positive and negative outcomes. *J exp psychol: general* 115:131-154.

Strotz RH (1955) Myopia and inconsistency in dynamic utility maximization. *Rev Econ stud* 23:165-180.

Tobler PN, Fletcher PC, Bullmore ET, Schultz W (2007a) Learning-related human brain activations reflecting individual finances. *Neuron* 54:167-175.

Tobler PN, O'Doherty JP, Dolan RJ, Schultz W (2007b) Reward value coding distinct from risk attitude-related uncertainty coding in human reward systems. *J neurophysiol* 97:1621-1632.

Tversky A (1969) Intransitivity of preferences. *Psych rev* 76: 31-48.

Tversky A, Kahneman D (1986) Rational choice and the framing of decisions. *J business* 59:s251-s278.

Tversky A, Kahneman D (1992) Advances in prospect theory: cumulative representation of uncertainty. *J risk uncert* 5:297-323.

Von Neumann J, Morgenstern O (1944) *Theory of games and economic Behavior*. Princeton. Princeton University Press: New Jersey.

Waite TA (2001) Intransitive preferences in hoarding gray jays (perisoreus Canadensis). *Behav ecol sociobiol* 50:116-121.

Winstanley CA, Theobald DE Cardinal RN, Robbins TW (2004) Contrasting roles of basolateral amygdala and orbitofrontal cortex in impulsive choice. *J neurosci* 24:4718-4722.

Winstanley CA, Theobald DE, Dalley JW, Cardinal RN, Robbins TW (2006) Double dissociation between serotonergic and dopaminergic modulation of medial prefrontal and orbitofrontal cortex during a test of impulsive choice. *Cereb cortex* 16:106-114.

Wolf M, Van Doorn GS, Leimar O, Weissing FJ (2007) Life-history trade-offs Favour the evolution of animal personalities. *Nature* 447:581-584.

In: Psychology of Decision Making in Education
Editor: Jeanine A. Elsworth, pp. 125-142

ISBN: 978-1-60021-933-7
© 2006 Nova Science Publishers, Inc.

Chapter 5

PROJECT TOWARDS NO DRUG ABUSE (TND): A NEEDS ASSESSMENT OF A SOCIAL SERVICE REFERRAL TELEPHONE PROGRAM FOR HIGH RISK YOUTH

Steve Sussman[*1,2]*, *Silvana Skara*[1] *and Patchareeya Pumpuang*[1]

[1] Institute for Health Promotion and Disease Prevention Research,
University of Southern California, Department of Preventive Medicine,
Keck School of Medicine
[2] University of Southern California, Department of Psychology

ABSTRACT

This chapter describes a quantitative and qualitative needs assessment of a potential social service resource telephone program component among high risk youth who received the Project Towards No Drug Abuse (TND) classroom-based program (approximately 1-year earlier). Information was obtained to determine whether the targeted youth would be interested and receptive, or even need the information available from such a program. Results supported youths' overwhelming receptiveness of a social service referral program. The vast majority of respondents indicated a strong desire for resource and referral information on vocational, educational, recreational, transportation, and mental health and drug counseling. Participants' responses will be used to better structure and tailor our booster program. Further research is needed to investigate the effectiveness of the provision of social service resource information on drug use among emerging adults.

* Correspondence to: Professor of Preventive Medicine and Psychology, Institute for Health Promotion and Disease Prevention Research University of Southern California, Department of Preventive Medicine, Keck School of Medicine, 1000 S. Fremont Avenue, Unit 8, Alhambra, California 91803, Email: ssussma@usc.edu

INTRODUCTION

Drug Use Consequences: Teens and Emerging Adults

Many negative consequences befall substance users during adolescence or in emerging adulthood, a period defined here as extending from approximately 16-25 years of age (coinciding with the developmental period when young persons transition to independent roles; Chassin et al., 1999; Kandel et al., 1986; Krohn et al., 1997; Maggs et al., 1997; Newcomb and Bentler, 1988; 1988b; O'Leary et al., 2002). These consequences include adverse immediate events (e.g., overdoses, accidents, and physical health problems), early involvement in family creation and divorce, and crimes such as stealing and vandalism. Additional negative consequences include dropping out of high school or college, seeking less skilled employment, developing unusual beliefs that interfere with problem-solving abilities (e.g., thinking about the "quick fix"), diminished adaptive coping and achievement behavior, and greater social isolation and depression. Finally, some adolescents and emerging adults suffer a sufficient number of negative consequences that classify them as suffering from substance abuse or dependence disorders (Sussman et al., 1997).

Developmental Transitions during Emerging Adulthood

Young people leaving high school are expected to seek new opportunities (Arnett, 2000; Bachman et al., 1997). These may include: (a) assuming career avenues and financial independence, (b) learning skills of independent living (e.g. buying or renting a place to live apart from one's parents; Bachman et al., 1997), (c) growth in self-care skills (e. g. cooking, cleaning, grooming, buying goods, and traveling), and (d) social adventures (e.g., love and young adult groups). Social adventures lead eventually to commitment in relationships (e.g., marriage and children). Youth may also transition from a relatively high level of family conflict in adolescence to the reduction of such conflicts in emerging adulthood, as one achieves an emotional distance from parental demands and begins to associate more as a junior peer (Aseltine and Gore, 2000). One may argue that youth enter a protracted life phase. Within this phase, there is a "trade-off" between what one commits to and new areas of exploration that must be abandoned. For example, getting married would tend to preclude further dating. Beginning a full-time job would tend to preclude taking on another full-time job with a different directional emphasis. Events characteristic of young and middle adulthood, such as taking on the role of a parent, economic provider, and nurturer, leads to new experiences but often in sacrifice for others and also leads to increasing law abidance, diligence, and conservatism (Stein et al., 1986).

Youth who receive parental support are academically and socially competent, strongly bonded to school, attend church, and hold normatively popular attitudes are relatively likely to transition smoothly into normatively defined young adult roles (Brook et al., 1995; Guo et al., 2001; Krohn et al., 1997; Maggs et al., 1997). Normatively popular attitudes include such sentiments as valuing one's health, affirming the importance of hard work, and expressing respect of family. On the other hand, youth that exhibit unconventional behavior (e.g., cheating, having a child out of wedlock), unconventional attitudes (e.g., tolerance of deviance and preference for sensation seeking), poor emotional control, anger, intrapsychic distress, and interpersonal difficulty are relatively likely to use drugs in emerging adulthood (Aseltine and Gore, 2000; Brook et al., 1997). These youth tend to enter adult roles early ("precocious development"), prior to being prepared to take them on. They tend to drop out of high school or attend part-time education, get married and quickly divorced, become a parent while relatively young, and take on relatively undesired full-time employment. Those teens who exhibit precocious development are at particularly high risk for drug use in emerging adulthood (Krohn et al., 1997). Successful marriage (often forestalled until later in emerging adulthood) is inversely related to drug use, possibly because social opportunities to use decrease, and relationship commitment and consideration of the other person may reduce one's desire to use. This effect applies to males and females, though more strongly for females. Pregnancy and parenthood, in the context of happy marital relationships, are statuses that are also inversely related to drug use. On the other hand, cohabitation, which is relatively strongly associated with holding nontraditional beliefs, is positively associated with drug use. Job stability in young adulthood is negatively related to drug use, although participation in the military or in hourly jobs may be relatively strongly associated with use of cigarettes and alcohol (Bachman et al., 1997). Another major predictor of drug use in emerging adulthood is drug use in adolescence (Brook et al., 2002). The stability of cigarette smoking from high school graduation over the next 10 years is very high, is moderately high for alcohol and marijuana use, but decreases dramatically for other illicit substance use (Bachman et al., 1997; Rohrbach et al., 2005). Finally, age is a major curvilinear predictor of drug use. Experimental drug use tends to peak during this period of emerging adulthood (Bachman et al., 1997), and then tends to decline later in young adulthood (around 25 years of age). Prevention programs focusing on emerging adulthood must not only acknowledge the features of emerging adulthood (e.g., increased exploration of various experiences) but also must link these features to feasible strategies of prevention (e.g., enhancing pro-social skills, providing job information).

Prevention Programming Relevant to Emerging Adulthood

Relatively few prevention programs have been completed among persons in emerging adulthood. A recent review by Sussman and colleagues (Sussman et al., 2004) examined all evidence-based (model or promising) targeted (indicated or selective) drug abuse prevention programs identified by the Blueprints program, SAMSHA, and in a literature search of Medline and PsycINFO. A total of 29 programs were identified (as of 2004). Of these programs, 16 included youth that were 16 years old at baseline. Of these 16 programs, any effects on drug use were reported for 13 of them. Of these 13 programs, effects that occurred or persisted into emerging adulthood (18-25 years of age) were reported in only four programs: Nurse-Family Partnership (N-F P), Project PATHE, Reconnecting Youth (RY), and Project TND. N-F P provided home visits and resource advocacy for first-time mothers with no income from pregnancy to 2 years after childbirth. This program emphasized environmental advocacy, counseling by highly trained counselors, and decision making instruction, and led to decreased smoking and alcohol use and reduced rates of child abuse. Project PATHE provided programming to youth 12-18 years of age who were of disadvantaged socioeconomic status, low achieving in school, and disruptive. School-based activities, peer counseling, academic skills, development of school-pride, and job seeking skills were provided. This program decreased drug involvement, school alienation, and discipline problems and increased graduation rates. RY was implemented with regular high school youth at risk for drop-out from high school. This program involved 90 class sessions and use of small student groups, and led to decreased hard drug use, and less perceived stress and improved grades at approximately a one-year follow-up. Finally, Project TND was implemented with alternative high school youth, as well as regular high school youth. This program involved 12-sessions, which helped motivate youth to change their perspectives on and perceptions of drug use, learn social and life skills to bond to pro-social institutions, and decision making to help them plan good solutions to complex, problem situations. Decreased use of cigarettes, alcohol, marijuana, hard drugs, and weapons carrying was found in this study at one-year follow-up. Effects on cigarette smoking, hard drug use, and marijuana use were maintained at a two-year follow-up. Together, these programs encouraged several changes. They sought to help youth change their drug use motivations, learn new skills (communication, self-control, academic, job seeking), and make good decisions. In addition, they sought to make the older teens' or emergent adults' current life situation more tolerable through providing leads on how to obtain new environmental resources. Extended programming appeared desirable.

Social Service Resource Telephone Program (SSRTP) and Booster Programming Considerations

Relatively little research exists documenting the influences of the provision of social services resource information on drug use among youth, as was indicated in the Sussman et al. review (Sussman et al., 2004). Still, availability of environmental resources has been proposed as a potential elaboration of the DSM axes (Scotti et al., 1996), and the importance of providing access to social-environmental resources is part of the fundamental justification within fields such as social work and urban planning. There is some suggestion of effectiveness on drug use in single-group studies by attendance of high risk preteens and teens at community-schools. These programs involve bringing in an intensive and costly in-house network of social service resources to teens under one roof (Coalition for Community Schools, 2004).

Availability or perception of availability of environmental resources such as access to jobs, education, recreation, transportation, or drug/counseling services in one's community could be enhanced among emerging adults by receiving such information through a telephone education service. If provided as booster programming following receiving drug prevention educational programming in school, this strategy could enhance hope for lifestyle stability with satisfactory self-fulfillment (Lesser and Escoto-Lloyd, 1999; Ward et al., 1982) in a time and location efficient way. However, the effects of provision of resources to emerging adults as an adjunct to drug abuse prevention education has not been attempted to our knowledge. Telephone education has been becoming a more popular modality of delivering information to teens and adults in such venues as smoking prevention (Elder et al., 1994; Skara and Sussman, 2003), smoking cessation (Leed-Kelly et al., 1996, with recovering alcoholics; Mermelstein et al., 2003; Miguez et al., 2002; Whelan et al., 1993; Zhu et al., 2000); at-risk drinking (Curry et al., 2003); prenatal substance abuse treatment (Laken and Ager, 1996);

medication adherence (Aubert et al., 2003; Tutty et al., 2000); pap screening behavior (Hou et al., 2004); mammography screening (Champion et al., 2000); exercise programming (Nies et al., 2003; Pinto et al., 2002); and nutrition behavior (Pierce et al., 2004), with demonstrable results across target behaviors in the vast majority of studies relative to no telephone education. Telephone education could be provided as a means of booster programming (of classroom-based drug use prevention programming) and to help refer emerging adults to nearby social-environmental resources.

Several conceptual models relevant to emerging adulthood have been advanced that provide a language to organize the interaction between developing persons and their environment (Mason et al., in press). Among these include psychosocial process models focusing on the role of social integration and perceived availability of support (Cohen, 1988) and "ecologically-relevant approaches" that seek to understand functional changes of individuals as they are constituted by particular settings and contexts (Bronfenbrenner, 1977; Green, et al., 1996; Mason et al., in press). Consistent with features of these models, the SSRTP component attempts to provide information to subjects to help network them with elements of their surrounding environment. Emerging adults are provided awareness that positive opportunities are "out there" in these systems and youth are motivated further to not select drug use as an alternative. As proposed herein, we believe that an SSRTP component will protect emerging adults from engaging in drug use by helping (Cohen, 1988; Eccles et al., 2003; Mason et al., in press; Millstein, 1994) in at least four ways which correspond to a MACH (mastery, attachment, cue, hope) model of helping early-stage emerging adults to transition successfully during emerging adulthood. First, participants will receive instruction to help them develop a sense of mastery and autonomy (e.g., planning how and where to get assistance in independent living). Receiving general instructions on how to accomplish a life function does provide a vicarious means of anticipating barriers and surmounting them. Further, just being prompted to learn by experience through accessing opportunities in one's environment may assist participants in achieving developmental goals of emerging adulthood (Arnett, 2000; Eccles et al., 2003; Millstein, 1994). Second, by providing information on available resources (jobs, education, transportation, recreation, and mental health or drug abuse counseling), participants might access alternative sources of institutional attachments (emerging adults linking to institutions that support healthy development), that might serve as constructive alternatives to a drug use-based lifestyle. This notion of alternative attachments is familiar within the "bonding" drug abuse prevention, social support, and ecological literatures (Bronfenbrenner, 1977; Aubert et al., 2003; Cohen, 1988; Green et al., 1995; Hawkins et al., 1987; Hawkins et al., 1992; Mason et al., in press). Third, the mere availability of the SSRTP is likely to cue participants to previously learned classroom-based program material; particularly the message that drug use/abuse is risky (Stacy et al., 1995; 1996; 1990a; 1990) this is consistent with suggested drug abuse prevention applications of the memory association literature (Stacy et al., 1996; Sussman, 2001). Since memory is sensitive to a variety of associated cues, links of classroom-based programming to the participants' experiences (prompted by the proposed SSRTP component) may subsequently lead to these life experiences cuing memories of program material. Finally, merely providing participants with the knowledge that there are numerous life options in their community or in southern California that they might think of tapping could instill hope that satisfying and stable life opportunities are available in the future. A future-directed orientation may lead emerging adults to desire to protect their health (Eccles et al., 2003; Millstein, 1994; Sussman and Dent, 2004).

Previous research shows that school-based drug use prevention programs have much greater chance of long-term success, especially for those youth who began using drugs before the prevention program was implemented, if such programs are "boosted" (Skara and Sussman, 2003). Booster programs typically involve implementation of one-to-three lessons or contacts six months to one or two years after the main program implementation. Booster lessons: (1) summarize previously taught material and (2) encourage discussion of how program material was utilized in post-program daily living. Phone boosters are feasible and promising in this population and are probably one of the only ways to reach the participants after high school. A randomized comparison is critical for future prevention efforts that consider implementing booster programs among these emerging adults. If relatively inexpensive (and easily implemented) boosters substantially enhance or maintain effects of a school-based program, then major progress would be made in understanding how to best improve effects of school-based prevention into emerging adulthood.

CHS Youth Subjects: Risk, Ethnic Diversity, and Contexts for Booster Programming.

Since 1992, we have investigated drug abuse prevention among youth across at least 80 continuation high schools (CHSs) in southern and northern California. CHS youth are at relatively high risk for drug abuse. When reaching high school age, those youth who are unable to remain in the regular school system for functional reasons, including lack of credits and consistent use of substances, are transferred to a CHS. These schools were established in 1919 pursuant to the California Educational Code (Section 48400), which requires continued (part-time) education for all California youth until reaching 18 years of age. Every school district that has an enrollment of over 100 students in 12th grade must have a CHS program; there are approximately 600 CHSs in the State of California. Usually students who are experiencing life difficulties when beginning comprehensive (regular) high school transfer to continuation high schools where hours are more flexible and the teacher-to-student ratio is twice as high (i.e., 1:15 versus 1:30). Drugs are used by a greater percentage of youth at CHS than at regular high schools, though. Drug use rates in the last month among CHS average: cigarettes, 57%; alcohol, 63%; marijuana, 54%; stimulants, 21%; hallucinogens, 13%; and all other drugs, 5-8% (e.g., Sussman et al., 2002; n=1861). These data are similar to that reported in a national cross section of alternative high school youth (Grunbaum et al., 2000). On the other hand, among 10th graders assessed concurrently at comprehensive high schools (RHS) from overlapping school districts (n=1208), use in the last month of these substances average: cigarettes, 24%; alcohol, 36%; marijuana, 22%; stimulants, 2%; hallucinogens, 2%, and all other drugs, 1-3%. In addition, there is rich ethnic heterogeneity in continuation high schools, particularly Latino, white, Asian American, and African American youth. Project TND was developed on this diverse population. For example, names of persons in the "talk shows" used in Project TND reflect this cultural diversity. The program was found to be generalizable among youth from different backgrounds (Sussman et al., 2002).

To reach emerging adults with effective programming, one should consider the contexts within which they are likely to spend their time. We followed up persons who received project TND-1 while attending continuation (alternative) high school five years later, while they were in emerging adulthood. We noted that only 25% of the sample was still in CHS at a 1-year follow-up, 5% at a 2-year follow-up, and none by 3-year follow-up. We generated descriptive statistics for subjects' demographic characteristics and living situation at the 5-year follow-up. These subjects did not differ on these variables from those at baseline that had left the pool, aside from baseline living situation (McCuller et al., 2002). Subjects were a mean age of 22 (sd=0.8); 57% male. Half of the subjects were Latino (51%), followed by 35% white, 6% African American, 4% Asian American, and 4% other ethnicity. A total of 67% of the sample reported having completed high school. During the prior 12 months, 42% of the sample had been in school or job training, with 17% in trade school (i.e., trucking, appliances, dent repair, machine operator, plumbing, financial/management, medical assistant, art, computer operator, electronics, insurance, beauty, cooking). Another 14% were in junior college, 7% in a four-year college, and 4% in adult education high school completion classes. Most (80%) longed for additional education training.

The majority (77%) was currently employed. Of those employed, 69% were working full-time (40 or more hours per week). Their job positions included skilled laborers (27%), semi-skilled laborers (16%), clerks or salespersons (14%), small business owners or managers (14%), and professionals (e.g., teacher or nurse; 11%); with 27% reporting they were unskilled laborers, unemployed, or housewives/husbands. A total of 75% of the working sample wanted to get a new job in the future. In terms of marital status, 65% were single, 30% were married or engaged, and 5% were divorced or separated. A total of 42% had at least one child. Many CHS emerging adults hope to continue educational and vocational training. In addition, their lives are busy, although not particularly satisfying. Programming for them should be concise and directed in contexts (i.e., at home by telephone) in which they have time to reflect on their behavior.

THE PRESENT STUDY

This chapter reports the results of a preliminary needs assessment study that was designed to assess interest in a potential social service referral telephone program (SSRTP) component for youth. A needs assessment is a very important step to any program development, implementation, and/or improvement because it allows for the identification of potentially beneficial interventions, as well as gaps in provision that health services could meet (Billings and Cowley, 1995; Stevens, 1998; Wright et al., 1998; Gilbody et al., 2002). This approach has been used more frequently in recent times especially due to limited resources. Needs assessments studies have been conducted in many different settings such as in the medical treatment of patients in hospitals (Man et al., 2004; Rainbird et al., 2004; Wood et al., 2004) or the provision of health promotion and prevention information to various populations, including methadone users at clinics (Morrow and Costello, 2004) and adolescents in peer-led sex education programs (Forrest et al., 2004). A legitimate needs assessment is particularly crucial in developing prevention or intervention programs and in effectively utilizing program resources. The current needs assessment follows a consumer-based perspective, in that it provides identification of the needs of health care and/or improvement in health or quality of life based on the perceptions of the target population rather than on the 'normative' or professionally defined needs. In other words, a consumer need approach is necessary because there is a potential that individual needs may be ignored, while the perceived needs of the health professionals are heeded; thus, there is a danger that the planning and provision of health services would follow a top-down approach, which may end up not matching the needs of the target population.

The participants for this needs assessment study are former students who received the Project TND 12-session classroom-based program (approximately 1-year earlier). Project TND is a school-based drug abuse prevention program funded by the National Institute on Drug Abuse since 1992 (e.g., Sussman et al., 2002). This program is considered a model or exemplary program by the U.S. D.O.E., SAMSHA/CSAP, NIDA, Health Canada, Colorado and Maryland Blueprints, and numerous other agencies. The target population of our ongoing research has been primarily youth from the alternative school system (continuation high schools, CHSs) in California. The average age at baseline of these youth is approximately 17 years old (93% of the sample is 16-18 years of age). While promising short-term program effects (Dent et al., 2001; Sussman et al., 1998; 2003) were obtained for the classroom-based program, and some effects were maintained over several years (see Sun et al., under review), it is believed that program effects could be better sustained during early emerging adulthood through use of booster programming (e.g., delivered by telephone). However, before implementing this social service referral telephone program, it is first necessary to determine, through a formal needs assessment, whether the targeted youth would be interested and receptive, or even need the information available from such a social service referral program.

METHODS

During the period from August to September 2004, we undertook a cross-sectional study involving a convenience sample of subjects who received the Project Towards No Drug Abuse (TND) classroom-based program (approximately 1-year earlier). Subjects were randomly selected from 5 southern California urban and suburban continuation high schools (CHSs). A total of 102 subjects (54 males and 48 females) completed telephone interviews (75 % response rate). The mean age of interview participants was 18.5 (range=17-22, SD=0.93). The sample included 40% Latino, 40% white, 10% African American, and 10% other ethnicity.

Following a standardized questionnaire format, the interviewer asked for the subject's opinions about a potential, new type of free telephone-based referral service for people who participated in Project TND while in high school. Specifically, the subject was told that well-trained telephone educators would call subjects multiple times to provide desired information on resources that people out of high school typically need such as jobs, work training, educational opportunities, transportation, recreational activities, and mental health or drug counseling resources. The educator would attempt to find resources within the subject's local area and zip code. For example, if the subject were interested in finding a job, the educator could discuss the subject's interests and provide some advice and ideas, and then give the subject information on where to go to either get a list of jobs available in the subject's area or, if needed, information on where to go to find out about training for the job. Further, the educator could also print and send mailed information to the subject about the resources (such as telephone numbers and maps).

Finally, the subjects were told that they could call our resource center as many times as wanted for information on our 1-800 telephone line from 10 a.m.-through 3 p.m., on Mondays through Fridays.

After the subjects were given this brief description of the social service referral telephone program, subjects were asked 14 questions in a 5-minute interview. On scales of 1 (not at all useful)-to-10 (very useful), they were asked about their perceptions of usefulness of the service to people who are recently out of high school; how useful job, education, recreation activities, transportation, mental health counseling, and drug counseling sources of information would be; overall interest in such a service; and perceived helpfulness in preventing people from abusing drugs (including cigarettes, alcohol, marijuana, or harder drugs). Subjects were also asked that if a counselor from the telephone resource center called to give resource information, would they talk to them (Yes/ No/ Not Sure), what an adequate number of calls from the educator might be within a 6 month period (1 time /2 times/3 times/4 times+), whether the subject would ever call this service on their own (Yes/ No/ Not Sure) and, if so, how often (1/2-5/6+ times in 6 months). Finally, subjects were asked if and why this service would help to prevent drug abuse (open-ended responses, multiple responses were permitted, and responses were coded into categories by two raters, with a 95% agreement).

RESULTS

Subjects were extremely receptive to the concept of the SSRTP. The overall usefulness mean score was 8.67 (SD=1.57). Usefulness by categories ranged from means=8.90 and 9.05, for job and education, respectively (SDs=1.58 and 1.29, respectively), to means of 8.36 and 8.63, for drug counseling resources and transportation, respectively (SDs=2.10 and 1.83, respectively), to mental health and recreation (means=8.00 and 8.06, SDs=2.30 and 2.01, respectively). Subjects reported being very interested in the service (mean=7.83, SD=2.54). Most subjects (76%) said that they definitely would be willing to talk with the telephone educator, and 22% said they were not sure (only 2% said they would not). Interestingly, subjects desired a mean of 2.53 calls every 6 months (SD=1.09). Also, 65% said that they definitely would call the telephone educator on their own as well (on the 800-line), and that they would call an average of 2-5 times, themselves, in a 6-month period.

Finally, 82% of the subjects reported that this service would help prevent drug abuse among themselves and their peers. A total of six categories were coded based on student responses to the open-ended question that assessed why this service might help to prevent drug abuse: (1) it would educate participants on risks of drug abuse (38%); (2) it would help those who are unsure how to ask for or obtain advice, and assist them in self-improvement, autonomy, or mastery (31%); (3) it can provide access to alternative attachments (e.g., jobs) that keep one busy (20%); (4) it can provide access to help for smoking or drug abuse cessation (6%); (5) it would help participants project their life into the future (6%); and (6) it would help participants to think more about others (2%). (Twenty subjects gave more than one response.) Subjects anticipated that the phone calls would take an average of 20 minutes to complete, although they desired having up to an average of 45 minutes of telephone time. All proposed 4 functions of the SSRTP component appeared to be represented; that is, attain mastery, access alternative attachments, cue program information on drug abuse risks, and future orientation/hope (MACH).

Approximately two weeks following the first telephone interview, we telephoned a random selection of 27 of these persons (13 males; 14 females) to assess if our merely contacting previous attendees of the Project TND classroom program regarding social services would prompt them to begin looking for services. Surprisingly, 8 of these subjects had taken action in the last 2 weeks (and attributed this to our call) by either calling a number after looking at job wanted ads (7 subjects), or visiting the local college to pick up a catalogue (2 subjects; 1 person looked for a job and school).

DISCUSSION

The results of this needs assessment study identified youths' strong interest and positive feedback regarding the provision of a potential social service resource telephone program (SSRTP) that was designed to offer information to individuals recently out of high school to help integrate them into emerging adulthood. This chapter is the first description, in the form of a needs assessment, of the perceptions and opinions of youth on the information and services that a telephone resource and referral center should provide. The findings are thus a major step forward in using the views of interested parties to provide a new service that may empower people who are at high risk for drug use.

The vast majority of respondents indicated a strong desire for resource and referral information on vocational, educational, recreational, transportation, and mental health and drug counseling services. However, the highest value was placed on vocational and educational information, which is not surprising given their recent transition from the high school context to a young adult "real world" context where they face increasing challenges to become financially independent from their parents. Subjects also reported being very interested in actually utilizing the service, with most indicating that they definitely would be willing to talk with the telephone educator if called, as well as call the telephone educator (on the 800-line) on their own. This reported interest may be due to an important aspect of SSRTP, which is the provision of a tailored service to emerging adults. Information on local and current resources will be provided to each subject based on where they live and what they want to achieve. This localized resource component decreases perceived barriers and increase self-efficacy (Hochbaum, 1958; Rosenstock, 1960). Findings from past research have shown that systematic barriers (i.e. time, location of resources, and transportation) have been a major problem in accessing these resources and hence, compliance (Flores et al., 1998; Fitzpatrick et al., 2004). In addition, providing emerging adults with information on how they can obtain their own information increases the feeling of self-efficacy or the perception that one can perform a certain task or tasks. Programs designed around the self-efficacy framework have been shown effective in enhancing compliance to particular behaviors in diverse fields such as in decreasing use of alcohol and tobacco among adolescents (Ellickson & Bell, 1990; Bell et al., 1993), taking medication (Buchmann, 1997), weight control in patients with end-stage renal diseases (Tsay, 2003), increase in patient-initiated partner notification for curable sexually transmitted infections among adolescents (Fortenberry et al., 2002), and in having healthy diets among adolescents (Ebbeling et al., 2003; Woo et al., 2004).

Another explanation for the strong enthusiasm about this service may be due to the delivery modality. Research has shown that telephone counseling can be a very favorable means in reaching emerging adults (Chen et al., 1995). In general, telephone services have been shown to be effective in improving health care delivery (McBride and Rimer, 1999; Ploeg et al., 2001; Wilkes et al., 2004). Using telephones to deliver interventions allows individualized services to broad sections of the target population as well as minimize logistics and systematic barriers (McBride and Rimer, 1999). Telephone services have also been shown effective when working with teens and tobacco cessation (Chen et al., 1995; Zhu et al., 2000). For example, telephone HELPLINES provided counseling to participants living in California in six different languages. It provided information on tobacco cessation, counseling and self-help kits. Compared to those who did not use the HELPLINES, participants who did were more likely to have tried to quit smoking recently and were ready to try to quit again if the first attempts were not successful. Using peer counselors to deliver important information and support have also been useful (Horton et al., 1997; Goldschmidt and Graves, 2003).

Needs assessment studies for establishing telephone health services have been conducted in the past. For example, Poncia et al. (2000) conducted a needs assessment for a next day telephone follow-up of the elderly after being discharged from the hospital. The results of this assessment revealed a need for improvements in care of elderly patients before and after discharge and thus, the importance of this telephone service (Poncia et al., 2000). The telephone assessment provided an inexpensive alternative to assessing the needs of patients and therefore, potentially decreasing unnecessary return visits to the emergency room. Baker et al. (1999) conducted a needs assessment via an after-hours telephone triage on the advice in private and non-private pediatric populations and found very important implications for improvements of such services (Baker et al., 1999). Thus far, it can be seen that the telephone needs assessment conducted in this current study plays a very critical role in development of the SSRTP program, especially among our target population. The SSRTP has the potential to provide time- and cost-efficient dissemination of imrtant information to emerging adults in a manner most suitable for them. Since many will be out of high school at the time of the telephone intervention, they are not easily reached and followed. Mailing information is difficult as students tend to move out of their parent's home and establish their own residence elsewhere. Mailing can also be costly when considered over long periods of time and is prone to getting lost or misplaced. Needs assessment of other young adults have been in favor of telephone interventions (Chen et al., 1995).

Interestingly, another indication of the great potential of this telephone service to influence high risk youth to engage in productive activities has been evidenced in the results of this study. That is, a follow-up survey to the initial needs assessment of the SSRTP has shown almost immediate positive feedback towards the telephone service. Our findings indicate that by just implementing the initial needs assessment study, several students (almost one-third of the small follow-up sample) were prompted to seek job and educational information on their own. These strong, albeit limited, data provide promising implications for significant program effects in the future.

Furthermore, participants in this study also provided open-ended, qualitative responses indicating that they believed that the Project TND prevention education offered in the classroom in high school plus the addition of this new continuing social resource service (i.e., the SSRTP) might be helpful in preventing people from using drugs (including cigarettes, alcohol, marijuana, or harder drugs). These data lend support to our hypothesis that a telephone booster component to Project TND will help emerging adults to integrate successfully into main stream adult lifestyles, while avoiding substance use. Specifically, it is feasible that including an SSRTP booster component could bolster preventive effects on drug use over a longer period of time, through review of drug abuse prevention program material, and by assisting former CHS youth better prepare themselves during emerging adulthood by helping with at least four ways which correspond to the MACH (mastery, attachments, cue previous material, and hope) model introduced earlier.

LIMITATIONS AND FUTURE DIRECTIONS

Our results should be interpreted in the context of a few methodological limitations. First, data in this study were generated from self-report surveys, the accuracy of which could not be independently verified. Thus, it is impossible to assess the extent to which such data may be biased, particularly in regard to social desirability. It is also important to understand that due to difficulty in contacting students for surveys, it eventually became a selective group of individuals who answered the survey questions. That is, only those who were willing to talk to us were the ones providing responses. Thus, it is likely that they would provide positive responses in support of our service. Those that may provide lower scores were those that declined, and thus, were not surveyed. Second, the results of this study are generalizable only to subjects who are similar to those examined in this study. Continuation high school students differ in many important ways from general population youth (Sussman et al., 1995; 1995) Also, this sample was quite heterogeneous ethnically. It is possible that these results differ from other, more ethnically homogeneous populations of youths.

Third, there was no comparison group for the findings presented in this study. However, results from this study were primarily intended to represent a preliminary needs assessment of our targeted sample to be used for the first phase of development of the SSRTP.

Despite these limitations, this study provides new evidence which suggests that continuation high school students have a strong interest in utilizing a potential social service resource telephone program (SSRTP) that was designed to offer information to individuals recently out of high school to help integrate them into emerging adulthood. The results provide feedback on how to better structure and tailor such a prevention intervention program. For example, the results reveal exactly for which topics (e.g., vocational and educational) the participants are interested in receiving information. Other programs with similar missions of developing a tailored social service referral and resource intervention may benefit from these findings.

Finally, it should be noted that he SSRTP intervention cannot stand alone; it is only a component of Project TND and serves as a supplement to the program. However, it is expected that this component will boost program effects and serve to enhance the lifestyles of emerging adults by reminding them of what was learned while in school and assist them in applying it to real life situations. Thus, once the SSRTP is developed, further experimental research is needed to investigate the effectiveness of the provision of the social service resource information component, as well as the Project TND classroom-based component on drug use among emerging adults.

REFERENCES

Arnett, J. J. (2000). Emerging adulthood: A theory of development from the late teens through the twenties. *American Psychologist, 55*, 469-480.

Aseltine, R. H., & Gore, S. L. (2000). The variable effects of stress on alcohol use from adolescence to early adulthood. *Substance Use & Misuse, 35*, 643-668.

Aubert, R. E., Fulop, G., Xia, F., Thiel, M., Maldonato, D., & Woo, C. (2003). Evaluation of a depression health management program to improve outcomes in first or recurrent episode depression. *American Journal of Managed Care, 9*, 374-380.

Bachman, J., Wadsworth, K., O'Malley, P., Johnston, L., & Schulenberg, J. (1997). *Smoking, Drinking, and Drug use in Young Adulthood: The Impacts of New Freedoms and New Responsibilities.* Mahway, NJ: Lawrence Erlbaum Associates.

Baker, R. C., Schubert, C. J., Kirwan, K. A., Lenkauskas, S. M., & Spaeth, J. T.. (1999). After-hours telephone triage and advice in private and nonprivate pediatric populations. *Archives of Pediatrics & Adolescent Medicine, 153*(3), 292-296.

Bell, R. M., Ellickson, P. L., & Harrison, E. R. (1993) Do drug prevention effects persist into high school? How project ALERT did with ninth graders. *Preventive Medicine, 22*, 463-483.

Billings, J., & Cowley, S. (1995). Approaches to community needs assessment: A literature review. *Journal of Advance Nursing, 22*(4), 721-730.

Brook, J. S., Balka, E. B., Gursen, M. D., Brook, D. W., & Shapiro, J. (1997). Young adults' drug use: A 17-year longitudinal inquiry of antecedents. *Psychological Reports, 80*, 1235-1251.

Brook, D. W., Brook, J. S., Zhang, C., Cohen, P., & Whiteman, M. (2002). Drug use and the risk of major depressive disorder, alcohol dependence, and substance use disorders. *Archives of General Psychiatry, 59*, 1039-1044.

Brook, J. S., Whiteman, M., Cohen, P., Shapiro, J., & Balka, E. (1995). Longitudinally predicting late adolescent and young adult drug use: Childhood and adolescent precursors. *Journal of the American Academy of Child Adolescent Psychiatry, 34*, 1230-1238.

Bronfenbrenner, U. (1977). Toward an experimental ecology of human development. *American Psychologist, 32*, 513-531.

Buchmann, W. (1997). Adherence: a matter of self-efficacy and power. *Journal of Advance Nursing, 26*(1), 132-137.

Champion, V. L, Skinner, C. S., & Foster, J. L. (2000). The effects of standard care counseling or telephone/in-person counseling on beliefs, knowledge, and behavior related to mammography screening. *Oncology Nursing Forum, 27*, 1565-1571.

Chassin, L., Pitts, S. C., & DeLucia, C. (1999). The relation of adolescent substance use to young adult autonomy, positive activity involvement, and perceived competence. *Development and Psychopathology, 11*, 915-932.

Chen, S. P., Dallas, C., & Chen, E. H. (1995). Teen voices on a proposed telephone health service. *ABNF Journal, 6*(1), 19-23.

Coalition for Community Schools. (2004). *Evaluation of Community Schools: An Early Look.* Retrieved September 2, 2004 from http://www.communityschools.org/evaluation/evalbrieffinal.html.

Cohen, S. (1988). Pyschosocial models of the role of social support in the etiology of physical disease. *Health Psychology, 7*, 269-297

Curry, S. J., Ludman, E. J., Grothaus, L. C., Donovan, D., & Kim, E. (2003). A randomized trial of a brief primary-care-based intervention for reducing at-risk drinking practices. *Health Psychology, 22*, 156-165.

Dent, C. W., Sussman, S., McCullar, W. J., Stacy, A. W. (2001). Project Towards No Drug Abuse: Generalizability to a general high school sample. *Preventive Medicine, 32*, 514-520.

Ebbeling, C. B., Leidig, M. M., Sinclair, K. B., Hangen, J. P., & Ludwig, D. S. (2003). A reduced-glycemic load diet in the treatment of adoelscent obesity. *Pediatrics & Adolescent Medicine, 157*(8), 773-779.

Eccles, J., Templeton, J., Barber, B., & Stone, M. (2003). Adolescence and emerging adulthood: The critical passage ways to adulthood. In M. H. Bornstein, L. Davidson, C. L. M. Keys & K. A. Moore (Eds.), *Well-being: Positive Development Across the Life Course* (pp. 383-406). Mahwah, NJ: Lawrence Erlbaum Associates, Inc.

Elder, J. P., Woodruff, S. I., & Eckhardt, L. (1994). Participation in a telephone-based tobacco use prevention program for adolescents. *American Journal of Health Promotion, 9*, 92-95.

Ellickson, P. L., & Bell, R. M. (1990). Drug prevention in junior high: a multi-site longitudinal test. *Science, 247*, 1299-1305.

Fitzpatrick, A. L., Powe, N. R., Cooper, L. S., Ives, D. G., & Robbins, J. A. (2004). Barriers to health care access among the elderly and who perceives them. *American Journal of Public Health, 94*(10), 1788-1794.

Flores, G., Abreu, M., Olivar, M. A., & Kastner, B. (1998). Access barriers to health care for Latino children. *Archives of Pediatrics & Adolescent Medicine, 152*(11), 1119-1125.

Forrest, S., Strange, V., Oakley, A., & The RIPPLE Study Team. (2004). What do young people want from sex education? The results of a needs assessment from a peer-led sex education programme. *Culture, Health & Sexuality, 6*(4), 337-354.

Fortenberry, J. D., Brizendine, E. J., Katz, B., P., & Orr, D., P. (2002). The role of self-efficacy and relationship quality in partner notification by adolescents with sexually transmitted infections. *Archives Pediatric & Adolescent Medicine, 156*(11), 1133-1137.

Gilbody, S., House, A., & Sheldon, T. (2002). Routine administration of Health Related Quality of Life (HRQoL) and needs assessment instruments to improve psychological outcome - a systematic review. *Psychological Medicine, 32*(8), 1345-1356.

Goldschmidt, R. H. & Graves, D. W. (2003). The National HIV Telephone Consultation Service (Warmline): a clinical resource for physicians caring for African-Americans. *Journal of the National Medical Association, 95*(2 Suppl 2), 8S-11S.

Grunbaum, J. A. Kann, L., Kinchen, S. A., Ross, J. G., Gowda, V. R., Collins, J. L., & Kolbe, L. J. (2000). Youth risk behavior surveillance National Alternative High School Youth Risk Behavior Survey, United States, 1998. *Journal of School Health, 70*, 5-17.

Green, L. W., Richard, L., & Potvin, L. (1996). Ecological foundations of health promotion. *American Journal of Health Behavior, 10*, 270-281.

Guo, J., Hawkins, J. D., Hill, K. G., & Abbott, R. D. (2001). Childhood and adolescent predictors of alcohol abuse and dependence in young adulthood. *Journal of Studies on Alcohol, 62*, 754-762.

Hawkins, J., Lishner, D., Jenson, J., & Catalano, R. (1987). Delinquents and drugs: What the evidence suggests about prevention and treatment programming. *Youth at High Risk for Substance Abuse*. Superintendent of Documents, U.S. Government Printing Office, DHHS ADM-D87-1537 (pp. 81-131). Washington, DC: National Institute on Drug Abuse.

Hawkins, J. D., Catalano, R. F., & Miller, J. Y. (1992). Risk and protective factors for alcohol and other drug problems in adolescence and early adulthood: Implications for substance use prevention. *Psychological Bulletin, 112*, 64-105.

Hochbaum, G. (1958). *Public Participation in Medical Screening Programs: A Sociopsychological Study. PHS Publication No. 572*. Washington, DC:U.S. Government Printing Office.

Horton, R., Peterson, M. G. E., Powell, S., Engelhard, E., & Paget, S. A. (1997). Users evaluate lupusline a telephone peer counseling service. *Arthritis Care &Research, 10*(4), 257-263.

Hou, S. I, Fernandez, M. E., & Parcel, G. S. (2004). Development of a cervical cancer educational program for Chinese women using intervention mapping. *Health Promotion Practice, 5*, 80-87.

Kandel, D. B., Davies, M., Karus, D., & Yamaguchi, K. (1986). The consequences in young adulthood of adolescent drug involvement. *Archives of General Psychiatry, 43*, 746-754.

Krohn, M. D., Lizotte, A. J., & Perez, C. M. (1997). The interrelationship between substance use and precocious transitions to adult statuses. *Journal of Health and Social Behavior, 38*, 87-103.

Laken, M. P. & Ager., J. W. (1996). Effects of case management on retention inn prenatal substance abuse treatment. *American Journal of Drug & Alcohol Abuse, 22*, 439-448.

Leed-Kelly, A., Russel, K. S., Bobo, J. K., & McIlvain, H. (1996). Feasibility of smoking cessation counseling by phone with alcohol treatment center graduates. *Journal of Substance Abuse Treatment, 13*, 203-210.

Lesser, J. & Escoto-Lloyd, S. (1999). Health-related problems in a vulnerable population: pregnant teens and adolescent mothers. *Nursing Clinics of North America, 34*, 289-299.

Maggs, J. L., Frome, P. M., Eccles, J. S., & Barber, B. L. (1997). Psychosocial resources, adolescent risk behaviour and young adult adjustment: is risk taking more dangerous for some than others? *Journal of Adolescence, 20*, 103-119.

Man, D. W. K., Lee, E. W. T., Tong, E. C. H., Yip, S. C. S., Lui, W. F., & Lam, C. S. (2004). Health services needs and quality of life assessment of individuals with brain injuries: a pilot cross-sectional study. *Brain Injury, 18*(6), 577-591.

Mason, M. J., Cheung, I., & Walker, L. (in press). Substance use, social networks and the geography of risk and protection of urban adolescents. *Substance Use & Misuse*.

McBride, C. M. & Rimer, B. K. (1999). Using the telephone to improve health behavior and health service delivery. *Patient Education & Counseling, 37*(1), 3-18.

McCuller, W. J., Sussman, S., Holiday, K., Craig, S., & Dent, C. W. (2002). Tracking procedures for locating high risk youth. *Evaluation and the Health Professions, 25*, 345-362.

Mermelstein, R., Hedeker, D., & Wong, S. C. (2003). Extended telephone counseling for smoking cessation: does content matter? *Journal of Consulting & Clinical Psychology, 71*, 565-74.

Miguez, M. C., Vazquez, F. L. & Becona., E. (2002). Effectiveness of telephone contact as an adjunct to a self-help program for smoking cessation: a randomized controlled trial in Spanish smokers. *Addictive Behaviors, 27*, 139-44.

Millstein, S.G. (1994). *Health promotion and disease prevention in the 21st century: Time for a paradigm shift? Paper presented at the State of the Art Symposium: Innovative Prevention Approaches for the 21st Century*, American Psychological Association 1994 Annual Meeting, Boston, MA.

Morrow, K. & Costello, T. (2004). HIV, STD and hepatitis prevention among women in methadone maintenance: a qualitative and quantitative needs assessment. *AIDS Care, 16*(4), 426-433.

Newcomb, M. D. & Bentler, P. M. (1988). *Consequences of Adolescent Drug Use*. Newbury Park, CA: Sage Publications, Inc.

Newcomb, M. D. & Bentler, P. M. (1988b) Impact of adolescent drug use and social support on problems of young adults: A longitudinal study. *Journal of Abnormal Psychology, 97*, 64-75.

Nies, M. A., Chruscial, H. L., & Hepworth, J. T. (2003). An intervention to promote walking in sedentary women in the community. *American Journal of Health Behavior, 27*, 524-535.

O'Leary, T. A., Brown, S. A., Colby, S. M., Cronce, J. M., D'Amico, E. J., Fader, J. S., Geisner, I. M., Larimer, M. E., Magges, J. L., McGrady, B., Palomer, R. S., Schulenberg, J., & Monti, P. M. (2002). Treating adolescents together or individually? Issues in adolescent substance abuse interventions. *Alcoholism: Clinical and Experimental Research, 26*, 890-899.

Pierce, J. P., Newman, V. A., Flatt, S. W., Faerber, S., Rock, C. L., Natarajan, L., Caan, B. J., Gold, E. B., Hollenbach, K. A., Wasserman, L., Jones, L., Ritenbaugh, C., Stefanick, M. L., Thomson, C. A., & Kealey, S. (2004). Telephone counseling intervention increases intakes of micronutrient- and phytochemical-rich vegetables, fruit and fiber in breast cancer survivors. *Journal of Nutrition, 134*, 452-458.

Pinto, B. M., Friedman, R., Marcus, B. H., Kelley, H., Tennstedt, S., & Gillman, M. W. (2002). Effects of computer-based, telephone-counseling system on physical activity. *American Journal of Preventative Medicine, 23*, 113-120.

Ploeg, J., Bichler, L., Willison, K., Hutchison, B., & Blythe, J. (2001). Perceived support needs of family caregivers and implications for a telephone support service. *Canadian Journal of Nursing Research, 33*(2), 43-61.

Poncia, H., Ryan, J., & Carver, M. (2000). Next day telephone follow-up of the elderly: a needs assessment and critical incident monitoring tool for the accident and emergency department. *Journal of Accident Emergency Medicine, 17*, 337-340.

Rainbird, K. J., Perkins, J. J., & Sanson-Fisher, R. W. (2004). The Needs Assessment for Advanced Cancer Patients (NA-ACP): A measure of the perceived needs of patients with advanced, incurable cancer. A study of validity, reliability and acceptability. *Psychooncology*, *14*(4), 297-306.

Rohrbach, L. A., Sussman, S., Dent, C. W., & Sun, P. (2005). A five-year longitudinal study from adolescence to emerging adulthood. *Journal of Drug Issues, 35*(3), 333-356.

Rosenstock, I. (1960). What research in motivation suggests for public health. *American Journal of Health Promotion, 50*, 295-301.

Scotti, J. R., Morris, T. L., McNeil, C. B., & Hawkins, R. P. (1996). DSM-IV and disorders of childhood and adolescence: can structural criteria be functional? *Journal of Consulting & Clinical Psychology, 64*, 1177-91.

Skara, S. & Sussman, S. (2003). A review of 25 long-term adolescent tobacco and other drug use prevention program evaluations. *Preventive Medicine, 37*, 451-474.

Stacy, A. W. (1995). Memory association and ambiguous cues in models of alcohol and marijuana use. *Experimental and Clinical Psychopharmacology, 3*, 183-194.

Stacy, A. W., Ames, S., Sussman, S., Dent, C. W. (1996). Implicit cognition in adolescent drug use. *Psychology of Addictive Behaviors, 10*, 190-203.

Stacy, A. W., Dent, C. W., Sussman, S., Raynor, A., Burton, D., & Flay, B. R. (1990a). Expectancy accessibility and the influence of outcome expectancies on adolescent smokeless tobacco use. *Journal of Applied Social Psychology, 20*, 802-817.

Stacy, A. W., Widaman, K. F., & Marlatt, G. A. (1990). Expectancy models of alcohol use. *Journal of Personality and Social Psychology, 58*, 918-928.

Stein, J. A., Newcomb, M. D., & Bentler, P. M. (1986). Stability and change in personality: A longitudinal study from early adolescence to young adulthood. *Journal of Research in Personality, 20*, 276-291.

Stevens, A. & Gillam S. (1998). Needs Assessment: from theory to practice. *British Medical Journal, 316*(7142), 1448-1452.

Sun, W., Skara, S., Sun, P., Dent, C. W., & Sussman, S. (2006). Project Towards No Drug Abuse: Long-term substance abuse use outcomes evaluation. *Preventive Medicine, 42*, 188-192.

Sussman, S. (2001). *Handbook of Program Development for Health Behavior Research and Practice.* Thousand Oaks, CA: Sage.

Sussman, S. & Dent, C. W. (2004). Five-year prospective prediction of marijuana use cessation among youth at continuation high schools. *Addictive Behaviors, 29*, 1237-1243.

Sussman, S., Dent, C. W., & Galaif, E.R. (1997). The correlates of substance abuse and dependence among adolescents at high risk for drug abuse. *Journal of Substance Abuse, 9*, 241-255.

Sussman, S., Dent, C. W., Simon, T.R., Stacy, A. W., Galaif, E. R., Moss, M. A., Craig, S., & Johnson, C. A. (1995). Immediate impact of social influence-oriented substance abuse prevention curricula in traditional and continuation high schools. *Drugs and Society, 8*(3/4), 65-81.

Sussman, S., Dent, C. W., & Stacy, S. (2002). Project Towards No Drug Abuse: A review of the findings and future directions. *American Journal of Health Behavior, 26*, 354-365.

Sussman, S., Dent, C. W., Stacy, A., & Craig, S. (1998). One-year outcomes of Project Towards No Drug Abuse. *Preventive Medicine, 27*, 632-642 (Erratum: 27(5, Pt.1), 766, 1998).

Sussman, S., Earleywine, M., Wills, T., Cody, C., Biglan, A., Dent, C. W., & Newcomb, M. D. (2004). The motivation, skills, and decision-making model of "drug abuse" prevention. *Substance Use & Misuse, 39*(10-12), 1971-2016.

Sussman, S., Stacy, A. W., Dent, C.W., Simon, T. R., Galaif, E. R., Moss, M. A., Craig, S., & Johnson, C. A. (1995) Continuation high schools: youth at risk for drug abuse. *Journal of Drug Education, 25*(3), 191-209.

Sussman, S., Sun, P., McCuller, W. J., & Dent, C. W. (2003). Project Towards No Drug Abuse: Two-year outcomes of a trial that compares health educator delivery to self-instruction. *Preventive Medicine, 37*,155-162.

Tsay, S. (2003). Self-efficacy training for patients with end-stage renal disease. *Journal of Advance Nursing, 43*(4), 370-375.

Tutty, S., Simon, G., & Ludman, E. (2000). Telephone counseling as an adjunct to antidepressant treatment in the primary care system. A pilot study. *Effective Clinical Practice, 3*, 170-8.

Ward, D. A., Bendel, R. B., & Lange, D. (1982). A reconsideration of environmental resources and the posttreatment functioning of alcoholic patients. *Journal of Health & Social Behavior, 23*, 310-7.

Whelan, V., McBride, D., & Colby, R. (1993). Public health department tracking of high-risk drug users. *Public Health Reports, 108*, 643-645.

Wilkes, L., Mohan, S., White, K., & Smith, H. (2004). Evaluation of an after hours telephone support service for rural palliative care patients and their families: A pilot study. *Australian Journal Rural Health, 12*(3), 95-8.

Woo, K., Chook, P., Yu, C. W., Sung, R. Y. T., Qiao, M., Leung, S. S. F., Lam, C. W. K., Metreweli, C., & Celermajer, D. S. (2004). Effects of Diet and Exercise on Obesity-Related Vascular Dysfunction in Children. *Circulation, 109*(16), 1981-1986.

Wood, I., Douglas, J., & Priest, H. (2004). Education and training for acute care delivery: a needs analysis. *Nursing in Critical Care, 9*(4), 159-166.

Wright, J., Williams, R., & Wilkinson, J, R. (1998). Health needs assessment: Development and importance of health needs assessment. *British Medical Journal, 316*(7140), 1310-1313.

Zhu, S. H., Anderson, C. M., Johnson, C. E., Tedeschi, G., & Roeseler, A. (2000). A centralised telephone service for tobacco cessation: the California experience. *Tobacco Control, 9*(Suppl 2), II48-II55.

Zhu, S. H., Tedeschi, G., Anderson, C. M., Rosbrook, B., Byrd, M., Johnson, C. E., & Gutierrez-Terrell, E. (2000). Telephone counseling as adjuvant treatment for nicotine replacement therapy in a "real-world" setting. *Preventive Medicine, 31*, 357-63.

In: Psychology of Decision Making in Education
Editor: Jeanine A. Elsworth, pp. 143- 162

ISBN: 978-1-60021-933-7
© 2006 Nova Science Publishers, Inc.

Chapter 6

AN ERROR-MINIMIZING RULE FOR ANIMAL DECISION-MAKING UNDER UNCERTAINTY

J.A. Devenport[1] and L.D. Devenport[2]
[1]University of Central Oklahoma USA
[2]University of Oklahoma, USA

ABSTRACT

Decision-making under uncertainty is to be expected in natural environments. The greatest source of uncertainty comes from the passage of time, because time—and the environmental variability it allows to proceed—discounts the reliability of information on which decisions are based. Information is most reliable if it can be acted on immediately, but as time passes, an average of past values of the alternatives is the best estimate of current value, since this subjective process matches the objective tendency of biological variables to regress to their means. The most optimal strategy, therefore, would be to flexibly shift from tracking the most recent outcomes to averaging across them. A model, the temporal weighting rule (TWR), accomplishes this transition. The output of TWR is a dynamic average whose rate matches the rate of environmental change. We review empirical studies showing the wide range of species that make dynamic foraging decisions consistent with TWR, the special predictions the model makes and their accuracy, its ecological relevance, and the memory mechanisms it appears to rely on. We conclude that this quantitative model and its accompanying decision rule, or something very similar to it, solve the one of the commonest problems animals face in their variable environments. TWR minimizes decision error made under uncertainty.

INTRODUCTION

In the natural world there are many reasons for incomplete information but one of the most important is variability. Change is inevitable and time is the fundamental cause. The quality of resources may degrade with time, and the quantity or availability of resources changes as competitors discover and utilize them, or natural factors, e.g., wind-dispersed seeds, alter conditions. So food resources that were once good will in time get worse but the reverse is also true; resources that were once poor will improve in time, as patches regenerate (Devenport, J. & Devenport, L. 1994).

Decisions made with incomplete information are said to be made under uncertainty. Most uncertainty results from not knowing the current probability or likelihood of a naturally varying outcome (reviewed in Dall, Giraldeau, Olsson, McNamara, & Stephens, 2005; Inglis, 2000). A decision-maker has incomplete information because it is uncertain whether the current state matches the previously sampled state.

Much of what we know about decisions under uncertainty comes from investigations of foraging decisions in animals. When an animal is foraging for food it often visits locations or patches that it has sampled in the past and therefore has information about the quality or quantity of food found in those patches. However, because natural resources vary, the difficulty of knowing the *current state* of a patch contributes to the uncertainty of information about it. We will argue that natural selection has equipped animals with a cognitive adaptation to deal with this problem.

Just as time leads to change, it necessarily discounts the reliability of information about the comparative value of alternatives, so uncertainty is dynamic. The degree of uncertainty is correlated with the amount of time that has passed. For example, a bird that finds a ripe fruit tree is likely to find fruit is still available an hour later, but as returns are postponed, the probability of fruit remaining declines progressively owing to harvesting by competitors. Correspondingly, the reliability of information about that alternative is diminished and should be discounted. This relationship between time and information reliability obtains for all resources or options that have some variability, which in the natural world is the rule (Stephens, 1989). What differs is the rate of change of resources (Devenport, L., & Devenport, J., 1994).

Regardless of the exact rate of change, choices made shortly after the information is obtained are (almost) completely deterministic. If a squirrel finds a nut tree and returns an hour later, it is a near certainty that there will still be nuts to harvest. A honey bee returning to a flower patch in 15 min will still find nectar or pollen. In such cases, where information is fresh, keeping track of where you have just been and repeating that choice provides the best outcome, provided the animal has not itself depleted the resource. There are many examples of animals tracking resources in both natural and laboratory settings (Bateson, 2003; Cowie, 1977; Stephens & Anderson, 2001). But this strategy, termed *tracking*, only works when information is recent and therefore predictive of current conditions. Delineating what is recent or fresh information is difficult because this is a *relative* not absolute measure and varies with the type of resource and prevailing conditions.

Information that is not recently acquired is more uncertain and less reliable because there has been a greater opportunity for change to occur, but knowledge acquired in the past still has worth because the long-term average value of the alternative can be used to predict its current condition, albeit with some added error. This strategy, termed *averaging*, is based on the assumption that variability has regularity or form, namely regression-to-the-mean (Devenport, L., 1998; Stephens, 1989). For instance, a dandelion plant produces flowers and seeds in succession so at any given time, the presence of seeds may be uncertain (depending on when the last assessment occurred). However, larger or healthier plants or those growing in more favorable microclimates will produce more seeds more rapidly. Ideally, a forager visiting that plant will be able to valuate the quality of that plant or *patch* as higher on average than another.

Because resources vary with time, good patches become bad, and bad ones become good. Even though the last visit to a patch might have resulted in no food, the forager could assume that the plant will regress to its mean (good) value in the long run so that when information has not been recently up-dated, choosing the alternative with the higher average value will give better returns than decisions based on tracking or random foraging. There is evidence that many foragers use averaging to assist with their foraging decisions (Cuthill, Haccou, & Kacelnik, 1994; Reboreda & Kacelnik, 1992), but just as with tracking, exclusive use of an averaging strategy will not result in the best use of information because even a typically poor patch can be temporarily good. This implies that individuals who use a combination of both strategies would have an advantage. However, flexibly deploying two different strategies requires a mechanism for transitioning from one to another.

Given the importance of decision-making and the inevitable effect of time on virtually all resources, it would be surprising if selective forces had not adapted animals to optimize decisions under uncertainty (Inglis, 2000). Such an adaptation would need to give an output of estimated patch values corresponding to the rate of environmental change. This would allow for a match between the reliability of information and the temporal changes in the real world. Because change unfolds in time, time itself could be the mechanism that guides the decision-making strategy.

We suggest that the best regulator of the progression from non-probabilistic to probabilistic outcomes would be an average obtained from patch experiences weighted by their temporal recency, i.e., how much time has passed since the visit. Such a weighted average is dynamic and would permit flexible shifts from tracking (using the most recent information) to averaging (regression-to-the-mean). Because time is compared as a ratio (Gibbon, 1977), the relative recency of information about alternatives could act as a weighting factor, automatically giving less weight to less recent experiences. Such an adaptation would require interval time perception and a decision rule.

Time is a basic element of the world and therefore perception of temporal durations or intervals is common throughout the animal kingdom. Interval time perception has been demonstrated in many species including birds, mammals, insects, fish and at least one reptile (reviewed in: Lejeune & Weardern, 1991; Matell & Mech, 2000) and some basic timing processes exist in many if not most animal species (reviewed in Gallistel, 1990).

Dynamic Averaging

We have developed a dynamic averaging model based on the functional properties of the environment and the psychological mechanisms of timing. The temporal weighing rule (TWR) model proposes that the value of an option whose objective value is known but variable, is weighted by the relative recency of information about that option and thus when information is recent, it is most heavily weighted, returning a high probability in favor of the last best alternative (Devenport, L., 1998). When information is not recent, the weighted average regresses to the mean and returns a value equivalent to the absolute long-term average. TWR is the only decision model that accomplishes this transition.

More formally, the output of the model is a weighted average of the subjective quality, Q_i, of an alternative weighted by it recency $1/T$, which is the time between previous experiences and when the decision is being made. The temporally weighted value of a given patch, e.g., x, would be represented as:

$$v_{wx} = \sum_{n=1}^{n=i} \left[Q_i \left(\frac{1}{T_i} \right) \right] \div \sum_{n=1}^{n=i} \left(\frac{1}{T_i} \right)$$

which is the sum of the n set of x patch quality experiences, Q_i, weighted by their respective recencies and then divided by the sum of the recencies. When choices need to be made between two alternatives, e.g., patches A and B, the weighted averages would be compared as a ratio. To illustrate, let the individual values of patch A = v_{wa} and patch B = v_{wb}. The *relative* weighted value of patch B (V_{wB}) is simply a proportion.

$$V_{wB} = v_{wb}/(v_{wa} + v_{wb}), \text{ where } V_{wA} = 1 - V_{wB}.$$

If the two weighted values are not discriminably different, choices for the two patches should be evenly divided. If the relative value of one patch is substantially greater than the other, choices should strongly favor that alternative (see Appendices in Devenport, L.,1998 and Devenport, L., & Devenport, J., 1994 for more details).

GENERAL EXPERIMENTAL APPROACH

The TWR model is based on inevitable resource variability and delays between when information is gathered and acted on. To test the model, animals were given foraging experiences in two experimental food patches that varied in availability and quality, such that animals experienced one patch that was good (full) when the other was bad (empty) and then after some time, conditions reversed. In some cases, the two patches were equal in overall (average) value and in some cases, they differed. When they differed, the patch with the higher value was experienced first. A third patch, that was never baited, was often provided to assess memory (see *Memory Mechanisms* below). Tests occurred either when information was fresh or after a delay, using independent groups. Patches never contained food during the choice test.

As an example of our methods and procedures, the initial observations and data for development of the model came from a field study of wild populations of least chipmunks and golden-mantled ground squirrels. We erected feeder stands in open meadows where these ground-dwelling rodents forage for seeds. We permitted free-ranging, tagged animals to visit a feeder that contained sunflower seeds. After a predetermined time, conditions changed so that the previously baited feeder was empty and another feeder contained seeds. Simultaneously, animals were given an equivalent amount of experience visiting the second feeder (patch) that varied inversely. When the first patch was good, it was bad and vice versa. We then imposed a delay to simulate normal interruptions in foraging that lasted either 1 or 48 hr, followed by a single test trial where the original feeders were again presented but were empty. Other studies were carried out with different animals in the field or laboratory, with variations in most key variables, but this example is typical and the simplest.

SPECIES SIMILARITIES IN DECISION-MAKING

One of our goals has been to investigate the generality of cognitive adaptations for decisions under uncertainty, especially those caused by temporal variation. Variability is one of the few constants in nature. Regardless of habitat or phyla, most animals are very likely to experience variable resources and interruptions in the flow of information and the resultant uncertainty. Therefore, adaptations for dealing with uncertainty should be common among species.

In our initial study we found no species differences between least chipmunks, *Tamias minimus* and golden-mantled ground squirrels, *Spermophilus lateralis* (Devenport, L., & Devenport, J., 1994). Both species made decisions consistent with TWR, choosing the most recently good patch when information was recent, but averaging when information was not recent. The species similarity could have been attributable either to relatedness (same family, *Sicuridae*) or similar selective pressures from a shared environment. We and others have subsequently studied several unrelated species that do not share evolutionary histories or similar environments.

Two laboratory species, rats (*Rattus norvegicus*) and pigeons (*Columba liva*), make an especially interesting comparison because, reared in stable environments, both have had no previous exposure to the extreme fluctuations in resources that might produce sensitivity to variability or uncertainty. Nevertheless, both species showed dynamic decisions (Devenport, L., Hill, Wilson, & Ogden, 1997; Mazur 1995; 1996) that were indistinguishable from those of wild populations of sciurids. They favored the last good outcome when choices were relatively recent, but progressively relied more on patch averages with increasing delays.

One reason for the consistency among these divergent species could be the similarity in type of diet. All primarily consume non-renewable foods that are high in energy content and spatially and temporally variable. The similarity in diet might especially favor a cognitive adaptation to deal with uncertainty, so we extended our investigation to species with very different types of diets: carnivores and herbivores.

Although most domestic dogs do not experience a strictly carnivorous diet, they have retained many of the characteristics of their wolf ancestors, especially foraging behaviors (Fox, 1965). We tested sporting and working breed pets in their home yards. We found that choices were time-dependent, with all dogs choosing the most recently good patch when it immediately followed training experiences, but with only half of the dogs choosing the last good patch when neither experience was recent, and weighted averages would have been equivalent (Devenport, J., & Devenport, L., 1993).

Herbivores have diets even more dissimilar from those of all the previously mentioned species; they consume foods low in caloric value, more homogeneously distributed, and that renew rather quickly, factors that could affect the role of uncertainty in foraging decisions. Despite these differences, herbivores make dynamic choices (Bailey & Sims, 1998). Cattle (*Bos spp.*) given daily trials foraging in an 8-arm radial maze baited with food (alfalfa) of moderate quality, followed by trials where two arms contained either preferred (grain) or non-preferred (straw) food, learned the locations and visited grain arms first and avoided straw arms. Following a 30 day interruption, visits to the non-preferred arms recovered as the higher values from the first trials were averaged in, consistent with TWR.

Similarly, quarter horses given variable patch experiences in a familiar pasture or arena found either patches of equal or unequal average value (independent groups). As predicted, horses made time-dependent decisions. When there was fresh information, regardless of the absolute value, all chose the most recently good patch but when tests were delayed so that no information was recent, patch choices matched unweighted patch averages (Devenport, J., Patterson, & Devenport, L., 2005).

Taken together, these studies show a remarkable similarity in decision-making across of a wide variety of species and all are consistent with predictions of TWR. (Also see Applications and Implications below for an insect example).

PREDICTIONS OF THE TWR MODEL

If a model is to functionally represent the environment, it should make accurate predictions based on the relevant properties of the environment. Several different variables have been studied, including the rate of patch change, the effects of different patch values, causes of variability in patch values, the nature of the transition from good to poor patch values, and the influence of non-food variables. We then compared decisions to TWR model predictions

Rate of Patch Change

It is obvious that different resources change at different rates. Some, e.g., pooled rainwater, can change quickly whereas others, e.g., nut trees, change slowly. The rate at which patch conditions change should alter the rate of regression from tracking to averaging and thus effect foraging decisions. We and others have assessed a wide range of rate changes in a number of ways.

When patches change in minutes to hours, the regression from tracking to averaging should shift relatively quickly. Calculations using of the midpoint of the durations of the good and bad states of patches were used to determine test times when weighted averages for the last good patch were very high or equivalent to the unweighted average. Animals overwhelmingly chose the patch with the higher recent value (tracking) at the early test and distributed choices equally between the two alternatives (averaging) at the delayed test (Devenport, L., & Devenport, J., 1994).

Using longer time-frames, independent groups experienced much slower rates of change, for example, where each patch was good for 4 hours and bad for 4 hours, separated by 32 hr. Using model predictions, we selected test times for high, medium, and low weighted averages for the last baited patch and found dynamic choices, with preference for the last, most recently good patch extended about 20 times longer than when the two states were temporally more contiguous and changes occurred more quickly (as described above).

If resources change very rapidly, e.g., on a scale of seconds to minutes, weighted averages should regress very quickly to unweighted average values. We tested this in the laboratory where animals made repeated visits to variable patches, and the pace of trials was controlled so that each patch state of the experiment was 20 min in length and independent groups were tested at a range of delay intervals. Animals made choices that were consistent with the weighted averages: when tested soon after experiencing the baited patches, all chose the most recently baited patch, but after a 4 hr delay, test choices mirrored unweighted averages (Devenport, L., et al., 1997).

Transition From Tracking to Averaging

The studies described above confirm another prediction of the model: the transition from tracking recent trends to relying on an average should be a smooth progression. We systematically chose test times that generated weighted averages that were high to very low and found that when relative values were above 0.6, groups of animals overwhelmingly choose that alternative, whereas when weighted estimates were less that 0.4, animals overwhelmingly preferred the other alternative. For patches with weighted values between 0.4 - 0.6, animals were indifferent (Devenport, L., et al., 1997). A smooth transition from tracking to averaging mirrors resource changes which are typical of the natural environment.

Different Patch Values

In nature there is considerable variability in quality between patches. We noticed for example, that most patches that chipmunks encounter are spatially and temporally variable but that some have higher productivity than others. Optimal foraging theory predicts that animals should select the patch with the absolute higher value (Charnov, 1976; Cowie, 1977), but as we have shown, time alters objective value. The TWR model predicts that patch choices should favor the most recent patch at short delays, *regardless* of absolute values in patch quality, but that at delayed tests there can be a complete preference reversal depending on whether the two patches being considered were of equal or unequal average quality.

In experiments where unweighted patch values were equal, choices split 50-50 when there was no recent information, paralleling the similar unweighted averages. However when the two patches had different unweighted values, e.g., one yielded for a longer time (Devenport, L., et al., 1997) or animals got more food at the first of two patches (Devenport, L., 1998; Devenport, J., et al., 2005) there was a complete reversal of choices as the patches regressed to different unweighted means. It is important to note that we are referring to groups of animals tested at different delays, and not individuals reversing preferences.

Quantification of Patch Averages

Natural patches can vary in a number of ways. Some patches, e.g., fungi, are edible only for a short time before they begin to degrade, making duration of yield the metric of patch value. Some patches vary in the amount of food an animal can extract on each visit. For instance, hoarding animals make multiple trips to a patch to cache food (reviewed in VanderWall, 1990). In that case, the run of good visits is a measure of patch value. Fast changing patches, e.g., seeds in wind shadows, can vary in the probability that conditions are good when the animal visits.

We have tested the importance of these patch metrics in a series of studies and found that all produce dynamic decisions. Whether we varied the amount of food available on each trial but held duration of yield constant (Devenport, J., et al., 2005) or held the amount of food available at each patch constant and varied the number of visits to a patch (Devenport, L., et al., 1997), choices were always time-dependent.

Probabilistic changes in patches have been investigated in operant paradigms where responses were reinforced on variable-interval schedules and the probability of reward was equal for several sessions, followed by several sessions where one key "patch" was substantially better than the other. In other conditions, the sequences were reversed. Regardless, choices were time-dependent, regressing to the unweighted average of past sessions following the 24 hr interruption between daily sessions but returning to the more recent averages within sessions as new information was acquired. (Mazur, 1995; 1996).

These results from probabilistic rewards mirror those from a field study where two patches were probabilistically baited for five days and one patch had a substantially higher probability of yield. Test choices were again dynamic, with animals choosing the last good patch irrespective of its unweighted mean at the early test, but reverting to averaging at the late test (Devenport, L., & Devenport, J., 1994).

TWR and Non-foraging Variables

Decisions are rarely made solely on the basis of one dimension and are usually a trade-off between two or more conflicting variables. Predation risk is one of the most important non-food related influences on foraging behavior (reviewed in Lima & Dill, 1990) and many foraging decisions reflect a compromise between patch quality and predation risk. This raises the question of whether variables like risk are treated like patch quality and could figure into a dynamic average.

Winterrowd & Devenport (2004) tested the predictions of TWR in a field study by giving animals a choice between patches that varied, but that had equivalent average food quality. Half of the patches (safe) were close to experimental rock piles where animals could find cover and half were in the open (risky). Perceived safety was independently quantified in groups that did not experience variable patches. Animals treated patch safety in much the same way as patch food value. Most chose the risky patch if it had yielded food relatively recently but when experience was not recent, risk took precedence and most chose the safe patch even though average food values had been equivalent. The TWR model easily accommodated safety as an added dimension of patch quality.

In much the same way, TWR has been used to predict sampling and exploration. Model simulations that incorporated hunger, patch location uncertainty, reward expectation, and reward uncertainty found TWR to be the best predictor of when a forager should seek information, i.e., sample, vs. spend time foraging (Inglis, Langton, Forkman, B., & Lazarus, 2001).

Grazing distribution patterns can also be predicted using a modification of TWR that incorporates physical and mechanical factors such as rate of turning, speed of movement, and abiotic factors such as slope of ground and location of other important resources, e.g., water or shade (Bailey, Gross, Laca, Rittenhouse, Coughenour, Swift, & Sims, 1996). Taken together these studies demonstrate that TWR can flexibly accept several different variables thought to be important influences on decisions, without modifying the basic structure of the model.

The Ecological Validity of TWR

Adaptations are the result of selective pressures for solving specific "problems" and in the case of foraging, interruptions and variable food resources are among them. If interruptions are common, foragers should be able to adjust to them. It would also be adaptive if foragers not only kept track of the rate at which external factors brought about change in food resources but were aware of the effect of their own behavior on resource variability. Below we review evidence showing that these conditions have a substantial impact on foraging behavior and discuss their importance in dynamic averaging models like TWR.

Interruptions in Foraging

The importance of time in understanding foraging is well recognized. From the first, optimal foraging models incorporated time into the search or discovery phase, in calculating the rate at which food was harvested and thus the giving up time (Charnov, 1976), and in the time cost involved in processing or handling prey items which determined whether prey items should be included in the diet or avoided (reviewed in Bateson, 2003; Shettleworth, 1998). But one aspect of time that has been largely ignored is that as animals forage, they often encounter unexpected interruptions in their foraging activities. Those interruptions arise from a variety of factors including unexpected events such as weather changes, the appearance of competitors, the need to escape or hide from predators, or to give parental care. There are also predictable interruptions in foraging, such as daily fluctuations of darkness or tides that suspend activities. For most animals interruptions in foraging probably occur very frequently. Whether anticipated or predictable, familiar or novel, interruptions all have the same effect on the reliability of information as discussed above. Models, like TWR, that incorporate interruptions are likely to be better predictors of foraging behavior.

Other Sources of Change

All of the studies described thus far have involved changes in the environment caused by forces external to the forager but the forager itself also contributes to changes in patch values by depleting patches as it forages and the objective value of the patch diminishes as prey are harvested. In order to forage optimally, it seems likely that animals should be able to take account of those changes in their patch valuations.

We tested whether animals were able to represent changes in patch value resulting from their own foraging by allowing chipmunks to partially deplete one of two buried seed patches. The following day all of the animals chose the patch from which fewer seeds had been taken. Even when we controlled the amount of depletion each animal was able to accomplish, all still chose the patch that they had least depleted. Animals refused to revisit fully depleted patches and would only do so if given an external signal of patch renewal (Devenport, L., Humphries, & Devenport, J., 1998). These experiments demonstrate that least one species does take account of their own foraging activities and discounts patch values based on its own behavior, representing resources in terms of future rather than past value. The only model to take self-depletion effects on future value into account is TWR.

MECHANISMS AND ALTERNATIVE INTERPRETATIONS

Memory Mechanisms

The temporal weighting rule incorporates three main variables: 1) patch item value, *what* type and quality of food items were discovered, 2) instances of patch quality changes, i.e. *when* patches yielded best, moderately, or worst, and 3), spatial location, *where* patches were found. It might be wondered if animals are capable of acquiring and retaining such rich representations of their foraging experience.

That many animals use sophisticated spatial representations is no longer doubted (Jacobs & Liman, 1991; Kamil & Balda, 1985; MacDonald, 1997). This generalization also applies to the wild animals we have used extensively in our studies (Devenport, J., & Devenport, L.,1994; Devenport, L., & Devenport, J., 1994). Of course, memory for the comparative quality and quantity of food items has long been established in the "preference" and "choice" literature and is taken for granted in the design of studies aimed at investigating higher order cognitive processes, such as "chunking" (Cook, Brown, & Riley, 1985), "transitivity" (Bond, Kamil, & Balda, 2003; Roberts & Phelps, 1994) and selective cache recovery (reviewed in Vander Wall, 1990).

To this list, TWR adds patch variability, because stability in nature is considered to be exceptional (Devenport, L., 1983; 1989; Stephens, 1989). Olton (1979) was among the first of many (reviewed in Shettleworth, 1998) to show that the absence or removal of reward is at least as memorable as the presence of reward. In fact, animals can transition flexibly between using (retrospective) memory of patches that have been visited and emptied, to using (prospective) memory of patches that still remain good in order to efficiently solve a harvesting problem involving 8-19 separate patches (Cook et al. 1985; Zentall, Steirn, & Jackson-Smith, 1990). The transition from the use of empty vs. full patches to guide choices is evidently based on which requires fewer cognitive resources (i.e., retention of fewest items in working memory). This research obviously bears on temporal memory as well. TWR, as we have formulated it, requires retrospective and, possibly, prospective memories.

Further evidence for the spontaneous encoding and use of time-based memories is now well documented (Cook, et al., 1985; Emory & Clayton, 2001) Research in the last quarter of the 20th century worked out important details of interval timing and the types of memory—i.e., working and reference—that enable it (Church & Gibbon, 1982; Gibbon, 1977). Recent studies (Naqshbandi & Roberts 2006; Raby, Alexis, Dickinson & Clayton, 2007) answer lingering skepticism about how long retrospective memories are retained and whether an animal's prospective representation of time could in any sense be used to guide behavior farther into the future than a few seconds or minutes (Roberts, 2002; Suddendorf & Busby, 2003). For example, after having learned that they will be restricted to a particular area for their morning foraging sessions, western scrub jays selectively provisioned this area during a free-food session on the preceding afternoon (Raby, Alexis, Dickinson & Clayton, 2007). Animals not only selectively pre-stocked this area with extra food when it otherwise promised to be empty, they assured a variety of food by caching a second type of food item when only a single type would ordinarily be present. Importantly, this "planning" behavior appeared in the absence of a motivational state specific to the plan (i.e., preparing for the eventual absence of food when it was still present), assuring that the behavior was not reflexive (Raby, Alexis, Dickinson & Clayton, 2007).

The remaining question is whether or not animals can simultaneously incorporate *what*, *when* and *where* information into their patch valuations and choices—i.e., use declarative memory (Tulving, 1983). Work by Clayton and her colleagues bears directly on this question. They have shown that scrub jays use time, place, and item type to decide where to search for food. For example, birds choose to harvest first a preferred food type (meal worms) over a somewhat less preferred type (peanuts) that they have previously cached. This in itself is not surprising. But if the opportunity to forage is considerably delayed, a different pattern appears: the animals now prefer to search in areas where the peanuts were previously cached and the meal worm caches are avoided (although none of the patches actually contained food items at test). This selective change in preference over time is related to the more rapid spoilage of the insects compared to the seeds. This is one in a series of studies showing that jays readily incorporate *what* (meal worms vs. peanuts), *when* (delay between discovery and subsequent test trials), and *where* (the spatially unique, hidden patches where the two food items are found) information into their foraging decisions (Clayton, Yu, & Dickinson, 2003; de Kort, Dickenson & Clayton 2005). Further evidence for the flexible use of declarative memory is found in the reaction of caching birds (Emory & Clayton, 2001) and rodents (Preston & Jacobs, 2001) to potential robbery by onlookers and in other complex decision-making tasks (Bird, Roberts, Abroms, Kit, & Crupi, 2003; Grosenick, Clement, & Fernald, 2007; Zentall, 2005). We think that similarly rich representations of experience are probably involved in the implementation of TWR.

Other Mechanisms

TWR is primarily a rule that that guides optimal decision-making over a continuum of near-certain to uncertain information. Because time-, quality-, and place-tagging of item information in memory appears to be an automatic and relatively effortless process (reviewed in Gallistel, 1990; see earlier discussion above), TWR was developed with those processes in mind. It will be recalled that there are no memory variables in the model, only patch quality, time, and place. Thus, the quantitative model of TWR is silent on the question of how it is implemented. The output of the model, which we have referred to as a dynamic average, could be executed by mechanisms other than declarative memory without altering the validity of the model. In this regard, "spontaneous recovery" phenomena are similar to dynamic averaging. Spontaneous recovery has historically been attributed to non-cognitive mechanisms (reviewed in Rescorla, 2004). It is therefore worth considering if this mechanism might qualify as an explanation of dynamic averaging, or if a more cognitive interpretation better explains both dynamic averaging and spontaneous recovery.

Spontaneous recovery reliably appears after an animal has been rewarded to perform some behavioral response and is then extinguished, i.e. by withholding reward until it no longer responds. Placed back into the training context at some later time, animals almost always begin performing again. For example, an animal running down a long alley for food does so vigorously for several trials, until food is withheld. After a few no-food experiences, the animal refuses to run. In a few hours or days, the running behavior can be expected to "recover"; i.e., reappear. This phenomenon is highly reliable, can be seen in virtually any training context, and is plainly time-dependent (reviewed in: Devenport, L., 1998; Robbins, 1990; Rescorla, 2004; Rescorla & Cunningham, 1978).

Spontaneous recovery can be seen as an instance of patch variability, but in this case variability in a single patch rather than the multiple patches we have used for our choice studies of TWR. The patch valuation function of TWR can, and has been (Devenport, L., 1998), applied to such instances in which the "choice" is between whether to perform the response or not. Early on, the weighted average TWR gives for a patch that was good and then bad will continue to be bad for some period of time, the length of which depends on the temporal pace of training and extinction, but the patch will progressively rise in subjective value and finally converge on the average of all training trials. At some point in this process, the increasing value will brighten the animal's prospects for obtaining food and it will once again perform the response. At least this is the explanation we prefer.

Current thinking in the animal learning literature favors a different interpretation, involving differential trace-decay mechanisms. The gist of the idea is that spontaneous recovery involves two associative memories (or "traces"), and that "inhibitory" traces (thought to be established by non-reward) decay more quickly than "excitatory" traces (thought to be established by reward). Thus, the inhibitory trace at first predominates, but soon becomes weaker than the more slowly decaying excitatory trace and thus trained behavior re-emerges (Bouton, 1993; 1994; Kraemer & Spear, 1993). Although somewhat ad-hoc, and not formalized into a quantitative model, this differential forgetting account seems to capture the essential features of spontaneous recovery and could conceivably be applied to more complex choice situations.

We therefore incorporated tests of memory into most of our experiments to determine if significant decay of any sort could be detected, and have found surprisingly little. In one paradigm (Devenport, J., & Devenport, L, 1993; Devenport, J., et al. 2005), three patches were used, but one was always empty. When two variable patches eventually converged on the same value (as given by the quantitative model of TWR), animals appeared to choose between them indiscriminately. This lack of discrimination could be attributed to the random behavior of animals who have forgotten what happened at the patches or it could be attributed to indifference—they remember what happened, but each patch seems as good a prospect as the other. The evidence falls in favor of the latter interpretation. Despite their indifference about the two variable patches after a long delay, virtually no responses were directed to the never-rewarded, never-extinguished patch (Devenport, J., & Devenport, L, 1993; Devenport, J., et al. 2005). Even when allowed a second choice, animals selected the other variable patch over the neutral one, indicating that they remembered the behavior of each patch.

Another way of assessing memory factors is by creating patches of unequal value. We usually did this by placing more food items in one patch when in its good state, than in the poorer patch when in its respective good state. Both patches were variable and went through identical states of non-reward. When sufficient time passes since the patches were sampled, a cognitive interpretation of TWR predicts that choices should be made on the basis of average patch quality, not the last state the patches were in. This requires a memory not only of which patch yielded rewards at some point in the past, but which one yielded the most when in its good state. As expected from our optimality perspective, animals chose the patch with the best average—a complete reversal from the choices animals made when much less time had elapsed (Devenport, J., et al. 2005; Devenport, L., 1998). From a functional perspective, this implies that patch memories remained intact; otherwise choices would have been random.

The memory issue can also be addressed by requiring a highly improbable response. Using a T-maze, animals not only experienced variable quality outcomes in the patches found in each of the two arms, one arm had a better overall average than the other. To make the correct response more difficult, an additional pair of choice points at the end of each arm required further spatial discrimination. Only one member of the sub-pair was baited when a particular arm was in its good state. As expected, animals at first preferred the arm (and subchoice) that was most recently baited, but with the passage of time, the arm (and subchoice) with the higher average was preferred. Now, if those final choices were made because the details of the experience with the alternative arm were forgotten, then when allowed to make a second choice and run into the non-preferred arm, the subchoice should have been little better than random. This was not the case. Animals accurately remembered the details of where food was once available within the non-preferred arm (Devenport, L., et al, 1997). In a follow-up experiment, animals were trained in the same way and tested at short or long delays but at test no arm choice was allowed. The door was closed to what would have been the preferred arm, forcing the animals to go into the less-preferred arm and choose between the two sub-options. Again, the animals performed almost flawlessly, indicating that their previous behavior was not guided by the selective absence of memory.

In one of our earliest experiments (Devenport, L., & Devenport, J., 1994), we varied the probability that a patch would yield. Animals were given repeated experience with three patches and then one of the patches was baited for a final time. This is a case in which, according to associative theory and research, the least frequently baited patch should be the most resistant to extinction, since it yielded on a leaner schedule. Thus, predictions from a cognitive account of TWR and a trace-decay account about how animals should select among the patches after a long delay were exactly opposite. The choices clearly fell in favor of the cognitive interpretation, indicating that an active choice was made among equally salient memories, and not just the appearance of a "choice" springing from a weak or absent competing memory.

One other observation bears on the memory issue. Memory decay is considered to proceed at an unspecified but fixed rate, perhaps because of steadily declining synaptic strength. TWR's cognitive account, on the other hand, predicts that patch valuations will not change at a fixed rate. Instead, they should be directly tied to the pace of change experienced at the patches. We demonstrated this experimentally, showing that preference shifts across train-test intervals were hastened or delayed proportionally by the previously experienced rate of patch change (Devenport, J., & Devenport, L.,1993; Devenport, L., & Devenport, J.,1994), consistent with the use of intact memories and inconsistent with the trace-decay hypothesis.

At present, we consider that TWR relies on declarative memory-type processes, not on forgetting.

Computational Considerations

Early optimal foraging theory was developed with overly optimistic assumptions about the cognitive architecture of animals. It concerned itself with the economics of time and energy budgets, hoping that a forager's cognitive adaptations would match the sophisticated economic formulations, which often required an exhaustive memory of experience. Some of the early results springing from this approach were disappointing (reviewed in Krebs, Houston, & Charnov, 1981). Animals did not always choose "optimally". Given the benefit of hindsight and historical developments, we can see that, more often then not, the formulations themselves were non-optimal. Still, the reaction by many in the animal behavior community was to swing in the opposite direction and assume that animals retain very little about their everyday experience and instead might rely on a set of (presumably innate) "rules-of-thumb" that would suffice to keep an animal competitive while making smaller computational demands (Cuthill, Kacelnik, Krebs, Haccou, & Iwasa, 1990; Dow & Lee, 1987; Kacelnik et al., 1987; Reboreda & Kacelnik, 1992). Several such "rules" have been suggested, and could probably serve the animal well enough, if not optimally, in some instances.

A more moderate position about animal cognition would admit that animals like humans, collect and process information selectively and do not remember irrelevant details of everyday life, nor do they retain an exhaustive record of relevant details. But, such limitations do not preclude flexible cognitive adaptations to improve decision-making. To illustrate, consider an animal that has visited a small set of patches that have varying histories. After attending to other concerns, it is now ready to resume foraging and needs to decide among these patches. There are only three simple rules of thumb available: 1) visit the patch that was good the last time, 2) visit the patch that has the best average, or 3) forage randomly. Rules 1 and 2 will often hold an advantage over random foraging, but not if the two patches are of equal value and perhaps not the same as other patches in the area. Under these conditions random foraging allows animals to sample the environment and discover unexpected opportunities. When Rules 1 and 2 do perform better, they will still be suboptimal because both fail to conform to the forces of patch variability that will tend to intervene before the animal returns. TWR handles this variability and provides a systematic transition from the predominant use of Rule 1 to the use of Rule 2, while transitioning through Rule 3.

How much more complex are the computations required by TWR? First, rules-of-thumb are not as simple as they seem. Remembering which patch was the last best one requires the time-tagging of experiences so that recency can be discriminated. The alternative is to erase records of earlier experiences so that only a memory of the last best patch remains. Of course, this option strips the forager of important knowledge, since the location and behavior of patches in its home range are surely among the most important things it can know. Rule 2, averaging, requires additional computation, but there is no doubt that animals carry out such operations. Faced with temporal variability (as in variable schedules of operant reinforcement) or variable quality of reward (as when magnitude or duration of reward varies), animals have no difficulty comparing and selecting the richest option, provided that the mean differences are of discriminable magnitude (Herrnstein,1970; Gallistel, 1990;

Reboreda & Kacelnik, 1992). Although animals can compute them, exclusive reliance on averages would leave an animal unable to adapt to change, e.g., when typically poor patches produce temporary bonanzas. The output from TWR passes through a relatively wide region of indifference, where sampling and exploration of patches would be encouraged, similar to (but not in fact) like random foraging.

The cognitive demands of TWR require little more than averaging, and rely on what might even be considered a computational weakness. TWR considers all patch valuations to be averages. But since they are weighted by recency, the averaging function is not apparent until time passes and the relative recency of each patch experience becomes almost equal. The progression from highly weighted to nearly unweighted averages is the work of the computational "weakness". Animals, including humans, compare time, distance, amount, and so forth by division, not subtraction (reviewed in: Gallistel, 1990; Gibbon, 1977; Reboreda & Kacelnik, 1992), as described by Weber's Law. If the comparison were by subtraction (as a human trained in mathematics might prefer), then something that happened 2 seconds ago would always be 5 seconds more recent than something that happened 7 seconds ago. But temporal perception computes the difference as a ratio. At first the last-visited patch is $7/2 = 3.5$ times more recent than the other. As time passes, this difference vanishes and automatically converges on 1.0. For example, after 5 min, the last-visited patch is only $307/302 = 1.02$ times more recent. Thus, no special weighting mechanism is required by TWR, just the timing mechanism that is already in place, Nor are excessive cognitive loads required since animals appear to use only a sample when computing an average based on large numbers of temporal events stored in memory (Gibbon, Church, Fairhurst, & Kacelnik, 1988).

Considering the gains to be made by conforming to a general rule of nature, i.e., regression-to-the-mean, and in light of the poorer rules of thumb available, which nevertheless require considerable computation, the cognitive resources needed for implementing TWR would, at least in theory, appear to be more than repaid in foraging success.

APPLICATIONS AND IMPLICATIONS

Many types of decisions are made under uncertainty and therefore dynamic averaging might be useful for several types of decisions. For example, reproductive decisions such as where to lay eggs can affect offspring size and the sex ratio of eggs laid (reviewed in Ode & Heinz, 2002). Females have to decide whether to accept or reject an ovposition site and past information may be useful.

Parasitic wasps (*Diglyphus isaea*) exposed to increasingly larger host sizes laid significantly more female eggs than did those who experienced invariant host sizes, whereas those exposed to decreasing host sizes decreased the proportion of female eggs laid. TWR produced estimates of the relative weighting of experiences, in this case favoring recent events which would be expected given the rapid rate of change (Ode & Heinz, 2002). In addition to broadening the settings in which dynamic decisions are useful, this is the first demonstration of time-dependent decisions in an invertebrate.

Time-dependent decisions could also be useful for less important choices. There is evidence that humans make dynamic choices for non-biological alternatives. Participants given a simple problem solving task ("Build A Stick"), where correct solutions varied from trial to trial, chose a strategy based on how well the solution matched the current problem and the history of success of that strategy. The more successful a strategy had been in the past, the more likely it was to be chosen, regardless of its current utility (Lovett & Anderson, 1996). Despite substantial differences in the type of decision, a dynamic average appeared to be used in assigning weights to past and current history (Lovett, 1998). In a study directly testing TWR, human participants played a game that involved finding hidden tokens in one of three boxes followed by an equivalent number of trials locating tokens in a second box. Test trials were given at different delays following the second set of trials, in independent groups. As predicted, decisions were time-dependent, with 65% choosing the last box where tokens were found when tested immediately but only 20% choosing the last box at the delayed test. When independent groups were given a 4:1 difference in token densities, 80% chose the last baited, lower density box at the immediate test whereas only 10% chose it at the delayed test (Devenport, J., unpublished observations). These results show that dynamic decisions are made in a variety of situations and temporal weighting is useful whenever there is variability in the state of one or more alternatives.

CONCLUSION

In conclusion, many decisions made by animals in the real world involve some degree of uncertainty, resulting from the passage of time. For many species that uncertainty appears to be minimized by a cognitive adaptation that takes time into account and weights the reliability of information by its relative recency. Dynamic decisions as specified by TWR have been demonstrated in a wide range of species, to aid decisions on a number of dimensions. The consistency in behavior seen in wild, domestic, and laboratory-bred species encourages us to think that TWR could serve as a flexible adaptation to assist decision-making under uncertainty. The variety of experimental settings, from field to laboratory, across long and short time spans, gives us confidence that dynamic decisions are easily implemented in real-world conditions and underscores the validity of the TWR model.

REFERENCES

Bailey, D.W., Gross, J.E., Laca, E.A., Rittenhouse, L.R., Coughenour, M.B., Swift, D.M., & Sims, P.L. (1996). Mechanisms that result in large herbivore grazing distribution patterns. *Journal of Range Management, 49*, 386-400.

Bailey, D.W., & Sims, P.L. (1998). Association of food quality and locations by cattle. *Journal of Range Management, 51*, 2-8.

Bateson, M. (2003). Interval timing and optimal foraging. In Meck, W. H. (Ed.), *Functional and neural mechanisms of interval timing* (pp. 113-141). Boca Raton, FL: CRC Press.

Bird, L.R., Roberts, W.A., Abroms, B., Kit, K.A., & Crupi, C. (2003) Spatial memory for food hidden by rats (*Rattus norvegicus*) on the radial maze: studies of memory for where, what, and when. *Journal of Comparative Psychology, 117*, 176-187.

Bond, A.B., Kamil, A.C., & Balda, R.P. (2003). Social complexity and transitive inference in corvids. *Animal Behaviour, 65, 479-487.*

Bouton, M.E. (1993). Context, time and memory retrieval in the interference paradigms of Pavolvian learning. *Psychological Bulletin, 114*, 80-99.

Bouton, M.E. (1994). Conditioning, remembering, and forgetting. *Journal of Experimental Psychology: Animal Behavior Processes, 20*, 219-231.

Charnov, E.L. (1976). Optimal foraging: the marginal value theorem. *Theoretical Population Biology, 9*, 129-136.

Church, R.M., & Gibbon, J. (1982). Temporal generalization. *Journal of Experimental Psychology: Animal Behavior Processes, 8*, 165-186.

Clayton, N.S., Yu, K.S., & Dickinson, A. (2003). Interacting cache memories: evidence for flexible memory use by western scrub jays (*Aphelocoma californicia*). *Journal of Experimental Psychology: Animal Behavior Processes, 29*, 14-22.

Cook, R.G., Brown, M.F., & Riley, D.A. (1985). Flexible memory processing by rats: use of prospective and retrospective information in the radial maze. *Journal of Experimental Psychology: Animal Behavior Processes, 17*, 12-20.

Cowie, J. (1977). Optimal foraging in great tits (*Parus major*). *Nature, 268*, 137-139

Cuthill, I., Haccou, P., & Kacelnik, A. (1994). Starlings (*Sturnus vulgaris*) exploiting patches: response to long-term changes in travel time. *Behavioral Ecology, 5*, 81-90.

Cuthill, I.C., Kacelnik, A., Krebs, J.R., Haccou, P., & Iwasa, Y. (1990). Starlings exploiting patches: the effect of recent experience on foraging decisions. *Animal Behaviour, 40*, 625-640.

Dall, S.R.X., Giraldeau, L-A., Olsson, O., McNamara, J.M., & Stephens, D.W. (2005). Information and its use by animals in evolutionary ecology. *Trends in Ecology and Evolution, 20*, 187-193.

de Kort, S.R., Dickinson, A., & Clayton, N.S. (2005). Retrospective cognition by western scrub-jays. *Learning & Motivation, 36*, 159-176.

Devenport, J.A., & Devenport, L.D. (1993). Time-dependent decisions in dogs. *Journal of Comparative Psychology, 107*, 169-173.

Devenport, J.A., & Devenport, L.D. (1994) Spatial navigation in natural habitats by ground-dwelling sciurids. *Animal Behaviour, 47, 747-749.*

Devenport, J. A., & Devenport, L. D. (1998). Foraging in squirrels: Cognitive adaptations. In M. Haraway & G. Greenberg (Eds.), *Comparative psychology: A handbook* (pp. 492-498). New York: Garland Press.

Devenport, J.A., Patterson, M.R., & Devenport, L.D. (2005). Dynamic averaging and foraging decisions in horses (*Equus callabus*). *Journal of Comparative Psychology, 119*, 352-358.

Devenport, L.D. (1983). Spontaneous behavior: inferences from neuroscience. In R.L. Mellgren (Ed.), *Animal cognition and behavior* (pp. 83-126). Amsterdam: Elsevier.

Devenport, L. (1998). Spontaneous recovery without interference: Why remembering is adaptive. *Journal of Experimental Psychology: Animal Behavior Processes, 26*, 172-181.

Devenport, L.D., & Devenport, J.A. (1994). Time-dependent averaging of foraging information in least chipmunks and golden-mantled ground squirrels. *Animal Behaviour, 47*, 787-802.

Devenport, L., Hill, T., Wilson, M., & Ogden, E. (1997). Tracking and averaging in variable environments: A transition rule. *Journal of Experimental Psychology: Animal Behavior Processes, 23*, 450-460.

Devenport, L.D., Humphries, T W., & Devenport, J.A. (1998). Future value and patch choice in least chipmunks. *Animal Behaviour, 55*, 1571-1581.

Dow, S.M., & Lea, S.E.G. (1987). Foraging in a changing environment: simulations in the operant laboratory. In M.C. Commons, A. Kacelnik, & S.J. Shettleworth (Eds.), *Quantitative analysis of behavior Vol. 6: foraging* (pp. 89-113). Hillsdale, NJ: Lawrence Earlbaum.

Emory, N.J., & Clayton, N.S. (2001). Effect of experience and social context on prospective caching strategies by scrub jays. *Nature, 414*, 443-445.

Fox, M.W. (1965). *Canine behavior*. Springfield, IL: Charles C. Thomas.

Gallistel, C.R. (1990). The organization of learning. Cambridge, MA: MIT Press.

Gibbon, J. (1977). Scalar expectancy theory and Weber's law in animal timing. *Psychological Review, 84*, 279-325.

Gibbon, J. Church, R.M., Fairhurst, S., & Kacelnik, A. (1988). Scalar expectancy theory and choice between delayed rewards. *Psychological Review, 95*, 102-114.

Grosenick, L., Clement, T.S., & Fernald, R.D. (2007). Fish can infer social rank by observation alone. *Nature, 445*, 429-432.

Herrnstein, R.J. (1970). On the law of effect. *Journal of the Experimental Analysis of Behavior, 13*, 243-266.

Inglis, I.R. (2000). The central role of uncertainty reduction in determining behaviour. *Behaviour, 137*, 1567-1599.

Inglis, I.R., Lanagton, S., Forkman, B., & Lazarus, J. (2001). An information primacy model of exploration and foraging behaviour. *Animal Behaviour, 62*, 543-557.

Jacobs, L.F., & Liman, E.R. (1991). Grey squirrels remember the locations of buried nuts. *Animal Behaviour, 41*, 103-110.

Kacelnik, A., Krebs, J.R., & Ens, B. (1987). Foraging in a changing environment: an experiement with starlings (*Sturnus vulgaris*). In M.L. Commons, A. Kacelnik, & S.J. Shettleworth (Eds.), *Quantitative analysis of behavior Vol. 6: foraging* (pp. 63-87). Hillsdale, NJ: Lawrence Earlbaum.

Kamil, A.C., & Balda, R.P. (1985). Cache recovery and spatial memory in Clark's nutcrackers. *Journal of Experimental Psychology: Animal Behavior Processes, 11*, 95-111.

Krebs, J.R., Houston, A.I., & Charnov, E.L. (1981). Some recent developments in optimal foraging. In A.C. Kamil & T.D. Sargent (Eds.), *Foraging behavior: ecological, ethological, and psychological approaches* (pp. 3-18). NY:Garland Press.

Kraemer, P., & Spear, N.E. (1993). Retrieval processes and conditioning. In T.R. Zentall (Ed.), *Animal cognition* (pp. 87-107). Hillsdale, NJ: Erlbaum.

Lejeune, H., & Wearden, J.H. (1991). The comparative psychology of fixed-interval responding: some quantitative analyses. *Learning and Motivation, 22*, 84-111.

Lima, S. L., & Dill L.M. (1990). Behavioral decisions made under the risk of predation: a review and prospectus. *Canadian Journal of Zoology, 68*, 619-640.

Lovett, M.C. (1998). Choice. In J.R. Anderson & C. Lebiere (Eds.), *The atomic components of thought* (pp. 255-296). Mahwah, NJ: L. Erlbaum.

Lovett, M.C., & Anderson, J.R. (1996). History of success and current context in problem solving: combined influences on operator selection. *Cognitive Psychology, 31,* 168-217.

MacDonald, I.M.V. (1997). Field experiments of duration and precision of grey and red squirrel spatial memory. *Animal Behaviour, 54,* 879-891.

Matell, M.S., & Meck, W. H. (2000). Neuropsychological mechanisms of interval timing behavior. *BioEssays, 22,* 94-103.

Mazur, J.E. (1995). Development of preference and spontaneous recovery in choice behavior with concurrent variable-interval schedules. *Animal Learning & Behavior, 23,* 93-103.

Mazur, J.E. (1996). Past experience, recency, and spontaneous recovery in choice behavior. *Animal Learning & Behavior, 24,* 1-10.

Naqshbandi, M., & Roberts, W.A. (2006). Anticipation of future events in squirrel monkeys (*Saimiri sciureus*) and rats (*Rattus norvegicus*): test of the Bischof-Kohler hypothesis. *Journal of Comparative Psychology, 120,* 345-357.

Ode, P.J., & Heinz, K.M. (2002). Host-size-dependent sex ratio theory and improving mass-reared parasitoid sex ratios. *Biological Control, 24,* 31-41.

Olton, D.S. (1979). Mazes, maps, and memory. *American Psychologist, 34,* 583-596.

Preston, S.D., & Jacobs, L.F. (2001). Conspecific pilferage but not presence affects Merriam's kangaroo rat caching strategy. *Behavioral Ecology, 12,* 517-523.

Raby, C.R., Alexis, D.M., Dickinson, A., & Clayton, N.S. (2007). Planning for the future by western scrub-jays. *Nature, 445,* 919-921.

Reboreda, J.C., & Kacelnik, A. (1992). Risk sensitivity in starlings: variability in food amount and food delay. *Behavioral Ecology, 2,* 301-308.

Rescorla, R.A. (2004). *Spontaneous recovery. Learning and Memory, 11,* 501-509.

Rescorla, R.A., & Cunningham, C.L. (1978). Recovery of the US representation over time during extinction. *Learning & Motivation, 9,* 373-391.

Robbins, S.J. (1990). Mechanisms underlying spontaneous recovery in autoshaping. *Journal of Experimental Psychology: Animal Behavior Processes, 16,* 235-249.

Roberts, W.A. (2002). Are animals stuck in time? *Psychological Bulletin, 128,* 473-489.

Roberts, W.A., & Phelps, M.T. (1994). Transitive inference in rats: a test of the spatial coding hypothesis. *Psychological Science, 5,* 368-374.

Shettleworth, S. (1998). *Cognition, evolution, and behavior.* Oxford: Oxford University Press.

Stephens, D.W. (1989). Variance and the value of information. *American Naturalist, 134,* 128-140.

Stephens, D.W., & Anderson, D. (2001). The adaptive value of preference for immediacy: when shortsighted rules have farsighted consequences. *Behavioral Ecology, 12,* 330-339.

Suddendorf, T., & Busby, J. (2003). Mental time travel? *Trends in Cognitive Science, 7,* 391-396.

Tulving, E. (1983). *Elements of episodic memory.* Oxford: Oxford University Press.

VanderWall, S.B. (1990). *Food hoarding in animals.* Chicago: University of Chicago Press.

Winterrowd, M.F., & Devenport, L.D. (2004). Balancing variable patch quality with predation risk. *Behavioural Processes, 67,* 39-46.

Zentall, T.R. (2005). Animals may not be stuck in time. *Learning & Motivation, 36,* 208-225.

Zentall, T.R., Steirn, J.N., & Jackson-Smith, P. (1990). Memory strategies in pigeons' performance of a radial-arm-maze analog task. *Journal of Experimental Psychology: Animal Behavior Processes, 16*, 358-371.

In: Psychology of Decision Making in Education
Editor: Jeanine A. Elsworth, pp. 163-183

ISBN: 978-1-60021-933-7
© 2006 Nova Science Publishers, Inc.

Chapter 7

RISK MANAGEMENT DECISION-MAKING IN A HIGH RISK RECREATIONAL ACTIVITY: LESSONS FROM MOUNTAINEERING

*Robert C. Lee[1],**** and Linda S. Cook[2]*
[1] University of New Mexico Department of Emergency Medicine
[2] University of New Mexico Department of Internal Medicine

ABSTRACT

Mountaineers can be viewed as "edgeworkers" who carefully manage risks in a voluntary activity that has the potential for serious injury or death. We maintain that the act of managing risks contributes to a sense of "flow" or transcendence that is a major psychological motivation for mountaineers. We also maintain that decisions associated with engaging in mountaineering as an activity, choices of particular types of mountaineering, locations, specific mountains, etc., and decisions associated with the act of mountaineering itself are conducted, implicitly or explicitly, within a rational multi-objective risk management framework. There are numerous risk-risk, risk-benefit, and benefit-cost tradeoffs throughout this risk management hierarchy. Furthermore, the risk management process is dynamic on a number of different levels. This rational process must be conducted within a context of uncertainty and fear, balanced with the sense of flow, and survival is sometimes at stake. Based on a review of the peer-reviewed, mountaineering association, and popular mountaineering literature, interviews with mountaineers and professional guides, and personal experience, we were unable to find any explicit exploration of dynamic hierarchical multi-objective risk management in voluntary, recreational risky activities. The psychology of decision-making in this context is also largely unexplored. Thus, we have developed a qualitative framework, based on Hammond, Raiffa, and Keeney's PrOACT framework, that helps elucidate and inform the

**** Correspondence to: Department of Emergency Medicine, MSC 10 5560, 1 University of New Mexico, Albuquerque NM 87131-0001, USA, Telephone: 505-272-1429, Fax: 505-272-6503, Email: rclee@salud.unm.edu

decision-making processes associated with mountaineering. This approach may help mountaineers and society understand the psychology and tradeoffs associated with this activity, and may be useful for risk management of other types of risky recreational activities.

INTRODUCTION

"There are only three sports: bullfighting, motor racing, and mountaineering; all the rest are merely games": attributed to Ernest Hemingway

". . .you have to be good when you take nasty risks, or you'll lose it, and then you're in serious trouble": Hunter S. Thompson

"Risky", "extreme", or "adventure" recreation (i.e. voluntary activities involving the potential for serious injury or death) are increasingly popular in developed countries. Such activities may include skydiving, SCUBA diving, surfing, mountain biking, skiing, hanggliding, and the like. Mountaineering is commonly viewed as one of these risky activities.

Risk is defined here in the formal sense; i.e. as a function of probability and consequence [Cox 2002]. A hazard is a potential risk. Mountaineering is defined here as mountain climbing or travel activities that routinely involve specialized techniques and equipment to manage risks (i.e. to reduce probability and/or consequences of adverse events), as opposed to, say, walking, hiking, or ski touring in non-glaciated terrain. Such equipment may include ropes, harnesses, fall protection (i.e. devices placed in rock, snow, or ice that are clipped to the person or rope and thus theoretically limit falls), helmets, and so forth. Thus, mountaineering may include rock climbing, waterfall ice climbing, glacier travel, "technical" mountain climbing, and ski mountaineering involving glacier travel. Mountaineering may be conducted as a solitary or group activity, and can be performed by amateurs or professionals.

The question of why individuals engage in mountaineering, which can be not only risky, but physically miserable and costly, has been discussed in the social science literature [Loewenstein 1999, Heywood 1994], as well as numerous popular books and articles. From a psychological perspective, there may be a popular perception among some non-mountaineers that mountaineers are risk-loving, and that pursuit of risk *per se* is a main driver for their activities. This may be true some individuals, but there is ample evidence that this is not the case for many mountaineers and similar recreationalists [Creyer et al. 2003, Delle Fave et al. 2003, Olivier 2006]. Further, mountaineering has been discussed as a means of escape from a rationalized world [Heywood 1994, Kiewa 2002], but the phenomenon is likely more deep-seated and complex than this. Lyng [1990, 2005], employing a term first used by the psychoactive-drug using popular writer Hunter S. Thompson [1974], has used the term "edgework" to describe seeking of gratification, self-actualization, or transcendence (what Csikszentmihalyi and colleagues [1991] refer to as "flow") via risky activities. However, edgeworkers must carefully manage the risks in order for the activities to be sustainable; hence the Thompson quote at the beginning of this chapter. We prefer the term "manage" rather than "control" (which is used by many authors), in that "control" may imply that the risk can be reduced to zero. This is never the case.

Lyng and colleagues (1990, 2005) draw many parallels between diverse edgeworkers such as drug addicts, high-stakes businessmen, and risky recreationalists. A consistent attribute is management or control of a risky situation, from which mountaineers and other edgeworkers derive satisfaction [Loewenstein 1999, Celsi et al. 1993]. Professional mountain guides exemplify this factor, in that they derive satisfaction from not only managing their risk, but that of their clients [Beedie 2003]. The explosion of "adventure" recreation and tourism in recent years may be symptomatic of a change in culture that may be spawning more edgeworkers, although in many cases this sort of "risky" adventure occurs in a carefully controlled environment, and is in reality quite safe. Examples include guided whitewater rafting [e.g. Holyfield et al. 2005] and expansion-bolt protected "sport" climbing. In these cases, the participants may essentially delude themselves into thinking that the activity is risky, similar to participants on an amusement park ride. The net psychological effect may be the same, although as discussed below the consequences of failure to manage risk may be vastly different between, say, sport climbing and high-altitude mountaineering.

Given that pursuit of flow along with management of risks are characteristic of edgeworkers in general, and mountaineers in particular, we propose that risk management in mountaineering can and must be conducted in a rational fashion, and thus can be framed within utility theory. This is independent of whether one considers the act of mountaineering *per se* to be rational. Although it has been argued that utility theory has its limitations as applied to recreation [McNamee et al 2001], and indeed proposed that mountaineering is a means of escape from a rationalized world [Heywood 1994, Kiewa 2002], Lowenstein [1999] compellingly argues that mountaineering decision-making can fit within a broad definition of utility, and indeed uses the example of mountaineering to call for a return from narrow, economics based views of utility to the original broad utility concepts of Bentham. Lowenstein, however, does not explore the complex dimensions of risk management associated with the activity. If we assume that the pursuit of flow or some similar objective is a strong motivator of behaviour and is strongly related to the value structure of the mountaineer, in order to attain that objective in a sustainable fashion we argue that risks should and indeed must be managed in a rational framework. The lucky, overly-romantic mountaineer may be able to blunder irrationally through many climbs and survive (and many have, according to the popular literature. . .), but the chances of survival are obviously increased if systematic risk management occurs.

Thus, interesting conflicts exists in the mind of the mountaineer. She seeks flow via management of risky situations, and deliberately puts herself in those situations. These situations may elicit a range of emotions from exalted joy to mild apprehension to crushing fear. A rational thought process must nonetheless occur throughout to maximize survival. This dynamic psychological state can present extreme challenges. Indeed, the physical challenges of mountaineering often pale in comparison.

We further propose that not only decisions associated with the acts or process of mountaineering, but also those associated with engaging in mountaineering itself as an activity, as well as choices of particular types and locations of mountaineering, can be framed within a multi-objective hierarchy. Multi-objective decision-making is an approach to informing risk management decision-making that explicitly addresses the objectives of the decision maker and the tradeoffs across multiple objectives [Keeney 1992]. There are numerous risk-risk, risk-benefit, and benefit-cost tradeoffs throughout the mountaineering decision hierarchy (examples are provided in Table 1). Additionally, the decision-making process is dynamic on a number of different levels. Multi-objective decision-making provides an informative structure in which to frame these complex decisions, and thus potentially refine the decision-making process of the mountaineer.

Table 1. E xamples of Risks, Benefits, and Costs Associated with Mountaineering; and Examples of Associated Tradeoffs

Risks: Human failure, equipment failure, foreign travel, ice conditions causing falls, ice fall, rock conditions causing falls, rock fall, avalanches, weather, getting disoriented/lost, cold temperatures, altitude, unstable political environments in developing countries, insect-, food- and water-borne illness.

Benefits: Physical fitness, mental fitness, exposure to wild natural environments (beauty, connection with "nature", etc.), exposure to different ecosystems and cultures, changes in brain chemistry (e.g. endorphin release), sense of "flow", sense of accomplishment.

Costs: Equipment, travel (air fare, vehicle, hotels, etc.), house/child sitting.

Risk-risk tradeoffs: Risk of proceeding up a climb with bad rock conditions vs. risk of descending with poor anchors, risk of climbing slowly in adverse conditions using much safety equipment vs. risk of inadequate safety equipment but climbing quickly, risk associated with climbing vs. risk of mental stress associated with not climbing.

Risk-benefit tradeoffs: **Risk of injury vs. benefit of physical fitness, risks of illness vs. bBenefits of travel to beautiful and interesting foreign environments**.

There is a rich literature on the psychology and nature of voluntary versus involuntary risk; e.g. Slovic [1986], McDaniels et al. [1992]; and a psychological/sociological literature on edgework, as previously mentioned. However, based on a review of the peer-reviewed, mountaineering association, and popular mountaineering literature, we were unable to find any exploration of dynamic hierarchical multi-objective risk management in voluntary, recreational risky activities. We conducted interviews with approximately 20 mountaineers and professional mountain guides to build on our personal experience (approximately 50 years of combined mountaineering experience) in developing a formal, qualitative description of an approach that informs the risk management decision-making processes inherent in mountaineering, and which adds to the edgework and similar literature. We based this approach on the PrOACT framework (Hammond et al. 1999). PrOACT incorporates consideration of 5 major elements; Problem, Objectives, Alternatives, Consequences, and Tradeoffs; and also uncertainty, risk tolerance, and linked decisions. This framework is based on 40 years of utility theory and application of decision science [e.g. Raiffa 1968] in a wide variety of contexts. We then apply this approach to a personal case study. Our intent is to not present a normative, prescriptive decision-making process, but rather an analytical framework to inform risky decisions that can aid complex mountaineering decisions that are often fraught with complex emotions. Our approach may be useful for informing risk management decision-making in other types of risky recreational activities.

Risks Associated with Mountaineering

The quote at the beginning of the chapter attributed to Mr. Hemingway implies that risk to life and limb is a necessary constituent of "sport". Mountaineering entails some risk, because people are routinely injured or die while they are doing it, but estimating the risk is difficult for three major reasons.

First, there is a wide variability across different types of mountaineering. For example, climbing a large, technically difficult wilderness mountain peak entails a much different set of risks than those associated with, say, fixed expansion-bolt protected sport rock climbing at the local cliff (Table 2).

Technical mountaineering risks may involve "objective" risks such as avalanches, storms, rock-fall, etc., as opposed to "subjective" risks such as misjudging the difficulty or length of a climb. Popular perception of risks associated with mountaineering is no doubt influenced by the literature and media coverage of high altitude (e.g. over 7000 metres) difficult mountaineering. This type of mountaineering entails a much higher degree of risk and tradeoffs than other types. However, this type of mountaineering is constrained to, at most, a few hundred individuals worldwide at any one time, and extrapolating these experiences to the vast majority of mountaineering activities results in a biased view of the risks.

Secondly, there is wide variability in the skill, training, experience, and judgement of mountaineers. Intuition and analysis of accidents [e.g. American Alpine Club 2004] indicate an approximate inverse relationship between these factors and the probability of injury and necessary rescue. Of course, there may be a positive correlation between the training and skill of mountaineers and the degree of difficulty of their objectives, cancelling out the previous effect. However, the degree of risk aversion in a particular climber must be accounted for, and sometimes even the best, most careful mountaineers are subject to uncontrollable risks, and simply suffer "bad luck". A special situation exists in the form of guided mountaineering trips; i.e. where the mountaineers are under the management of professional guides, who are essentially professional risk managers. There is a general lack of statistics regarding numbers of different types of mountaineers, and the skill level of those mountaineers. This makes estimation of denominators (i.e. populations at risk) difficult. Typical statistics, such as British surveys of climbing popularity [Crowe et al. 2004], do not account for these differences.

Lastly, there is a great deal of uncertainty regarding the magnitude of risk itself, even within any particular arena of mountaineering. Reliable statistics on injury or death rates for most mountain areas or types of mountaineering simply do not exist. A recent article [Athern 2004] discussed the accident related death rates associated with two mountains for which statistics do exist (Mt. Rainier in Washington and Denali in Alaska, USA). The author noted a drop in the total number of accident related deaths in recent years, but that the risk of death associated with climbing these mountains was lower than other risks such as dying of heart disease, and comparable to driving a car. However, Huey and Hornbein [2004], in another analysis which adjusted for exposure duration, estimated that the annual death rate associated with climbing Mt. Rainier is 115 times the age-standardized rate for death from heart disease. Huey and Eguskitza [2000] estimate that the death rate for climbing and descending Mt. Everest is 1 in 29, and for K2 (the second highest peak in the world and much more technically difficult than Mt. Everest) as 1 in 7, which is risky indeed (i.e. on a par with

Russian roulette). It is obviously important for mountaineers who attempt such peaks to realize what they are getting into.

Table 2: Comparative Aspects of Different Types of Mountaineering (note that risk associated with normal travel to climbs (e.g. driving a car) is associated with all levels)

Type	Hazards	Cost[2]	Popularity[3]	Degree of risk[4]
Bolted sport climbing[1]	Human failure, equipment failure, travel, rock fall	Low	High	Low
Multi-pitch (i.e. more than one rope length) rock climbing	Human failure, equipment failure, travel, unstable rock conditions causing falls, rock fall, weather, getting disoriented/lost	Medium	Medium	Medium
Ski mountaineering, glacier climbing	Human failure, equipment failure, travel, suboptimal snow conditions causing falls, crevasse falls, avalanches, weather, getting disoriented/lost, cold temperatures	High	Medium	Medium to high
Waterfall ice climbing	Human failure, equipment failure, travel, unstable ice conditions causing falls, ice fall, avalanches, weather, getting disoriented/lost, cold temperatures	High	Medium	High
Alpine mountain climbing (i.e. involving technical rock, snow, ice)	Human failure, equipment failure, travel, ice conditions causing falls, ice fall, rock conditions causing falls, rock fall, avalanches, weather, getting disoriented/lost, cold temperatures	High	Low	High
High-altitude (e.g. over 7000 metres) alpine mountain climbing (i.e. involving technical rock, snow, ice)	Human failure, equipment failure, foreign travel, ice conditions causing falls, ice fall, rock conditions causing falls, rock fall, avalanches, weather, getting disoriented/lost, cold temperatures, altitude, unstable political environments in developing countries, insect-, food- and water-borne illness[5]	Very high	Very low	Very high

1: Baseline comparator used is bolted sport climbing, as this is likely the safest type of outdoor climbing. Bolted climbing involves relatively "clean" rock, use of permanent expansion bolts placed in the rock for protection, typically single pitch (i.e. one rope-length) or shorter in length, close to road access.

2: Inferred from personal experience

3: Statistics are difficult to estimate, but relative popularity can be inferred from mountain club surveys such as the British Mountaineering Council (2003).

4: Relative degree of risk is inferred from accident statistics (e.g. American Alpine Club, 2005)

5: These risks are present in any outdoor activity; however, the risks are much higher in many developing countries where this type of climbing takes place.

Semi-quantitative information from organizations such as the American Alpine Club [2004], although subject to many biases and of limited utility for estimating the degree of risk, allows rough ranking of risks and thus potentially informs risk management (Table 2). For instance, according to these statistics, if one wants to avoid serious injury or death one should avoid high-altitude or waterfall ice climbing, and stick to bolted sport climbing. Relying solely upon such statistics, however, is not optimal for risk management decision-making, as will be discussed below.

Of course, risks to life and limb are only a subset of a larger suite of risks that mountaineers expose themselves to, including financial costs, impacts to careers, impacts to family and other personal relationships, and so on. These risks are harder to objectify, yet the psychological consequences can be severe. For example, a compelling account of the potentially severe impacts on the friends and families of mountaineers is found in Coffey [2005]. Regardless, at a high level in a broad risk management framework these risks should be accounted for and balanced against benefits in decision-making.

Benefits Associated with Mountaineering

There are benefits associated with mountaineering, but these are even more difficult to characterize and quantify than the risks. We (via our interviews and personal experience) and others have tried, but it is difficult. Some of the benefits likely and directly relate to the state of being in and managing a risky situation, as previously discussed. Many mountaineers seek some altered mental and physiological state that is a result of exertion, pain, and altitude, and with being exposed to a wide variety of difficulties and hazards. The extreme focus that is required for the simple acts of moving on a mountain and surviving the experience is addicting. In this sense, the benefit is not very different than a psychotropic drug induced state, and in a few cases is just as pathological and self-destructive (i.e. a small proportion of climbers who essentially continue to climb more and more difficult objectives, seeking these stimuli, until they exceed the limits of their abilities and they die climbing). However, for most mountaineers there is a more complex set of benefits that relate to not only the risk, but the experience of being in a wild natural environment, the camaraderie of companions, the fulfilment of a goal, and so on. Additionally, the benefits of attempting a particular mountain or route can be roughly scaled according to the "attractiveness" in terms of the condition of the rock or ice, the purity of the climbing line, the size of the route, the difficulty, and other factors.

One way of characterizing the quality of interaction between a mountaineer and a mountain is whether the mountaineer attains a state of "flow" (according to Csikszentmihalyi et al. [1991]). This transcendent state is likely what many mountaineers seek from their activity, but it can be highly transient and variable in intensity, ranging from non-existent on an unpleasant climb to many hours or even days when there is a good "match" between the person(s) and the environment. The type and degree of flow is highly dependent on the person(s), the degree of skill and training, and so forth. For example, a highly experienced mountaineer may experience a state of flow on a long, highly technical route, and indeed may seek such routes, whereas a novice may simply find the experience frightening and laborious. Of course, if mountaineering is conducted in a pair or team, there must be some degree of concordance of flow, or the partners may not attain it.

Management of risk is likely an important objective for most mountaineers, whether viewed as part of the flow phenomenon, or as a separate benefit (i.e. flow can be attained in a relatively "safe" fashion via distance running, etc.; i.e. activities not requiring the same degree of risk management). Our interviews and the literature have indicated that the continuous act of risk management is indeed a desirable objective for many mountaineers; especially those with a great deal of experience (in which case they may manage risks for apprentice partners) or for professional mountain guides. In our interviews with guides (e.g. "why do you enjoy guiding?"), as well as other studies [Beedie 2003], management of risks for clients is a consistent "reward" for guiding. Of course, there is variability in the degree of risk that guides are willing to expose clients to, ranging from simple scrambles to long difficult routes. We have asked guides "what is the most difficult climb that you would guide?", and the consistent answer was that it depended on both the experience level and risk tolerance of both the guide and the client, often with a premium added to the financial cost of the experience. In any event, the guides approach climbs that do not involve clients quite differently (e.g. they may engage in much more difficult and risky climbs). As several guides have told us, "guiding is not climbing".

It is quite unclear as to how carefully the typical mountaineer weighs benefits versus risks. We do not question the judgement of mountaineers in terms of engaging in a risky activity; rather, assuming that there are compelling reasons for individuals to engage in mountaineering, we propose that the risks can be managed in a rational, systematic fashion in a multi-objective framework. Some of the more important means and the tradeoffs are discussed below.

Risk Management in Mountaineering

As previously mentioned, some of the risks associated with mountaineering can be managed via safety equipment, procedures, and training, fitness, and other means (Table 3).

These reflect Reason's "layers of safety" concept that is often used as a model in the safety field [Reason 1998]. Reason's model is represented as a series of filters (e.g. slices of Swiss cheese) that sequentially reduce the probability that a person who is exposed to a hazardous scenario will experience an adverse event.

If one chooses to expose oneself to the mountains, there is limited ability to manage some "objective" risks such as rock-fall, avalanches, hidden crevasses (cracks in glaciers), extreme weather, altitude, and the like. However, careful observation and the experience to judge when to turn around or "bail" can be effective in managing these risks. In some cases, a risk-averse mountaineer may choose to avoid some types of climbing entirely due to an unwillingness to expose herself to these risks; e.g. many mountaineers choose not to climb high altitude peaks or waterfall ice for this reason. The tradeoff here relates to depriving oneself of what might be very rewarding or even life-changing experiences.

Table 3. Equipment, Materials, and Methods for Risk Management in Mountaineering (note that in all cases proper training and experience is assumed, and professional guiding may also be a means for risk management).

Type	Methods	Cost	Degree of experience required	Overall effectiveness in managing risk
Bolted sport climbing[1]	Rope[2], permanent bolts, clip protection[3], belay[4], helmet (sometimes)[5], footwear, water and nutrition	Low	Low	High
Multi-pitch (i.e. more than one rope length) rock climbing	Rope, permanent bolts, rock protection[6], clip protection, belay, helmet, footwear, clothing, water and nutrition, communication[7], first aid, navigational aids	Medium	Medium	Medium
Ski mountaineering, glacier climbing	Rope, snow protection[8], ice protection[9], prussiks[10], avalanche rescue equipment[11], crevasse rescue[12], footwear, clothing, ski equipment, ice ax, water and nutrition, communication, first aid, navigational aids, bivouac equipment[13]	High	High	Medium
Waterfall ice climbing	Rope, ice protection, belay, helmet, footwear, clothing, ice tools, crampons, water and nutrition, communication, first aid, navigational aids	High	High	Medium
Alpine mountain climbing (i.e. involving technical rock, snow, ice)	Rope, snow protection, ice protection, belay, prussiks, rock protection, ice tools, crampons, helmet, crevasse rescue, footwear, clothing, water and nutrition, communication, first aid, navigational aids, bivouac equipment	High	High	Medium to low
High-altitude (e.g. over 7000 metres) alpine mountain climbing (i.e. involving technical rock, snow, ice)	Rope, snow protection, ice protection, belay, prussiks, rock protection, ice tools, crampons, helmet, crevasse rescue, footwear, clothing, water and nutrition, communication, first aid, navigational aids, bivouac equipment, oxygen[14]	Very high	Very high	Low

1: Baseline comparator used is bolted sport climbing, as this is likely the safest type of climbing.

2: "Rope" means use of modern dynamic rope(s), a sit harness, and an appropriate method of joining the two.

3: "Clip protection" means use of aluminium carabiners, nylon slings, and/or other appropriate means of joining the rope to protection placed in rock, ice, or snow.

4: "Belay" means one partner is feeding the rope through a friction device while the "leader" climbs and places protection, thus controlling the amount of distance the leader will fall. Once the leader reaches an appropriate stance, she can then belay the partner from above. In sport climbing, it is often possible to "toprope" or place a rope so that all climbers are belayed from above.

5: Sport climbers often do not wear helmets, as the probability of rock fall is perceived as low. This practice, in the author's opinion and based on accident statistics, is highly questionable. Ski mountaineers usually do not wear helmets unless they plan to ascend a technical peak.

6: "Rock protection" means aluminum or steel devices, other than expansion bolts, that are placed in cracks or pockets in the rock. There are typically removed and re-used as the team progresses up the climb.

7: "Communication" means radios, cell phones, satellite phones as appropriate

8: "Snow protection" involves devices that can be hammered into or buried in snow.

9: "Ice protection" means hollow screw-like devices that are screwed or hammered into ice.

10: "Prussiks" means devices that are placed on the rope to allow climbing up the rope itself in the event of a fall into a crevasse.

11: "Avalanche rescue equipment" involves electronic transceivers, shovels, probes, balloon packs (i.e. personal airbags), etc. that allow finding and retrieving buried victims. These are routinely used only in ski mountaineering. In other forms of mountaineering, the weight of carrying such items is traded off the utility in terms of rescue; thus they are usually not carried.

12: "Crevasse rescue" means knowledge of processes to extract a disabled person from a crevasse. This may involve a range of processes from simply pulling someone out to complex pulley systems, rappelling into the crevasse, etc. Ski mountaineers do not typically belay each other, but they are exposed to crevasse hazards on glaciers.

13: "Bivouac equipment" means minimal camping equipment such as a sleeping bag, stove, light tent or cover bag, etc., as opposed to full camping equipment used at a base camp. Carrying such equipment depends on the length of the climb.

14: The use of oxygen on very high peaks (e.g. over 8000 metres) has historically been a risk management measure. However, in recent years many high-altitude climbers have been eschewing oxygen, under the concept that the use of oxygen is not "fair means" (attributed to the Austrian climber Reinhold Messner, who was the first person to summit Mt. Everest without oxygen). This likely increases risk many-fold.

Use of safety equipment is an important risk management technique. For instance, a rope can prevent major injuries or death by limiting the distance of a fall, and wearing a helmet can prevents the same outcomes via reduction of head trauma in the case of rock or ice fall. All this comes at a price; modern active mountaineers typically spend thousands of dollars per year on equipment and technical clothing. The degree to which equipment can alter the risk profile of an individual is dependent on the degree of training with and thoughtful use of the equipment; accident reports corroborate this as a major factor in many accidents [American Alpine Club 2004]. An odd cognitive phenomenon among some users, especially with regard to wearing a rope, is that mere donning of the equipment confers some level of safety. This is obviously fallacious.

The degree of physical and mental fitness of the climber is paramount in mountain safety. A fit climber is able to move faster and more confidently, and to retain clear thinking in a state of fatigue. Speed is an oft-overlooked risk management strategy; many successful climbers take an approach to safety that involves getting up and down a climb as fast as possible (e.g. Easton [2005]). This is rational because the time of exposure to uncontrollable hazards is reduced if one climbs as fast as possible. Of course, there are tradeoffs; the safest strategy, all other things being equal, is to stay out of the mountains entirely, and if one climbs too hastily one might make fatal errors. Assuming one exposes oneself to the mountains, one must climb often to gain the degree of fitness necessary to climb fast; i.e. for training there is no substitute for actual climbing. Thus, an odd tradeoff exists in which the safest climber is one who climbs fast, but in order to climb fast one must climb often (thus increasing exposure time). Thus, the two factors may indeed cancel each other out in terms of cumulative risk. Additionally, in order to climb fast, one must generally carry less weight, which means less equipment, food, and water. Many of the risks associated with high altitude mountaineering relate to compromised physical and mental functioning; e.g. mountaineers make mistakes at high altitude that they would never make at lower altitudes. For example, the popular book "Into Thin Air" [Krakauer 1999] is a highly critical exploration of how rational decision-making is compromised at high altitude (in this case, Mt. Everest).

A critical variable in mountaineering safety relates to one's partner(s). In roped climbing one partner leads while the other follows, and a variety of techniques have been developed so that the partners manage each other's safety. Additionally, the state of mind of the partners may influence each other in both positive and negative directions. In many instances, the life of one partner is literally in the hands of the other. A fascinating account of partners who found themselves in an extreme decision to compromise the security of the rope is found in the book (and subsequent documentary) "Touching the Void" [Simpson 1989], in which one partner cuts the rope (believing the other partner to be dead, which turned out to be false) to save himself. We have asked many climbers whether they would do this, and despite the clear mental torture that resulted from this act and is well-communicated in the book, the majority have said yes. This may reflect an over-riding sense of self-preservation, or simple lack of concern for the other party; the spread of psychological reasons behind this is likely to be large. Our personal experience is unusual because we are married climbing partners, and we expect that such a choice would be extremely difficult.

Professional guides manage the risks, to the extent possible, for their clients. They have therefore developed a series of techniques and decision rules for their business. Guides will not generally take clients on highly difficult routes, as the degree to which the guide can manage the risks is reduced as the climb becomes more difficult. The tradeoffs for the client relate to expense and loss of some control over the experience of the climb. The tradeoffs for the guide may relate to having to manage the client, as opposed to simply climbing with a partner, although they are compensated for this by their fee.

Rescue is the ultimate retroactive risk management method in the event of a non-fatal accident. The existence of timely and efficient rescue capability is highly variable, however, ranging from a high degree of capacity in some US national parks and some areas of Europe to non-existence in remote wilderness ranges. The question as to whether existence of rescue capacity (and ready communication in the form of mobile and satellite telephones) has an impact on the behaviour of mountaineers is unanswered. Regardless, the ability of a team to self-rescue or facilitate rescue likely has a large impact on the survival of injured mountaineers in many instances.

Mountaineering is thus a sport of numerous multi-objective tradeoffs. In the next section we explore this in greater detail using a case study, and introduce the concept of dynamic multi-objective risk management under the PrOACT framework.

CASE STUDY: CLIMBING MT. ROBSON

We use the case of Mt. Robson, which at 3954 metres is the highest peak in the Canadian Rockies. It is considered a "classic" mountain in terms of its size, its beauty, and the difficulty of attaining the peak. We present a hierarchical multi-objective structure, based on PrOACT, for disaggregating the decisions involved in climbing this peak. "Macro-" level decisions involve lifestyle decisions around "whether to climb", including the type of mountaineering to pursue. "Meso-" level decisions involve "what and where to climb". "Micro-" level decisions involve "how to climb", including risk management on a continuous and dynamic basis (Table 4). An objectives hierarchy is presented in Figure 1.

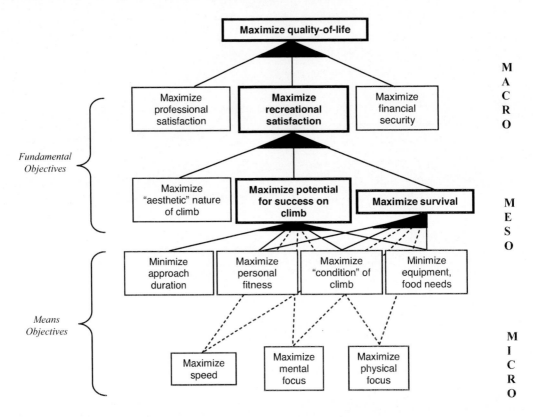

Figure 1: Objectives hierarchy for mountaineering decisions. The bolded boxes are fundamental objectives for which the illustrated means objectives are relevant. Note that for clarity the hierarchy is only partially completed; it focuses on objectives that are directly related to the act of mountaineering itself.

Table 4. The PrOACT framework as Applied to Multiple Levels of Mountaineering Decision-Making. (note that these are examples only; a complete assessment would involve many more considerations. Uncertainties, risk tolerance, and linked decisions are discussed in the text.

Level	Problem	Objectives	Alternatives	Consequences	Tradeoffs
Macro	How does one maximize quality of life? How does recreational satisfaction fit into this? Should one engage in mountaineering?	Maximize recreational satisfaction (f)[1]; also maximize professional satisfaction (f), maximize financial security (f)	Multiple; outdoor activity examples include walking, cycling, skiing, mountaineering, etc.	Positive: physical and mental fitness, enjoyment of nature, sense of accomplishment Negative: injury, illness, death	Increase in recreational satisfaction results in potentially limited career choices, increases in cost Choice of mountaineering results in increased physical fitness, but exposes one to risk
Meso	Where/what does one climb?	Maximize "aesthetic" nature of climb (f), maximize potential for success (f), minimize travel time (f), minimize duplication of climbs (f), minimize approach duration (m)[2], maximize person fitness (m), maximize "condition" of climb (m), minimize equipment and food needs (m)	Multiple; depending on the type of climbing one chooses and where one lives	Positive: enjoyment of climb, feeling of success, travel to new area Negative: unpleasant or adverse conditions, sense of failure	Choosing a large peak such as Mt. Robson maximizes "aesthetic" nature of climb, but limits potential for success Choosing a peak that is difficult provides challenge, but potentially more risk
Micro	How does one climb fast yet safely?	Maximize survival (f), maximize success (f), maximize speed (m), maximize physical and mental fitness/focus (m0, maximize safety equipment (m), maximize nutrition and hydration (m)	Choice of training, equipment (including accounting for rare risks), how much and what kind of nutrition	Positive: completing the climb safely Negative: unintended bivouac, injury or death	Increased training time vs. actual climbing time Too much equipment vs. too little

1: "f" represents a fundamental objective

2: "m" represents a means objective

Macro Decisions

Problem: We want to maximize our quality-of-life. How should mountaineering be part of this?

Objectives: We want to maximize our recreational satisfaction, as well as professional satisfaction and financial security (Table 4).

Alternatives: There are innumerable options in terms of recreational activities, ranging from reading books about climbing mountains to actually climbing them. Why a particularly risky and costly choice? The benefits of mountaineering must outweigh the risks and costs.

Consequences: The positive consequences of mountaineering, as opposed to other activities, include a high degree of physical and mental fitness, a sense of flow, gratification from managing risks, an increased appreciation for the natural environment, and so on. The negative consequences of mountaineering can be severe, including disability and death. Aside from obvious health and safety risks and impact on families, there are consequences that impact our non-climbing lives. For example, we choose to live near mountains, which can be professionally constraining and stressful. We spend an appreciable amount of money and time on travel and mountaineering, so we must choose jobs that pay enough to be able to do this and which allow flexible time.

Tradeoffs: There are large degrees of tradeoffs across the objectives in Table 4. In choosing mountaineering over other activities to maximize recreational satisfaction, we are limited in our jobs and where we live, and we spend a lot of money. If, for example, we chose to read books about mountaineering for recreation, we would be able to live anywhere and perhaps would not have to make as much money. However, we would not enjoy the benefits of mountaineering.

At the time of this writing, considering the tradeoffs, we chose to live near the Canadian Rockies, thus shorter scale decisions centred on that mountain range. For example, a yearly-level decision in 2004 was where to spend our annual holiday. We decided on a number of objectives, based on the appeal of the climbs and our projected ability to complete them.

Meso Decisions

Choosing and planning a particular climb represents the next level of decision-making. The PrOACT framework for this level is illustrated in Table 4. We desired to climb an "elegant" route on a major peak that we had not climbed before, and which was well within our capabilities and our available time. The choices were somewhat limited, as we had already climbed many peaks in the Rockies. We chose a relatively straightforward but classic route, the Kain Route on Mt. Robson (named after the person who guided the first ascent in 1913), which involves a long hike, extensive glacier travel to a base camp, a 500 metre 50 degree snow and ice face (the "Kain Face"), and another 300 metres of steep snow and ice ridge to the summit.

Getting to the mountain involved a 5 hour drive from our home, thus includes some degree of risk, cost, and time commitment even before reaching the mountain. Typically, parties allow a week to climb the mountain (to allow for the approach, the climb, and descent, and delays due to bad weather). After discussions with professional guides, we decided to avoid the approach by flying via helicopter to the base of the Kain Face in order to maximize our chance of success (but which of course introduces a new set of risks!). The reasonable expense of flying and the risk of flying were outweighed by the avoidance of a 30 kilometer hike with 25 kilogram backpacks and travel across a heavily crevassed glacier, which can be quite risky.

As we had previously climbed many similar glaciated peaks and were accustomed to this sort of climbing, we did not need to buy any additional equipment or undergo any training, other than climbing to stay fit. We did need to carefully consider our equipment, clothing, and food; for camping in a harsh environment as well as climbing (including a satellite phone for rescue, if necessary). In order to complete the climb safely in a day from a base camp, a team has to move continuously and fast. Also, the mountain becomes more amenable to climbing later in the season, as the amount of arduous snow climbing (as opposed to ice, which is faster) is reduced. Thus, we chose to attempt the mountain at the end of our summer holiday, when we would have been climbing for a couple of weeks and would be as fit as possible, and the mountain would be in good condition. However, this also meant that the length of day was reduced (compared to early summer), thus some amount of climbing in the dark was necessary, which is riskier.

A major source of uncertainty at this level of decision-making regarded the weather. Based on climate statistics, the timing of our trip was marginal; i.e. there was a better-than-even chance that we would have bad weather. However, we "lucked out", and the weather was good (we had backup plans in case the weather was too bad for the helicopter to fly). We arrived on the mountain, and the next level of decision-making began.

Micro Decisions

See Table 4 for the PrOACT framework applied at this level. Once on the mountain, the fundamental objectives are maximizing success and survival. There were decisions as to equipment to take on the day of the climb (i.e. as little as possible, while keeping a reasonable margin of safety), food and water needs, timing and "style". Based on experience, we decided to take the "clothes on our backs", a minimum of climbing equipment, and enough food and water to sustain us for approximately 20 hours. We also carried lightweight radios to facilitate communication between us. We planned to leave camp as early as possible in the morning while getting a modicum of sleep (i.e. 2 a.m.). This of course meant that we would have to climb by headlamp for several hours, which obviously can be riskier than climbing in the daylight. We awoke to a clear starry sky (a critical decision-point) the next morning, and the climb began.

Once climbing, the level of decision-making becomes much more focused and micro-scale. We decided to use the style know as "simul-climbing" in which we both moved continuously on a rope, with ice screws placed into the glacier ice between us at all times to theoretically stop a fall (as opposed to belaying and moving one at a time). There is a risk-risk tradeoff here; belaying would be safer in the event of a fall, but it is slower, and as previously discussed, speed is safety. However, the main form of security on a steep ice face is to ensure that one is connected to the mountain at all times via ice tools for the hands and crampons (spikes) on the feet. There are second-by-second decisions as to placement of hands and feet, and a wrong decision can be deadly. There is no reason or indeed opportunity to consider whether the bills had been paid before we left, how much the new ice tool cost, or whether another mountain would have been more rewarding. The state of rapid risk assessment and management, which indeed occurs at an "automatic" (i.e. without conscious thought) level to some extent, exists for as long as the climber is moving, and can be more draining mentally than physically. However, this is part of the attraction of technical climbing for most people; the focus on moving safely can be rewarding in itself as a source of flow. At its simplest level, climbing becomes a single-objective problem: maximizing survival. Risks are not ignored, but managed on a move-by-move basis and performed at an instinctual, intuitive level that is only gained by experience.

Time is an enemy to a mountaineer. On a long climb like Mt. Robson, survival is maximized by completing the climb as quickly as possible. Neither of us wear watches on our wrists, because we have found that knowing the rate of time passage impedes our abilities to attain a sense of flow. There is also a sense (for us at least, but this is by no means universal as we discovered via interviews) that if we know the actual rate of time passage, that we become apprehensive that we are climbing too slowly. Yet, it is useful (*sans* observations of the sun or other indications) to know if it is getting too late to complete the climb; thus we carry a watch hidden in a pocket until it is needed to inform major decisions.

It becomes more difficult to maintain focus as the climber becomes fatigued, thus careful attention to hydration and blood sugar levels is important. Recent advances in sports nutrition have resulted in products such as energy drinks and glucose packets that allow rapid ingestion and absorption, thus allowing more continuous climbing without the need to stop for extended periods of time.

Additionally, there are minute-by-minute and hour-by-hour choices regarding the route itself in terms of condition and ease of ascent. We chose a line on the Kain Face that was the most direct and icy route to the summit ridge (for the sake of efficiency and speed), yet this line was exposed to serac (section of unstable glacier ice) hazard. This was managed by completing the Face before the sun arose; it would have been much riskier later in the day. On this particular mountain, a major uncontrollable variable was the weather. Mt. Robson, like many big mountains, can create its own weather patterns. A cloud cap can form on the mountain that can result in "white-out" and windy conditions where it is difficult or impossible to see for more than a few yards. Such conditions are highly risky, as it becomes easy to become disoriented and indeed, at worst, to step off a cliff or cornice (overhanging snow) into oblivion. As we climbed the mountain, a cloud cap started to form, thus the "need for speed" intensified. However, by this point the snow was knee-deep (despite our planning) and climbing fast was difficult. Minute-by-minute decisions were made regarding the speed of formation of the cloud cap versus our own speed of ascent. We found ourselves in a conflicted state, as the line between benefit (attaining the summit) and risk became more and more "fuzzy". This corresponds to the mountaineer/writer David Roberts' "moments of doubt" [Roberts 1986]. At such a point, it was advisable to facilitate rational thinking via a brief rest, food, and water. As we were returning the same way, we were able to make the rational decision that we would be able to follow our track, even if it became cloudy. Thus, we were able to attain the summit and enjoy spectacular views. However, we were not able to spend much time enjoying this, as we had to immediately start our descent given the change in the weather.

Descending a mountain is often just as or more risky than ascending. Rappelling (sliding down the rope in a controlled fashion using a friction device) down a climb is one of the most risky aspects of climbing, because one is totally dependant on the integrity of the anchors that are set (as opposed to using one's hands and feet to hold on), plus it is often slower than down-climbing. In our case, we chose to rappel the steepest parts of the descent (the upper part of the Kain Face), but mainly down-climbed for the sake of speed. We made it back to camp 15 hours later, with the upper part of the mountain now immersed in cloud.

As the weather had deteriorated and in order to physically recover, we made the choice to spend the next day at our base camp. However, it is risky to spend time at this elevation on the mountain, as the weather can be extreme. We managed this risk by using a very strong tent and building snow walls around the tent. Despite being ensconced in such a "bombshelter", it is difficult to sleep, and most mountaineers have a sense of apprehension, ranging from mild concern to an overwhelming dread of being blown away (a nontrivial concern on high mountains).

We had previously decided not to fly out, due to the expense, plus we wanted to experience what is commonly considered as one of the most scenic walks in the Canadian Rockies. Unfortunately, the conditions were such that we had to bypass the typical route down the upper Robson Glacier due to its instability (i.e. teetering seracs the size of houses), and take a more circuitous and unpleasant ridge that involved exposed rock climbing with heavy packs. Regardless, a day's worth of glacier travel (which involves continuous, dynamic, and draining decision-making as to choice of route in order to avoid crevasses and detours) and a long day's hike later we completed our climb. The mental relief that is felt by the simple state of being off the mountain and in a hot tub is indescribable.

Additional Proact Considerations: Uncertainty, Risk Tolerance, and Linked Decisions

The PrOACT framework includes consideration of uncertainty as an important step in informed decisions. As described above, mountaineering is rife with uncertainty. In particular, there is always an element of "luck", bad or good, in mountaineering, which can be characterized as random influences that are highly uncertain. For example, a novice mountaineer may cross an avalanche slope unscathed, while a highly skilled and trained mountaineer who has performed multiple stability tests may still be caught in an avalanche. The mountain environment is by its very nature highly complex and uncertain, and risks cannot be entirely managed. Acknowledgement of this fact is necessary for informed decision-making.

Risk tolerance of mountaineers is highly variable, both within an individual and across individuals. Within an individual, it may indeed depend on how well the person feels, how much coffee she has consumed, the "intimidation factor" of a particular climb, and so on. There is some average degree of risk tolerance that may exist, and which for example may determine the type of climbs that are chosen at the meso level, but at the micro-level raw fear may outweigh any sort of rational behaviour if the individual's risk tolerance is exceeded. Being aware of and not exceeding one's risk tolerance level is thus critical for rational decision-making.

Linked decisions are also important at all levels of the mountaineering decision-making process. As we have presented, most of these decisions are hierarchical; the decision to engage in mountaineering influences the decisions on what to climb, which in turn influences the micro-level decisions. The hierarchy is also reversed; ones' experience on a particular climb (positive or negative) may influence macro-level decisions. A wrong decision at the micro-level can change or end one's life in a split second.

CONCLUSION

Decision making under "risk" has been studied extensively for decades (e.g. Raiffa [1968]). However, the "risk" in the majority of case studies relates to simple opportunity cost, and in most cases is defined for a single strategy or decision [Loewenstein 1999]. This paper has explored dynamic, hierarchical decision making under risk where the risks involve personal injury or death, and where the activity is completely voluntary.

We have not presented a quantitative analysis (e.g. a formal decision analysis) for several reasons. First, the intent of our paper was to explore the psychology and demonstrate a way of thinking about voluntary risk that may clarify what may be, in some instances, life-and-death decisions. In our opinion, the critical aspect of this decision-making exercise is to recognize that there are substantial tradeoffs associated with choosing to engage in and actually engaging in risky recreation. Second, quantitative information associated with different types and aspects of mountaineering is sadly lacking. Indeed, there is little peer-reviewed literature at all related to such activities. Third, as previously discussed, there is difficulty in quantifying or even scaling objectives such as the benefits associated with mountaineering. Fourth, in order to properly model these decisions a complex hierarchical and dynamic probabilistic model would have to be employed. Few (if any) people would actually use such a model in making voluntary risky decisions, yet many may use a qualitative framework for informing their personal risky choices. Indeed, land managers and regulators responsible for areas where such activities take place may use similar frameworks in making programmatic and planning decisions. Last, there are aspects of decision-making throughout the hierarchy that are intuitive as opposed to conscious, particularly at the micro-level, which obviously makes quantification difficult.

However, we argue that qualitative multi-objective thinking is nonetheless useful and informative. Our discussions with professional guides have confirmed this, particularly in terms of educating less-experienced mountaineers about risk management. It would be difficult to estimate, say, the marginal utility of using our framework versus not using it, but as there essentially are no disutilities or downsides associated with using it, the marginal utility is likely to be positive.

We have not explored the myriad heuristic biases inherent in mountaineering decisions. For example, "projection bias" relates to making non-objective judgements about the future or the past, because the risks or benefits are "distant" in time and may not be evaluated properly [Loewenstein ct al. 2003]. A common experience among mountaineers is to unfairly weight the benefits of an unpleasant climb as the memory of the unpleasant aspects fades (in fact, without this heuristic bias, many mountaineers would quit!). Group behaviour may obviously influence individual decision-making in either positive or negative directions. Considerations such as age and family may affect individual risk aversion. Although discussions of these issues are common in the popular literature, there has been little primary research, and thus may be fertile ground.

Considering the increasing popularity of "extreme" or "adventure" recreation, it may behoove participants, organizers/guides, and land managers to think more carefully about the risks and management of the risks, or decisions may end up in the hands of risk-averse arbiters such as lawyers or government agencies. For instance, the lack of injury and death statistics in mountaineering, and likely even more so in other risky activities, makes it difficult to conduct risk assessments. Societal risk related decisions in the face of uncertainty are often driven by media attention and reaction or public outcry, rather than proactive and careful consideration. There is ample opportunity for primary research in decision-making under risk and uncertainty in this area.

We have no illusions that mountaineering itself is, in the popular view, a rational activity. However, we have illustrated a framework and process of rational thinking and risk management and how it may contribute to safety for a risky sport. Our multi-objective framework may be useful for both individuals and society in understanding risk management in such activities. We hope to follow-up with studies designed to collect empirical data on how such a framework may contribute to safety in recreational mountaineering.

ACKNOWLEDGEMENTS

This work was funded by the Calgary Health Technology Implementation Unit (University of Calgary, Alberta, Canada). The authors would like to thank the following individuals (all experienced mountaineers with professional and/or academic appointments) for useful discussions and comments: Dr. Bruce Jamieson, Dr. Ian McCammon, Dr. Pascal Haegeli, and Ian Tomm. We would also like to thank several mountain guides and professional and amateur mountaineers who provided useful input, as well as reviewers of initial drafts of this chapter. Some of the ideas presented in this paper were presented to an audience of professional mountain guides at a Canadian Avalanche Association workshop, "Professionalism at a Crossroads", in Penticton, BC in May 2005.

REFERENCES

American Alpine Club (2004). *Accidents in North American Mountaineering.* Vol. 8, No. 4, Issue 57.

Athern, L. (2004) The risks of mountaineering put in perspective. *American Alpine Club News,* Vol. 11, No. 246. www.americanalpineclub.org.

Beedie, P. (2003) Mountain guiding and adventure tourism: Reflections on the choreography of the experience. *Leisure Studies* 22, pp. 147-167.

Celsi, R.L., Rose, R.L., Leigh, T.W. (1993) An exploration of high-risk leisure consumption through skydiving. *Journal of Consumer Research* 20, pp. 1-23.

Coffey, M. (2005) *Where the Mountain Casts Its Shadow : The Dark Side of Extreme Adventure* (St. Martins Griffin).

Cox, L.A. (2002) *Risk Analysis: Foundations, Models, and Methods* (Boston, Kluwer Academic Publishers).

Creyer, E.H., Ross, W.T., Evers, D. (2003) Risky recreation: An exploration of factors influencing the likelihood of participation and the effects of experience. *Leisure Studies* 22, pp. 239-253.

Crowe, L., Mulder, C. (2004) *Demand for Outdoor Recreation in the English National Parks* (Sheffield Hallam University, Centre for Environmental Conservation and Outdoor Leisure).

Csikszentmihalyi, M. (1991) *Flow: The Psychology of Optimal Experience* (New York, Harper Collins).

Delle Fave, A., Bassi, M., Massimini, F. (2003) Quality of experience and risk perception in high-altitue rock climbing. *Journal of Applied Sport Psychology* 15, pp. 82-98.

Easton, S. (2005) How (not to) climb under seracs. *Rockies Ice Specialists.* http://www.rockies-ice.com/detail_news.php?nid=17.

Hammond, J.S., Keeney, R.L., Raiffa, H. (1998) *Smart Choices: A Practical Guide to Making Better Decisions* (Cambridge, Harvard Business Review).

Heywood, I. (1994) Urgent dreams: Climbing, rationalization, and ambivalence. *Leisure Studies* 13, pp. 179-194.

Holyfield, L., Jonas, L., Zajicek, A. (2005). Adventure without risk is like Disneyland. In: Lyng S. (ed.) *Edgework: The Sociology of Risk-Taking* (New York, Routledge).

Huey, R., Eguskitza, X. (2000) Supplemental oxygen and mountaineer death rates on Everest and K2. *Journal of the American Medical Association* 284(2) p. 181.

Huey, R., Hornbein, T. (2004) Risks of mountaineering. *American Alpine Club News*, Vol. 11, No. 247. www.americanalpineclub.org.

Keeney, R.L. (1992) *Value-Focused Thinking: A Path to Creative Decisionmaking* (Cambridge, Harvard University Press).

Kiewa, J. (2002) Traditional climbing: Metaphor of resistance or metanarrative of oppression? *Leisure Studies* 21, pp. 145-161.

Krakauer, J. (1999) *Into Thin Air: A Personal Account of the Mt. Everest Disaster* (New York, Anchor Publishing).

Loewenstein, G., O'Donoghue, T., Rabin, M. (2003) Projection bias in predicting future utility. *Quarterly Journal of Economics,* 118, pp. 1209-1248.

Lowenstein, G. (1999) Because it is there: The challenge of mountaineering for utility theory. *Kyklos* 52, pp. 315-343.

Lyng, S. (1990) Edgework: A social psychological analysis of voluntary risk taking. *American Journal of Sociology* 95(4), pp. 851-886.

Lyng, S. (2005) *Edgework: The Sociology of Risk-Taking* (New York, Routledge).

McDaniels, T.L., Kamlet, M.S., Fischer, G.W. (1992) Risk perception and the value of safety. *Risk Analysis,* 12(4), 495-503.

McNamee, M.J., Sheridan, H., Buswell, J. (2001) The limits of utilitarianism as a professional ethic in public sector leisure policy and provision. *Leisure Studies* 20, pp. 173-197.

Olivier, S. (2006) Moral dilemmas of participation in dangerous leisure activities. *Leisure Studies* 25, pp. 95-109.

Raiffa, H. (1968) *Decision Analysis: Introductory Lectures on Choices under Uncertainty* (Reading, Addison-Wesley).

Reason, J.T. (1998). *Managing the Risks of Organizational Accidents* (Hampshire, Ashgate Publishing Ltd.).

Roberts, D. (1986) *Moments of Doubt and Other Mountaineering Writings* (Seattle, Mountaineers Books)

Simpson, J. (1989) *Touching the Void: The True Story of One Man's Miraculous Survival* (New York, Harper-Collins).

Slovic, P. (1986) Informing and educating the public about risk. *Risk Analysis*, 6(4), pp. 403-415.

Thompson, H. (1974) Interview by *Playboy Magazine*, November, available at http://www.playboy.com/features/features/hunterthompson/04.html

In: Psychology of Decision Making in Education
Editor: Jeanine A. Elsworth, pp. 185-206

ISBN: 978-1-60021-933-7
© 2006 Nova Science Publishers, Inc.

Chapter 8

DECIDING ABOUT RISKY PROSPECTS: A PSYCHOLOGICAL DESCRIPTIVE APPROACH

Petko Kusev[1] and Paul van Schaik[2,]*

[1] Department of Psychology, School of Social Sciences, CityUniversity,
Northampton Square, London, EC1V 0HB, United Kingdom.
[2] Psychology subject group, School of Social Sciences and Law, University of Teesside,
Borough Road, Middlesbrough, TS1 3BA, United Kingdom.

ABSTRACT

Results from many studies suggest that people violate the principles of rational choice in both the domain of gain and that of loss. People usually treat probabilities non-linearly by overweighting low and underweighting moderate and large probabilities. The violations of rational choice in human decision-making were disregarded by the normative point of view (von Neumann & Morgenstern's (1947) Expected Utility theory, EUT) until Allais (1953) and Kahneman and Tversky (Kahneman & Tversky, 1979; Tversky & Kahneman, 1981, 1986, 1992) developed a descriptive theoretical approach. In this chapter we investigate what might affect decision-makers' preferences with respect to described real-world protective prospects. People's precautionary ('protective') decision-making in the face of risk implies that they may judge and weight the probability of risky events in characteristic ways that deviate from both normative EUT and psychological descriptive theory of decision-making tested with abstract gambles. The following theoretical frameworks contribute to an explanation of protective decision-making: (a) experience-based decision-making models - past and immediate experience affect decision-makers' preferences (Dougherty et al., 1999; Frisch, 1993; Hertwig, Barron, Weber & Erev, 2004; Stewart, Chater & Brown, 2006; Tversky & Koehler, 1994)

* Correspondence to: Psychology subject group, School of Social Sciences and Law, University of Teesside,Middlesbrough,TS1 3BA,United Kingdom e-mail: P.Van-Schaik@tees.ac.uk, Tel.: 01642 342320/342301 (from UK); +44 1642 342320/342301 (from abroad), Fax: 01642 342399 (from UK); +44 1642 342399 (from abroad), Web: http://sss-studnet.tees.ac.uk/psychology/staff/Paul_vs/index.htm

- and (b) accessibility of information (Higgins, 1996; Kahneman, 2003; Koriat & Levy-Sadot, 2001) - not all available observations of risks are equally accessible in memory.

1. INTRODUCTION

Existing decision-making research has used formal models that are assumed to apply equally to (a) both rational and human decision-making and (b) both hypothetical and real-world tasks that humans perform. However, research has shown that human-decision making is not necessarily rational and there is increasing evidence that humans perform hypothetical and given real-world tasks differently. In this chapter, we attempt to demonstrate the complexity of people's judgments and decision-making under risk and uncertainty with given real-world tasks, focusing on precautionary ('protective') real-world decision-making tasks and hypothetical decision-making tasks (using abstract gambles). We define protective decisions as those that involve participants deciding whether or not to adopt a specified precaution with a known cost in the face of a described risk. Indeed, precautionary behavior can be described as behavior where people aim to avoid or reduce risks by taking protective actions.

As discussed in this chapter, research findings contradict two main types of theory of decision-making - normative (e.g., von Neumann & Morgenstern, 1947) and descriptive psychological (e.g., Kahneman & Tversky, 1979; Tversky & Kahneman, 1992). Both types assume that people's risk preferences and decisions under risk and uncertainty are task-independent and can be represented as hypothetical gambles. The nature of the content area being contemplated may influence judgments of the degree of risk and benefit (e.g., Slovic, 1987), but most prominent decision theories assume that, once these judgments are made, decision-making with risky prospects is not influenced by factors associated with this content and is independent of the decision-task. For instance, the decision whether or not to insure my luggage worth £500 for a cost of £5 where the risk of loss is 1% is identical to the decision to pay £5 or take a gamble where I have a 1% chance of losing £500, but the results of decision-making in these two scenarios differ (Kusev, Ayton, van Schaik & Chater, 2006, 2007). Therefore, although existing studies of decision-making using hypothetical (abstract) gambles corroborate the need for a distinction between normative and descriptive accounts, evidence suggests they cannot provide all the answers that we need to explain observable behavior in the face of risk. We can assume that given hypothetical tasks do not have a similar experienced 'background' as given real-world protective tasks (e.g., insurance decisions) and this can account for (a) predominantly risk-averse preferences and (b) a lack of loss aversion, where the risk associated with the protective category is exaggerated.

The aim of this chapter is to argue for a differentiation between models developed to account for precautionary decision-making and models of other types of decision-making under risk (Kusev et al., 2006, 2007) and to offer possible psychological mechanisms which might affect people's risk preferences in precautionary-decision-making tasks. We first outline the normative theory of decision-making and its violations by human decision-makers. We then present the psychological descriptive approach that attempts to account for these violations. However, because this approach cannot account for differences between human decision-making in hypothetical decision tasks and that in given real-world decision tasks, we discuss theoretical approaches that contribute to an explanation of protective decision-making as well as hypothetical decision-making.

2. NORMATIVE THEORY OF DECISION-MAKING UNDER RISK AND UNCERTAINTY

2.1 The Normative Approach

The study of decision-making contains both normative and descriptive directions. Normative analysis is concerned with the nature of rationality and the logic of decision-making, while descriptive analysis is concerned with people's beliefs, preferences and imagination as they are, not as they should be (Kahneman & Tversky, 1984). The dominant normative approach to or the theory of rational choice - Expected Utility theory (EUT) (von Neumann & Morgenstern, 1947) - can be interpreted as a theory describing the behavior of an idealized human decision-maker. EUT is an early normative theory of decision-making, originally formulated by Bernoulli (1954), revived and axiomatized by von Neumann and Morgenstern (1947) and then extended by Savage (1954) to non-monetary outcomes and conditions of uncertainty rather than risk. The theory argues that if people are willing to accept a number of axioms or basic principles of behavior (some of which are discussed below), then this logically defines a unique criterion for rational choice.

EUT maintains that, facing uncertainty, people behave (in a descriptive interpretation) or should behave (in a normative interpretation) as if they were maximizing the expectation of some utility function of the possible outcomes. One of the central topics of decision theory is providing a justification for making wise or rational decisions under conditions of risk and uncertainty. EUT provides such a rational criterion, demonstrating that if individuals' preferences satisfy certain basic axioms of rational behavior then their decisions can be described as the maximization (minimization) of expected utility (disutility) (see Figure 1). Maximization of expected utility (EU) appears to be a basic characteristic of rational behavior because it is obtained from axiomatic principles that presumably would be accepted by any rational human (Slovic, 2000).

If we consider a gamble that gives P_i chance at outcome X_i, the EU of this gamble is $\sum P_i U(X_i)$, where $U(X_i)$ measures the *utility* of receiving X_i. The basic principle of EUT is that decisions under risk are made so as to maximize EU and to minimize the losses (disutility). Traditionally, the process of maximization and minimization is represented by the shape of the utility or disutility function; it has been assumed that the functions are concave for utility of wealth - maximization of wealth, and convex for disutility of loss - minimization of loss, as in Figure 1.

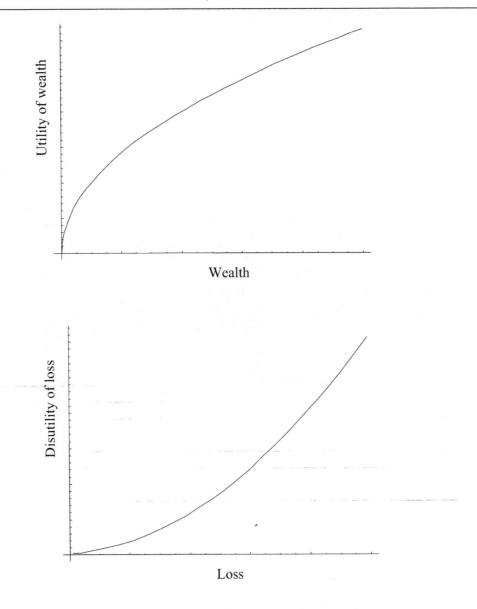

Figure 1. Traditional functions of utility and disutility.

Savage's generalization of EUT (Savage, 1954) allows it to be applied to decision situations where no objective mathematical probabilities are available and where judgments may be no more than expressed individual beliefs about likelihoods or *subjective probabilities* (Ayton, 2005). According to Subjective Expected Utility theory (SEUT), if decision-makers violate one or more of the axioms, then their choices will not maximize EU and will not be normative. Some important principles of EUT related to the psychology of decision-making are *cancellation*, *dominance* and *invariance*. The cancellation principle argues that with a prospect of two *risky* alternatives, a choice between two alternatives should depend only on those attributes that differ, not on outcomes that are the same for both alternatives, that is common factors should cancel out. The dominance principle proclaims that perfectly rational decision-makers should never choose a dominated option, even if the strategy is only weakly dominated. For example, according to EUT a decision-maker should never choose product B, if product A strongly dominates product B (e.g., A has better price and quality) or product A weakly dominates B (e.g., A has better quality than product B but is equivalent in cost). The invariance principle assumes that decision-makers are not affected by the format of presented prospects. For example, a rational decision-maker should have no preferences between (a) a compound gamble and (b) a simple gamble to which (a) can be reduced (e.g., one stage lottery) (Plous, 1993).

In the next section, we begin by discussing the systematic and overwhelming evidence of violations of the predictions of EUT and SEUT. We then present two of the leading psychological alternative (descriptive) theories that are vying to replace the normative models.

2.2 Violations of Normative Decision Theory

Despite the intuitive appeal of the rational paradigm, EUT and SEUT models suffer from some serious problems. Most critically, studies using both experimental and *real-world* evidence have repeatedly found that individuals often do not behave in a manner consistent with these models. The paradoxical choices identified by Allais (1953) and Ellsberg (1961) demonstrated the first doubts regarding the still popular rational EUT paradigm. However, the main problem for EUT and supporting economics models is their failure to explain the lack of stability in people's risk preferences - people demonstrate both risk-aversive and risk-seeking preferences with different forms (concave and convex) of the utility and disutility function (Kahneman & Tversky, 1979; Tversky & Kahneman, 1992). In particular, there are differences among the different decision domains (gain and loss) in terms of the value function and probability-weighting function, as discussed in this chapter.

EUT does not offer an account for common problems in decision-making and choice phenomena affected by uncertainty and probability - problems, which have dominated decision research over the years. For example, the Allais paradox (also known as common consequence effects and common ratio effects) played a particularly significant role in stimulating and shaping the development of alternatives to EUT. Following the rationality of EUT's independence and cancellation principles, a choice between two alternatives should depend only on how those two alternatives differ and not on any factor that is the same for both alternatives, but human decision-makers typically violate this assumption. As another example, Ellsberg (1961) presented what became famous as the Ellsberg paradox - individuals systematically show a preference for well-defined probabilities and violate EUT's cancellation principle.

Another violation of EUT - a lack of transitivity, has been proposed by Tversky (1969). In a hypothetical (abstract) gamble experiment, Tversky found an effect violating the EUT's *transitivity* axiom. In Tversky's intransitivity phenomenon, when two alternatives have very close (similar) probability of winning, for example:

A.   7/24 chance of winning £5 (EV = £1.46)

Or

B. 8/24 chance of winning £4.75 (EV = £1.58),

participants choose the option with the higher payoff (£5) of winning. In contrast, when the difference in probabilities is large, for example:

A. 7/24 chance of winning £5 (EV = £1.46)

or

B. 11/24 chance of winning £4 (EV = £1.83),

participants chose the option with high probability (11/24) of winning. The intransitivity phenomenon has been an important direction in decision-making science and has high applicability to many hypothetical (descriptive) decision-making applications involving probabilities and values.

Another well-known phenomenon, often interpreted as a failure of the *invariance* principle (stating that preferences over prospects are independent of the method used to elicit them), is the preference reversal phenomenon, observed first by Lichtenstein and Slovic (1971). Reversals of preferences (see also Grether & Plott, 1979) are observed when a so-called $-bet (offering a high money prize with low probability) is assigned a higher reservation price than a P-bet (offering a lower money prize, but with a higher probability), but is subsequently not chosen in a direct choice between the two. The preference reversal phenomenon is an example of growing evidence in recent years that very minor changes in the presentation or *framing* of hypothetical prospects can have marked impacts upon the choices of decision-makers.

A well-known example of a framing effect, violating the invariance principle, was first reported by Tversky and Kahneman (1981), in which two groups of participants were presented with an Asian-disease story. The choice was between two pairs of medical policy options, which are probabilistically equivalent - one with a certain outcome and one with a risky outcome, having higher potential gain. The only difference was that the information in one experimental condition was presented in terms of lives saved while in the other experimental condition the information was presented in terms of lives lost. Tversky and Kahneman found a strong effect demonstrating the violation of EUT's invariance principle: 72% of participants preferred the first policy when it was described as lives saved, while only 22% of participants preferred this option when it was described in terms of lives lost.

Economic theory traditionally assumes that economic agents (decision-makers) have the ability to use information in the real world and to make rational decisions under risk, without being influenced by their risk own preferences and the domain of the decision problem (i.e., loss or gain). On the other hand, psychologists and social scientists have criticized the use of such strong assumptions, arguing for the existence of individual and contextual specificity. Psychologists became interested in EUT soon after its publication. As an alternative to the maximization hypothesis, Simon (1955, 1956) introduced the principle of *bounded rationality*, stating that cognitive limitations of decision-makers force them to construct a simplified model of the world in order to cope with it. EUT is concerned with probabilities, payoffs and the combination of these factors - people's expectations for a particular outcome (EU). The problem of comparing the worth of one consequence with the worth of another consequence is solved directly by translating both into a common scale of utility. Simon's concept assumes that the goal of the decision-makers is to reach a *satisficing* rather than a maximizing decision, that is they set an aspiration level which, if achieved, they will be happy enough with; otherwise, they will try to change either their aspiration level or their decision. Decision-makers are constrained by limitations of perception and memory, and bounded rationality forces them to proceed by trial and error, modifying plans that do not ensure *satisficing* outcomes and maintaining those that do until they fail.

Normative decision-making theory assumes that a rational decision-maker maximizes EU for gains and minimizes EU for losses. Decision theory provides a model, based on the maximization (minimization) of EU, which serves as a normative or rational basis for making decisions. This view has been adapted in the light of criticism of EUT, for example, Simon's (1955, 1956) concept of bounded rationality. Such criticisms have led to the development of Prospect Theory, a descriptive model of decision-making under uncertainty proposed by Daniel Kahneman and Amos Tversky (1979). This, in turn, was extended into Cumulative Prospect Theory (Tversky & Kahneman, 1992; Tversky & Fox, 1995).

3. DESCRIPTIVE THEORY OF DECISION-MAKING UNDER RISK AND UNCERTAINTY

3.1 A Psychological Alternative to the Normative Approach

Kahneman and Tversky (1979) proposed Prospect Theory (PT) as a psychological alternative to the dominant EUT. In this theory, based on hypothetical decision problems (experiments with simple hypothetical gambles), choice is modeled as a two-phase process - editing followed by evaluation. In the first phase, prospects are *edited*, using a preliminary analysis of the offered prospects (hypothetical gambles), which results in a simple representation of these prospects. For example, a compound gamble prospect [£300, 30%; £300, 30%] can be reduced to [£300, 60%], using Kahneman and Tversky's *combination* operation.

The editing phase contains six specific operations (principles) that transform the outcomes and probabilities associated with the offered prospects (Kahneman & Tversky, 1979). According to *coding* operation, people normally perceived outcomes from hypothetical prospects as gains or losses rather than as final states of wealth or welfare. Gains and losses are defined relative to some neutral reference point (usually corresponding to the current asset position). Coding may be affected by the formulation of the offered prospects. In the *combination* operation, prospects are simplified by combining probabilities associated with identical outcomes (see above). The *segregation* operation states that some prospects contain a riskless component that is segregated from the risky component in the editing phase. The prospect [£300, 80%; £200, 20%] is naturally decompressed into a sure gain of £200 and a risky prospect [£100, 80%]. Another 'loss' example for a segregation is the prospect [-£400, 40%; -£100, 60%], which might be seen to consist of a sure loss of £100 and of the prospect [-£300, 40%]. The *cancellation* operation states that the components that are shared by the offered prospects are discarded. Participants may ignore the first part of a sequential game. For example, [£200, 20%; £150, 50%; -£100, 30%] and [£200, 20%; £100, 50%; -£50, £30] can be reduced by cancellation to a choice between [£150, 50%; -£100, 30%] and [£100, 50%; -£50, 30%]. The *simplification* operation supposes a simplification of prospects by rounding probabilities and outcomes. For example, the prospect [£101, 49%] is likely to be perceived as [£100, 50%]. The *detection of dominance* operation, involves scanning of offered prospects to detect a dominated alternative, which might be rejected without further evaluation.

In the evaluation phase, decision-makers evaluate each of the edited prospects and choose the prospect with the highest value. In the first version of PT (Kahneman & Tversky, 1979), the overall value of an edited prospect is expressed in terms of two functions - the value function and probability-weighting function. The evaluation of positive and negative prospects follows a different rule. In this phase, choices among edited prospects are determined by a reference function (value function), in which outcomes are interpreted as gains and losses relative to a reference point (e.g., status quo). The reason for treating consequences in this way is that it allows gains and losses to be evaluated differently. The main postulate of PT states that losses loom larger than corresponding gains. PT also differs from EUT in the way it deals with the probabilities attached to particular outcomes. EUT assumes that a decision-maker evaluates, for example, a 50% chance of winning as exactly as 50% of winning, whereas PT treats human preferences as a function of decision (probability) *weights*, assuming that these weights do not always correspond to the real level of probability - people tend to overweight small probabilities and underweight moderate and high probabilities (Kahneman & Tversky).

Another claim made by PT is in agreement with the extant psychophysical approach in psychology (Helson, 1964; Garner, 1954; Medin & Schaffer, 1978; Nosofsky, 1986), in particular that humans' perceptual apparatus is attuned to the evaluation of changes or differences rather than to the evaluation of absolute magnitudes - people's judgments are affected by the set of stimuli in the task. The response to single psychophysical stimuli differing in for example brightness, loudness or temperature depends on immediate or previous experience with stimuli in the task. Kahneman and Tversky (1979) assumed that the same principle applies to non-sensory attributes such as health, prestige and wealth.

The basic principle of EUT is that decisions under risk are made to maximize people's EU for gains and minimize EU for losses (von Neumann and Morgenstern, 1947) and that equivalent formulations of a choice problem should give rise to the same preference order. Kahneman and Tversky's (1979, 1984) and Tversky and Kahneman's (1986, 1991, 1992) concept of loss aversion suggests an alternative functional form, different for the domains of gain and loss - a value function that is steeper (convex) for losses (the curve lying below the horizontal axis) than for gains (see Figure 2), implying that people feel losses more than they do gains of equivalent value. Contrary to the normative assumption, it was concluded that a framing effect (in terms of gains and losses) leads to systematically different preferences with people's decisions (Tversky & Kahneman, 1986).

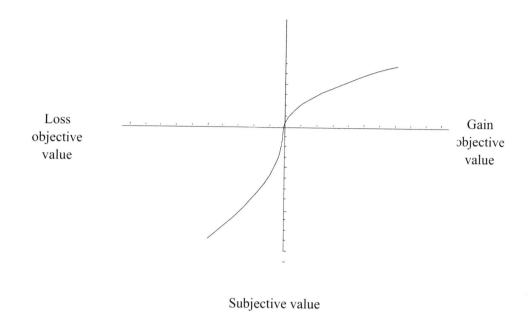

Subjective value

Figure 2. S-shaped value function for hypothetical decision-making tasks (Kahneman & Tversky, 1979).

However, recent research has shown that loss aversion is not a stable phenomenon and can vary depending on the decision task (abstract gamble or real-world protective task, the latter resulting in an absence of loss aversion) (Kusev et al., 2006, 2007), demographic differences (less loss aversion with a higher level of education) (Johnson, Gachter & Herrmann, 2006) or experience with the attributes probability and value (experts are less loss-averse) (Camerer, Babcock, Loewenstein & Thaler, 1997; List, 2003, 2004).

3.2 Probability Prospects - Cumulative Prospect Theory

Anticipated-Utility theory (AU) and its Rank-Dependent Expected-Utility model (RDEU) were originally proposed by Quiggin (1982) and later extended by Yaari (1987) to explain the Allais paradox. RDEU is typically applied to problems that have well-defined probabilities and are formulated in terms of hypothetical lotteries. AU is a generalization of EUT, where RDEU incorporates transformations of both a prospect's probabilities as well as its outcomes. One characteristic of RDEU is that it uses the transformation of the cumulative distribution of a prospect's probabilities (where the prospect's outcomes are ordered by attractiveness) rather than the direct transformation of probabilities that is hypothesized in PT. RDEU offered a new representation (called rank-dependent or cumulative functional) that transforms cumulative rather than individual subjective probabilities. This use of the cumulative distribution makes the weighting of an outcome dependent on its rank, hence the name RDEU. Quiggin (1982) proposed an S-shaped function for humans' perceptions of probabilities that was later generalized by Tversky and Kahneman's (1992) Cumulative Prospect Theory (CPT).

Tversky and Kahneman (1992) proposed CPT as an extension of PT. In this extended version of PT, the problem of how people estimate probabilities (subjective probabilities) is central. CPT uses the same basic principles as original PT, a value function, defined over gains and losses, and a probability-weighting function that captures people's risk preferences. The major technical innovation is the use of the cumulative functional rank-dependent form to extend PT to uncertain and risky prospects with many hypothetical probabilities (ranks) and different numbers for outcomes.

The new theory incorporates the basic principles of PT and can explain descriptive violations of EUT: (a) *framing effects* in terms of gains and losses - EUT assumes description invariance, that is equivalent formulations of a choice problem should give rise to the same preference order, but human decision-makers violate this assumption; (b) *nonlinear preferences* - according to EUT's maximization principle, the utility of a prospect under conditions of risk is linear in outcome probabilities, but Allais (1953) successfully challenged this principle; (c) *source dependence* - Ellsberg (1961) observed that individuals systematically show a preference for well-defined probabilities, in contrast to EUT's rationality; and (d) *risk-seeking behavior* - people prefer a prospect with a small probability of winning a large prize over another prospect with larger probability and smaller prize. People prefer risk-seeking in choice between a sure loss and a substantial probability of a larger loss. However, risk-aversion is generally assumed in economic analyses of decision under uncertainty based on EUT (Tversky & Kahneman, 1992). Kusev et al. (2006, 2007) demonstrate that such a difference in risk preferences could be a result of the decision task given to the participants.

Tversky and Kahneman (1992) presented a comprehensive, empirical test of CPT consisting of two sessions, where participants' cash equivalents (certainty equivalents - CE) for a number of hypothetical gambles were calculated as a midpoint between the lowest accepted and highest rejected value in the second session. The prospects involved the domains of gain and loss, with different probabilities and outcomes. The vast majority of participants exhibited the four-fold pattern of risk attitudes, in particular risk-seeking preferences for low-probability ($p \leq 10\%$) gains and high-probability ($p \geq 50\%$) losses and risk-averse preferences for high-probability ($p \geq 50\%$) gains and low-probability ($p \leq 10\%$) losses (see Table 1).

A parametric regression analysis of the CEs produced a value function of the form of Figure 2 and a probability-weighting function of the form of Figure 3. As in the original prediction made by PT, Kahneman and Tversky's (1992) result demonstrates that the value function is concave for gains (above the reference point of 0) and convex for losses (below the reference point of 0) (see Figure 2). The function is also steeper for losses than for gains, implying the principle of loss aversion according to which losses loom larger then corresponding gains.

The one-parameter model proposed by Tversky and Kahneman (1992) to described the probability-weighting function has several specific features: (a) it has only one parameter irrespective of decision task (hypothetical or real-world), but this feature was not confirmed by experimental evidence from recent research by Gonzalez and Wu (1999); (b) it encompasses weighting functions with both convex and concave regions; and (c) it provides a reasonably good approximation to both aggregate and individual data for probabilities in the range between .05 and .95, demonstrating people's tendency to overweight small probabilities and underweight the large ones. Consequently, people are relatively insensitive to probability differences in the middle of the range. The pattern of probability estimates demonstrates that the probability weights for hypothetical gambles with gains and losses are relatively similar, although the probability functional form for gains is slightly more curved for gains (see Figure 3) (Abdellaoui, 2000; Camerer & Ho, 1994; Prelec, 1998; Stewart et al., 2006; Tversky & Kahneman, 1992; Tversky & Fox, 1995).

Table 1. Risk-Seeking and Risk-Averse Choices for Hypothetical Decision-Making Tasks (Tversky & Kahneman, 1992)

	Hypothetical, gain		Hypothetical, loss	
	$p \leq .1$	$p \geq .5$	$p \leq .1$	$p \geq .5$
Risk-seeking	78%[a]	10%	20%	87%[a]
Risk-averse	10%	88%[a]	80%[a]	6%

Note. Percentages are mean values.

[a] Values corresponding to the fourfold pattern of risk-seeking (Tversky & Kahneman, 1992).

Many other studies, using a variety of methodologies, agree or find inverse S-shape functions as shown in Figure 3 (e.g., Abdellaoui, 2000; Camerer & Ho, 1994; Tversky & Fox, 1995). Abdellaoui (2000) agrees with the introduction of probability-weighting functions in CPT, but also notes the observed tendency that participants treat probabilities differently when passing from gains to losses and vice versa (see Figure 3). Abdellaoui suggests that CPT's experimental findings can be seen as a confirmation that the traditional utility elicitation methods could produce distorted utility functions. Camerer and Ho (1994) argue for a model that is nonlinear in probability in order to capture people's risk preferences. Their results are consistent with both CPT and RDEU models, assuming an inverse S-shaped weighting function. Other studies with hypothetical prospects (gambles) have produced similar parameter estimates as those found by Tversky and Kahneman (1992), even though these exercises varied considerably in terms of the data used and estimation techniques (see Abdellaoui, 2000; Camerer & Ho, 1994; Tversky & Fox, 1995; Wu & Gonzalez, 1996).

In accordance with humans' adeptness at evaluating changes or differences, another important feature of CPT is that the value function and the probability-weighting function exhibit *diminishing sensitivity* with distance from a reference point (Tversky & Fox, 1995). The characteristic of diminishing sensitivity gives rise to an S-shaped value function that is concave for gains and convex for losses. For probability, there are two natural reference points - 0% (impossible) and 100% (certain), which correspond to the endpoints of the scale. Diminishing sensitivity implies that increasing the probability of winning a prize by 10% has more impact when it changes the probability of winning from 90%-100% or from 0%-10% than when it changes the probability from 40%-50% or from 50%-60% (see Figure 3). However, the stability of the principle of diminishing sensitivity is questionable (Kusev et al., 2006, 2007); in particular, this phenomenon could vary depending on the given decision task.

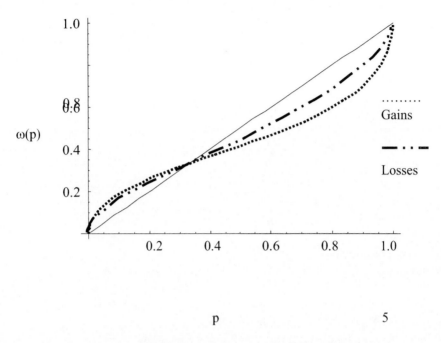

Figure 3. Inverse S-shaped probability-weighting function for hypothetical decision-making tasks (Tversky & Kahneman, 1992). *Note.* ω(p): humans' estimate of probability.

Despite CPT's general applicability to abstract gambles, the model is unlikely to be accurate in specific contexts, in particular the probability-weighting might be sensitive to the formulation of the prospects and types of prospect. In this chapter, we suggest that such sensitivity is due to the format of the decision prospects, for example hypothetical or given protective real-world task. Although existing studies of decision-making, using hypothetical (abstract) gambles, corroborate the need for a distinction between normative and descriptive accounts, evidence presented by recent research (e.g., Gonzalez & Wu, 1999) suggests they cannot provide all the answers that we need to explain people's behavior in the face of risk. As a consequence, various recent theoretical developments have specifically addressed decision-making with real-world prospects under risk.

4. THEORETICAL DIRECTIONS IN PROTECTIVE DECISION-MAKING

Why are people attracted to *protective* options such as insurance contracts, savings accounts, life- and health-assurance? In this section, we investigate what might affect people's probability-weighting with respect to described protective decision prospects. People's reactions in the face of risk imply that they may judge and weight the probability of risky events in characteristic ways that deviate from existing theory. We may expect a discrepant tendency concerning the probability-weighting process with precautionary behavior (Baron, Gurmankin & Kunreuther, 2007; Kunreuther, 2001; Slovic, Fischhoff &

Lichtenstein, 1987) compared to decisions with abstract gambles (still the main context for investigating economic behavior).

We specifically address the applicability of PT and CPT, proposing a protective-decision-making approach. People can reduce risks by engaging in protective behaviors such as washing their hands before eating, wearing a seat belt, taking health-screening tests, avoiding second-hand smoke, limiting alcohol consumption and installing a smoke detector. Governments and other organizations often set up programs to try to encourage people to undertake such protective behaviors (Baron et al., 2007). The research on precautionary behavior is also focused on what factors lead people to adopt a particular precautionary behavior and what interventions are likely to increase its adoption. For example low-risk, highly devastating events (e.g., natural disasters) could stimulate people's precautionary behavior (Kunreuther, 2001). In this section, we review two approaches that contribute towards the explanation and prediction of human decision-making in both hypothetical and precautionary decision scenarios.

4.1 The Role of Experience in People's Judgments under Risk: Implications for Protective Decision-Making

In their everyday decisions (e.g., regarding insurance decisions, pension plans, savings) people may exaggerate the risk of described risky options, when protecting themselves against the risk of real-world negative outcomes. Instances of some protectable risks are encountered in everyday life (via TV, newspapers, advertisements and individual experience) disproportionately frequently and might affect the probability-weighting process with given protective (real-world) scenarios. We could suppose that there are differences in the shape (modality) of the probability-weighting function in different domains of judgment - hypothetical (abstract) gambles and described real-world protective prospects. This notion is supported by evidence from research in subjective probability - in particular, that different descriptions of the same event can prompt different subjective probabilities (e.g., Tversky & Koehler, 1994) - and insurance-decision studies (e.g., Viscusi, 1995; Wakker, 2003; Wakker, Thaler & Tversky, 1997).

Even today, many economists interpret people's insurance preferences in terms of and within the framework of EUT. The descriptive psychological alternatives (PT and CPT) revealed the reasons why we should question its descriptive adequacy. For example, Murray (1972) and Neter, Williams and Whitmore (1968) found that utility functions scaled individually for each participant failed to predict their lottery and insurance preferences. It has therefore been suggested that the application of a utility and a disutility function as proposed by EUT for decision-making is not successful.

Behavior inconsistent with EUT has been confirmed in many problems, including insurance choices. For example, EUT cannot account for insurance-purchasing behavior if rates are actuarially unfair - a very expensive product with extremely low risk-probability (Hogarth & Kunreuther, 1992; Hershey, Kunreuther & Schoemaker, 1982). Decisions about insurance protection (e.g., natural disasters) are usually based on a lack of knowledge about relevant probabilities and in these situations people are often ambiguity-averse - they prefer known probability distributions over uncertain ones. Actuaries suggest higher warranty prices for ambiguous probabilities than for well-specified probabilities and underwriters set higher insurance premiums for ambiguous probabilities and losses than for well-specified probabilities and losses (Hogarth & Kunreuther, 1992; Kunreuther, 2001). However, Kusev et al. (2006, 2007) present experimental evidence showing that even well-defined (fairly presented) high and low real-world probabilities can be exaggerated.

Investigating insurance prospects, Camerer and Kunreuther (1989) assumed that most people have difficulties in evaluating small probabilities, arguing that decision-makers often ignore the information regarding small probabilities (underweighting). In contrast, Viscusi and Chesson (1999) argue that people are *averse* to ambiguous probabilities, demonstrating that preference for a known probability is most prevalent for low-probability losses and high-probability gains. In addition, Johnson, Hershey, Meszaros and Kunreuther (1992) found that manipulation of descriptions in an insurance-decision task leads decision-makers to violate EUT's basic principles regarding probabilities and values. Participants exhibit distortions of risk; in particular, the way that an insurance premium is framed can determine attractiveness of the insurance, in agreement with PT's *framing* effect - framing the prospects as gains or losses affects people's choices.

The theories of judgment and decision-making, ranging from normative frameworks that assume rational behavior to descriptive psychological concepts, differ in their approach to major issues. The descriptive psychological alternatives of EUT demonstrate that, breaching rational agents' rules, people usually treat probabilities non-linearly, overweighting low and underweighting high probability (Abdellaoui, 2000; Gonzalez & Wu, 1999; Prelec, 1998; Tversky & Kahneman, 1992; Tversky & Wakker, 1995). In EUT, every rational decision-maker should be able to trade off the value of all the possible outcomes by the likelihood of obtaining them (Ayton, 2005), highlighting that we all well deal with probabilities and monetary outcomes. However, there appears to be no evidence that normative EUT and descriptive theories of decision-making (tested with abstract gambles) - such as PT and CPT - can account for people's protective decision-making. The meaning of probability for decisions under risk and uncertainty has been the subject of numerous studies and the issues are still far from settled.

Research on decision-making (e.g., Simon, 1956; Ellsberg, 1961; Allais, 1953; PT and CPT) has suggested that people violate the principles of rational choice (EUT) and these violations are different in the domains of gain and loss. However, Baron et al.'s (2007) comparative approach demonstrates that real-world behavior is more complex and in some cases could be rational. The authors suggest that people's precautionary behavior might be rational (i.e., consistent with EUT) when considered in isolation, but not when considered in the context of other precautionary behaviors - people are less willing to undertake a precautionary behavior when they are considering several precautionary behaviors at the same time. People might have 'precautionary behavior budgets' - the extent to which people engage in a particular precautionary behavior decreases as the number of precautionary behaviors that they consider increases.

Further evidence of the complexity of people's real-world judgments has been presented by experience-based decision-making models, which recently gained popularity as psychological models of decision-making (Dougherty, Gettys & Ogden, 1999; Frisch & Jones, 1993; Fiedler, 2000; Gilboa & Schmeidler, 2001; Hertwig et al., 2004; Stewart et al., 2006; Tversky & Koehler, 1994). Kunreuther (2001) offered the notion of *fear*, based on individual experience with protective decision-making, as a powerful emotional factor; for example, people's fear of crime is what makes people more willing to spend on various precautionary measures. However, EUT does not predict a role of *affect* and *emotions* in people's precautionary behavior.

Case-Based Decision Theory - CBDT (Gilboa & Schmeidler, 2001) makes very similar predictions as Kunreuther, that is decisions under uncertainty are made by analogies to previously-encountered problems. The theory postulates a similarity function over decision problems and a utility function on outcomes, such that acts are evaluated by a similarity-weighted sum of the utility they yielded in past cases in which they were chosen. According to CBDT, decision-makers are not rational as EUT predicts - they count on their experience rather than attempt to figure out what the outcomes of available choices will be.

In agreement with the *experienced* decision-making orientation, Viscusi and Chesson (1999) assumed that there are in fact, few risks where probabilities are known with precision and decision-makers very often make risky decisions, in some instances after receiving highly divergent risk information. The authors proposed that people exhibit fear in response to the ambiguity associated with small probabilities and loss and *hope* in response to large probabilities. Ignoring the *accessibility* paradigm (see Section 4.2 below), Kunreuther (2001) has suggested the notion of *fear-and-prudence* decisions, where only past individual experience with anxiety or fear have an important influence on decisions of whether or not to invest in protective measures.

The experience-based view suggests that estimates of probabilities are made by retrieving exemplars from memory and that frequently-occurring probabilities will be more strongly represented in memory. People's estimation of the distribution of probabilities is dependent on their experience with small or large probabilities (Stewart et al., 2006). According to Stewart et al.'s theory - Decision by Sampling (DbS), the attributes that constitute the decision sample come either from memory or from the immediate context of the decision and the distribution of values in memory is assumed to reflect the distribution of attribute values in the world. DbS accounts for a convex utility function (in accordance with existing psychological models) - losses loom larger than gains and decision weights are distorted (the overweighting of small probabilities, and the underweighting of large probabilities).

Fiedler's (2000) theoretical framework, suggests that the sampling process may draw on the external world or on internal memories. Because people lack the meta-cognitive ability to understand and control for sampling constraints, sampling biases carry over to subsequent judgments. Human behavior appears to be affected by a reliance on relatively small samples of information and overweighting of recently sampled information and there is evidence that people distinguish between decisions based on experience and decisions based on description (Hertwig et al., 2004). Recently, Hertwig, Pachur and Kurzenhäuser (2005) suggested two decision mechanisms - availability by recall and regressed frequency, where the former mechanism assumes that participants' risky judgment is a function of the number of cases recalled from participants' social circles and the latter offers the assumption that people keep track of the frequency of occurrences of risk. The two mechanisms were formally stated as follows:

$$Choice\ proportion_{Risk\,a} = \frac{\sum recalled\ instances_{Risk\,a}}{\sum recalled\ instances_{Risk\,a} + \sum recalled\ instances_{Risk\,b}}$$

(recall)

and

$$Choice\ proportion_{Risk\,a} = \frac{\sum occurrences_{Risk\,a}}{\sum occurrences_{Risk\,a} + \sum occurrences_{Risk\,b}}$$

(regressed frequency).

In the framework of illness scripts, proposed as a pertinent type of knowledge structure operating in medical contexts (e.g., Charlin, Tardiff, & Boshuizen, 2000) - including decision-making (van Schaik, Flynn, van Wersch, Douglass & Cann, 2005), three types of knowledge component are distinguished. One of these components ('enabling conditions' - both medical and non-medical contextual patient-related factors that influence the probability of disease) develops as a function of experience and affects decision-making over and above and in interaction with 'objective' knowledge components ('consequences') (van Schaik et al., 2005), again highlighting the role of experience-based knowledge in decision-making.

4.2 The Effect of Accessibility on Decision-Making under Risk

In this chapter, we suggest that people's past experience with the frequency of risks has an important influence on decisions whether or not to invest in protective measures. According to our assumption, in judging prospects in protective-decision scenarios, people's risk preferences may be affected by their subjective experience and the accessibility of frequencies of hazardous events (Higgins, 1996; Kahneman, 2003; Koriat, 1993, 1995; Koriat & Levy-Sadot, 2001; Schwarz, 1998; Tulving & Pearlstone, 1966), that is not all available observations of risks are equally accessible in memory.

It seems that the probability associated with highly accessible features or events tends to be exaggerated (see e.g., Kusev et al., 2006, 2007), whereas events of low accessibility (e.g., gambles and inaccessible real-world events) in memory are largely ignored. People judge highly accessible hazards in memory as more likely than less accessible events. Indeed, we do not have memory for any particular experienced frequencies with sampling of abstract gambles (or the capability of retrieving examples of abstract gambles from our memory, even though abstract gambles have typically been used in decision-making research), unrealistic gain insurance scenarios or low-accessibility risks.

The concept of *accessibility* originates from research on memory (Koriat, 1993; Tulving & Pearlstone, 1966) and social cognition (Higgins, 1996; Schwarz, 1998). According to Tulving and Pearlstone's theoretical framework, it is important to draw a distinction between what information or what traces are available in memory storage and what are accessible. Based on one experiment ($N = 948$), they proposed that availability refers to whether information is stored in memory, whereas *accessibility* is the ease of retrieving information that is available. This distinction parallels that between retention and recall or the distinction between trace storage and trace utilization.

More recent developments in *accessibility* (Koriat, 1993, 1995; Koriat & Levy-Sadot, 2001) report that when participants fail to recall an answer, their judgments of feeling-of-knowing are based on the amount and intensity of the partial information accessed in the course of the search for the target. The assumption is that even if the retrieval attempt is unsuccessful, it may generate a variety of partial clues and activations, such as fragments of the target (e.g., semantic and episodic attributes). These partial clues may induce the subjective feeling that the target is stored in memory although there is no direct access to the accuracy of the partial clues that come to mind.

In social-cognition research, *accessibility* is defined as the activation potential of available knowledge (Higgins, 1996; Schwarz, 1998). This definition is useful because it separates the concepts of *accessibility* and availability, which are often confused. However, in distinguishing the availability heuristic (Tversky & Kahneman, 1973) from accessibility, Kahneman (2003) described *accessibility* as a continuum that has characteristics of perception and of the intuitive system; specifically, *accessibility* might be viewed as an intuitive judgment or preference where particular solutions come to mind. There appears to be a lack of evidence that the most accessible features are also the most relevant to making a good decision.

It is difficult for humans to make judgments about given real-world options and their possible outcomes. The complexity of the real-world environment, our risk preferences and individual experience make the decision process an arduous task. In contemplating most real-world risks, people suffer from a lack of knowledge about the probabilities of hazardous events (e.g., natural disaster, health and safety risk). As a consequence, most of our decisions will be based on accessibility of the frequencies of real-world observations - often via news reports on TV, newspapers and advertisements. Recent results (Kusev et al., 2007) show that risk exaggeration is caused by experienced frequencies and their accessibility in memory. We could explain the exaggeration of the risk of hazardous events by assuming that instances of some protectable risks are encountered in everyday life disproportionately frequently. The findings indicate that people estimate probability differently and are willing to drastically exaggerate given real-world high-frequency risks even when the probabilities are known and fairly presented.

The evidence presented by Kusev et al. (2006, 2007) demonstrates that individuals magnify the probability of given protective options compared to probabilities in hypothetical gamble scenarios in the domain of loss. In contrast, the well-known fourfold pattern of risk attitudes (Tversky & Kahneman, 1992; Tversky & Fox, 1995) suggests predominantly risk-seeking preferences for losses with medium-sized and large probabilities (see Table 1). People's risk preferences in hypothetical decision tasks (gambles), when using a repeated measures design - including a mix of trials with losses and trials with gains, are characterized by risk-seeking behavior for small ($p \leq .1$) probabilities of gains and risk-aversion for small ($p \leq .1$) probabilities of loss, as well as risk-aversive behavior for high ($p \geq .5$) probabilities of gains and a risk-seeking predilection for high ($p \geq. 5$) probabilities of loss (see Table 1) (Tversky & Kahneman, 1992; Tversky & Fox, 1995). However, people's protective choice behavior (Kusev et al., 2006, 2007), as represented in Figure 4 and Table 2, highly overweights small and moderate probabilities and underweights or almost behaves neutrally in response to high probabilities; the pattern of risk-seeking preferences in protective decision-making (see Table 2) is different from that in abstract gambles (see Table 1).

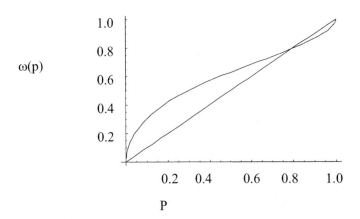

Figure 4. Probability-weighting function for protective decision-making tasks (Kusev et al., 2006, 2007). *Note.* ω(p): humans' estimate of probability.

Table 2. Risk-Seeking and Risk-Averse Choices for Hypothetical and Protective Decision-Making Tasks (Kusev et al., 2006, 2007)

	p =.01	.01 < p ≤ .1	p ≥ .5	p =.01	.01 < p ≤ .1	p ≥ .5
	Hypothetical, gain			Hypothetical, loss		
Risk-seeking	78%[a]	57%	11%	13%	30%	88%[a]
Risk-averse	22%	43%	89%[a]	87%[a]	70%	12%
	Protective, gain			Protective, loss		
Risk-seeking	76%	56%	7%	0%	12%	45%
Risk-averse	24%	44%	93%	100%	88%	55%

Note. Percentages are mean values. The pattern of results shows similarity among tasks in risk-seeking with gain, but inconsistency among tasks in risk-seeking preferences with loss.
[a] Values corresponding to the fourfold pattern of risk-seeking (Tversky & Kahneman, 1992).

In the past few decades, the question how people make decisions and deal with real-world choice options has become of fundamental significance to cognitive psychologists. Although it seems that the existing theories, models and concepts are adequate and well established, recent debate in decision-making demonstrates that we are far away from any general behavioral conclusions regarding core decision-making dimensions such as value or utility, probability, loss and gain.

People's incapacity to simultaneously deal with complex multidimensional tasks and the failure of existing models to explain the complexity of real-world decisions in terms of value, probability, loss and gamble motivated the notions presented in this chapter. Kusev et al. (2006, 2007) identified two independent probability-related psychological constructs: *probability discriminability* and *protective willingness*, which together affect probability-weighting for protective decision-making, resulting in significant overweighting of probability. Descriptive and normative models fail to explain the probability-weighting function for this type decision-making (see Figure 4), in which small and moderate probabilities are highly overweighted and higher probabilities are almost accurately estimated.

5. CONCLUSION

The normative approach to the study of decision-making (EUT, SEUT) does not distinguish between rational and human decision-making. The descriptive psychological approach (PT, CPT) does account for various violations of normative theory by human decision-making, but does not distinguish between decision-making in hypothetical and given real-world tasks.

Various theoretical approaches contribute to an explanation of decision-making in protective decision-making. In contrast to hypothetical decision-making, protective decision-making appears to be influenced by emotions, conceptualized for example as fear and prudence (Kunreuther, 2001), and hope and fear (Viscusi & Chesson, 1999). Furthermore, more than one decision-making parameter affects humans' risk preferences, in particular protective willingness is involved in protective decision-making (Kusev et al., 2006, 2007). The exaggeration of the risk of hazardous events can be explained by assuming that instances of some protectable risks are encountered in everyday life disproportionately frequently. In deciding about real-world risks, people suffer from a lack of knowledge about the probabilities of hazardous events, indicating that risk exaggeration is caused by experienced frequencies and their accessibility in memory.

Future research should investigate the range of situations under which risk exaggeration occurs and the influence of experience and accessibility in different tasks. It is important therefore that any future research expands the scope of enquiry to include data from populations with more varied demographic characteristics, using a range of decision environments (e.g., real-world applications and computer-controlled individually administered experiments).

REFERENCES

Abdellaoui, M. (2000). Parameter free elicitation of utilities and probability weighting functions. *Management Science, 46*, 1497-1512.

Allais, M. (1953). Le comportment de l'homme rational devant le risqué: Critique des postulats et axioms de l'ecole americaine. *Econometrica, 21*, 503-546.

Ayton, P. (2005). Judgment and decision making. In N. Braisby & A. Gellatly (Eds.), *Cognitive psychology* (pp. 382-413). New York: Oxford University Press.

Baron, J., Gurmankin, A. & Kunreuther, H. (2007). The comparative approach to protective behavior. *Journal of Behavioral Decision Making* (under review).

Bernoulli, D. (1954). Exposition of a new theory on the measurement of risk. *Econometrica, 22*, 23-36. (Original work published 1738)

Camerer, C., Babcock, L., Loewenstein, G. & R. Thaler. R. (1997). Labor supply of New York City cabdrivers: One day at a time. *Quarterly Journal of Economics, 112*, 407-41.

Camerer, C. F. & Ho, T. H. (1994). Violations of the betweenness axiom and nonlinearity in probability. *Journal of Risk and Uncertainty, 8*, 167-196.

Camerer, C.F. & Kunreuther, H.C. (1989). Experimental markets for insurance. *Journal of Risk and Uncertainty, 2*, 265-300.

Charlin, B., Tardiff, J., & Boshuizen, H. (2000). Scripts and medical diagnostic knowledge: Theory and applications for clinical reasoning instruction and research. *Academic Medicine, 75*, 182–190.

Dougherty, M. R. P., Gettys, C. F. & Ogden, E. E. (1999). MINERVA-DM: A memory process model for judgments of likelihood. *Psychological Review, 106*, 180-209.

Ellsberg, D. (1961). Risk, ambiguity, and the Savage axioms. *Quarterly Journal of Economics, 75*, 643-79.

Fiedler, K. (2000). Beware of samples! A cognitive-ecological sampling theory of judgment biases. *Psychological Review, 107*, 659-676.

Frisch, D. (1993). Reasons for framing effects. *Organizational Behavior and Human Decision Processes, 54*, 399-429.

Frisch, D. & Jones, S.K. (1993). Assessing the accuracy of decisions. *Theory and Psychology, 3*, 115-135.

Garner, W. R. (1954). Context effects and the validity of loudness scales. *Journal of Experimental Psychology, 48*, 218-224.

Gilboa, I. & Schmeidler, D. (2001). *A theory of case-based decisions*. New York, Cambridge University Press.

Gonzalez, R. & Wu, G. (1999). On the shape of the probability weighting function. *Cognitive Psychology, 38*, 129-166.

Grether, D.M. & Plott, C.R. (1979). Economic theory of choice and the preference reversal phenomenon. *American Economic Review, 69*, 623-638.

Helson, H. (1964). *Adaptation-level theory*. New York: Harper & Row.

Hershey, J.C., Kunreuther, H.C. & Schoemaker, P. (1982). Sources of bias in assessment procedures for utility functions. *Management science, 28*, 936-954.

Hertwig, R., Barron, G., Weber, E. & Erev, I. (2004). Decisions from experience and the effect of rare events in risky choice. *Psychological Science, 15*, 534-539.

Hertwig, R., Pachur, T., & Kurzenhäuser, S. (2005). Judgments of risk frequencies: Test of possible cognitive mechanisms. *Journal of Experimental Psychology: Learning, Memory, and Cognition, 4*, 621-642.

Higgins, E. T. (1996). Knowledge activation: Accessibility, applicability, and salience. In E. T. Higgins & A. Kruglanski (Eds.), *Social psychology: Handbook of basic principles* (pp. 133-168). New York: Guilford.

Hogarth, R. M. & H. Kunreuther. (1989). "Risk, Ambiguity and Insurance," *Journal of Risk and Uncertainty 2*, 5-35.

Johnson, E., Gachter, S. & Herrmann, A. (2006). Exploring the nature of loss aversion. Manuscript in preparation.

Johnson, E. J., Hershey, J., Meszaros, J. & Kunreuther, H. (1992). Framing, probability distortions, and insurance decision. *Journal of Risk and Uncertainty, 7*, 35-51.

Kahneman, D. (2003). A perspective on judgment and choice: Mapping bounded rationality. *American Psychologist, 58*, 697-720.

Kahneman, D. & Tversky, A. (1979). Prospect theory: An analysis of decision under risk. *Econometrica, 47*, 263-291.

Kahneman, D. & Tversky, A. (1984). Choices, values, and frames. *American Psychologist, 39,* 341-350.

Koriat, A. (1993). How do we know that we know? The accessibility model of the feeling of knowing. *Psychological Review, 100,* 609-639.

Koriat, A. (1995). Dissociating knowing and the feeling of knowing: Further evidence for the accessibility model. *Journal of Experimental Psychology: General, 124,* 311-333.

Koriat, A. & Levy-Sadot, R. (2001). The combined contributions of the cue-familiarity and accessibility heuristics to feeling of knowing. *Journal of Experimental Psychology: Learning, Memory, and Cognition, 1,* 34-53.

Kunreuther, H. (2001). Protective decisions: Fear or prudence. In Hoch, S., & Kunreuther, H. (Eds.), *Wharton on Making Decisions.* New York: Wiley.

Kusev, P., Ayton, P., van Schaik, P. & Chater, N. (2006). Taking precautions is not the same as choosing gambles: Prospect theory and use of probability in risky choices. *The 37th Annual Conference of the Society for Judgment and Decision Making.* Houston, Texas. November 17-20, 2006.

Kusev, P., Ayton, P., van Schaik, P. & Chater, N. (2007). Exaggerated risk. *The 21st Bi-annual Conference on Subjective Probability, Utility and Decision Making.* Warsaw. August 19-23, 2007.

Lichtenstein, S. & Slovic, P. (1971). Reversal of preference between bids and choices in gambling decisions. *Journal of Experimental Psychology, 89,* 46-55.

List, J. A. (2003). Does market experience eliminate market anomalies? *Quarterly Journal of Economics, 118,* 41-71.

List, J. A. (2004). Neoclassical theory versus prospect theory. Evidence from the marketplace. *Econometrica, 72,* 615-625.

Medin, D. L. & Schaffer, M. M. (1978). Context theory of classification learning. *Psychological Review, 85,* 207-238.

Murray, M. (1972). Empirical utility functions and insurance consumption decisions. *Journal of Risk and Uncertainty, 1,* 31-41.

Neter, J., Williams, C. A. & Whitmore, G. A. (1968). Comparison of independent and joint decision-making for two insurance decisions. *Journal of Risk and Uncertainty, 1,* 87-105.

Nosofsky, R. M. (1986). Attention, similarity, and the identification-categorization relationship. *Journal of Experimental Psychology: General, 115,* 39-57.

Plous, S. (1993). *The psychology of judgment and decision making.* New York: McGraw-Hill.

Prelec, D. (1998). The probability weighting function. *Econometrica, 66,* 497-527.

Quiggin, J. (1982). A Theory of Anticipated Utility. *Journal of Economic Behavior and Organization 3,* 323-343.

Savage, L. (1954). *The foundations of statistics,* New York, Wiley.

van Schaik P., Flynn D., van Wersch A., Douglass, A. & Cann, P. (2005). The influence of illness script components and medical practice on medical decision-making. *Journal of Experimental Psychology: Applied, 11,* 187-199.

Schwarz, N. (1998). Accessible content and accessibility experiences: The interplay of declarative and experiential information in judgment. *Personality and Social Psychology Review, 2,* 87-99.

Simon, H. A. (1955). A behavioral model of rational choice. *Quarterly Journal of Economics, 69,* 99-118.

Simon, H. A. (1956). Rational choice and the structure of the environment. *Psychological Review, 63,* 129-138.

Slovic, P. (1987). Perception of risk. Science, 236, 280-285.

Slovic, P. (2000). The perception of risk. London: Earthscan publication.

Slovic, P., Fischhoff, B. & Lichtenstein, S. (1987). Behavioral decision theory perspectives on protective behavior. In N.D. Weinstein (Ed.), *Taking care: Understanding and encouraging self-protective behavior* (pp. 14-41). New York: Cambridge University Press.

Stewart, N., Chater, N., & Brown, G. D. A. (2006). Decision by sampling. *Cognitive Psychology, 53,* 1-26.

Tulving, E. & Pearlstone, Z. (1966). Availability versus accessibility of information in memory for words. *Journal of Verbal Learning and Verbal Behavior, 5,* 381-391.

Tversky, A. (1969). Intransitivity of preferences. *Psychological Review, 76,* 31-48.

Tversky, A. & Fox, C. R. (1995). Weighting risk and uncertainty. *Psychological Review, 102,* 269-283.

Tversky, A. & Kahneman, D. (1973). Availability: A heuristic for judging frequency and probability. *Cognitive Psychology, 5,* 207-232.

Tversky, A. & Kahneman, D. (1981). The framing of decisions and the psychology of choice. *Science, 211,* 453-458.

Tversky, A. & Kahneman, D. (1986). Rational choice and the framing of decisions. *Journal of Business, 59,* 251-278.

Tversky, A. & Kahneman, D. (1991). Loss aversion in riskless choice: A reference dependent model. *Quarterly Journal of Economics, 106,* 1039-1061.

Tversky, A. & Kahneman, D. (1992). Advances in prospect theory: Cumulative representation of uncertainty. *Journal of Risk and Uncertainty, 5,* 204-217.

Tversky, A. & Koehler, D. J. (1994). Support theory: A nonextensional representation of subjective probability. *Psychological Review, 101,* 547-567.

Tversky, A. & Wakker, P. (1995). Risk attitudes and decision weights. *Econometrica, 63,* 1255-1280.

Viscusi, K. & Chesson, H. (1999). Hopes and fears: The conflicting effects of risk ambiguity. *Theory and Decision, 47,* 153-178.

Viscusi, W. K. (1995). Government action, biases in risk perception, and insurance decisions. The *Geneva Papers on Risk and Insurance Theory, 20,* 93-110.

von Neumann, J. & Morgenstern O. (1947). *Theory of games and economic behavior.* Princeton, N.J., Princeton University Press, 2nd Edition.

Wakker, P. (2003). The data of Levy and Levy (2003) "Prospect theory: Much ado about nothing?" actually support prospect theory. *Management Science, 49,* 979-981.

Wakker P.P., Thaler, R.H. & Tversky A. (1997). Probabilistic insurance. *Journal of risk and uncertainty, 15,* 7-28.

Wu, G. & Gonzalez, R. (1996). Curvature of the Probability Weighting Function. *Management Science, 42,* 1676-1690.

Yaari, M. (1987). The dual theory of choice under risk. *Econometrica 55,* 95-117.

In: Psychology of Decision Making in Education
Editor: Jeanine A. Elsworth, pp. 207-226

ISBN: 978-1-60021-933-7
© 2006 Nova Science Publishers, Inc.

Chapter 9

EXPLORING GENDER DIFFERENCES IN DECISION-MAKING USING THE IOWA GAMBLING TASK

Ruud van den Bos, Esther den Heijer,*
Suzanne Vlaar and Bart Houx

Ethology & Welfare, Faculty of Veterinary Sciences, Utrecht University, Yalelaan 2, NL-3584 CM Utrecht, the Netherlands

ABSTRACT

Human and non-human animals essentially face the same problem: how to find the best long-term option within an environment that contains uncertainty for relevant items. Against this background the Iowa Gambling Task is a biologically relevant task to study such decision-making processes. We have recently developed an animal analogue of this task in rodents. An interesting cross-species finding in this task is that performance differences exist between males and females: while males tend to focus exclusively on long-term goals, females tend to balance short- and long-term interests, in other words males shift from exploration to exploitation, while females remain exploratory. In this chapter we try to answer the question what may underlie these differences between males and females, focussing thereby on humans. First, we discuss a neurobehavioural model for the Iowa Gambling Task. Subsequently, we look at the contribution of the menstrual cycle using both data from the literature and an experiment that we conducted. We conclude that the menstrual cycle is not a decisive factor for these differences to occur. Finally, we discuss the possibility that differences in choice behaviour may be due to differences in the general dynamics of neurotransmitter systems. Based on recent experiments we conclude that differences in brain serotonergic and dopaminergic activity may contribute to the observed behavioural differences.

---

* Correspondence to: Ethology & Welfare, Faculty of Veterinary Sciences, Utrecht University, Yalelaan 2, NL-3584 CM Utrecht, the NetherlandsTel: ++31-30-2534373; fax: ++31-30-2539227; e-mail: r.vandenbos@vet.uu.nl

INTRODUCTION

The Iowa Gambling Task (IGT) was originally developed as tool to diagnose patients suffering from lesions in the ventromedial prefrontal cortex (VMF; Bechara et al., 1994). Patients with such lesions are characterised in their everyday life by the absence of establishing profitable long-term behavioural strategies in both social and non-social affairs (Damasio, 1994). The Iowa Gambling Task was meant to model the development of everyday life long-term profitable strategies. Test subjects have to develop a long-term profitable monetary scenario in a situation of uncertainty and a conflict between the chance of encountering an immediate large reward (100$) in two long-term losing decks (A and B; -250$ per 10 cards) and the chance of encountering an immediate small reward (50$) in two long-term winning decks (C and D; +250$ per 10 cards; Bechara et al., 1994). Normal subjects develop a preference for the so called 'good' or advantageous decks C and D over the course of the experiment, while VMF patients do not (Bechara et al., 1994).

While much effort has been devoted to substantiate and characterize the effects observed in VMF patients using physiological measurements, such as skin conductance responses, and by comparing the test results of VMF patients with those of patients suffering from other kinds of brain lesions (Bechara et al., 1997, 1998, 1999, 2000; Clark et al., 2003; Manes et al., 2002; Tranel et al., 2000, 2002), little effort has been devoted to put the test in a biological context. Yet, this test may be positioned in the context of animal research that studies similar phenomena, such as optimal foraging and risk sensitive foraging: how to find the best long-term strategy in an environment in which costs and benefits vary at different sites and at different times (Van den Bos, 2004).

Inglis and colleagues (1997, 2001) have described a model of animal exploration and foraging behaviour in an environment containing uncertainty, i.e. *the information primacy model*, which in essence may capture the problem underlying the Iowa Gambling Task. In short, uncertainty in environments arises because of three factors: fluctuating patch quality (broadly taken as overall cost-benefit relationships), location specificity (broadly taken as spatio-temporal stimuli characterising a location), and recency of information (broadly taken as 'when was I here last time'). To reduce uncertainty to zero – Has a site changed in quality? Have stimuli characterising a site changed? Have I been here before today? - an individual should be everywhere anytime. However, as this is physically impossible, and runs right against fulfilling physiological needs, such as obtaining enough food, daytime ongoing behaviour is a compromise between 'information gathering' and 'satisfying physiological needs': when hungry go to the best sites, i.e. the easiest to find sites with the lowest cost-benefit ratios, when not, or less, hungry, explore - update information - and eat while on the way. All information gathered on the way might be useful at a later stage (De Valois, 1954). So, in order to be successful the organism has to build a cognitive and affective map of its surroundings which contains the 'when, where, what' and 'what's the value' features of environmental stimuli respectively.

The Iowa Gambling task may be seen as an environment that contains uncertainty and through exploration the individual has to decipher what this environment looks like. The order of win and loss cards per deck differs per block of 10 cards and no information is present which indicates that decks will remain the same throughout the game. The individual has to pay attention to the amount of money he or she has (cf. a physiological need), and create and update an 'affective' and a 'cognitive' map.

In this chapter we explore differences between men and women in IGT performance. For, such differences have been reported in the literature (Bechara and Martin, 2004; Bolla et al., 2004; Reavis and Overman, 2001; Overman, 2004; Overman et al., 2004, 2006). Figure 1 shows the results of our own studies (data from Van den Bos, 2004; Van den Bos et al., 2006a) which are in line with those from the literature: regardless of the specific experimental set up, it turns out that female subjects take more cards from the disadvantageous decks than male subjects, especially in the second half of the task. One could therefore argue that male subjects shift their behaviour from exploration to exploitation while female subjects remain exploratory. In an animal analogue of this task we observed similar gender differences in mice (Van den Bos et al., 2006b) and rats (unpublished data; see later sections of this chapter).

Choices from disadvantageous decks

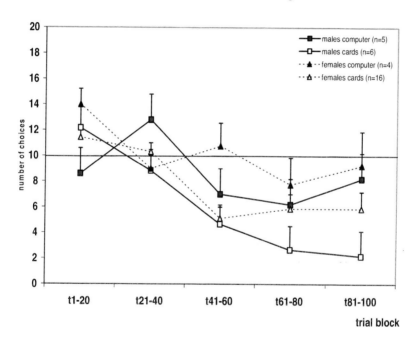

Figure 1. IGT test performance in men and women expressed as the number of cards taken from decks A and B (AB) per block of 20 choices (mean+SEM). The data are taken from two experiments (Van den Bos, 2004; Van den Bos et al., 2006a). Differences existed between the two experiments. In the cards-experiment (Van den Bos, 2004) subjects were subjected to the original experiment using cards as described by Bechara et al. (1994). In the computer-experiment (Van den Bos et al., 2006a) subjects were subjected to a computerised version. Subjects in the first experiment were older (average age±SEM: 36.3±2.4 yr) than subjects in the second experiment (average age±SEM: 27.2±3.0 yr). Statistical analysis revealed that regardless of gender or experiment subjects chose fewer and fewer AB cards as the IGT progressed (three-way ANOVA with gender and experiment as independent factors and trial-block as repeated measurement: $F(4,108)= 9.978$, $p \leq 0.001$). Regardless of experiment women chose more AB cards than men ($F(1,27)=4.622$, $p \leq 0.041$), whereas regardless of gender subjects chose more AB cards in the computer than in the cards version ($F(1,27)=10.670$, $p \leq 0.003$). The latter may be age- rather than version-related (see Crone & Van der Molen, 2004).

In the following sections we shall explore what may underlie these differences. First, we will present a neurobehavioural model of the performance in the IGT. Subsequently we will discuss as well as present data that the menstrual cycle may not contribute to the observed differences. We will then turn to the question what exactly may characterize the performance differences between males and females using a recently developed formal mathematical model to analyse IGT behaviour. We will conclude that men and women may engender different strategies to approach problems such as presented in the IGT and that differences in neurotransmitter activity may explain differences in performance between men and women.

THE IOWA GAMBLING TASK: A NEUROBEHAVIOURAL MODEL

Thus far studies have shown that the amygdala and ventromedial prefrontal cortex are important structures in developing a choice for the long-term winning decks C and D (Bechara et al., 1997, 1998, 1999). It has recently been shown that reducing dopamine levels in healthy volunteers by a mixture containing the branched-chain amino acids (BCAA) valine, isoleucine and leucine led to more choices for the disadvantageous decks (Sevy et al., 2006). Earlier findings suggested that the dopaminergic system may be important in the early stages of the test (Bechara et al., 2001), i.e. when representations may be formed of the different options (Sevy et al., 2006). As discussed by others this dopaminergic activity may also be related to exploring the different decks and responding to rewards (Fiorillo et al., 2003). The ventral striatum may also be critically involved herein (Knutson et al., 2001).

A serotonergic component appears to be present in the later stages of the test (Bechara et al., 2001). This serotonergic activity may be related to regulating the extent to which individuals continue or maintain their choice behaviour for the best long-term option, as opposed to being tempted to visit the long-term losing decks that contain immediate large rewards, i.e. self-control, as serotonin has been implicated in controlling levels of impulsive behaviour (Higley et al., 1996a,b; Mehlman et al., 1994, 1995) or controlling the extent to which mesolimbic dopaminergic activity gains control over behaviour (Katz, 1999). Recent studies in female rats in which serotonin levels have been elevated in the brain by genetically affecting serotonin-reuptake are in line with these findings (Homberg et al., 2007; see later sections of this chapter). The dorsolateral prefrontal cortex may be critically involved in this later stage of the test as well (Ernst et al., 2002; McClure et al., 2004; Ridderinkhof et al., 2004).

The differential involvement of these neurotransmitter systems suggests a transition from one set of neuronal structures to another as the test progresses, i.e. from the reward system, necessary for learning the best long-term option by assessing and integrating trial-by-trial wins and losses, to a cognitive control system, aiding in maintaining to choose once chosen options for which pay-off lies ahead in the future (Figure 2; Bechara & Damasio, 2002; Ernst et al., 2002; McClure et al., 2004; Ridderinkhof et al., 2004; Tanaka et al., 2004; Tranel et al., 2000; Shizgal & Arvanitogiannis, 2003). McClure and colleagues (2004) have demonstrated that the activity of this cognitive control system (delta system in their nomenclature) is stronger than the activity of the reward system (beta system) when decisions are made for options where pay-off lies ahead in the future, while the beta system has a slightly higher activity than the delta system when decisions are made for which pay-off is immediate. The

IGT contains a conflict between immediate and long-term pay-off. It has been shown that individual differences exist in the extent to which subjects are able to withhold responding to the immediate pay-offs of the disadvantageous decks (Bechara & Damasio, 2002; Van den Bos, 2004; Crone et al., 2004).

Neurobehavioural Model of the IGT

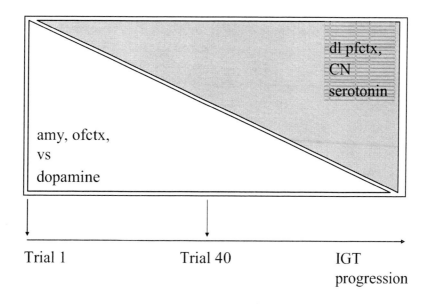

Figure 2. Neurobehavioural model of the IGT. The horizontal axis represents the progression of the task. The upper and lower triangle represent the relative contribution of the different brain systems which may be involved in the different stages of the test, learning the relevant task-features and choosing cards from the long-term winning decks (see text for further explanation). Abbreviations: amy: amygdala; ofctx: orbitofrontal cortex; vs: ventral striatum; dl pfctx: dorsolateral prefrontal cortex; CN: caudate nucleus.

We have not as yet validated all aspects of the model (Van den Bos et al., 2006a; Van den Bos & De Ridder, 2006). However, we do have data supporting features of the model.

Firstly, we conducted a recent study on the relationship between dieting and self-control (Kuijer et al., 2007). This study revealed that self-control moderated IGT choice behaviour of women scoring high or low on food restraint in the second half of the test (trials 41-100) but not the first half (trials 1-40). Women scoring high on restraint with low self-reported self-control took more cards from the disadvantageous decks in the second half of the task than women scoring high on restraint who also scored high on self-reported self-control (Kuijer et al., 2007). These data are in line with the model, as they show that self-control plays an important role in the second but not the first half of the task.

Secondly, data from a recent student-practical experiment revealed that stimulating elements of the reward system in the second half of the task disrupted task performance (Van den Bos & Houx, unpublished data). In this experiment we presented young male subjects (average age ±SEM: 22.4±0.3 yr, n=90 subjects) at trials 41, 61 and 81, i.e. during the second half of the task, blocks of three pictures each consisting of beautiful ('hot') or average ('not') women. As control pictures, pictures of flowers were used. Participants were awarded 3 Euro upon completion of the task. In addition they received 1 Euro for every 1000 Euro they earned in the task. We used the computerised form of the standard IGT (for details see Bechara et al., 1994; Van den Bos et al., 2006a). It has been reported that pictures of beautiful women enhance activity in the ventral striatum of men, which is related to their willingness to exert effort for viewing them (Aharon et al., 2001) and may be related to an activated mesolimbic ventral striatal dopamine system, which subserves willingness to exert effort, even up to the point of risk-taking behaviour or tolerating negative cost-benefit outcomes (Cardinal et al., 2001; Fiorillo et al., 2003; Matthews et al., 2004; Richards et al., 1999; Salamone & Correa, 2002; Spruijt et al., 2001). So, we predicted that pictures of beautiful women may compromise men's monetary decision-making, as these pictures weaken cognitive control, needed to maintain a long-term perspective, by activating the ventral striatum and increase the temptation to engage in less than optimal options. In a recent study such an effect was observed using a temporal discounting paradigm (Wilson & Daly, 2004). Men settled for a smaller immediate amount of money after viewing pictures of beautiful women than after viewing pictures of average women. It would appear that they tolerate a less than optimal cost-benefit balance. The results of our study are shown in Figure 3. The men clearly rated the pictures of beautiful women higher than those of average women, which is in line with literature findings (Figure 3, panel A; cf. Wilson & Daly, 2004). No differences were observed with respect to viewing times for the different pictures, suggesting that IGT effects were not related to attentional differences for the different classes of pictures or mnemonic differences for the different classes of pictures due to the fact that the task was interrupted (Figure 3, panel B). The data from the IGT showed that viewing pictures of beautiful women slightly increased risk-taking behaviour compared to viewing pictures of average women or flowers (Figure 3, panel C). It is clear that the effect was small, which is partly due to the fact that the range over which disturbances may be found in this age group is small, given that the performance after 100 trials is still poor in males as also shown in Figure 1 (cf. Crone & Van der Molen, 2004). Thus any factor interfering with their performance may mask the results. During the student-practicals many disturbing factors were present. Indeed, a replication of this study in another student-practical may have failed for this reason. Nevertheless, the present data are in line with the prediction of the model.

THE MENSTRUAL CYCLE AS A FACTOR IN THE IOWA GAMBLING TASK

So, if the model holds, one obvious explanation for the difference between men and women therefore would be the way these brain systems operate in men and women. As dopaminergic and serotonergic activity fluctuate across the menstrual/oestrus cycle in humans and animals (Becker, 1999; Dluzen & Ramirez, 1985; Fernández-Ruiz et al., 1991; Ho et al., 2001; Justice & De Wit, 1999; Nördstrom et al., 1998; Rubinow et al., 1998; Shimizu & Bray, 1993; Thompson & Moss, 1997) we hypothesised that the performance of women may depend on the phase of their menstrual cycle.

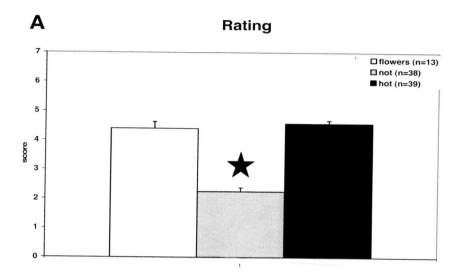

Figure 3, panel A: Mean (+SEM) rating scores of pictures offered during the second half of the IGT (scale 1-7; see text). Pictures were taken from the 'hot/not' internet site (cf. Daly & Wilson, 2004). Beautiful women ('hot') were ranked >9 at this site, average ('not') women <5 (scale:1-10). One-way ANOVA: $F(2,87)=106.077$, $p\leq0.001$; *: $p\leq0.05$, significantly different from the other two groups (Student-Newman Keuls test).

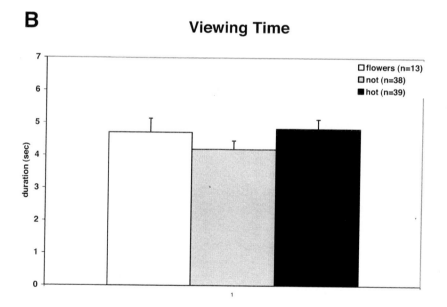

Figure 3, panel B: Mean (+SEM) picture viewing times of pictures offered during the second half of the IGT (see text). One-way ANOVA: $F(2,87)=1.453$, NS.

C Relative Performance Trial 41-100 Versus Trial 1-40

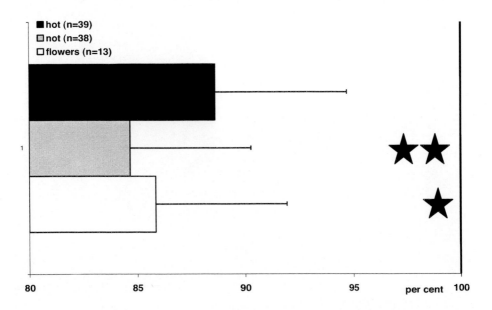

Figure 3, panel C: Mean (+SEM) per cent of choices from the disadvantageous decks during trials that were intermitted by pictures of hot- and not-women or flowers (trial 41-100) compared to baseline (trial 1-40). Statistics were paired t-tests (hot: t=1.879, df=38, p≤0.07; not: t=2.742, df=37, p≤0.009; flowers: t=2.335, df=12, p≤0.038). Initially data were expressed as the number of choices from the disadvantageous decks per block of 20 trials. We noted that the hot-group did not improve its performance from blocks 1 and 2 to blocks 3, 4 and 5. The not-group did improve its performance but more weakly than expected which may have been due to the presentation of the pictures. This masked the difference between the hot- and not-group. Therefore we decided to analyse the data using a within-subject analysis. We compared the average scores of blocks 1 and 2 with the average scores of block 3, 4 and 5. This is shown in the figure.

Data of one recent study suggested that the menstrual cycle has no effect on choosing cards from disadvantageous decks in the IGT (Reavis & Overman, 2001). However, the absence of an effect may depend on the magnitude of reward used. We showed that by increasing the differences between the immediate rewards of decks A and B versus decks C and D, risk-taking behaviour may be enhanced which could be due to a prolonged or increased dopaminergic activity (Van den Bos et al., 2006a). Female subjects are more sensitive to stimulation of dopaminergic activity in the follicular than the luteal phase of the menstrual cycle (Justice & De Wit, 1999; White et al., 2002). We therefore tested female subjects in the follicular and luteal phase in a within design using the IGT with increased reward magnitude differences (Van den Bos et al., 2006a). We hypothesised that subjects would make more choices for disadvantageous options in the follicular than the luteal phase of the menstrual cycle. We also tested subjects in a newly developed 'speed IGT' in order to explore the effect of a different type of reward. We reasoned that increased or decreased computer speed as reward or punishment would affect the subjects more directly than the more indirect wins and losses of abstract money. We expected that this 'speed IGT' would be more sensitive to potential effects of the menstrual cycle. We hypothesised that subjects would make more choices for disadvantageous options in the follicular than the luteal phase of the menstrual cycle.

Forty-one female subjects (average age±SEM: 21.5±0.5 yr) fulfilling strict criteria with respect to cycle irregularities, mood disorders and drug use, were tested in the follicular phase (until day 9 after menses) and luteal phase (day 3-8 before menses). We used two versions of the Iowa Gambling Task, i.e. the standard 'money IGT' and the newly developed 'speed IGT'.

The basic instructions of the 'speed IGT' were similar as to those of the 'money IGT'. The overall goal in the 'speed IGT' was to keep the speed of a black square (puppet) at a high level rather than earning as much money as possible as in the 'money IGT'. On a computer screen subjects saw four coloured boxes ('food patches') that were connected by a central area. At the start of each trial the puppet was present in the middle of the central area. When subjects clicked on one of the four boxes using the mouse the puppet would move towards that box. Subjects could then obtain 'good' or 'bad' food by their choice instead of winning or losing money. While 'good' food increased the puppet's speed, 'bad' food slowed it down. Upon returning to the central area the puppet would adopt its new speed as well as on its journey to the next box in the next trial. The monetary values of the original IGT were used to calculate increases and decreases in speed. The feedback that subjects obtained was the same as for the 'money IGT' in terms of absolute values, so they could see whether they had wins or losses. The puppet's speed was indicated graphically by a speedometer as well as numerically by a value to the left of the boxes. The four boxes represented the four decks of cards of the 'money IGT': upper left: A (green), upper right: B (blue), lower left: C (red) and lower right: D (orange-brown). A bar and numbers indicated how many choices remained for each box. Just as in the 'money IGT' 40 choices per box existed.

The experimental design was such that subjects either started with the 'money IGT' or the 'speed IGT' in either the follicular or the luteal phase according to a complete cross-over design. Thus they visited our institute twice. They were awarded course credits or money (6 Euro) upon completing the task.

A 4-way ANOVA [menstrual cycle phase, IGT-version, trial-block (repeated), visit-order (repeated)] showed that: (i) regardless of phase, IGT-version or visit-order, all subjects gradually decreased the number of choices from the disadvantageous options as the IGTs progressed (trial-block: $F(4,40)=8.559$, $p \leq 0.001$) and (ii) regardless of IGT-version or phase, subjects improved performance on their second IGT (visit-order: $F(1,35)=5.586$, $p \leq 0.024$). As the latter may mask phase differences, we analysed the subjects' performance separately for each visit.

Only for the first visit a menstrual cycle effect was found. The data are shown in Figure 4. It would appear that women performed better on the 'money IGT' in the follicular phase than the luteal phase while the opposite was true for the 'speed IGT', which was supported by a near significant ($F(4,148)=2.284$, $p \leq 0.063$) three-way interaction term, trial-block * phase * IGT-version. Subsequent two-way ANOVAs showed that only for blocks 3-5 of the 'speed IGT' significant differences existed between the follicular and luteal phase (phase: $F(1,19)=5.384$, $p \leq 0.032$). Furthermore, a significant trial-block effect ($F(4,76)=4.095$, $p \leq 0.005$) as well as IGT-version effect ($F(1,19)=6.986$, $p \leq 0.016$) was found for the follicular phase.

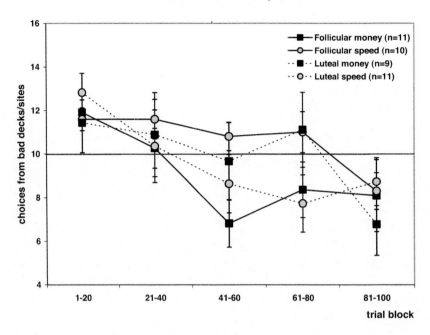

Figure 4: Mean (±SEM) number of choices from 'bad' decks/sites during the follicular and luteal phase. See text for further explanation.

In none of the analyses did the performance on the 'money IGT' differ from the performance on the 'speed IGT' per se, suggesting that the two Gambling Tasks are equivalent.

In line with earlier findings (Reavis & Overman, 2001) we did not observe clear menstrual cycle phase differences in performance on the 'money IGT', even when we increased the conflict between 'good' and 'bad' decks (Van den Bos et al., 2006a). If anything, we observed that women tended to perform more poorly on the 'speed IGT' in the follicular phase than the luteal phase. Whether this is related to differences in metabolic rate in these phases (Buffenstein et al., 1995) or differences in perceptual motor skills in these phases (Kimberly Epting & Overman, 1998) remains to be determined.

The fact that the menstrual cycle has little effect on IGT performance is supported by recent studies that suggest that gender differences in IGT performance already occur early in life, i.e. from the age of 7 years onwards (Crone et al., 2005; Overman, 2004; Overman et al., 2004), that is, well before the onset of puberty and the period in which the menstrual cycle starts.

Differences between Males and Females Revisited: Neurobiology

Having discarded the menstrual cycle as a possible confound in the monetary IGT, we now again turn to the question what may underlie performance differences between men and women. To this end we first describe the choice behaviour of men and women in slightly more detail. The test instruction in the IGT is to win as much money as possible. Figure 5 shows the amount of money won by men and women in the experiment that was shown in Figure 1. It is clear that men and women have earned the same amount of money at the end of the game. Also when the amount of money was analysed for the different trial blocks no differences were observed (data not shown). Thus in terms of complying with the task instructions no major differences existed between men and women. The only difference is that women take more cards from the disadvantageous decks than men, and thereby take the risk of losing money, yet in return gain information on whether the disadvantageous decks may have changed or not. In fact, a few cards from the disadvantageous decks, although the choices nevertheless are risky, may lead to high immediate pay-off. As we have argued earlier (Van den Bos, 2004) the performance in the IGT may be a balance between exploration and exploitation.

To assess whether men and women are differently sensitive to wins and losses, we analysed the data in Figure 1 using the Expectancy-Valence model (EV model; Stallen, 2006), which has been shown to be useful for analysing choice behaviour in the IGT (Busemeyer & Stout, 2002; Sevy et al., 2006; Yechiam et al., 2005).

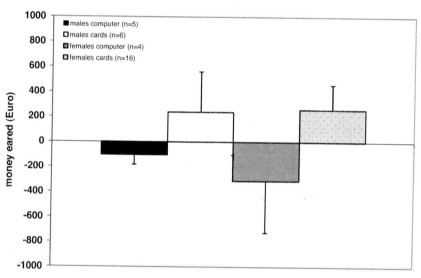

Amount of money earned after 100 trials

Figure 5: The mean (+SEM) amount of money earned after 100 trials. A two-way ANOVA [experiment, gender] revealed no significant differences: experiment: $F(1,27)=2.263$, NS; gender: $F(1,27)=0.093$, NS; experiment*gender: $F(1,27)=0.142$, NS.

In general the model seems to describe the behaviour of men better than that of women, as the percentage of subjects in which the model does not do better than a random model is higher in women than in men (women versus men: 35 % (n=20) versus 9.9% (n=11)), and the test-statistic (G^2 statistic; Busemeyer & Stout, 2002, page 258) that describes its usefulness is higher (but not significantly so) in men than in women for those individuals in which the EV model did better than a random model (mean ±SEM: men versus women: 43.7±12.1

(n=10) versus 26.8±6.0 (n=13)). This model contains three different parameters, each describing a different feature of task performance.

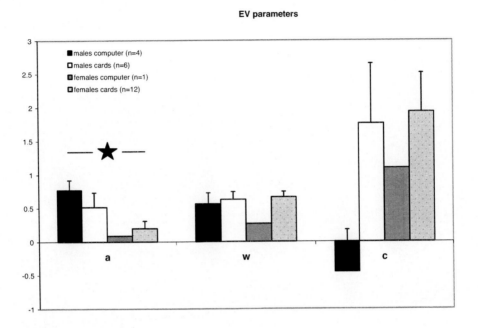

EV parameters

Figure 6: Mean (+SEM) values of different parameters from the Expectancy-Valence model. See text for an explanation on parameters a, w and c. Only for the learning rate parameter (a) a significant gender-difference was observed (two-way ANOVA [experiment, gender]: gender effect: $F(1,19)=$ 3.879, $p\leq0.064$; since in the computer version only one woman was present we also analysed the data using a one-way ANOVA with gender as factor: $F(1,21)=6.316$, $p\leq0.020$); gender effect: *$p\leq0.05$.

Firstly, the attention to losses/wins parameter *w*, which measures the relative weight given to losses and wins and ranges from 0 (attention to wins only) to 1 (attention to losses only). As Figure 6 shows no differences exist between men and women on this parameter. This suggests that women and men are equally sensitive to rewards or punishments. Indeed, when the original IGT was changed such that the immediate reward conflict between decks A and B versus C and D was eliminated by having only the chance to win 50 Euro maximally in all decks, while keeping the net gains and losses per 10 cards the same, i.e. –250 Euro (AB) and +250 Euro (CD), no differences were observed between men and women in choice behaviour (re-analysis of data of Van den Bos et al., 2006a), suggesting that women and men do not differ in at least their sensitivity to losses.

Secondly, the recency parameter *a*, which represents the updating rate of recent information. The value of this parameter ranges from 0 to 1. A value of 0 means long associative memories, that is, information of the valence of decks is kept over long lags of choices, and thus little updating of information. A value of 1 means short associative memories, rapid forgetting and a strong urge to update information. As Figure 6 shows, men show higher values on this parameter than women. This would suggest that women retain information of the valences of different decks across longer lags than men, i.e. women have longer associative memories than men.

Thirdly, the choice consistency parameter c, which measures how consistent subjects are in their choices across trials. This parameter is related to response mechanisms. Its value ranges from -5 to $+5$. Negative values mean that the subject's choices are random and not led by expectancies. Positive values mean that the subject behaves according to deck expectancies. No differences were observed between men and women on this parameter.

Thus is seems that only on the recency parameter men and women differ. As already mentioned above, it was recently shown that this parameter is sensitive to manipulation with the dopaminergic system (Sevy et al., 2006). Lowering dopaminergic activity led to higher values of the parameter and a weaker performance in the IGT, which was interpreted as being due to destabilizations of representations in the orbitofrontal cortex, and thereby to more attention to recent events (Sevy et al., 2006). Combined, the present data suggest that dopaminergic activity in women may be higher than in men while their performance appears to be worse than that of men as judged by the number of cards from disadvantageous decks. One way to reconcile this apparent contradiction is to suggest that females 'emotionally' know the differences between decks, but remain, despite this knowledge, exploratory or do not yet form a routine of choosing only cards from decks C and D. That is, they do not make the switch to the other system as readily as men do. This suggests that a difference with respect to serotonergic activity or dorsolateral prefrontal cortical activity may contribute to these differences in choice behaviour. Indeed, evidence for this may be found in the literature and our own experiments.

In the rodent version of the IGT, we observed that female rats chose the 'bad' arms more often than male rats as the rat-IGT progressed, as was also observed earlier in mice (Van den Bos et al., 2006b). However, female rats lacking the serotonin reuptake transporter gene completely (homozygous rats) or partially (heterozygous rats) showed a performance similar to that of male rats, that is, they gradually started to choose the 'good' arm more often as the rat-IGT progressed (Homberg et al., 2007). Reuptake of serotonin is an important mechanism for regulating serotonergic tone (Murphy et al., 2004). Both homozygote and heterozygote rats have higher levels of serotonin release in brain structures than wild-type rats (Homberg et al., unpublished data). These data suggest that an increase of brain serotonin levels in female rats leads to a suppression of the continuing tendency to explore.

Combined, the findings in rats and humans suggest gender differences in dopaminergic and serotonergic regulation, that is, in males the balance between the two systems might be in favour of serotonin, while in females this balance might be in favour of dopamine.

From the foregoing it may be predicted that differences between men and women disappear when the dopaminergic system is strongly activated in both sexes. In an earlier published study we increased reward magnitude differences between advantageous and disadvantageous decks (AB:CD=200:50 Euro or 300:50 Euro) while keeping the overall gains and losses per 10 cards of the different decks the same (AB:-250 Euro; CD: +250 Euro) to test how sensitive the emotional system is to manipulation (Van den Bos et al., 2006a). We hypothesised that the increased preference for the disadvantageous decks and concomitant increased loss of money was due to a strong activation of the dopaminergic system. When the data were reanalysed with women and men as a separate factor it turned out that the differences between men and women that were observed in the original 100-50 IGT condition disappeared in the 200-50 and 300-50 IGT condition (re-analysis of data of Van den Bos et al., 2006a). This is in line with the hypothesis formulated above.

A study using PET-scans while subjects performed the IGT observed differences in several brain structures between male and female subjects (Bolla et al., 2004). A within-subject analysis revealed that men activated extensive regions of the right and left lateral orbitofrontal cortex and right dorsolateral prefrontal cortex, whilst women activated only the left medial orbitofrontal cortex. Starting from these within-subject differences Overman and colleagues (2006) predicted that personal moral dilemmas, which activate the lateral dorsal prefrontal cortex, would reduce IGT performance differences between men and women. Indeed their study showed that such dilemmas either contemplated during or before the IGT led women to choose the same number of advantageous cards as men as the test progressed, i.e. during the second half of the task (Overman et al., 2006). They attributed this to an increased cognitive control due to activation of the dorsolateral prefrontal cortex. These data also support our neurobehavioural model of the IGT.

Overall, these neurobiological data suggest that women do not activate the cognitive control system to the same extent as men. From this it may be predicted that when tasks are made more difficult, i.e. when subjects have to pay more attention to the test features, leading to activation of the dorsolateral prefrontal cortex (e.g. MacDonald et al., 2000), gender differences may disappear. Indeed we observed that when task-conditions were made more difficult, differences between men and women disappeared (Vlaar, 2007), suggesting that differences between men and women actually may depend on task-conditions and thus in this sense are not fixed.

An intriguing finding that we have not yet discussed is the observation that differences also occur between men and women at the level of individual decks. These differences will be discussed in the next paragraph.

Male-Female Differences at the Level of Individual Decks

Overman and colleagues (2006; Overman, 2004; cf. Hooper et al., 2004) noted that men and women differed with respect to the decks they choose. Within the disadvantageous decks A and B both men and women chose more cards from deck B than from deck A. However, women also chose more cards from deck B than men, which accounts for the overall performance difference. Within the advantageous decks C and D men had no preference for cards from deck C or D, while women preferred cards from deck D over cards from deck C. We also observed such differences (Figure 7), regardless of whether reward magnitude differences were increased (re-analysis of data of Van den Bos et al., 2006a). When we made the long-term differences between decks AB versus CD smaller (-100 Euro versus +100 Euro) the differences between men and women with respect to decks C and D remained (Vlaar, 2007).

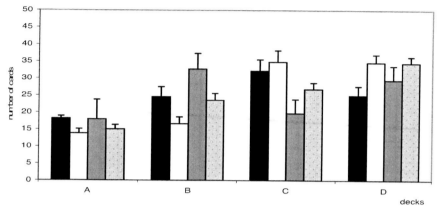

Figure 7: Mean (+SEM) number of choices from the different decks for women and men in different test-conditions. A three way ANOVA [experiment, gender, deck as repeated measure] showed a significant deck effect (F(3,81)=15.160, p≤0.001), a significant deck*experiment effect (F(3,81)=5.052, p≤0.003) and a significant deck*gender effect (F(3,81)=5.098, p≤0.003). Gender effects existed for deck B (two way ANOVA [gender, experiment]: F(1,27)=6.084, p≤0.02) and deck C (F(1,27)=10.668, p≤0.003). Experiment effects existed for deck B (F(1,27)=7.878, p≤0.009) and deck D (F(1,27)=6.669, p≤0.016). Gender effects: *: p≤0.05; **: p≤0.01.

The differences between decks lie in the frequency with which wins and losses occur. While deck A and C stand out by the fact that wins and losses follow one another on a regular basis (frequent loss decks), decks B and D stand out by the fact that losses only occur after long series of wins (infrequent loss decks; see scheme in Bechara et al., 1994). Thus, these gender differences seem to suggest a differential sensitivity to the way information is presented and decisions are made, which in turn may affect the overall task performance. It may thus be concluded that women have a tendency to select decks with infrequent losses and thereby may thus not perform optimally in this task. However, data of recent exepriments done in our laboratory using several variants of the IGT suggest that frequency alone is not a decisive factor for the differences between men and women (Vlaar, 2007; cf. Garon & Moore, 2007). Alternatively, therefore, the data may imply that women are more sensitive to punishment and thus avoid regular losses (Hooper et al., 2004). However, the EV model did not support such a notion as shown in Figure 6. Thus it remains to be determined why women and men are differentially sensitive to frequent or infrequent losses under some test-conditions.

CONCLUSION

Although evidence is accumulating that differences exist between men and women in the performance on the Iowa Gambling Task, little is known about why such differences exist and what they mean. In this chapter we have explored these differences and suggested that neurobehavioural differences may explain why men and women differ in their performance. Women tend to be more flexible in the way they organise their responses: they pay attention to both long-term and short-term aspects. In contrast men appear to be more focussed on long-term goals (Overman, 2004; Overman et al., 2006). While men tend to focus exclusively on exploitation, women combine exploration and exploitation. Thus women gain and update information in return for losing some resources, while men focus solely on the latter. Whether this may be framed within an evolutionary framework remains speculative, but if so, it may be related to the differences in the roles men and women may have had in ancient times. Men may have been more goal-directed, related to for instance their hunting trips, while women were more flexible, since they were sedentary. Furthermore, men may have needed to pay more attention to energy resources than women, for instance to secure their competitive and hunting potential, and as such do not take too many risks in such decision making processes. However, such explanations remain just-so stories if they cannot be put to test. For instance therefore, it may be hypothesised that women become more goal-directed, when they are pregnant, i.e. when energy resources are more important. It is clear that more experiments are needed in human as well as non-human animals to assess how these differences emerge, what they mean and why they have evolved.

REFERENCES

Aharon, I., Etcoff, N., Ariely, D., Chabris, C.F., O'Connor, E. & Breiter, H.C. (2001) Beautiful faces have variable reward value: fMRI and behavioral evidence. *Neuron, 32*, 537-551.

Bechara, A., Damasio, A.R., Damasio, H. & Anderson, S.W. (1994) Insensitivity to future consequences following damage to human prefrontal cortex. *Cognition, 50*, 7-15.

Bechara, A., Damasio, H., Tranel, D. & Damasio, A.R. (1997) Deciding advantageously before knowing the advantageous strategy. *Science, 275*, 1293-1295.

Bechara, A., Damasio, H., Tranel, D. & Anderson, S.W. (1998) Dissociation of working memory from decision making within the human prefrontal cortex. *The Journal* of *Neuroscience, 18*, 428-437.

Bechara, A., Damasio, H, Damasio, A.R. & Lee, G.P. (1999) Different contributions of the human amygdala and ventromedial prefrontal cortex to decision-making. *The Journal of Neuroscience, 19*, 5473-5481.

Bechara, A., Tranel, D. & Damasio, H. (2000) Characterization of the decision-making deficit of patients with ventromedial prefrontal cortex lesions. *Brain, 123*, 2189-2202.

Bechara, A., Damasio, H. & Damasio, A.R. (2001) Manipulation of dopamine and serotonin causes different effects on covert and overt decision making. Society of Neuroscience Abstracts 465.5.

Bechara, A. & Damasio, H. (2002) Decision-making and addiction (part I): impaired activation of somatic states in substance dependent individuals when pondering decisions with negative future consequences. *Neuropsychologia, 40*, 1675-1689.

Bechara, A. & Martin, E.M. (2004) Impaired decision making related to working memory deficits in individuals with substance addictions. *Neuropsychology, 18*, 152-162.

Becker, J.B. (1999) Gender differences in dopaminergic function in striatum and nucleus accumbens. *Pharmacology, Biochemistry & Behavior, 64*, 803-812.

Bolla, K.I., Eldreth, D.A., Matochik, J.A. & Cadet, J.L. (2004) Sex-related differences in a gambling task and its neurological correlates. *Cerebral Cortex ,14*, 1226-1232.

Bos, van den R. (2004) Emotions and Cognition. In: M. Bekoff (Ed.) *Encyclopedia of Animal Behavior* (pp.554-557) Westport (CT): Greenwood Press.

Bos, van den R., Houx, B.B. & Spruijt, B.M. (2006a) The effect of reward magnitude differences on choosing disadvantageous decks in the Iowa Gambling Task. *Biological Psychology, 71*, 155-161.

Bos, van den R., Lasthuis, W, Heijer, den E., Harst, van der J. & Spruijt, B. (2006b) Towards a rodent model of the Iowa Gambling Task. *Behavior Research Methods, 38*, 470-478.

Bos, van den R. & Ridder, de D. (2006). Evolved to satisfy our immediate needs: Self-control and the rewarding properties of food. *Appetite, 47*, 24-29.

Buffenstein, R., Poppitt, S.D., McDevitt, R.M. & Prentice, A.M. (1995) Food intake and the menstrual cycle: a retrospective analysis, with implications for appetite research. *Physiology & Behavior, 58*, 1067-1077.

Busemeyer, J.R. & Stout, J.C. (2002) A contribution of cognitive decision models to clinical assessment: Decomposing performance on the Bechara Gambling Task. *Psychological Assessment, 14*, 253-262.

Cardinal, R.N., Pennicot, D.R., Sugathapala, C.L., Robbins, T.W. & Everitt, B.J. (2001) Impulsive choice induced in rats by lesions of the nucleus accumbens core. *Science, 292*, 2499-2501.

Clark, L., Manes, F., Antoun, N., Sahakian, B.J. & Robbins, T.W. (2003) The contributions of lesion laterality and lesion volume to decision-making impairment following frontal lobe damage. *Neuropsychologia, 41*, 1474-1483.

Crone, E.A. & Molen, van der M.W. (2004) Developmental changes in real life decision making: performance on a gambling task previously shown to depend on the ventromedial prefrontal cortex. *Developmental Neuropsychology, 25(3)*, 251-279.

Crone, E.A., Somsen, R.J.M., Beek, van B. & Molen, van der M.W. (2004) Heart rate and skin conductance analysis of antecedents and consequences of decision making. *Psychophysiology, 41*, 531-540.

Crone, E.A., Bunge, S.A., Latenstein, H. & Molen, van der M.W. (2005) Characterization of children's decision making: sensitivity to punishment frequency, not task complexity. *Child Neuropsychology, 11*, 245-263.

Damasio, A.R. (1994) *Descartes' error. Emotion, reason and the human brain.* New York: Avon Books.

Dluzen, D.E. & Ramirez, V.D. (1985) In vitro dopamine release from the rat striatum: diurnal rhythm and its modification by the estrous cycle. *Neuroendocrinology, 41*, 97-100.

Ernst, M., Bolla, K., Mouratidis, M., Contoreggi, C., Matochik, J.A., Kurian, V., Cadet, J-L., Kimes, A.S. & London, E.D. (2002) Decision-making in a risk-taking task : a PET study. *Neuropsychopharmacology, 26*, 682-691.

Fernández-Ruiz, J.J., Hernandez, M.L., Demiquel, R. & Ramos J.A. (1991) Nigrostriatal and mesolimbic dopaminergic activities were modified throughout the ovarian cycle of female rats. *Journal of Neural Transmission - General section, 85 (3)*, 223-229.

Fiorillo, C.D., Tobler, P.N. & Schultz, W. (2003) Discrete coding of reward probability and uncertainty by dopamine neurons. *Science, 299*, 1898-1902.

Garon, N. & Moore, C. (2007) Developmental and gender differences in future-oriented decision-making during pre-school period. *Child Neuropsychology, 13*, 46-63.

Higley, J.D., Mehlman, P.T., Poland, R.E., Taub, D.M., Vickers, J., Suomi, S.J. & Linnoila, M. (1996a) CSF testosterone and 5-HIAA correlate with different types of aggressive behaviors. *Biological Psychiatry, 40*, 1067-1082.

Higley, J.D., Mehlman, P.T., Higley, S.B., Fernald, B., Vickers, J., Lindell, S.O., Taub, D.M., Suomi, S.J. & Linnoila, M. (1996b) Excessive mortality in young free-ranging male nonhuman primates with low cerebrospinal fluid 5-hydroxyindoleacetic concentrations. *Archives of General Psychiatry, 53*, 537-543.

Ho, H-P., Olsson, M., Westberg, L., Melke, J. & Eriksson, E. (2001) The serotonin reuptake inhibitor fluoxetine reduces sex steroid-related aggression in female rats: an animal model of premenstrual irritability? *Neuropsychopharmacology, 24*, 502-510.

Homberg, J.R., Heijer, den E., Suer, R., Spruijt, B., Bos, van den R. & Cuppen, E. (2007) Modulation of decision making in the Iowa Gambling Task by partial and complete genetic ablation of the serotonin transporter in the rat and the human serotonin transporter polymorphism. Endo-Neuro-Psycho meeting 5th-8th June 2007, Doorwerth, the Netherlands.

Hooper, C.J., Luciana, M., Conklin, H.M. & Yarger, R.S. (2004) Adolescents' performance on the Iowa Gambling Task: Implications for the development of decision making and ventromedial prefrontal cortex. *Developmental Psychology, 40*, 1148-1158.

Inglis, I.R., Forkman, B. & Lazarus, J. (1997) Free food or earned food? A review and fuzzy model of contrafreeloading. *Animal Behaviour, 53*, 1171-1191.

Inglis, I.R., Langton, S., Forkman, B. & Lazarus, J. (2001) An information primacy model of exploratory and foraging behaviour. *Animal Behaviour, 62*, 543-557.

Justice, A.J.H. & Wit, de H. (1999) Acute effects of d-amphetamine during the follicular and luteal phases of the menstrual cycle in women. *Psychopharmacology, 145*, 67-75.

Katz, L.D. (1999) Dopamine and serotonin: Integrating current affective engagement with longer-term goals. *Behavioral and Brain Sciences, 22*, 527.

Kimberly Epting, L. & Overman, W.H. (1998) Sex-sensitive tasks in men and women: A search for performance fluctuations across the menstrual cycle. *Behavioral Neuroscience, 112*, 1304-1317.

Knutson, B., Fong, G.W., Adams, C.M., Varner, J.L. & Hommer, D. (2001) Dissociation of reward anticipation and outcome with event-related fMRI. *Neuroreport, 12*, 3683-3687

Kuijer, R., Ridder, de D., Ouwehand, C. Houx, B. & Bos, van den R. (2007) Dieting and behavioural decision making. *Appetite* (submitted).

MacDonald, A.W III, Cohen, J.D., Stenger, V.A. & Carter, C.S. (2000) Dissociating the role of the dorsolateral prefrontal and anterior cingulate cortex in cognitive control. *Science, 288*, 1835-1838.

Manes, F., Sahakian, B., Clark, L., Rogers, R., Antoun, N, Aitken, M.. & Robbins, T.W. (2002) Decision-making processes following damage to the prefrontal cortex. *Brain, 125*, 624-639.

Matthews, S.C., Simmons, A.N., Lane, S.D. & Paulus, M.P. (2004) Selective activation of the nucleus accumbens during risk-taking decision making. *Neuroreport, 15*, 2123-2127.

McClure, S.M., Laibson, D.I., Loewenstein, G. & Cohen, J.D. (2004) Separate neural systems value immediate and delayed monetary rewards. *Science, 306*, 503-507.

Mehlman, P.T., Higley, J.D., Faucher, I., Lilly, A.A., Taub, D.M., Vickers, J., Suomi, S.J. & Linnoila, M. (1994) Low CSF 5-HIAA concentrations and severe aggression and impaired impulse control in nonhuman primates. *American Journal of Psychiatry, 151*, 1485-1491.

Mehlman, P.T., Higley, J.D., Faucher, I., Lilly, A.A., Taub, D.M., Vickers, J., Suomi, S.J. & Linnoila, M. (1995) Correlation of CSF 5-HIAA concentration with sociality and timing of emigration in free-ranging primates. *American Journal of Psychiatry, 152*, 907-913.

Murphy, D.L, Lerner, A., Rudnick, G. & Lesch, K-P. (2004) Serotonin transporter: gene, genetic disorders, and pharmacogenetics. *Molecular Interventions, 4*, 109-123.

Nördstrom A., Olsson, H. & Halldin, C. (1998) A pet study of D_2 dopamine receptor density at different phases of the menstrual cycle. *Psychiatry Research: Neuro-imaging section, 83*, 1-6.

Overman, W.H. (2004) Sex differences in early childhood, adolescence, and adulthood on cognitive tasks that rely on orbital prefrontal cortex. *Brain and Cognition, 55*, 134-147.

Overman, W.H., Frassrand, K., Ansel, S., Trawalter, S., Bies, B. & Redmond, A. (2004) Performance on the IOWA card task by adolescents and adults. *Neuropsychologia, 42*, 1838-1851.

Overman, W., Graham, L., Redmond, A., Eubank, R., Boettcher, L., Samplawski, O. & Walsh, K. (2006) Contemplation of moral dilemmas eliminates sex differences on the Iowa gambling task. *Behavioral Neuroscience, 120*, 817-825.

Reavis, R. & Overman, W.H. (2001) Adult sex differences on a decision-making task previously shown to depend on the orbital prefrontal cortex. *Behavioral Neuroscience, 115*, 196-206.

Ridderinkhof, K.R., Wildenberg, van den W.P.M., Segalowitz, S.J. & Carter, C.S. (2004) Neurocognitive mechanisms of cognitive control: The role of prefrontal cortex in action selection, response inhibition, performance monitoring, and reward-based learning. *Brain and Cognition, 56*, 129-140.

Rogers, R.D., Everitt, B.J., Baldacchino, A., Blackshaw, A.J., Swainson, R., Wynne, K., Baker, N.B., Hunter, J., Carthy, T., Booker, E., London, M., Deakin, J.F.W., Sahakian, B.J. & Robbins, T.W. (1999) Dissociable deficits in the decision-making cognition of chronic amphetamine abusers, opiate abusers, patients with focal damage to prefrontal cortex, and tryptophan-depleted normal volunteers: evidence for monoaminergic mechanisms. *Neuropsychopharmacology, 20*, 322-339.

Rubinow, D.R., Schmidt P.J. & Roca C.A. (1998) Estrogen-serotonin interactions: implications for affective regulation. *Biological Psychiatry, 44*, 839-850.

Salamone, J.D. & Correa, M. (2002) Motivational views of reinforcement: implications for understanding the behavioral functions of nucleus accumbens dopamine. *Behavioural Brain Research, 137*, 3-25.

Sevy, S., Hassoun, Y., Bechara, A., Yechiam, E., Napolitano, B., Burdick, K., Delman, H & Malhotra, A. (2006) Emotion-based decision–making in healthy subjects: short-term effects of reducing dopamine levels. *Psychopharmacology, 188*, 228-235.

Shimizu, H. & Bray, G.A. (1993) Effects of castration, estrogen replacement and estrus cycle on monoamine metabolism in the nucleus accumbens, measured by microdialysis. *Brain Research, 621*, 200-206.

Shizgal, P. & Arvanitogiannis, A. (2003) Gambling on dopamine. *Science, 299*, 1856-1858.

Spruijt, B.M., Bos, van den R. & Pijlman, F.T.A. (2001) A concept of welfare based on reward evaluating mechanisms in the brain: anticipatory behaviour as an indicator for the state of reward systems. *Applied Animal Behaviour Science, 72*, 145-171.

Stallen, M. (2006). *Excel application of the Expectancy-Valence model.* Technical Report, University of Amsterdam.

Tanaka, S.C., Doya, K., Okada, G., Ueda, K., Okamaoto, Y., & Yamawaki, S. (2004). Prediction of immediate and future rewards differentially recruits cortico-basal ganglia loops. *Nature Neuroscience, 7*, 887-893.

Thompson, T.L. & Moss, R.L. (1997) Modulation of mesolimbic dopaminergic activity over the rat estrous cycle. *Neuroscience Letters, 229*, 145-148.

Tranel, D., Bechara, A. & Damasio, A.R (2000). Decision making and the somatic marker hypothesis. In : M.S. Gazzaniga (Ed). *The new cognitive neurosciences* (pp.1047-1061). Cambridge (MA): A Bradford book.

Tranel, D., Bechara, A & Denburg, N.L. (2002) Asymmetric functional roles of right and left ventromedial prefrontal cortices in social conduct, decision-making, and emotional processing. *Cortex, 38*, 589-612.

Valois, De R.L. (1954) The relation of different levels and kinds of motivations to variability of behaviour. *Journal of Experimental Psychology, 47*, 392-398.

Vlaar, S. (2007) *Three new variants of the Iowa Gambling Task: deck structure effects and gender differences.* Master Thesis, Utrecht University, Utrecht, the Netherlands.

White, T.L., Justice, A.J.H. & Wit, de H. (2002) Differential subjective effects of d-amphetamine by gender, hormone levels and menstrual cycle phase. *Pharmacology, Biochemistry & Behavior, 73*, 729-741.

Wilson, M., & Daly, M. (2004). Do pretty women inspire men to discount the future? *The Royal Society. Biology Letters 271 nr. S4*, 177-179.

Yechiam, E., Busemeyer, J.R., Stout, J.C. & Bechara, A. (2005) Using cognitive models to map relations between neuropsychological disorders and human decision-making deficits. *Psychological Sciences, 16*, 973-978.

In: Psychology of Decision Making in Education
Editor: Jeanine A. Elsworth, pp. 227-241

ISBN: 978-1-60021-933-7
© 2006 Nova Science Publishers, Inc.

Chapter 10

YOUNG CHILDREN'S DECISIONS
ABOUT THE POWER OF INFERENCE

Norman H. Freeman, Angeliki Varouxaki**
*and Katerina Maridaki-Kassotaki***

*University of Bristol, UK
**Harokopio University, Athens, Greece

ABSTRACT

Seeing in a box is a direct way of knowing what is in the box. There is evidence that 4-year-olds engage with the idea that equally reliable knowledge can also be gained indirectly, via inference. For example, if you see that there is one cup to each saucer, the cups can be put away out of sight, and just by counting the saucers you can infer the number of the uncounted cups. But sometimes it is possible to make an inferential mistake. We review recent evidence of young children's decisions on whether people know things via inference, and add new evidence to test a claim about a false inference test. That test involved asking children to judge another's knowledge through inference when the other was misled to input the wrong premises into her calculation. The finding that children performed better in the false inference task compared to the true inference task, together with their explicit verbal justifications, attests to children's theoretical understudying of inference. We suggest that that is the growth point for the next round of research.

INTRODUCTION

The human mind makes much use of inference. Three-year-olds use inference in planning action in very simple tasks (Halliday, 1977). Four-year-olds, as reported by Pears and Bryant (1990), are prepared to use transitive inference about spatial position without any prior training when working out how to organise their actions in building a tower (e.g. if the blue block has to go higher than the red block, and the red block has to go higher than the green block, then the inference is that the red block will be lower than the blue block). That is, in deciding what to do in simple situations, preschool children come to rely on inference: but to what extent do the children understand what it is that underpins their decisions? It has been argued by Karmiloff-Smith (1992) that once children achieve practical behavioural mastery of something, they normally progress towards a theory of what they are doing, eventually becoming aware of their theory. So the question of how explicitly children can explain their inferential judgements bears closely on assessment of the speed of representational change in normal childhood.

One way of thinking about childhood representational change is to posit that children start by (a) grasping that seeing manifestly causes knowing, and then (b) progress to conceptualising unobservable inference as a generator of knowledge. Sodian and Wimmer (1987, p.432) suggested that a young child might come to make 'an amplification of his or her empiricist theory of knowledge'. Another testable hypothesis is that children's minds teem with ideas, and they have problems in discriminating (a) when they know something, from (b) when merely hopeful guesses arise in their minds. Children have to learn that there are permission conditions for claiming knowledge; and a sign of that would be a readiness to acknowledge their ignorance even when it would be easy to make a hopeful guess. In that light, inference can be regarded as a constraint on knowledge: if you follow a chain of inference, your mind is channelled towards one piece of knowledge. It is possible that children do not so much need to realise that inference *generates* knowledge as that inference constrains knowledge.

In this chapter, we consider some new and old evidence on

a)   children's use of inference under different conditions,
b)   children's adeptness in spotting conditions under which inference is safe and apposite,
c)   children's readiness to give satisfactory explanations of how their own and other people's inferences operate, and
d)   children's readiness to extend their expertise into more than just solving problems, into the situation where they are asked to predict when an inference will or will not lead to knowledge.

STUDIES ON YOUNG CHILDREN'S GRASP OF INFERENCE

One line of work on young children's efficiency at making inferences in action planning (Halliday, 1977; Pears and Bryant, 1990) was noted at the outset. Such work is invaluable in identifying the earliest manifestations of inferential decision-making, but is not so suitable for investigating further development towards reflective awareness. Here, another line of work seems to be proving its worth. The work stems from that of Sophian, Wood and Vong (1995) on numerical decisions. Briefly, children watched as a few Hawaiian frogs went to a party, each frog in its own boat. The frogs hopped into the party (actually a box that was then closed up, each frog leaving its boat moored outside. From counting the number of boats one can infer how many frogs were at the party; and one cannot infer how many dolphins had gone to the party because the dolphins swam in a group, leaving no visible traces outside the party. Sophian et al reported that with encouragement, something like half the preschoolers inferred the number of frogs, and appropriately refrained from using the boats to infer the number of dolphins who were at the party. The dolphin control condition gives one confidence that the successes with frogs were not a mechanical procedure, e.g. due to the children merely repeating the last number-word that was in their heads after counting boats: the last-word repetition tendency is always a worry in number research (Freeman, Antonucci & Lewis, 2000). In short, the 'frogboats paradigm' seems suitable for gaining evidence on children's adeptness in spotting conditions under which inference is safe and apposite. For follow-up research on 4-year-olds' numerical inference see Muldoon, Lewis and Freeman (2003); Muldoon, Lewis and Towse (2005). For confirmation of a contribution of logical reasoning to the learning of mathematics in primary school see Nunes et al (2007). We shall return to numerical inference below. For the present, we note one final line of study on inference. The work stems from an interest in children's dawning understanding of the power of the mind.

An early mentalistic insight is understanding that seeing can lead to knowing. Thus, many 3-year-olds grasp that a person who looks in a box knows what is in the box, and that someone who has not looked in a box does not know what is in it (Pillow, 1989; Pratt and Bryant, 1991). A discrimination between 'seeing is knowing' and 'not-seeing is not-knowing' is immensely useful as a step in grasping that there are causes of knowledge. But it can become counterproductive if held to too firmly; because under some conditions, inference can safely be used as a *substitute* for direct observation. Imagine that instead of one box, there are two boxes: you and your partner see a red pen and a green pen on the table, and do not see which pen goes into which box. Your partner need only look into one box to infer what is in the *second* box. You in turn infer that she knows because you apply a 'seeing is knowing' rule to the box she looks into, and then set aside the rule (a) that she has to see into the second box in order to know what is in it, in favour of (b) its inferential *functional equivalent* for the second box with its unseen contents. That is a complex procedure where a seeing rule has to be switched in and then inhibited; especially if you yourself had not looked into any box and knew that you did not know what your partner knew, so not-seeing is still not-knowing for you. The test formed part of the design invented by Keenan, Ruffman and Olson (1994). The work provoked interest, see Friedman, Griffin, Brownell & Winner (2003); Rai and Mitchell (2006). Yet there is one limitation on what the work showed. There was little evidence bearing on the question of children's readiness to give satisfactory explanations of how their own and other people's inferences operate. That was studied by Varouxaki and Freeman (1998);

Varouxaki et al (1999). Briefly, many of the many preschoolers studied managed to give satisfactory explanations of how their own and other people's inferences operated in the two-box game. Further, there was evidence of children's readiness to extend their expertise into the situation where they are asked to predict when an inference will or will not lead to knowledge. We shall return to that shortly. Before doing so, it is useful to take a close look at the method used to study children's inferential knowledge.

We shall adopt the notation used in Sodian and Wimmer (1987, Table 1) who first tested for a concept of inference as a source of knowledge, and label the basic task as '-+'. That symbol order means that the child does not know (-) the colour of the item that the *second* person does know (+). Suppose a child gives correct answers to two inference questions in this test: 'Do you know the colour in the other person's box? and 'Does the other person know the colour in your box?' by answering 'no' and 'yes' respectively. There is a danger of a false positive, in that the child might credit the other person with omniscience, so one needs the converse +- condition to elicit 'yes' for self and 'no' for other. In Keenan et al's (1994) Experiment 2, only a meagre 4/16 of their 4-year-olds seemed to show complete success. The majority error was to neglect the other's inference. In the authors' Experiment 3, efforts were made to remind children that the other remembered the items seen at the start, and success rose to 9/16. Before that point in the paper the authors had given up asking the children to explain their answers, because they had encountered very uninformative replies, so one cannot chart the progress of those children towards fully explicit understanding. But it seems that at least some 4-year-olds have enough of a concept of inference to make correct judgements in practice. Development seems to be a slow process: Keenan et al (1994) found that success on their inference test showed little and nonsignificant improvement from 4-year-olds to 5-year-olds, and lagged behind success on a false belief test. There are, though, three things to find out in order to explain what achievement some children had shown.

The first worry relates to what Keenan et al (1994) did which just about doubled the success level between their second and third experiments. Just before asking the critical questions the Experimenter intervened with words and pictures to stress the facts that the other had seen two colours (shapes) initially and knew what they were. We are concerned that some children might then have solved the task by contrasting seeing with remembering in the following way. In the -+ condition, the child might think something along the lines of 'I am being asked if the other knows what he cannot see; I have just been told that the other knows the two things, so he must be remembering the other thing he knows'. In the +- condition, the child might be able to work out that the other knows two things and is not looking into any box so cannot give a one-box answer. Certainly, inference is involved, but there is more to inference than realising that others might have good reiterative memory for some knowledge that had just been explicitly mentioned. The minimal step one can think of is to make the inferential demand more generative: the task should involve coming up with an answer that had not been explicitly stated up to then. Thus, one can have tests where items varied in number, and the child and other count them together. If there are, say, four items, to be divided between two boxes, any one box could contain one, two, or three items, so an inference involves coming up with a new cardinal number. In short, placing either a red or a green item inside a box does not alter the items' colour-identity, whereas dividing a set of items between two boxes generates subsets of new numerosity. There is an additional benefit from using simple arithmetic: counting out loud might draw to children's attention that something needs to be worked out. It was reported by Varouxaki and Freeman (1998); Varouxaki et al (1999) used tests that dispensed with the questionable intervention noted above, and reported that there was no difference between colour-inference and number inference results. So an understanding of inference as a source of knowledge has some degree of generality across tests.

The second thing one wants to know concerns the extent to which 4-year-olds who succeed on the test have a theoretical understanding of what they are doing. One source of evidence was mentioned at the outset: to ask the child to explain her judgements in order to tap whether she uses her ideas in explanatory manner (see Wellman, 1990). Another source of evidence for the existence of a theory is needed, namely that a child should be ready to use it to make predictions (see Perner, 1991). One can incorporate a test to find out if the child can *predict* whether she and another person would infer what is in a particular closed box under hypothetical viewing conditions. In such a situation, it was reported by Varouxaki et al (1999, Experiment 1) that the preschoolers made some 89% correct predictions, mostly with lucid explanations. Here is an excerpt from a child in a later replication we ran: 5-year-old Ella in a – condition, volunteered that if she were to look inside the other person's box she would know how many pens were in her own box: 'There were four pens and he'll have some and I'll have some, and I'll know how many I've got 'cause how many he's got. If he's got two I'll have two'. There can be not a shadow of a doubt that a child such as that feels safe in basing her decisions upon an inferential process that runs from observable to unobserved displays.

The third thing that one wants to check concerns whether the children realise that other people can think in precisely the same way that they themselves do. Riggs and Robinson (1995) recently found evidence of young children having a greater awareness of the workings of their own minds than that of others. At first sight, the phenomenon of a child in the +- condition saying that she knows what is in the second box without looking into it and denying that someone else in the -+ condition can gain knowledge by inference ('inference neglect') is congruent with the notion that children solve advanced mentalistic problems for self before other. The strongest evidence for a representational theory of mind is if, whenever a new mentalistic insight occurs, it occurs simultaneously for first-person and third-person application (Gopnik, 1993). Yet here we have a type of a judgement which sometimes reliably occurs for self before being extended to others (Sodian and Wimmer, 1987; Keenan *et al*, 1994), and sometimes does not (Varouxaki and Freeman, 1998; Varouxaki et al, 1999). Again, there was one phenomenon that was noted in the very first experiment of Sodian and Wimmer (1987) where 88% of all wrong answers to the question of whether the child herself knew the colour came from the child claiming to know when she actually could not know. So it seems that many 4-year-olds both overestimate their own knowledge and underestimate another's knowledge, thus treating other minds as very much 'stupider' than their own in two respects. The tendency of children up to the age of 6 years or so to fail to acknowledge their own ignorance has long been documented (e.g. Beal and Flavell, 1982; Markman, 1977; Mitchell and Robinson, 1992; Sophian and Somerville, 1988). Acknowledging when oneself is ignorant is a key step in coming to grips with the problem of knowledge, since it involves the realisation that there are constraints on knowledge. From that perspective, realising that other people can attain knowledge via inference might merely be part of the general problem of extending a grasp of constraints from one's own mind to that of others. Accordingly, one needs a design that will make it easy to track whether those particular children who are ready to acknowledge their own ignorance are also ready to credit others with knowledge via inference. That can be done by studying the full Sodian-Wimmer matrix of --, +-, -+ and ++ conditions where Keenan *et al* (1994) used only the +- and -+ conditions. It was from using the full matrix that enabled Varouxaki and Freeman (1998); Varouxaki et al (1999) to report that the child's understanding of inferences for self kept pace with inferences for others.

One of the long-term aims of research is to model the emergence of new ideas in competition with old ideas. Kuhn (1992, p.256) produced the general argument that "The most formidable problem for subjects appears to be not the acquisition and consolidation of new strategies but rather the ability to abandon old less adequate strategies -- a reversal of the way in which we typically think about development". It might indeed be the case that 4-year-olds understand that inference leads to knowing but overvalue the immensely useful rule that seeing is knowing, so their competence is masked. It is there that the -+ and -- conditions are so useful: the child cannot see into any box so she cannot know what is in either box, and any false claim to knowledge must be in despite of 'seeing is knowing'. In that light, one looks to whether a readiness to acknowledge own ignorance is a predictor of crediting others with inferential knowledge, as part of an emerging theory of constraints on knowledge.

EVALUATION OF THE RESEARCH SO FAR

Keenan *et al* (1994) were correct to assert that the fifth year of life is about right for a test of a fledgling understanding that inference leads to knowledge. The similarity in results between Colour and Number found by Varouxaki et al (1999) enhances confidence in generalizing from the test. Some children had reached the highest level of articulating reflective awareness; other children were still showing inference neglect. We concentrate next on them.

The test involves converse inference: the child is asked whether she can infer the contents of the other's box and whether the other can infer the contents of the child's box. So success cannot come from egocentric reiteration since different colours/numbers are asked about even in the ++ condition where both protagonists have knowledge. That ++ condition should be the easiest in the matrix of conditions, since the child can see that it is possible for her to make an inference and that the other has a comparable experience. Yet inference neglect occurred in a third of those children who correctly assessed own knowledge. A crucial new finding by Varouxaki et al (1999) wass that when attention was focused on those children who avoided inference neglect, there was no significant drop in the frequency with which inferential explanations were given of how the other knew compared with how self knew. So another's mind was treated the same as own mind: in making a judgment of *whether* another knew and in reflecting on *how* the other knew. That is not congruent with the argument of Karmiloff-Smith (1992) that children mentally represent what they know more than once as they develop, with conscious awareness coming at the end of a process of what she termed 'explicitation'. Note that a two-step process has been suggested before for a lower-level problem in theory of mind: another's false belief is computed at an implicit level before becoming available for judgment at the verbal level (Clements and Perner, 1994; Freeman, Lewis and Doherty, 1991). It would be prudent to leave open the possibility that advance in technique might eventually show that the child's encounter with the problem of inferential knowledge similarly involves a step of collating own and other minds more than once. It is possible to be more precise about the developmental issue via the following consideration of the problem of knowledge.

Sodian and Wimmer (1987) argued that children need to 'enrich' their theory of mind to give inference equivalent weight to seeing as a source of knowledge. Keenan *et al* (1994), in their Discussion section emphasized the importance of not over-valuing seeing is knowing. The emphasis is on the acquisition of a generative theory of mind to encompass the notion that other people generate knowledge from inference. We suggest that the data on acknowledgment of own ignorance helps make an account less one-sided by focusing attention on the functional point that both seeing and inferring are ways of constraining belief. Seeing provides one constraint which can be directly experienced for oneself and observed in the behaviour of another person, inference provides another constraint which cannot be directly observed in others' behaviour.

THE NEXT RESEARCH STEP

The coding of experimental conditions as +-/++/--/-+ was possible because there are two possible states of mind in the experiment: either (a) someone cannot make an inference on that trial and so they are left uninformative about the hidden item(s), or (b) someone can make an inference and the result will be correct and informative about the hidden item(s). Yet it is commonly easy to be able to make an inference yet it turn out to be wrong. It would arise if the child were to watch someone who miscounted the frogboats, so that person would tell you a wrong number for how many frogs she inferred to be at the party. So that is an interesting case to study, to find out whether the child's conception of inference encompasses only true inference and does not yet extend to false inference. A person who is making a false inference is doing so in all honesty because she has a false belief about the number of frogboats. Accordingly, we need briefly to consider the acquisition of an understanding of false belief.

In experiments concerned with the developmental contingency between having a concept of inference and understanding false belief, Keenan et al (1994) found that performance on a false belief test preceded understanding of inference, whereas Varouxaki et al (1999) reported no pattern of association between children's performance on the two tests. Yet one would expect an association, if the following brief argument is on the right lines. In an inference test, to be correct children need to grasp that the other person has no direct access to the critical fact but that she does have access to information that allows her to make an inference. Similarly to pass the false belief test, children have to grasp that another person (a) has no direct access to an actual state, but that she (b) has access to relevant yet misleading information (Wimmer et al, 1988). If this 'informational access' approach accounts for difficulties in understanding both inference and false belief, then children should perform consistently across tests. There is an alternative approach: young children have difficulty with the representational complexity involved in false belief (Wimmer and Perner, 1983). The difficulty for the child arises because of the necessity of representing that the other holds a certain proposition as a true representation whilst this very same proposition represents misrepresentation. The mental truth of the other's belief needs to be represented rather than the child's own truth. The representational complexity of representing conflicting truth values does not apply to the Sodian and Wimmer and Keenan et al types of inference, because the same premise information holds true for the child and the story protagonist. So it might be comprehensible why different researchers have obtained different findings on the relations between false-belief and inference understanding: wherever there is a task-demand mismatch, error may enter into the data. Accordingly, we add a third test to those two: a false inference test. Here, we adopt the frogboats design and the child sees the other person miscount the boats. In total, two studies were conducted, and children's performance on the false inference and standard false belief test was cross-compared. Before reporting what happened, it is well worth briefly scanning the existing literature on true and false inference tests.

TRUE AND FALSE INFERENCES

Research into the child's theory of mind began with the problem of false belief. That is, preschool children were often adept at spotting when someone held a true belief about a state of affairs yet could not seem to understand that someone could hold a false belief. So the children's' problem was held to be that of mastering a particular type of mentalistic 'representational complexity'. Children's performance would naturally vary under particular conditions, but the order of acquisition of true belief first then false belief was reliable (a 'true-belief advantage'). A problem arose when Riggs and Simpson (2005) found a situation in which both true and false beliefs were equally easy, or equally hard, for preschoolers to ascribe. That finding generated puzzlement; and in respect of false belief it was suggested that 'we should think harder about it' (Russell, 2005). Russell, Hill and Franco (2001) had independently also reported no difference between true belief and false belief success in a novel intention-reporting test (and for more standard null results under various conditions see Garnham & Ruffman, 2001; Roth and Leslie, 1998; Surian and Leslie, 1999). Lohmann, Carpenter and Call (2002) reported conditions under which the true-belief advantage only appeared under low processing demands; that is, the particular tasks effectively modulated the true-belief advantage. Now let us return to the inference test. What would one predict for an inference test that involved the participant forming a false belief? Would the child be as ready to ascribe inference to that participant as in the usual situation where the participant formed a true belief? Some insight into that may be gained from Ruffman (1996) who reported that children performed reliably *better* on the false inference test: a reversal of the true-belief advantage that had started the whole theory-of-mind tradition. Yet note that Ruffman (1996) preceded the Think question (what colour the protagonist thinks the sweet in the box is) with a Know question (whether the protagonist knows what colour the sweet is) as in the true belief inference condition. That pegged question-order was by design, to suit Ruffman's ingenious prediction of a false-belief advantage. Once children had judged the protagonist not to know what colour sweet was in the box, they should then attribute a false belief about the colour in order to be consistent(knowing is linked to true belief, not knowing therefore cannot be: the concept of a 'lucky guess' might be beyond preschoolers). But the procedure then needs amending to drop the Know question, cutting out any possibility of carry-over from that question to the Belief question. That is, we need to make the procedure, asking simply what the protagonist thinks without preamble so as to make the inference test comparable to the standard false belief test. And there is a need to avoid ambiguity possibly attendant on the lucky guess problem, and on worries about a protagonist who might not know if something was true compared with a protagonist who did know about something, only they knew the wrong thing resulting in an inferential falsity, see Bradmetz and Bonnefoy-Claudet (2003). We can ensure that the protagonist knows the wrong thing as follows.

We pick up on numerical one-to-one correspondence as an inferential cue. It was noted earlier on that there was an interesting instance of numerical inference pioneered by Sophian, Wood and Vong (1995) whereby children watched as frogs went to a party, each frog in its own boat, with the boats being left outside. From counting the number of boats one can infer how many frogs were at the party. Roughly half the preschoolers succeeded (for extensions of the work see Muldoon, Lewis and Freeman, 2003); Muldoon, Lewis and Towse, 2005). The 'frogboats paradigm' gives one evidence on children's adeptness in spotting conditions under which inference is safe and apposite.. The paradigm can readily be adapted for judgement of self and other's inference. And one can easily ask for explanations to track the emergence of verbalisable explicit awareness. One can add a condition in which the protagonist happens to end up with a miscount, so making a false numerical inference

We worked with 47 four-year-old children (22 girls and 25 boys) attending a primary school in a middle class residential area in Avon. They ranged in age between 49 to 60 mo (mean age $M = 54$ mo and $SD = 4$ mo).

The procedure always began with a version of the standard false belief task before any of the inference conditions. The procedure for the standard false belief test was a version of Gopnik and Astington's (1998) deceptive container test. Children were shown an egg-box with its true contents replaced with eggs and were asked what they thought was inside. Then, the box was opened revealing onions. The box was closed up and children were asked 'When somebody else from your classroom sees the box, all closed up like this, what will she think is inside?', then 'What really is inside?'

For the inference tests, the material was as follows. A total of 18, hand-drawn four page picture booklets were for the inference ++, 6 for the inference +-, and 6 for the false inference conditions. For each condition there were three sets of stories (a cooking story, cake story, and a picnic story). For each story there were two versions varying the number of target items. For the standard false belief test, there was an egg box with the normal contents replaced with onions. All testing took place in a quiet room outside the classroom.

Children received three conditions: inference ++, inference +-, and false inference. Three orders of conditions were created according to a balanced Latin square design. For the purpose of simplicity the following description of methods will be based on the cooking story; for the cake and picnic stories, the questions and prompts were phrased appropriately.

Each booklet showed two protagonists about to cook some fish. There were five experimental groups. One group were asked to count the number of fishes on the plates, while the other groups counted the plates on the table. There was always one extra plate next to the ones containing the fishes and it was pointed out to the children that this plate was left empty because it was cracked. The children who counted plates were either asked to count forwards or backwards (counting backwards means that counting ends up with the number 'one', so that the half of the children there cannot rightly simply reiterate their last-mentioned number in answer to the inference question). Of those children who counted the plates half were asked to include the empty, cracked plate, while the other half were instructed to ignore it (again that forces half the children to verbalise a last number that is different from the number they need because of the over-run onto that irrelevant plate). Then one of the protagonists left the room, whilst the other put some fishes into a saucepan and closed the lid. The children recounted the fishes/plates on the table. They were the asked the Know question about their *own* inference e.g. "Do you know how many fishes are in the pan? [If the child had not spontaneously given a number, she was then asked "How many"? to ensure that she was ascribing a true inference to the story protagonist], followed by a request for explanation "How do you (why don't you) know that?" Then the absent protagonist returned, re-counted and the target child was asked the Know question about the *other's* inference: "Does s/he know how many fishes are inside the saucepan"? (again if necessary asking how many, followed by a request for explanation).

The +- and false belief inference trials followed the same procedure, except that (a) in the +- condition the absent protagonist never returned to the kitchen and (b) in the false inference condition a cat ate some of the fishes left on the plates before the protagonist's return. Because the fishes that were left on the plates and those now in the pan do not add up to the initial number of fishes on the table, and because the absent protagonist had not seen the fishes being transferred into the pan, he could not know how many were really in it. Participants were asked the false belief Think question: 'How many fishes does he think are inside the pot?' and the Reality control question 'How many are really in the pan?'. It may be recalled that Ruffman (1996) in his study of true inference preceded the Think question with a Know question as in the true belief inference condition. We chose not to do so here because traditionally tests that are concerned with false beliefs in self and others rely on the Think question, children's answers to the Think question were sufficient to gain an insight into their understanding of inference as set out by our research questions, and we were concerned about children mechanically going in for response switching.

We begin the analysis with the basic data of yes/no answers to the question of whether self or other knows the number of items transferred into an opaque container over five questions (two for self and three for other). Inspection of the data revealed that there was no effect of the counting manipulations (counting targets versus plates, forward or backward, with or without the inclusion of the extra plate) on total correct responses, confirmed by one way Analysis of Variance ($F(4, 42) < 1$). Hereafter these are not considered as variables.

Individual response patterns. The correct response pattern was to say (a) 'yes' for one's own and the other person's knowledge in the ++ condition, and (a) 'yes' for self but 'no' for the other in the +- and false belief inference condition. There were 17/47 (36%) children who were completely correct. Two incorrect response patterns were identified. Inference neglect involved neglecting the other's inference in the ++ trial whilst being correct for self --17/47 children (36.2%) showed this pattern. The remaining 13 children (27.6%) were either yea/no-saying, response switching, overestimating the other's knowledge, or giving uninterpretable responses.

The standard false belief test which was passed by 23/47 (48.9%) children was not a significant predictor of performance on the inference task. An analysis of covariance where standard false belief is the independent variable, inference is the dependent variable and age is the covariate showed a significant main effect of standard false belief understanding on the total number of correct responses on the inference task, $F(1, 44) = 8.83, p < .01$. Age did not have a significant effect as a covariant $F(1, 44) < 1$. The suggestion is that children who pass the false belief test are likely to give more correct answers on the inference trials.

Yet more correct answers do not necessarily translate into a correct response pattern. Table 1 is a cross-tabulation of children's false belief performance and response patterns for Inference. There was a significant difference between the 17 children who were correct for Inference and the remaining 30 children in whether they passed or failed the false belief test, $\chi^2(1, n = 47) = 8.08, p < .01$. Passing the false belief test is not a sufficient condition for understanding inference as 9 out of the 17 children who showed neglect on the inference task had passed the standard false belief test. In fact there was no significant difference between the 17 children who were correct in the inference trials and those 17 who showed neglect in whether or not they passed the false belief test, $\chi^2(1, n = 34) = 2.06, p > .05$. That (a) 23 children passed the false belief test but only 13 were completely correct for inference together with (b) the absence of a pattern of association in children's performance on the two tests supports Wimmer at al's (1988) claim that understanding inference is a distinct and later attainment than understanding false belief.

Table 1. Cross-tabulation of performance on the standard false belief test and inference response patterns

False Belief	Inference Response Pattern		
	Correct	Neglect	Other
Pass	13	9	1
Fail	4	8	12

There was no significant difference in the number of children (31/46 = 66.0%) who passed the false inference test and the 49% of children who had passed the standard false belief test (binomial $p > .05$). Table 2 shows the contingency between performance on the new false inference test and the traditional deceptive container test. In Table 2 the association between the false belief inference and traditional false belief tests was high, $\chi^2 (1, N = 47) = 17.7, p < .001$. There were 37/47 children (78.7%) who either passed both or failed both the deceptive container and false inference task. Of the remaining 10 children, 9 passed the traditional false belief test and failed the new false inference task whilst only one child showed the reverse pattern. The results are congruent with the hypothesis that both false belief and inference require an appreciation of the contingency between informational access and the resulting knowledge.

Table 2. Cross-comparison of performance on the false inference and standard false belief tasks

False Inference	Standard False Belief	
	Pass	Fail
Pass	22	1
Fail	9	15

An analysis of covariance where false belief inference is the independent variable, inference is the dependent and age is the covariate showed a significant main effect of false belief inference understanding on the total number of correct responses on the inference task, $F(1, 44) = 6.56, p = .01$. Age was not a significant covariant $F (1, 44) < 1$. Next, we examined whether success on the false inference task predicts the patterns of children's responses on the inference conditions, Table 3.

There was no significant difference between the 17 children who were correct on the inference trials and the remaining 30 children in whether they passed or failed the false inference test, $\chi^2(1, n = 47) = 1.84, p = .17$. Importantly, 17 children passed the false inference task but not the inference task and only 3 showed the reverse pattern, Binomial $p = .03$. Children actually found it easier to ascribe an inferential false belief than to ascribe an inferential true belief.

Table 3. Cross-tabulation of performance for false inference and true inference response patterns

False Inference	True Inference		
	Correct	Neglect	Other
Pass	14	14	3
Fail	3	3	10

Children's explanations were considered inferential when sufficient information was given of how reasoning had been involved. We classified children's explanations across conditions for self and other as: (a) equal proportions of inferential explanations for self and other, (b) proportionately more inferential explanations for self, (c) proportionately more inferential explanations for other, (d) no inferential explanations, and (e) insufficient evidence (it was possible to have insufficient evidence because children who showed inference neglect had no opportunity to give inferential explanations for other). On inspection of the data there were 19/47 children (40.4%) for whom we had insufficient evidence to classify the pattern of their explanations.

Contrary to Keenan et al's (1994) study, all the remaining children were able to give sufficient information to see how reasoning had been implicated in solving the inference. Of the 28 children for whom we had sufficient evidence 24 children (88.9%) gave equal proportions of inferential explanations for self and other, 2 children (7.4%) gave proportionately more inferential explanations for self, and 2 children (7.4%) gave proportionately more inferential explanations for other than for self. These data are consistent with Ruffman (1996) and Varouxaki et al (1999).

On cross-comparison of the pattern of children's responses with the pattern of their explanations, 17/19 children for which we had insufficient evidence had shown neglect whilst the remaining 2 children were 'other'. There is no discernible difference between the remaining 17 children who were correct and those 11 who were 'other', in whether they gave equal proportions of inferential explanations for self and other or were biased (Fisher's Exact Probability Test $p = .57$).

There was no discernible difference between the 24 children who gave equal proportions of inferential explanations for self and other and the remaining 23 children in whether they had passed or failed (a) the standard false belief test, and (b) the false inference test. Twelve and 13 children had passed false belief respectively. The respective numbers for the false inference test were 14 and 17.   The results of the true inference test are in line with past research (Sodian and Wimmer, 1984; Varouxaki et al, 1999): over a third of the children were completely correct, an equal proportion neglected another's knowledge through inference, and with the remaining children showing no understanding that the task was inferential. As with Keenan et al (1994) children's performance for inference lagged behind understanding false belief. A new finding was that there was a strong association between children's Think judgements on the false inference test and the standard false belief test. An important finding was that children found the new false inference task easier than the true inference task. The view that children at this age hold a theoretical understanding of inference was further supported by their explanations.

CONCLUSION

The main finding to take forward into the future was the children's readiness to spot when someone was basing an inference on a false belief compared with when they were basing inference on a true belief. That is an interesting reversal of the usual because the theory-of-mind accounts in the literature agree that false belief understanding is a later accomplishment than true belief understanding. Could it be that children are ready primed to spot when someone is, as it were, riding for a fall, inferentially speaking?

REFERENCES

Beal, C. R. & Flavell, J. H. (1982). The effects of increasing the salience of message ambiguities on kindergartners' evaluations of communicative success and message adequacy. *Developmental Psychology, 18*, 43-48.

Bradmetz, J., & Bonnefoy-Claudet, C. (2003). Do young children acquire the meaning of *to know* and *to believe* simultaneously or not? *International Journal of Behavioral Development, 27*, 109-115.

Clements, W. A., and Perner, J. (1994). Implicit understanding of belief. *Cognitive Development, 9,* 377-395.

Freeman, N.H., Antonucci, C., & Lewis, C. (2000). Representation of the cardinality principle: early conception of error in a counterfactual test. *Cognition, 74,* 71-89.

Freeman, N. H., Lewis, C., & Doherty, M. (1991). Preschoolers' grasp of a desire for knowledge in false-belief prediction. *British Journal of Developmental Psychology, 9,* 139-157.

Friedman, O., Griffin, R., Brownell, H., & Winner, E., (2003). Problems with the seeing = knowing rule. *Developmental Science, 6,* 505-513.

Garnham, W. A., & Ruffman, T. (2001). Doesn't see, doesn't know: is anticipatory looking really related to understanding of belief? *Developmental Science,, 4,* 94-100.

Gopnik, A. (1993). How we know our own minds: The illusion of first-person knowledge of intentionality. *Behavioral and Brain Sciences, 16,* 1-14.

Gopnik, A., & Astington, J. W. (1988). Children's understanding of representational change and its relation to the understanding of false belief and the appearance-reality distinction. *Child Development, 59,* 26-37.

Halliday, M. S. (1977). Behavioural inference in young children. *Journal of Experimental Child Psychology, 23,* 378-390.

Karmiloff-Smith, A. (1992). *Beyond modularity: A developmental perspective on cognitive science.* MIT Press, London.

Keenan, T., Ruffman, T., & Olson, D. R. (1994). When do children understand logical inference as a source of knowledge? *Cognitive Development, 9,* 331-353.

Kuhn, D. (1992). Cognitive development. In M. H. Bornstein and M. E. Lamb (Eds.), *Developmental psychology: An advanced textbook* (pp. 211-272). Hillsdale NJ: Erlbaum.

Lohmann, H., Carpenter, M., & Call, J. (2002). Guessing versus believing – and seeing versus believing – in false belief tasks. *British Journal of Developmental Psychology,23,* 451-469.

Markman, E. M. (1977). Realizing that you don't understand: A preliminary investigation. *Child Development, 48*, 986-992.

Marsh, R. W. (1967). Tables for testing the significance of difference between proportions. *Australian Journal of Psychology, 19,* 223-229.

Mitchell, P. & Robinson, E. J. (1992). Children's understanding of the evidential connotation of 'know' in relation to overestimation of their own knowledge. *Journal of Child Language, 19*, 167-182.

Muldoon, K., Lewis, C., & Freeman, N. H. (2003). Putting counting to work: preschoolers' understanding of cardinal extension. *International Journal of Educational Research, 39*, 695-718.

Muldoon, K., Lewis, C., & Towse, J. (2005). Because it's there! Why some children count, rather than infer numerical relationships. *Cognitive Development, 20,* 472-491.

Nunes, T., Bryant, P., Evans, D., Bell, D., Gardner, S., Gardner, A., & Carraher, J. (2007). The contribution of logical reasoning to the learning of mathematics in primary school. *British Journal of Developmental Psychology, 25*, 147-166.

Pears, R., and Bryant, P. (1990). Transitive inferences by young children about spatial position. *British Journal of Psychology, 81*, 497-510.

Perner, J. (1991). *Understanding the Representational Mind.* Cambridge, MA: MIT Press.

Pillow, B. H. (1989). Early understanding of perception as a source of knowledge. *Journal of Experimental Child Psychology, 47*, 116-129.

Pratt, C., & Bryant, P. E. (1991). Young children understand that looking leads to knowing (so long as they are looking into a single barrel). *Child Development, 61,* 973-982.

Rai, R., & Mitchell, P. (2006). Children's ability to impute inferentially-based knowledge. *Child Development, 77*, 1091-1093.

Riggs, K. J. & Robinson, E. J. (1995). What people say and what they think: Children's judgments of false belief in relation to their recall of false messages. *British Journal of Developmental Psychology, 13*, 271-284.

Riggs, K. J., & Simpson, A. (2005). Young children have difficulty ascribing true beliefs. *Developmental Science, 8, F27-F30.*

Roth D., & Leslie A. M. (1998). Solving belief problems: Toward a task analysis. *Cognition. 66*, 1-31. 1998.

Ruffman, T. K. (1996). Do children understand the mind by means of simulation or a theory? Evidence from their understanding of inference. *Mind and Language, 11*, 388-414.

Russell, J. (2005). Justifying all the fuss about false belief. *Trends in Cognitive Sciences, 9,* 307-308.

Rusell, J., Hill, E.L., & Franco, F. (2001). The role of belief veracity in understanding intentions-in-action: Preschool children's performance on the transparent intentions task. *Cognitive Development, 16, 775-792.*

Sodian, B., & Wimmer, H. (1987). Children's understanding of inference as a source of knowledge. *Child Development, 59*, 703-718.

Sophian, C., Wood, A. M., & Vong, K. I. (1995). Making numbers count: The early development of numerical inferences. *Developmental Psychology, 31*, 263-273.

Sophian, C. & Somerville, S. C. (1988). Early developments in logical reasoning: Considering alternative possibilities. *Cognitive Development, 3*, 183-222.

Surian L, & Leslie A. M. (1999). Competence and performance in false belief understanding: A comparison of autistic and normal 3-year-old children. *British Journal of Developmental Psychology. 17, 141-155.*.

Varouxaki, A., & Freeman, N. H. (1998). Young children's understanding of other people's inferences. *Psychologia: Journal of the Hellenic Psychology Society, 5,* 20-30.

Varouxaki, A., Freeman, N. H., Peters, D., & Lewis, C. (1999). Inference neglect and ignorance denial. *British Journal of Developmental Psychology, 17,* 483-499.

Wellman, H. M. (1990). *The child's theory of mind.* Cambridge, MA: MIT Press.

Wimmer, H., Hogrefe, G. J., & Sodian, B (1988). A second stage in children's conception of mental life: Understanding informational accesses as origins of knowledge and belief. In J. W. Astington, P. L. Harris & D. R. Olson (Eds.), *Developing theories of mind* (pp. 173-192). Cambridge University Press.

Wimmer, H, & Perner, J (1983). Beliefs about beliefs: Representation and constraining function of wrong beliefs in young children's understanding of deception. *Cognition, 13,* 103-128.

In: Psychology of Decision Making in Education
Editor: Jeanine A. Elsworth, pp. 243-255
ISBN: 978-1-60021-933-7
© 2006 Nova Science Publishers, Inc.

Chapter 11

THE ROLE OF FILIAL PIETY IN THE CAREER DECISION PROCESSES OF POSTGRADUATE STUDENTS IN CHINA

Leili Jin, Mantak Yuen, and David Watkins
The University of Hong Kong

The research attention paid to career decision making among Mainland Chinese adolescents and college students is of recent origin (e.g., Creed & Wong, 2006; Hampton, 2005). Such attention is mainly due to major changes in two salient policy areas by the government of the People's Republic of China (PRC). Firstly, the labor distribution system has been changed from a planned to a market economic system in which employers and graduates are free to choose each other. Before the middle of the 20th century in the PRC, college graduates had to accept the jobs assigned by the government. The freedom of selection by both employers and fresh employees has stimulated Chinese graduates to consider how to choose a suitable career for their own sake. Secondly, higher education in the PRC is undergoing a radical transformation from an elite to a mass system. The increasing intake of the youth into college had led to the sharp competition in the labor market, which in turn has produced the employment pressure among college graduates. The number of college graduates pouring into the labor market each year has increased from 1.15 million in 2001 to 4.2 million in 2006 (China Ministry of Education, 2005). Meanwhile, graduate school admission has become a top priority for the majority of undergraduates: 0.714 million senior undergraduates sat for the national entrance examination for a Master's Degree in January, 2007[1]. Although the need for career and other counseling services in the Mainland is continually increasing (Zhang, Hu, & Pope, 2002), it is obvious that the antecedents of adaptive career decision making among Chinese postgraduates still remain unclear.

---

[1] http://www.moe.edu.cn/edoas/website18/info23746.htm , 12-12-2006

Career Commitment and Decision Making Self-Efficacy

Theoretically, the process of career decision making covers sequential stages starting from a pre-awareness and moving through awareness, planning (exploration and crystallization), commitment, and implementation (Gottfredson, 2002; Harren, 1979; Jordaan, 1963; Super, 1957). For late adolescents and young adults entering into the transition from school to work, a salient achievement of career decision making is a strong commitment to a career choice through sufficient exploration of self and the world of work. Those who endorse higher career commitment are likely to have a clear sense of occupational preference, be awareness of the potential barriers and the willingness to overcome them; a confidence in abilities to achieve objectives; and actively preparing to implement a set of particular vocational goals (Blustein, Ellis, & Devenis, 1989; Harren, 1979; Jordaan & Heyde, 1979; Marcia, 1966; Super, 1957). Blustein et al. (1989) defined *vocational exploration and commitment* (VEC) as one's progress in attaining commitment to a career choice along with a process ranging from an uncommitted or exploratory phase to a highly committed and confident phase. They further asserted that there were individual differences in the means used to achieve career commitment. Some people may accept various experiences encountered in the career commitment process, while others would hastily make a career choice in order to avoid the ambiguous, uncertainty and anxiety. Such phenomena is defined as the tendency to foreclose reflecting "the desire to commit to important educational and career decisions as soon as possible and an analogous attempt to adhere to these choices even in the face of disconfirming evidence" (Blustein et al., 1989, p. 347). Presumably, such a tendency would restrict one's career exploratory space and yield a premature decision, which in turn hinder one's career satisfaction and success.

The construct of *career decision self-efficacy*[2] has been identified in the literature as a salient social cognitive factor in the career decision-making process. This construct is based on Bandura's (1997) self-efficacy theory and reflects beliefs in personal abilities to successfully complete tasks necessary in making career decisions (Taylor & Betz, 1983). Numerous studies have consistently showed that career decision self-efficacy is positively related to indices of adaptive career decision making, including career maturity, career exploratory activities, vocational identity, career certainty, and negatively to career indecision (see Betz, Hammond, & Multon, 2005; and Betz & Luzzo, 1996 for reviews). Therefore, career commitment, tendency to foreclose and career decision self-efficacy were used as outcome variables related to adaptive career decision making in the current study.

Familial Factors and the Career Commitment Process

Researchers have called for more attention to the relationships between contextual / cultural factors and the process and content of career decision making (Blustein, 1997; Lent, Brown, & Hackett, 1994, 2000; Vondracek, Lerner, & Schulenberg, 1986a). This represents a

---

[2] The original construct was named Career Decision-Making Self-Efficacy. As stated by Nancy Betz and Karen Taylor, Career Decision-Making Self-Efficacy has been changed into Career Decision Self-Efficacy because another author has copyright of the term career decision making already. In the current study, we adopt the term career decision self-efficacy in order to be consistent with what Betz and Taylor propose.

shift of research focus from individual differences and self-implementation to individuals embedded in a real social or relational context (Blustein, 2004). Among the contextual factors, family relationships have been indentified as salient in the personal career decision process, including attachment to and conflictual independence from parents, multiple indices of family environment (see Vondracek, Lerner, & Schulenberg, 1986b; and Whiston & Keller, 2004 for reviews), and perceived parental support and family barriers (Leal-Muniz & Constantine, 2005). Although past studies are quite impressive, the nature and magnitude of family relationship on career decision making still remain unclear (Blustein et al., 1991). In particular, Leong and Brown (1995) argued that some cultural- specific variables might miss when the existing career theories developed from the Western culture and value system are applied to culturally different populations.

For adolescents and young adults who endorsed collectivist values, family relationships presumably play a more prominent role in career decision making(Lent et al., 2003). A few of past studies reported that family involvement directly exerted a significant impact on career choices, inferring that Asian Americans (41.3% were Chinese Americans in their sample) who tended to follow their parent's wishes were more likely to choose careers in traditional areas. Although career self-efficacy was found to significantly predict career choices, it was not predicted by either family SES or family involvement as expected (Tang, Fouad, & Smith, 1999). In addition, higher levels of intergenerational or acculturation conflicts within families would likely lead to higher career indecision and lower career aspiration among Asian American youths. However, relational-interdependent self-construal was significantly predictive of career certainty, suggesting that individuals who had a closer relationship with their parents and an inclination to consult parents' opinions for the future were more likely to make a definite career decision (Constantine & Flores, 2006; Ma & Yeh, 2005).

Theorists generally assume that the intention of collectivists to consider or even follow parents' advice on career choices (Leong & Serafica, 1995) can be partially attributed to the high values placed on respect for seniors or obedience to authority (Ma & Yeh, 2005; Moy, 1992). Such values partially due to the obligation or responsibility to financially support the family and care for aged parents (Leong & Chou, 1994; Leong & Leung, 1994), and partially to the aspiration to bring honor to the family (Ying, Coombs, & Lee, 1999). The abovementioned devotion of children to the parents is typically reflected by the filial piety construct. To date, little research has examined the relations of filial piety and adaptive career decision making among Chinese students who are from a representative collectivist culture (Oyserman, Coon, & Kemmelmeier, 2002).

Filial Piety

Filial piety addresses how children should treat toward their parents, living or dead, as well as attitudes toward their ancestors, which is a prominent ethical rule guiding intergenerational or interpersonal relationships in Chinese families and society (Ho, 1996). Recently, Yeh and associates have proposed a dual filial piety model to reflect the developmental changes of filial piety in the contemporary era (Yeh, 1997a, 2003). The dual model involves four common dimensions. "Respecting and Loving Parents" and "Supporting and Memorializing Parents" were combined into one higher order factor termed reciprocal filial piety, whereas "Oppressing Oneself" and "Glorifying Parents" formed another superfactor labeled authoritarian filial piety.

Reciprocal filial piety is defined as "emotionally and spiritually attending to one's parents out of gratitude for their efforts in having raising one, and physical and financial care for one's parents as they age and when they die for the same reason" (Yeh & Bedford, 2003, p. 216). In other words, the harmonious relationships with and the responsibility to care about the seniors out of affection and gratitude are underlined by reciprocal filial piety based on the principle of reciprocity and favoring the intimate(Yeh, 2003; Yeh & Bedford, 2004). *Authoritarian filial piety* is characterized as "suppressing one's own wishes and complying with one's parents' wishes because of their seniority in physical, financial or social terms, as well as continuing the family lineage and maintaining one's parents' reputation because of the force of role requirements" (Yeh & Bedford, 2003, p. 216). It accentuates hierarchy and submission, as well as oppresses independence and self-autonomy based on the principle of absolute obedience for superiors (Yeh, 2003). Generally, researchers acknowledge that absolute observance, obedience and subjugation of individual needs are not emphasized as much as before, but affective consideration and care of parents are still affirmed among Chinese people (Yeh & Bedford, 2003; Yuc & Ng, 1999).

The dual model has only been applied to date to examine the relationships of filial piety to indices of intrapersonal differences and the frequencies and treatment of family conflict (Yeh & Bedford, 2003, 2004). This study will first probe its potential effectiveness in the realm of career decision making. More specific, we will examine the relationships between two types of filial piety and career commitment process and career decision self-efficacy.

Researchers (Yeh, 1997a; 2003; Yeh & Bedford, 2003) propose that the effects of reciprocal filial piety on family relationships and individual development would be consistent with the positive evidence documented by the past research. For instance, higher filial piety yields better intergenerational relationships, family cohesion and solidarity (Cheung, Lee, & Chan, 1994; Lawrence, Bennett, & Markides, 1992; Roberts & Bengtson, 1990), low frequencies of parent-child conflict (Yeh, 1997b). Higher filial piety makes children feel more obligated to offer financial, physical and emotional support for parents and more responsible for caring for them (Ishii-Kuntz, 1997). Family obligation facilitates adolescents to discuss personal issues with family members, actively involves in positive social interaction and seeks help with peers, and promotes their educational aspirations and expectations (Fuligni, Tseng, & Lam, 1999). Specifically, both relational factors (i.e. respect for and a sense of indebtedness to parents) and parental factors (i.e., expectation, pressure, and social support) were significantly predictive of Korean adolescents' self-efficacy, achievement motivation, and studying time, which in turn promoted their academic achievement (Kim & Park, 2006). More direct evidence showed that reciprocal filial piety was positively related to openness and negatively to conventionalism (Yeh & Bedford, 2003). Therefore, we expect that reciprocal filial piety is positively related to career decision self-efficacy and progress in career commitment but negatively to the tendency to foreclose.

One the other hand, authoritarian filial piety would be likely to play a harmful role in interpersonal relationships and individual development as also partially evidenced by previous research. For example, parents' strong filial piety attitudes would produce children's *rigidity* and impede their *cognitive complexity* (Boey, 1976). Children who trained according to traditional filial attitudes were inclined to show cognitive conservatism in performing various problem-solving tasks, that is, they were more likely to adopt a passive uncritical and uncreative orientation toward learning, to hold fatalistic, superstitious, and stereotypic beliefs, and to be authoritarian, dogmatic, and conformist (Ho, 1994). They were also more likely to engage in superstitious practices, such as consulting an almanac or fortunetellers in making decisions (Ho, 1990). A sense of obedience to one's parents would force children to give up self-fulfillment, suppress self-expression in terms of impulse control. In a recent qualitative research to explore how child-parent relationships affect career and educational choices with a sample of senior undergraduates from the PRC, Deutsch (2004) found that parents' education backgrounds, individual history, family financial situation and social network (guanxi) strongly influenced children's career and further education options and geographic location. Especially, when parents disagreed with children's career or educational decisions, the majority of participants tended to follow their parents' wishes in terms of parents' attitudes and needs rather than fulfill personal occupation preferences. Deutsch argued that less obedience to parents' expectations would facilitate Mainland Chinese college students to more commit to their career goals. More direct evidence has further shown that authoritarian filial piety was positively associated with Neuroticism, Authoritarian Aggression and Conventionalism, and Particularism, negatively with Openness and Extroversion (Yeh & Bedford, 2003). Therefore, we hypothesized that authoritarian filial piety is negatively related to career decision self-efficacy and progress in career commitment but positively to the tendency to foreclose.

METHOD

Participants

Convenience sampling was used to recruit 374 postgraduate students were recruited from a large comprehensive university in Beijing. Of these, 158 (42.2%) were male and 216 (57.8%) female, with a mean age of 23.9 (SD=1.16).

Measures

Filial Piety Scale (FPS; Yeh & Bedford, 2003). This 16-item scale assesses both reciprocal and authoritarian filial piety. The instructions and item statements were slightly modified to be suitable for Mainland postgraduates. Participants are asked to indicate their agreement with the items on a 6-point scale from Extremely Unimportant (0) to Extremely Important (5). Examples of items measuring reciprocal filial piety include, "Hurry home upon the death of a parent, regardless of how far away you live" and "Be grateful to parents for raising you". Authoritarian items include, "Live with parents even after marriage" and "Compliment your parents when needed to save their face". Yeh and Bedford (2003) reported the Cronbach alpha's coefficient of .90 for the reciprocal FPS (8 items) and .79 for the authoritarian scale (8 items).

Commitment to Career Choices Scale (CCCS; Blustein et al., 1989). The Vocational Exploration and Commitment (VEC) subscale of the Commitment Career Choices Scale taps a dimension that ranges from an uncommitted, exploratory phase to a highly committed phase of career exploration, and uses 19 items to assess one's progress in attaining commitment to career choices. Lower scores on the VEC represent a greater commitment in one's career exploration and choice process. Reliability of the VEC scale has been reported with Cronbach's alpha coefficients ranging from .92 (for a sample of 565 US college students) to .91 (for a sample of 571 US college students). In terms of validity, Blustein et al. (1989) reported a correlation of -.72 between VEC and the Decision Making Task: Occupations scale of the Assessment of Career Decision Making (Harren, 1984) in a sample of 117 college students. Betz and Serling (1993) reported that VEC correlated .62 with the Fear of Commitment Scale (Serling, 1988) and .83 with the Career Indecision from Career Decision Status (Osipow, Carney, Winer, Yanico, & Koschier, 1976) in a sample of 138 US undergraduates.

The Tendency to Foreclose subscale (TTFS) is a 9-item scale to assess how one commits to career choices. Participants are asked to indicate their agreement with the items on a 6-point scale from Never true about me (1) to Always true about me (6) on both VEC and TTFS subscales. Low scores on the TTFS indicate being less foreclosed in commitment to a career choice. The TTFS has been found to have Crobach's alpha coefficients of .82 (for a sample of 565 college students) and .78 (for a sample of 571 college students). In terms of validity, Blustein et al. reported that the TTFS was related to a measure of foreclosure (Bennion & Adams, 1986) as expected.

Career Decision Self-efficacy –Short Form (CDSE-SF; Betz, Klein, & Taylor, 1996). This 25-item scale measures the degree of one's belief concerning his/ her ability to successfully complete tasks necessary to make career decisions on five hypothesized dimensions, including self-appraisal, gathering occupational information, goal selection, making plans to implement the decision, and problem solving. Betz et al. (1996) reported subscale reliabilities ranging from .73 (Self- Appraisal) to .83 (Goal Selection) and a Cronbach alpha coefficient of .94 for the total score. In terms of validity, Betz et al. (1996) reported that CDSE-SF correlated significantly with the Certainty and Indecision subscales of the Career Decision Scale (Osipow, Carney, Winer, Yanico, & Koschier, 1976), and with the Vocational Identity subscale of the My Vocational Situation Scale (Holland, Daiger, & Power, 1980) in a sample of 184 undergraduates. Betz, Hammond, and Multon (2005) recently provided extensive evidence to support the reliabilities and validities of the CDSE-SF.

Two items were excluded in the current study because they were not suitable for postgraduates in our sample. These two items are "Find information about graduate or professional schools" and "Select one major from a list of potential majors you are considering". The modified version of CDSE-SF consists of 23 items. The participants indicated how confident they feel about each statement along a 5-point Likert scale from No Confidence At All (1) to Complete Confidence (5).

Demographic questionnaire. A demographic questionnaire was used to collect background information regarding the participants' gender, age, academic major and year in study.

Procedure

In order to guarantee the literal accuracy of instruments, Commitment to Career Choices and Career Decision Self-Efficacy-Short Form were translated from English to Chinese by the researcher and back-translated from Chinese into English by a Chinese PhD. student with an English major. A native English PhD. student compared the back-translated version with the original English version, leading by a minor revision of the Chinese version. The Filial Piety Scale was not included in this procedure as it was developed in Chinese.

The data were obtained in first semester of the 2006-2007 academic year. Participants were solicited in public classes and by dormitory fliers and personal contact. The questionnaires were distributed and administered in classrooms or dorms. Those who endorsed the informed consent forms spent about 35 minutes completing the questionnaires and received a small gift for their contribution.

RESULTS

Means, SDs and Cronbach's α coefficients for all measures are presented in Table 1. In order to examine the potential impacts of gender, a one-way multivariate analysis of variance (MANOVA) was performed using the two filial piety factors (i.e., RFP and AFP) as dependent variables, and gender as an independent variable. MANOVA indicated a significant gender main effect (Wilks' Lambda= .97, F (2, 371) = 5.32 $p<.01$). Follow-up univariate analyses further showed the significant main effect of gender on AFP [F (1, 372) = 5.55, $p<.05$], indicating that males were more likely to held stronger beliefs of authoritarian filial piety than females. However, there were no significant differences in reciprocal filial piety between males and females. Therefore, we conducted the following analyses in terms of gender.

Table 1. Means , Sds and Cronbach's α Coefficients for all Variables

	Male (n=158)			Female (n=216)			Total (N=374)		
	M	SD	α	M	SD	α	M	SD	α
1. RFP	4.41	.47	.79	4.48	.40	.76	4.45	.43	.78
2. AFP	2.34	.84	.82	2.14	.82	.84	2.22	.83	.83
3. CDSE	3.51	.52	.91	3.37	.48	.91	3.43	.50	.91
4. VEC	3.36	.60	.84	3.47	.54	.83	3.43	.57	.84
5. TTF	3.14	.70	.73	2.94	.66	.79	3.03	.68	.77

Note: **RFP**= reciprocal filial piety, **AFP**= authoritarian filial piety. **CDSE**= career decision self-efficacy. **VEC**= vocational exploration and commitment, **TTF**= tendency to foreclose.

Zero-order correlations were computed between two types of filial piety and CDSE, VEC and TTF by gender separately (see Table 2). For both men and women, reciprocal filial piety was significantly and moderately correlated with career decision self-efficacy (men, $r=.37$, $p<.001$; women, $r=.29$, $p<.001$), inferring that higher levels of reciprocal filial piety are associated with stronger perceived career decision self-efficacy across gender. Moreover, reciprocal filial piety was modestly but significantly related to vocational exploration and commitment for men($r=-.18$, $p<.05$), but not for women ($r=-.10$, $p>.05$). These results indicated that there may be gender differences in the correlations between reciprocal filial piety and vocational exploration and commitment. Authoritarian filial piety was consistently found to be significantly and moderately associated with the tendency to foreclose for both men ($r=.27$, $p<.001$) and women ($r=.37$, $p<.001$), indicating that stronger authoritarian filial piety was related to a greater tendency to foreclose regardless of gender.

Contrary to our hypotheses, for both genders, reciprocal filial piety was not significantly related to the tendency to foreclose, and authoritarian filial piety was not significantly related to either career decision self-efficacy or vocational exploration and commitment.

Table 2. Zero-Order Correlations for all Variables by Gender

	1	2	3	4	5
1. RFP	---	.22***	.29***	-.10	.05
2. AFP	.19**	---	-.02	.07	.37***
3. CDSE	.37***	-.01	---	-.37***	.05
4. VEC	-.18*	-.03	-.34***	---	-.18**
5. TTF	-.02	.27***	.03	-.18*	---

Note: **RFP**= reciprocal filial piety, **AFP**= authoritarian filial piety. **CDSE**= career decision self-efficacy, **VEC**= vocational exploration and commitment, and **TTF**= tendency to foreclose. Zero-order correlations for men are presented in the below diagonal, and those for women in the above. $*p<.05$, $**p<.01$, $***p<.001$ (1-tailed).

CONCLUSIONS

This study examined the relationships between two types of filial piety and adaptive career decision making (i.e., career commitment and decision self-efficacy) from an indigenous perspective. The findings partially support our hypotheses that reciprocal filial piety is likely to enhance career decision self-efficacy and progress in career commitment, while authoritarian filial piety is positively associated with the tendency to foreclose. It is very important for career theorists and counseling practitioners to understand the adaptive process of career decision making among Chinese postgraduates.

For hypothesis 1, the anticipated significant and positive relationship between reciprocal filial piety and career decision self-efficacy was moderate for both men and women, indicating that those who reported stronger reciprocal filial piety perceived higher levels of self-efficacy for their career decision-making. This finding is consistent with previous research that indicated filial piety may benefit the specific-domain self-efficacy, such as academic self-efficacy in Kim and Park's(2006) research and career decision self-efficacy in this study. It is possible that respect for and a sense of indebtedness to parents, and duties to financially and emotionally support the whole family among those with collectivist values are likely to foster more confidence in personal abilities to deal with their own career decisions. In addition, less family conflict and more expressive freedom have been documented to be associated with higher career decision self-efficacy (Hargrove, Creagh, & Burgess, 2002). Since reciprocal filial piety emphasizes children's initiative to maintain the harmonious and equal intergenerational relationships, the significant correlations of reciprocal filial piety with career decision self-efficacy would not surprise us.

The relation between reciprocal filial piety and vocational exploration and commitment was mixed. For men, higher levels of reciprocal filial piety were significantly and modestly associated with greater progress in career commitment, but not significantly for women. Such findings partially shed light on past research that family obligation (i.e., a combination of respect and care for parents) is likely to promote educational aspiration/ expectations (Fuligni, Tseng, & Lam, 1999). Here, we further provided the empirical evidence that, at least for men in this study, respect and care for parents tapped in reciprocal filial piety also benefit for young people to make progress in attaining career commitment. For women, reciprocal filial piety may only exert an indirect effect on progress in career commitment through career decision self-efficacy. However, such hypothesis merits further examination.

Contrary to our hypothesis, reciprocal filial piety was not observed to be significantly related to the tendency to foreclose across gender, although past research reported that reciprocal filial piety was positively related to openness and negatively to conventionalism (Yeh & Bedford, 2003). The confounding results are warranted to investigate more.

With respect to hypothesis set 2, as we had expected, for both men and women, those who endorsed higher authoritarian filial piety would likely show stronger tendency to foreclose. One possibility is authoritarian filial piety holders would likely submit to the authority and comply for parents' wishes. To avoid the intergenerational conflicts and parents' pressure in career choices, they tend to commit to a career choice as soon as possible out of obedience or suppression based on the requirements of social roles in the Collectivism culture, no matter whether they have clarified their own occupational preferences. This finding seems to partially support Blustein et al.'s (1989) findings that lack of autonomy was correlated with the tendency to foreclose. Another explanation is higher authoritarian filial piety has been identified to be related to higher Neuroticism personality (Yeh & Bedford, 2003), and less open-mindedness and future-orientation (Yang, 1996), which tended to lead authoritarian filial piety holders to adopt dogmatic or dualistic attitudes to approach the tasks of committing to career choices.

Contrary to our expectations, authoritarian filial piety was not significantly negatively related to career decision self-efficacy and progress in career commitment. Although previous research proposed that less bond to obey parents' expectations would facilitate Mainland Chinese college students to more commit to their career goals(Deutsch, 2004), or authoritarian filial piety holders tended to make decisions dependent on superstitious prediction, our study failed to identify that authoritarian filial piety would impede either progress in career commitment or career decision self-efficacy. The absence of significant relations may be explained by that some students would have a firm career commitment although they comply with parents' suggestions without in-depth exploration by themselves(Marcia, 1980). Given that career choice is conceived of as a means to represent interdependent self close to family (Hardin, Leong, & Osipow, 2001) or a reciprocal alternative for both self and family (Leong & Serafica, 1995) in a collectivist culture, Chinese students may have partly internalized parents' values as their own preferences, especially for those who would likely honor the family and keep the familial lineage (as partially reflected by authoritarian filial piety).

The findings of this study are very meaningful to career counseling practice. It helps us to understand the process of career decision making from a perspective of Chinese culture, above and beyond the previous angles of intrapersonal differences in cognition and personality, or adolescent development. Concerning the important effects of filial piety on career decision making, counselors are suggested to take the child-parent relationships stemming from filial piety into consideration when they design interventions for and counsel individuals endorsed the collectivist values. For example, elements regarding the enhancement of clients' gratitude and responsibilities to parents are suggested to add into career interventions in order to enhance young people's career decision self-efficacy and career commitment. It is also suggested that counselors should be sensitive to examine the antecedents of one's tendency to foreclose. If he or she commits to a premature choice purely caused by obedience to parents' authority, which in turn would reduce anxiety and pressure resulting from intergenerational conflicts, counselors had better remind the client to aware the negative possibilities of a tendency to foreclose for career success and satisfaction from a long-term career development perspective. If the tendency to foreclose is associated to one's cognitive limitations (i.e., dogmatic or dualistic thinking styles), counselors would better provide more career exposure to broaden clients' horizon.

REFERENCES

Bandura, A. (1997). *Self-efficacy: The exercise of control*. New York: Freeman.

Bennion, L. D., & Adams, G. R. (1986). A Revision of the Extended Version of the Objective Measure of Ego Identity Status: An identity instrument for use with late adolescents. *Journal of Adolescence Research, 1*, 183-198.

Betz, N. E., Hammond, M. S., & Multon, K. D. (2005). Reliability and Validity of Five-Level Response Continua for the Career Decision Self-Efficacy Scale. *Journal of Career Assessment, 13*(2), 131-149.

Betz, N. E., Klein, K. L., & Taylor, K. M. (1996). Evaluation of a short form of the Career Decision-Making Self-Efficacy Scale. *Journal of Career Assessment, 4*(1), 47-57.

Betz, N. E., & Luzzo, D. A. (1996). Career assessment and the Career Decision-Making Self-Efficacy Scale. *Journal of Career Assessment Special Issue: Assessing career beliefs, attitudes, and values, 4*(4), 413-428.

Betz, N. E., & Serling, D. A. (1993). Construct validity of fear of commitment as an indicator of career indecisiveness. *Journal of Career Assessment, 1*, 21-34.

Blustein, D. L. (1997). A context-rich perspective of career exploration across the life roles. *The Career Development Quarterly, 45*, 260-274.

Blustein, D. L. (2004). Moving from the inside out: Further explorations of the family of origin/career development linkage. *The Counseling Psychologist, 32*, 603-611.

Blustein, D. L., Ellis, M., & Devenis, L. (1989). The development and validation of a two-dimensional model of the commitment to career choice process [Monograph]. *Journal of Vocational Behavior, 35*, 342-378.

Blustein, D. L., Walbridge, M. M., Friedlander, M. L., & Palladino, D. E. (1991). Contributions of psychological separation and parental attachment to the career development process. *Journal of Counseling Psychology, 38*(1), 39-50.

Boey, K. W. (1976). *Rigidity and cognitive complexity: An empirical investigation in the interpersonal, physical, and numeric domains under task-oriented and ego-oriented conditions.* Unpublished doctoral dissertation, University of Hong Kong.

Cheung, C. K., Lee, J. J., & Chan, C. M. (1994). Explicating filial piety in relation to family cohesion. *Journal of Social Behavior and Personality, 9,* 565-580.

Constantine, M. G., & Flores, L. Y. (2006). Psychological distress, perceived family conflict and career development issues in college students of color. *Journal of Career Assessment, 14,* 354-369.

Creed, P. A., & Wong, O. Y. (2006). Reliability and validity of a Chinese version of the career decision-making difficulties questionnaire. *International Journal for Educational and Vocational Guidance, 6,* 47-63.

Deutsch, F. M. (2004). How parents influence the life plans of graduating Chinese university students. *Journal of Comparative Family Studies, 35,* 393-421.

Fuligni, A. J., Tseng, V., & Lam, M. (1999). Attitudes toward family obligations among American adolescents with Asian, Latin American, and European backgrounds. *Child Development, 70,* 1030-1044.

Gottfredson, L. S. (2002). Gottfredson's theory of circumscription, compromise, and self-creation. In D. Brown & Associates (Eds.), *Career choice and development* (4 ed., pp. 85-148). San Francisco: Jossey-Bass.

Hampton, N. Z. (2005). Testing for the structure of the Career Decision Self-Efficacy Scale-Short Form among Chinese college student. *Journal of Career Assessment, 13,* 98-113.

Hardin, E. E., Leong, F. T. L., & Osipow, S. H. (2001). Cultural relativity in the conceptualization of career maturity. *Journal of Vocational Behavior, 58,* 36-52.

Hargrove, B. K., Creagh, M. G., & Burgess, B. L. (2002). Family interaction patterns as predictors of vocational identity and career decision-making self-efficacy. *Journal of Vocational Behavior, 61*(2), 185-201.

Harren, V. A. (1979). A model of career decision making for college students. *Journal of Vocational Behavior, 14,* 119-133.

Harren, V. A. (1984). *Assessment of career decision making.* Los Angeles: Western Psychological Services.

Ho, D. Y. F. (1990). Chinese values and behavior: A psychological study: Unpublished manuscript, University of Hong Kong.

Ho, D. Y. F. (1994). Filial piety, authoritarian moralism, and cognitive conservatism in Chinese societies. *Genetic, Social, and General Psychology Monographs, 120,* 347-365.

Ho, D. Y. F. (1996). Filial piety and its psychological consequences. In M. H. Bond (Ed.), *The handbook of Chinese psychology* (pp. 155-165). Hong Kong: Oxford University Press.

Holland, J. L., Daiger, D. C., & Power, P. G. (1980). *My Vocational Situation.* Palo Alto, CA: Consulting Psychologists' Press.

Ishii-Kuntz, M. (1997). Intergenerational relationships among Chinese, Japanese, and Korean Americans. *Family Relations, 46,* 23-32.

Jordaan, J. P. (1963). Exploratory behavior: The formation of self and occupational concepts. In D. E. Super (Ed.), *Career development: Self-concept theory* (pp. 42-78). New York: College Entrance Examination Board.

Jordaan, J. P., & Heyde, M. B. (1979). *Vocational maturity during the high school years.* New York: Teachers College Press.

Kim, U., & Park, Y. (2006). Indigenous psychological analysis of academic achievement in Korea: The influence of self-efficacy, parents, and culture. *International Journal of Psychology, 41*, 287-292.

Lawrence, R. H., Bennett, J. M., & Markides, K. S. (1992). Perceived intergenerational solidarity and psychological distress among older Mexican-Americans. *Journal of Gerontology, 47*, S55-S65.

Leal-Muniz, V., & Constantine, M. G. (2005). Predictors of the career commitment process in Mexican American college students. *Journal of Career Assessment, 13*(2), 204-215.

Lent, R. W., Brown, S. D., & Hackett, G. (1994). Toward a unifying social cognitive theory of career and academic interest, choice, and performance [Monograph]. *Journal of Vocational Behavior, 45*, 79-122.

Lent, R. W., Brown, S. D., & Hackett, G. (2000). Contextual supports and barriers to career choice: A social cognitive analysis. *Journal of Counseling Psychology, 47*(1), 36-49.

Lent, R. W., Brown, S. D., Schmidt, J., Brenner, B., Lyons, H., & Treistman, D. (2003). Relation of contextual supports and barriers to choice behavior in engineering majors: Test of alternative social cognitive models. *Journal of Counseling Psychology, 50*(4), 458-465.

Leong, F. T. L., & Brown, M. (1995). Theoretical issues in cross-cultural career development: Cultural validity and cultural specificity. In W. B. Walsh, & Osipow,S.H., (Ed.), *Handbook of vocational psychology* (2nd ed., pp. 143-180). Hillsdale, NJ:: Erlbaus.

Leong, F. T. L., & Chou, E. L. (1994). The role of ethnic identity and acculturation in the vocational behavior of Asian Americans: An integrative review. *Journal of Vocational Behavior, 44*, 155-172.

Leong, F. T. L., & Leung, S. A. (1994). Career assessment with Asian Americans. *Journal of Career Assessment, 2*, 240-257.

Leong, F. T. L., & Serafica, F. C. (1995). Career development of Asian Americans: A research area in need of a good theory. In F. T. L. Leong (Ed.), *Career development and vocational behavior of racial and ethnic minorities* (pp. 67-102). Hillsdale, NJ: Lawrence Erlbaum.

Ma, P. W., & Yeh, C. J. (2005). Factors influencing the career decision status of Chinese American youths. *The Career Development Quarterly, 53*, 337-347.

Marcia, J. E. (1966). Development and validation of ego-identity. *Journal of Personality and Social Psychology, 3*(5), 551-558.

Marcia, J. E. (1980). Identity in adolescence. In J. Adelson (Ed.), *Handbook of adolescent psychology* (pp. 159-187). New York: John Wiley.

Moy, S. (1992). A culturally sensitive, psychoeducational model for understanding and treating Asian-American clients. *Journal of Psychology and Christianity, 11*, 358-369.

Osipow, S. H., Carney, C. G., Winer, J. L., Yanico, B., & Koschier, M. (1976). *The Career Decision Scale* (3rd rev. ed.). Columbus, OH: Marahon Consulting & Press and (1987) Odessa, FL: Psychological Assessment Resources.

Oyserman, D., Coon, H. M., & Kemmelmeier, M. (2002). Rethinking Individualism and Collectivism : Evaluation of theoretical assumptions and meta-analyses. *Psychological Bulletin, 128*, 3-72.

Roberts, R. E. L., & Bengtson, V. L. (1990). Is intergenerational solidarity a unidimensional construct? A second test of a formal model. *Journal of Gerontology, 45*, S12-S20.

Serling, D. A. (1988). Development of a fear of commitment inventory: Unpublished master's thesis, Ohio State University, Columbus.

Super, D. E. (1957). *The psychology of careers*. New York: Harper & Row.

Tang, M., Fouad, N. A., & Smith, P. L. (1999). Asian Americans' career choice: A path model to examine factors influencing their career choices. *Journal of Vocational Behavior, 54*, 142-157.

Taylor, K. M., & Betz, N. E. (1983). Applications of self-efficacy theory to the understanding and treatment of career indecision. *Journal of Vocational Behavior, 22*(1), 63-81.

Vondracek, F. W., Lerner, R. M., & Schulenberg, J. E. (1986a). *Career development: A life span approach*. Hillsdale, NJ: Lawrence Erlbaum.

Vondracek, F. W., Lerner, R. M., & Schulenberg, J. E. (1986b). *The influences of the family of origin on career development: A review and analysis*. Hillsdale, NJ: Lawrence Erlbaum.

Whiston, S. C., & Keller, B. K. (2004). The influences of the family of origin on career development. *Society of Counseling Psychology, 32*, 493-568.

Yang, K. S. (1996). The psychological transformation of the Chinese people as a result of societal modernization. In M. H. Bond (Ed.), *The handbook of Chinese psychology*. Hong Kong: Oxford University Press.

Yeh, K. H. (1997a). Changes in the Taiwanese people's concept of filial piety. In L. Y. Cheng, Y. H. Lu & F. C. Wang (Eds.), *Taiwanese Society in the 1990s* (pp. 171-214): Institute of Sociology, Academia Sinica, Taipei (in Chinese).

Yeh, K. H. (1997b). Parent-child conflicts and their solution types: Discussion from the viewpoint of flial piety [in Chinese]. *Bulletin of the Institute of Ethnology, Academia Sinica, 82*, 65-114.

Yeh, K. H. (2003). The beneficial and harmful effects of filial piety: An integrative analysis. In K. S. Yang, P. B. Hwang & P. Daibo (Eds.), *Asian Social Psychology: Conceptual and Empirical Contributions*: Greenwood Publishing Group, Inc., Connecticut.

Yeh, K. H., & Bedford, O. (2003). A test of the Dual Filial Piety model. *Asian Journal of Social Psychology, 6*, 215-228.

Yeh, K. H., & Bedford, O. (2004). Filial belief and parent-child conflict. *International Journal of Psychology, 39*, 132-144.

Ying, Y. W., Coombs, M., & Lee, P. E. (1999). Family intergenerational relationship of Asian American adolescents. *Cultural Diversity and Ethnic Minority Psychology, 5*, 350-363.

Yue, X., & Ng, S. H. (1999). Filial obligations and expectations in China: Current view from young and old people in Beijing. *Asian Journal of Social Psychology, 2*, 215-226.

Zhang, W., Hu, X., & Pope, M. (2002). The evolution of career guidance and counseling in the People's Republic of China. *Career Development Quarterly, 50*, 226-236.

In: Psychology of Decision Making in Education
Editor: Jeanine A. Elsworth, pp. 257-270

ISBN: 978-1-60021-933-7
© 2006 Nova Science Publishers, Inc.

Chapter 12

DECIDING WITH WHOM TO MATE:
DO FEMALE FINCHES FOLLOW FASHION?

John P. Swaddle and Earl Clelland

Institute for Integrative Bird Behavior Studies, Biology Department, College of William and Mary, Williamsburg, VA 23185

ABSTRACT

Choosing an appropriate mate is one of the most important decisions that any animal has to make. The traditional view in non-human systems is that animals are largely slaves to their genes and an individual's mate choice is handed down from their parents. However, in recent years it has become clear that many animals show active decision making in who to mate with and that females may copy mate preferences from other females in the population. In other words, females' mating decisions are affected by the current fashion in their population. Here, we explore whether "mate choice copying" occurs in a model monogamous mating system—the zebra finch. Females were given the opportunity to observe another female courting a particular type of male (we manipulated male appearance by placing small colored leg bands on each bird). In preference tests, our focal females significantly shifted their mate preferences towards the type of male that they had observed as being courted by other females. Therefore, female finches do seem to copy mate preferences, implying that there is social inheritance of information that fundamentally affects mating decisions. This is one of the first demonstrations of mate choice copying in any monogamous system and implies that many other birds may also use social information to affect their mating decisions. We need to rethink evolutionary models of mate choice and sexual selection incorporating this form of social decision making process.

INTRODUCTION

Although selecting a mate is one of the most important decisions in an animal's life, there is surprisingly little discussion and exploration of decision making in traditional studies of mate choice (e.g., Andersson 1994; Shuster & Wade 2003; Andersson & Simmons 2006). Evolutionary studies of mate choice are dominated by gene-centered explanations of among-individual variation in mate preferences (Brooks & Endler 2001; Kokko et al. 2002; Kokko et al. 2003; Shuster & Wade 2003; Andersson & Simmons 2006), stating that mate choice is largely determined by genetically inherited factors. However, it is becoming increasingly clear that mate choice and the benefits of choosing an appropriate mate are more plastic than commonly thought, varying within-individuals as well as among-individuals (Patricelli et al. 2002; Rodriguez & Greenfield 2003; Welch 2003; Greenfield & Rodriguez 2004; Lynch et al. 2005; Lynch et al. 2006). Plasticity is the manifestation of how environmental factors increase variation (in both additive and epistatic effects) above and beyond any genetic contribution to variation in mate preferences. Even this approach to mate choice tends to ignore actual decision making processes and largely represents plasticity as either environmentally determined noise in mate preference or a correlate of changes in life stage and physiology, rather than as the result of definable cognitive process that alter mate choice.

Recently, behavioral ecologists have started to merge the individual level processes of cognitive psychology with the population level processes of evolutionary biology to explain how mate choice is affected by decision making. One example of this is the study of mate choice copying (Pruett-Jones 1992; Dugatkin 1996a; Schlupp & Ryan 1997; Brooks 1998, 1999; Freeberg et al. 1999; Galef & White 2000; Westneat et al. 2000; White & Galef 2000; Swaddle et al. 2005; Uehara et al. 2005). In mate choice copying, the choosing individual (classically females) copies the mate preferences they observe in the population and expresses this copied preference through mate choice. In other words, mate preferences are inherited through social cues that are filtered through cognitive processes (White & Galef 2000; Swaddle et al. 2005). Females view what kind of male is successful and make a decision to mate with that type of male.

Mate choice copying has been demonstrated in a handful of polygynous or lekking species, but has only recently been explored in a monogamous species (Doucet et al. 2004; Swaddle et al. 2005). It makes sense for polygynous females to copy a mate preference as it would be in a female's interest to find quickly the few high quality males in the population. Mate choice copying promotes rapid acquisition of information that relates to mate quality. In contrast to polygynous mating systems, many males will be mated in a monogamous mating system and mate quality will be more evenly distributed across the population. Therefore, mate choice copying may not skew mating success substantially in a monogamous species and, hence, not be strongly selected for through sexual selection. However, mate choice copying could still be selected for in monogamous species where there is the opportunity to observe other mated individuals, such as in colonial breeders, and/or where the costs of developing an independent mate choice are high (Pruett-Jones 1992; Stohr 1998; White & Galef 1999). In other words, mate choice copying by monogamous females may be a cheap way of getting reliable information about male quality.

Even though we are currently unsure about the evolutionary origins or consequences of mate choice copying (Kirkpatrick & Dugatkin 1994; Laland 1994; Agrawal 2001), it is clear that animals must engage in various elements of decision making to copy mate preferences. For example, the age and sexual experience of individuals affects how females copy mate preferences (Dugatkin & Godin 1993; Ophir & Galef 2004; Amlacher & Dugatkin 2005). In addition, the information that females learn about males through mate choice copying can be generalized to new males (White & Galef 2000; Godin et al. 2005; Swaddle et al. 2005). In other words, if a hypothetical female sees males with red bills as being chosen by other females, then the copying female will be more likely to favor any male with a red bill, not just those particular individual males she saw as chosen. Hence, in some species, copying females are able to internalize copied information and make mate choice decisions dependent on the age, aggression, and sexual experience of the demonstrating female or the copied males. These are clearly cognitively complex decision making processes that push mate choice well beyond the confines of genetically inherited mate preferences.

Previously, we have shown that the monogamous zebra finch can copy mate preferences and that females can generalize information about preferred males to affect future mate preferences (Swaddle et al. 2005). This was the first convincing evidence of mate choice copying in a monogamous species (Brown & Fawcett 2005). Here, we report an experimental study further investigating how female zebra finches make decisions about mate preference and how mate choice copying is affected by social cues.

Our previous evidence for mate choice copying by female zebra finches relied on test (i.e., observer) females observing demonstrator females actually mating and starting to build nests with males for a two week period (Swaddle et al. 2005). Test females copied the preference for types of males they saw as being mated with other females. In the natural ecology of this species, archetypal copying females are probably unmated for shorter periods than two weeks (Zann 1996). Also, in other monogamous species, it is more likely that a potentially copying female would observe courtship between demonstrator females and males rather than prolonged periods of actual mating (i.e, copulations and nest building). Therefore, we investigated whether observing courtship for short bouts was sufficient to elicit mate choice copying in female zebra finches. In addition we investigated whether a known pre-existing preference for physical symmetry, manipulated by placing colored plastic leg bands on the males' legs in symmetric and asymmetric arrangements (Swaddle & Cuthill 1994a; Swaddle & Cuthill 1994b; Swaddle 1996), could be eroded by mate choice copying. In general, it is unclear how the decision making associated with mate choice copying can override or accentuate pre-existing (e.g., genetically inherited or sexually imprinted) mate preferences (Dugatkin & Godin 1992; Dugatkin 1996b).

Specifically, we examined how female zebra finches' preferences for symmetrically and asymmetrically leg banded males changed from before to after exposure to courting females and males. We predicted that females would show a general preference for symmetrically banded males before the observation period, consistent with previous studies (Swaddle & Cuthill 1994b; Swaddle 1996). We also predicted that females would increase their preference, from before to after the observation period, for males wearing the band patterns that they observed being courted by other females. In other words, we predicted that observation of conspecific courtship would be sufficient to change mate choice decisions in female zebra finches.

METHODS

Experimental Subjects and General Housing Conditions

We used 24 virgin adult male zebra finches, 15 virgin adult test (observer) females, and eight virgin adult demonstrator females in this study. Birds were randomly selected from our outbred zebra finch colony and were either one or two generations from wild caught stock. Males and females were housed in visual but not acoustic isolation from each other in same sex group cages at approximately 20 °C. The males were housed in groups of three while the observer and demonstrator females were housed in groups of four. The birds were housed in wire cages (approximately 60 x 30 x 40 cm) and provided nutritionally complete seed and water *ad libitum*. The birds were kept on a 14:10 light:dark photoperiod under full spectrum lighting to maintain their readiness to breed (Zann 1996). None of the birds had prior experience with other individuals in the study.

The experiment was separated into three phases. First, we assessed test females' preferences for males wearing symmetric and asymmetric arrangements of red and yellow plastic leg bands. Then test females observed demonstrator females display apparent preferences for new males wearing particular arrangements of these same leg bands. Finally, we tested whether test females' altered their mate preferences in favor of males wearing the leg band arrangements that demonstrator females preferred. In other words, we tested whether test females copied preferences from the demonstrator females.

Pre-Observation Mate Preference Trials

We assessed test females' preference for males wearing three arrangements of red and yellow plastic leg bands, in a three chamber preference apparatus (Figure 1). There were three arrangements of plastic leg bands: right asymmetric, left asymmetric, and symmetric. (a) In the right asymmetric arrangement the leg bands were positioned so that males wore three units of red color and one of yellow on their right leg, while wearing three units of yellow and one of red on their left leg (Figure 2a). (b) This band arrangement was mirror reflected for the left asymmetric treatment group (Figure 2b). (c) In the symmetric leg band arrangement each male wore two units of red and two of yellow on each leg, with the red part of the bands in the center of the arrangement (Figure 2c). It is important to note that there was the same amount of red and yellow color in each band treatment group, hence reducing the effect that particular colors would have on mate preferences.

To commence a mate preference trial, a test female was placed in the preference apparatus for two hours to acclimate to the cage (Figure 1). After the acclimation period, one cage of three males was randomly selected and banded according to each of the three leg band arrangements (i.e., one wore the right asymmetric treatment, one wore the left asymmetric treatment, and one wore the symmetrically arranged bands). These three males were randomly assigned to display cages in the preference apparatus to minimize positional bias across the series of preference trials. An opaque curtain that temporarily separated the display cages from the female part of the chamber was removed so that the female could observe the display males. The female's cage was arranged so that she could view only one male at a time

(Figure 1). There were opaque dividers between male display cages so that males could not visually interact with each other. During preference trials, all birds had *ad libitum* access to seed and water.

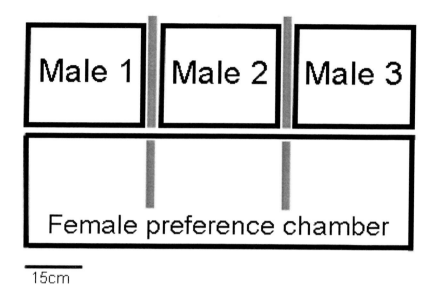

Figure 1. Plan view of the mate preference apparatus. Each of the stimulus males were placed in a small cage, separated by opaque barriers (gray bars). The test female was placed in a long chamber so she could observe each of the stimulus males. Each observation compartment was separated with an opaque barrier so that a female could see only one male at a time. There were abundant perches throughout all the cages. We used the proportion of time females spent displaying in the compartment immediately in front of each male as an index of female preference. All birds had *ad libitum* access to food and water throughout trials.

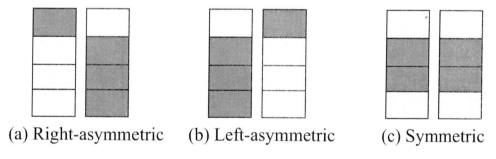

(a) Right-asymmetric   (b) Left-asymmetric   (c) Symmetric

Figure 2. Cartoon representations of the three colored plastic leg band arrangements used for this study: (a) the right-asymmetric; (b) left-asymmetric; and (c) symmetric band treatments. These small plastic leg bands were easily removed and replaced on birds between trials.

After a further 10 minute acclimation period, we videotaped (with a Sony digital video camera) all interactions among the birds for a 1-hour preference trial. We analyzed the tapes to record the amount of time a female spent performing ritualized display behaviors (short hops) in front of each male (Zann 1996; Swaddle et al. 2005). Quantification of this behavior is known to reflect actual mate choice in larger aviary cages and in the wild (Burley 1988; Swaddle & Cuthill 1994b; Swaddle 1996; Zann 1996). We used the relative amount of time a female spent displaying in front of each male as a measure of her mate preference for each leg band treatment. Each female experienced one mate preference trial and then was returned to her housing cage.

Observation Trials

Observation (mate choice copying) trials were conducted in a modified preference apparatus. We placed three female demonstrator cages between the three male display cages and the larger test female observation cage (Figure 3). The demonstrator female could visually interact with only the single male she was placed in front of; she could not move into any other cages of the observation apparatus. This arrangement of cages was intended to simulate the demonstrator female displaying a preference for a particular male (i.e., the male she was placed in front of) over the other males. The test female was free to observe this female and all the males; hence, she could gain information about which male was apparently preferred over other males.

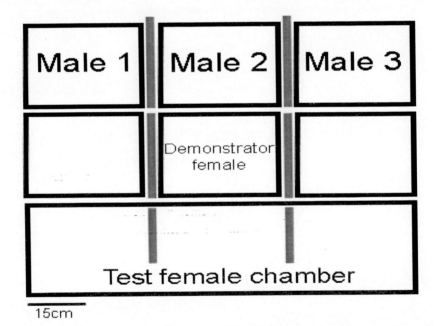

Figure 3. Plan view of the test observation chamber. Each of the stimulus males were placed in a small cage, separated by opaque barriers (gray bars), as in Figure 1. A demonstrator female was placed in one of three small cages in front of each of the stimulus males. A demonstrator female could see only one stimulus male. The test (observing) female was placed in a long chamber so she could see each of the stimulus males (one at a time) and also see the demonstrator female courting one of these stimulus males. The position of the demonstrator female changed between trials (see Methods section for more details). Here we have illustrated an example where the demonstrator female is placed in the middle cage. All birds had *ad libitum* access to food and water throughout trials.

The 15 test females were randomly allocated to two groups: one that was reinforced to prefer the right-asymmetric males in observation trials ($N = 7$), and one that observed left-asymmetric males as being preferred ($N = 8$). To begin an observation trial, we randomly selected a cage of three males to serve as stimuli for the observations and banded them as before. Next we placed a randomly selected demonstrator female in the appropriate demonstrator cage (according to which type of male should appear to be preferred). Then we introduced the test female, allowed for a 10 minute acclimation period and videotaped the test female's activity for a 1-hour observation trial. These videotapes verified that test females viewed all of the males during each observation trial. Every test female experienced ten 1-hour observation trials, only nearly consecutive days. For each observation trial, females observed different males than they had experienced in the pre-observation mate preference trials. Following each observation trial, all birds were returned to their housing cages.

Post-Copying Mate Preference Test

A new set of 24 males (additional to the original 24) was used in the post-copying preference test trials so that the test females' preferences were not confounded with familiarity with particular males. We followed the same procedure as for the pre-observation mate preference trials, with display males being randomly assigned to each of the three leg band treatments (right-asymmetric, left-asymmetric, and symmetric; Figure 2) and randomly assigned to cage positions in the preference apparatus (Figure 1). Again, we analyzed the videotapes to discern test females' preferences for males wearing these leg band treatments.

Statistical Analyses

All proportional preference data were arc-sine square-root transformed to improve normality. We tested for differences in the pre-observation preferences among leg band treatments using a one-way ANOVA. We compared pre-observation to post-observation leg band preferences with a paired t-test to determine whether test females' preferences shifted toward the band arrangement that they were reinforced to copy. All statistical tests were performed with SPSS v.13 and employed two-tailed tests of significance.

RESULTS

In the pre-observation mate preference trials, females consistently preferred the symmetrically banded males over the asymmetric males ($F_{2,42} = 3.61$, $P = 0.036$; Figure 4). This is consistent with previous data concerning general symmetry preferences among female zebra finches (Swaddle & Cuthill 1994a; Swaddle & Cuthill 1994b; Bennett et al. 1996; Swaddle 1996; Waas & Wordsworth 1999).

Test females significantly changed their mate preference from pre- to post-observation trials, with test females shifting band preferences toward the arrangement that was courted by demonstrator females in the observation trials ($t_{14} = 2.48$, $P = 0.026$; Figure 5). In other words, test females who observed an apparent preference for right-asymmetric banded males shifted their preference toward this type of male, and females who observed an apparent preference for left-asymmetric banded males increased their preference for that type of male.

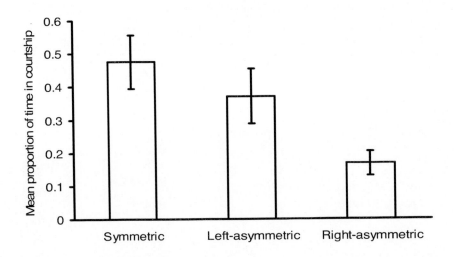

Figure 4. Mean (± s.e.m.) preference for leg band arrangements in the pre-observation mate preference trials. Before observation trials, females had a general preference for males wearing the symmetric band arrangement

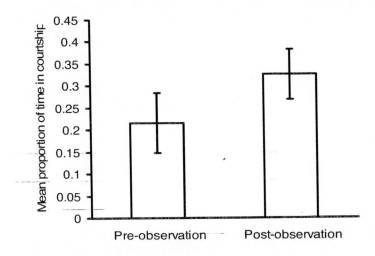

Figure 5. Mean (± s.e.m.) preference for males wearing the reinforced (i.e., courted by another female in the observation trials) leg band arrangement in the pre- and post-observation trials. Females significantly increased their preference for novel males wearing the reinforced band arrangement (whether that was the left- or the right-asymmetric band treatment) indicating that they copied apparent mate preferences displayed in the observation trials.

CONCLUSION

Our study indicates that observations of short bouts of stereotypical courtship are sufficient to stimulate mate choice copying in female zebra finches. This is important as unmated female zebra finches are very likely to observe other courting females over several days in natural conditions. These birds breed in small colonies where fledglings mature quickly (in a matter of months) and quickly join the breeding population (Zann 1996). A young female, maturing into her first breeding attempt, will consistently be surrounded by older breeding females from which she could copy a mate preference. Therefore, our results indicate that social information could affect mate choice decision making in wild birds. At the very least, we have shown that female zebra finches' mate preference decisions are altered by information about who other females court in the local population. Females shift their preference toward the phenotype of other courted males—they follow the current fashion in mate preferences. It is also relevant that observing courtship appears sufficient to elicit mate choice copying in other species, such as quail *Coturnix coturnix* (White & Galef 1999, 2000) and the guppy *Poecilia reticulata* (Dugatkin 1996b; Amlacher & Dugatkin 2005). However, our study is the first to show that courtship is a cue which guides mate choice decisions in a monogamous species.

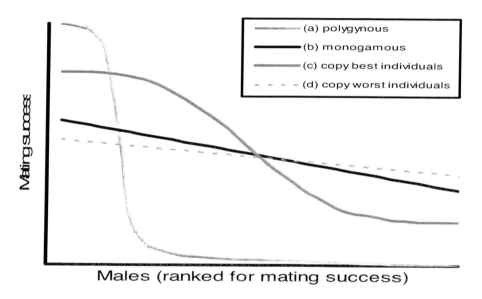

Figure 6. Hypothetical mating skew in (a) polygynous and (b) monogamous mating systems. In the polygynous situation a small number of males get most of the matings. In the monogamous mating system most males will get a mate in any one breeding season; hence, the slope of mating skew is much more shallow than in the polygynous situation. The slope of the mating skew curve indicates the strength of sexual selection acting on males. In the monogamous situation, if mate choice copying shifts mating toward the already successful males, the mating skew and strength of sexual selection can increase, as indicated by line (c) on the graph. However, if mate choice copying favors the least successful males, the mating skew could become flatter and sexual selection weaker, as indicated by line (d) on the graph. Therefore, this simple model can help visualize the outcome of decision making on the strength of sexual selection in a monogamous mating system where mate choice copying occurs.

As test females shifted their preference toward new males who wore the same band patterns as the courted males in the observation period, we provide further evidence that female zebra finches can generalize copied preferences to new males (Swaddle et al. 2005). In a species that mates for life (i.e., a male-female pair-bond is commonly only broken by death or emigration of either partner) this is an important finding, as mating can then be skewed toward unpaired (i.e., available) males who happen to share phenotypic characters with mated (or courted) males. Potentially, this could skew mating preferences toward particular male phenotypes, therefore increasing the strength of sexual selection for those particular traits (see Figure 6). An unanswered question is whether copied preferences for male traits can also skew extra-pair mating decisions (i.e., copulations and fertilizations outside the pair-bond). Although wild zebra finches show relatively low levels of extra-pair paternity (Birkhead et al. 1990), it is still possible that social information could mediate this small degree of fitness variation—which could have an effect on evolutionary processes. We postulate that social observations of courtship and/or copulations among other conspecifics may be a significant factor in affecting extra-pair mating decisions in other species. As yet, this question is unexplored from both empirical and theoretical perspectives.

Consistent with previous studies (Swaddle & Cuthill 1994b; Swaddle 1996), female finches preferred symmetrically banded males (Figure 4). Importantly, the pre-observation symmetry preference gave us the opportunity to examine how social information can affect a pre-existing mate preference. At least in terms of leg band symmetry preferences, copying of preferences indicated by biased courtship significantly eroded a pre-existing symmetry preference. Therefore, mate choice copying could change mate choice decisions sufficiently to alter evolutionary selection pressures; thereby increasing the evolutionary significance of this form of decision making.

Our study, in general, sheds light on the evolutionary significance of the decision making associated with mate choice copying. As stated above, our results indicate that social information could skew mating preferences consistently toward particular male phenotypes. However, the pattern and strength of this change in mating skew depends on cognitive processes. If female finches decide to copy the most successful (i.e., fittest) phenotype, then the slope of mating skew could easily increase (Figure 6). An increase in mating skew would result in stronger sexual selection pressures for that male phenotype. However, if mate preferences are copied at random, or the least successful phenotypes are copied, then the slope (and sexual selection pressure) could be reduced in some scenarios (Figure 6). As, by definition, the most successful males are the ones that are most likely to provide the courtship cues that could be copied, we hypothesize that the form of copying process we have indicated here has the potential to increase the strength of sexual selection, even in a monogamous species.

However, if the copied preferences are ephemeral and are quickly forgotten, or are easily replaced with other copied preferences, then the evolutionary implications are diminished. Copied preferences have to last over at least one genetic generation to have an evolutionary effect, but last for longer for noticeable directional change. Hence, copied preferences must also likely be stored in some form of longer term memory, further emphasizing the importance of exploring the cognitive processes involved in making a mate choice decision. Outside of one study reporting that copied preference can last for 24 hours in female sailfin mollies *Poecilia latipinna* (Witte & Massmann 2003), there is very little known about the erosion and stability of copied mate preferences. Our own preliminary data from a follow-up study of female zebra finch preferences indicates that copied preferences can last for over a month and, hence, can last between consecutive nesting attempts (J. P. Swaddle, unpublished data).

At this stage in our explorations it is not clear whether mate choice copying is adaptive in zebra finches. It is possible that what we have documented in this chapter and our previous study (Swaddle et al. 2005) is a by-product of other evolved cognitive and decision making processes. For example, zebra finches show sexual imprinting at a young age (Oetting & Bischof 1996; Bischof & Rollenhagen 1999; ten Cate & Vos 1999), in other words the mate preferences and sexual displays they exhibit at maturity are affected by the social (parental) environment in which chicks are raised. Perhaps these early age processes result in the ability of mature adults to acquire information about mate preferences, but that mate choice copying itself has not been directly selected for. Mate choice copying could be a by-product of selection for sexual imprinting.

Despite how mate choice copying evolved it is clear that these small birds use socially available courtship cues to develop their mate preferences. They appear to make decisions about which males to pay attention to and, further, they generalize the appearance of these apparently preferred males and apply that information to assessing new, unpaired males. Therefore, the experimental results we report here are an important step toward showing that mate choice copying and complex decision making play important roles in establishing mate preferences in a monogamous species. To extrapolate beyond the zebra finch, it may be that this form of decision making is much more prevalent than we commonly think. The zebra finch is a classic monogamous species, with low rates of extra-pair paternity (Birkhead et al. 1990; Burley et al. 1996). In other words, this species is both socially and genetically monogamous. Mate choice copying is not expected to be common in such situations and, hence, may be even more common in other socially monogamous species that show higher levels of extra-pair paternity (genetic polygamy). This would mean that mate choice copying and social decision making could occur in many monogamous species that have the opportunity to observe courtship among other individuals in the population. We predict that complex decision making and the social inheritance of mate preferences will be discovered in many other animals, including many socially monogamous species.

ACKNOWLEDGEMENTS

We thank Paul Heideman and Dan Cristol for comments on an earlier draft of this chapter. Funding was provided by the National Science Foundation (IOB-0133795 and EF-0436318) awards to JPS.

REFERENCES

Agrawal, A. A. (2001). The evolutionary consequences of mate copying on male traits. *Behavioral Ecology and Sociobiology, 51*, 33-40.

Amlacher, J., & Dugatkin, L. A. (2005). Preference for older over younger models during mate-choice copying in young guppies. *Ethology Ecology and Evolution, 17*, 161-169.

Andersson, M. (1994). *Sexual Selection*. Princeton, NJ: Princeton University Press.

Andersson, M., & Simmons, L. W. (2006). Sexual selection and mate choice. *Trends in Ecology and Evolution, 21*, 296-302.

Bennett, A. T. D., Cuthill, I. C., Partridge, J. C., & Maier, E. J. (1996). Ultraviolet vision and mate choice in zebra finches. *Nature, 380*, 433-435.

Birkhead, T. R., Burke, T., Zann, R. A., Hunter, F. M., & Krupa, A. P. (1990). Extrapair paternity and intraspecific brood parasitism in wild zebra finches, *Taeniopygia guttata*, revealed by DNA fingerprinting. *Behavioral Ecology and Sociobiology, 27,* 315-324.

Bischof, H.-J., & Rollenhagen, A. (1999). Behavioural and neurophysiological aspects of sexual imprinting in zebra finches. *Behavioural Brain Research, 98,* 267-276.

Brooks, R. (1998). The importance of mate copying and cultural inheritance of mating preferences. *Trends in Ecology and Evolution, 13,* 45-46.

Brooks, R. (1999). Mate choice copying in guppies: Females avoid the place where they saw courtship. *Behaviour, 136,* 411-421.

Brooks, R., & Endler, J. A. (2001). Female guppies agree to differ: Phenotypic and genetic variation in mate-choice behavior and the consequences for sexual selection. *Evolution, 55,* 1644-1655.

Brown, G. R., & Fawcett, T. W. (2005). Sexual selection: Copycat mating in birds. *Current Biology, 15,* R626-R628.

Burley, N. (1988). Wild zebra finches have band-colour preferences. *Animal Behaviour, 36,* 1235-1237.

Burley, N. T., Parker, P. G., & Lundy, K. (1996). Sexual selection and extrapair fertilization in a socially monogamous passerine, the zebra finch (*Taeniopygia guttata*). *Behavioral Ecology, 7,* 218-226.

Doucet, S. M., Yezerinac, S. M., & Montgomerie, R. (2004). Do female zebra finches (*Taeniopygia guttata*) copy each other's mate preferences? *Canadian Journal of Zoology, 82,* 1-7.

Dugatkin, L. A. (1996a). Copying and mate choice. In: Heyes, C. M., & Galef, B. G., Jr. (Eds.), *Social Learning in Animals: The Roots of Culture* (pp. 85-105). New York, NY: Academic Press.

Dugatkin, L. A. (1996b). The interface between culturally-based preferences and genetic preferences: female mate choice in *Poecilia reticulata. Proceedings of the National Academy of Sciences, USA, 93,* 2770-2773.

Dugatkin, L. A., & Godin, J. G. J. (1992). Reversal of female mate choice by copying in the guppy (*Poecilia reticulata*). *Proceedings of the Royal Society of London B, 249,* 179-184.

Dugatkin, L. A., & Godin, J. G. J. (1993). Female mate choice copying in the guppy (*Poecilia reticulata*): age dependent effects. *Behavioral Ecology, 4,* 289-292.

Freeberg, T. M., Duncan, S. D., Kast, T. L., & Enstrom, D. A. (1999). Cultural influences on female mate choice: an experimental test in cowbirds, *Molothrus ater. Animal Behaviour, 57,* 421-426.

Galef, B. G., & White, D. J. (2000). Evidence of social effects on mate choice in vertebrates. *Behavioural Processes, 51,* 167-175.

Godin, J. G. J., Herdman, E. J. E., & Dugatkin, L. A. (2005). Social influences on female mate choice in the guppy, Poecilia reticulata: generalized and repeatable trait-copying behaviour. *Animal Behaviour, 69,* 999-1005.

Greenfield, M. D., & Rodriguez, R. L. (2004). Genotype-environment interaction and the reliability of mating signals. *Animal Behaviour, 68,* 1461-1468.

Kirkpatrick, M., & Dugatkin, L. A. (1994). Sexual selection and the evolutionary effects of copying mate choice. *Behavioral Ecology and Sociobiology, 34,* 443-449.

Kokko, H., Brooks, R., Jennions, M. D., & Morley, J. (2003). The evolution of mate choice and mating biases. *Proceedings of the Royal Society of London B, 270,* 653-664.

Kokko, H., Brooks, R., McNamara, J. M., & Houston, A. I. (2002). The sexual selection continuum. *Proceedings of the Royal Society of London B, 269,* 1331-1340.

Laland, K. N. (1994). Sexual selection with a culturally transmitted mating preference. *Theoretical Population Biology, 45,* 1-15.

Lynch, K. S., Crews, D., Ryan, M. J., & Wilczynski, W. (2006). Hormonal state influences aspects of female mate choice in the Tungara Frog (Physalaemus pustulosus). *Hormones and Behavior, 49,* 450-457.

Lynch, K. S., Rand, A. S., Ryan, M. J., & Wilczynski, W. (2005). Plasticity in female mate choice associated with changing reproductive states. *Animal Behaviour, 69,* 689-699.

Oetting, S., & Bischof, H.-J. (1996). Sexual imprinting in female zebra finches: changes in preferences as an effect of adult experience. *Behaviour, 133,* 387-397.

Ophir, A. G., & Galef, B. G., Jr. (2004). Sexual experience can affect use of public information in mate choice. *Animal Behaviour, 68,* 1221-1227.

Patricelli, G. L., Uy, A. C., Walsh, G., & Borgia, G. (2002). Sexual selection: Male displays adjusted to female's response. *Nature, 415,* 279-280.

Pruett-Jones, S. (1992). Independent versus nonindependent mate choice - do females copy each other. *American Naturalist, 140,* 1000-1009.

Rodriguez, R. L., & Greenfield, M. D. (2003). Genetic variance and phenotypic plasticity in a component of female mate choice in an ultrasonic moth. *Evolution, 57,* 1304-1313.

Schlupp, I., & Ryan, M. J. (1997). Male sailfin mollies (*Poecilia latipinna*) copy the mate choice of other males. *Behavioral Ecology, 8,* 104-107.

Shuster, S. M., & Wade, M. J. (2003). *Mating Systems and Strategies.* Princeton, NJ: Princeton University Press.

Stohr, S. (1998). Evolution of mate-choice copying: a dynamic model. *Animal Behaviour, 55,* 893-903.

Swaddle, J. P. (1996). Reproductive success and symmetry in zebra finches. *Animal Behaviour, 51,* 203-210.

Swaddle, J. P., Cathey, M. G., Correll, M., & Hodkinson, B. P. (2005). Socially transmitted mate preferences in a monogamous bird: a non-genetic mechanism of sexual selection. *Proceedings of the Royal Society of London B, 272,* 1053-1058.

Swaddle, J. P., & Cuthill, I. C. (1994a). Female zebra finches prefer males with symmetric chest plumage. *Proceedings of the Royal Society of London B, 258,* 267-271.

Swaddle, J. P., & Cuthill, I. C. (1994b). Preference for symmetric males by female zebra finches. *Nature, 367,* 165-166.

ten Cate, C., & Vos, D. R. (1999). Sexual imprinting and evolutionary processes in birds: a reassessment. *Advances in the Study of Behavior, 28,* 1-31.

Uehara, T., Yokomizo, H., & Iwasa, Y. (2005). Mate-choice copying as Bayesian decision making. *American Naturalist, 165,* 403-410.

Waas, J. R., & Wordsworth, A. F. (1999). Female zebra finches prefer symmetrically banded males, but only during interactive mate choice tests. *Animal Behaviour, 57,* 1113-1119.

Welch, A. M. (2003). Genetic benefits of a female mating preference in gray tree frogs are context-dependent. *Evolution, 57,* 883-893.

Westneat, D. F., Walters, A., McCarthy, T. M., Hatch, M. I., & Hein, W. K. (2000). Alternative mechanisms of nonindependent mate choice. *Animal Behaviour, 59,* 467-476.

White, D. J., & Galef, B. G., Jr. (1999). Mate choice copying and conspecific cueing in Japanese quail, *Coturnix coturnix japonica. Animal Behaviour, 57,* 465-473.

White, D. J., & Galef, B. G., Jr. (2000). 'Culture' in quail: social influences on mate choices of
  female *Coturnix japonica*. *Animal Behaviour*, *59*, 975-979.
Witte, K., & Massmann, R. (2003). Female saiflin mollies, *Poecilia latipinna*, remember
  males and copy the choice of others after 1 day. *Animal Behaviour*, *65*, 1151-1159.
Zann, R. A. (1996). *The Zebra Finch: A Synthesis of Field and Laboratory Studies*. Oxford,
  UK: Oxford University Press.

In: Psychology of Decision Making in Education
Editor: Jeanine A. Elsworth, pp. 271-281

ISBN: 978-1-60021-933-7
© 2006 Nova Science Publishers, Inc.

Chapter 13

DEVELOPMENTAL TRENDS IN DECISION MAKING: THE CASE OF THE MONTY HALL DILEMMA

Wim De Neys[1]

University of Leuven, Tiensestraat 102
3000 Leuven, Belgium

ABSTRACT

The Monty Hall Dilemma (MHD) is a notorious brain-teaser where people have to decide whether switching to another option in a game is advantageous. Most adults erroneously believe that chances of winning remain equal or that they should stick to their original choice. The present study tested the impact of cognitive development on MHD reasoning to examine possible differences in the nature of the erroneous intuitions. Twelve to seventeen year old high school students were presented the MHD and selected one of three responses (switch, stick, or chances equal). Results showed that whereas maturation decreased adherence to the erroneous "stick with your first pick" belief, the "chances are equal" belief became more dominant with increasing age. Consistent with predictions, children who selected the latter response also scored better on a syllogistic reasoning task. Results further showed that twelve year old eighth graders selected the correct switching response more frequently than senior high school students. Implications for popular reasoning and decision making theories are discussed.

[1] Correspondence to: Lab Experimentele Psychologie, K.U. Leuven Tiensestraat 102 3000 Leuven Belgium, E-mail: Wim.Deneys@psy.kuleuven.be, Homepage : http://ppw.kuleuven.be/reason/wim/, Fax: +32 16 326099 Tel: +32 16 326143

DEVELOPMENTAL TRENDS IN MONTY HALL DILEMMA REASONING

Imagine you're the final guest in a TV quiz. Monty, the show host, is asking you to choose one of three doors. One of the doors conceals a BMW sports car but the two other doors only contain a bunch of toilet paper. If you choose the right door you will be the proud owner of the fancy BMW. However, after you finally select one of the doors, host Monty does not open it immediately. First, he opens one of the doors you did not choose to reveal it contained toilet paper. Monty now actually offers you the possibility to chance your mind and pick the other unopened door. What should you do to have most chance of winning the car of your dreams? Stay with your first choice, switch to the other unopened door, or doesn't it matter whether you switch or not?

The above switching problem is known as the "Monty Hall Dilemma" (MHD) after the host of the American TV show "Let's make a deal" where it was introduced. Contrary to most people's intuition the correct answer is that switching to the other door will actually increase the chance of winning. The counter-intuitive solution hinges on the crucial fact that Monty will never open the door concealing the prize, and obviously, he will not open the door the guest initially picked either. The probability that you initially select the correct door is one out of three. In this case it would be better not to switch. However, in the other two thirds of the cases the non-chosen closed door will hide the prize and switching is advantageous. Hence, switching yields a 2/3 chance of winning.

If you failed to solve the problem correctly you may find some comfort in the fact that you're in good company. Empirical studies show that typically less than 10% of educated adults give the correct switching response (e.g., Burns & Wieth, 2004; Friedman, 1998; Granberg & Brown, 1995; Krauss & Wang, 2003; Tubau & Alonso, 2003) and even ace mathematicians do not seem to be immune to MHD errors (e.g., Burns & Wieth; vos Savant, 1997). Most people have the strong intuition that whether they switch or not the probability of winning remains 50% either way. Research indicates that this powerful intuition is based on the so called number-of-cases heuristic ("if the number of alternatives is N, then the probability of each one is 1/N", see Shimojo & Ichikawa, 1989, and Falk, 1992). Since only two doors remain people will automatically assign a 50% chance to each door and fail to take the "knowledgeable host" information into account. The "equal chance" heuristic is so self-evident that it will literally dominate our thinking.

Over the last decades numerous studies have demonstrated that similar intuitive responses are biasing people's performance in a wide range of reasoning tasks (e.g., Evans & Over, 1996; Kahneman, Slovic, & Tversky, 1982). Influential dual process theories of reasoning and decision making have explained this "rational thinking failure" by positing two different human reasoning systems (e.g., Epstein, 1994; Evans, 2003; Evans & Over, 1996; Sloman, 1996; Stanovich & West, 2000). Dual process theories come in many flavours but generally they assume that a first system (often called the heuristic system) will tend to solve a problem by relying on intuitions and prior beliefs whereas a second system (often called the analytic system) allows reasoning according to normative standards. The heuristic default system is assumed to operate fast and automatically whereas the operations of the analytic system would be slow and heavily demanding of people's computational resources. Although the fast and undemanding heuristics can provide us with useful responses in many daily situations they can bias reasoning in tasks that require more elaborate, analytic processing (e.g., Sloman, 1996; Stanovich & West, 2000; Tversky & Kahneman, 1983). That is, both systems will sometimes conflict and cue different responses. In these cases the analytic system will need to override the automatically generated intuitive response. Since the inhibition of the heuristic intuitions and the computations of the analytic system draw heavily on people's limited cognitive resources, most people will be tempted to stick to mere intuitive reasoning. Therefore, correct analytic reasoning would be characteristic of those highest in cognitive capacity (Stanovich & West, 2000).

De Neys and Verschueren (2006) recently examined the relation between people's cognitive capacities and Monty Hall reasoning. Over 200 participants were presented the MHD and a test to measure their working memory capacity. Consistent with Stanovich and West's (2000) dual process predictions participants who did manage to solve the MHD correctly were specifically those highest in working memory span. Experimentally burdening the cognitive resources with a secondary task also decreased the rate of correct switching responses. These findings supported the basic claim that the analytic override of heuristic thinking draws on people's cognitive working memory resources.

Although the dual process framework has been quite influential in the reasoning and decision making community it has also been criticized severely (e.g., Gigerenzer & Regier, 1996; see commentaries on Evans & Over, 1997, or Stanovich & West, 2000, for an overview). One of the critiques focuses on the the framework's postulation of a single heuristic system that unitarily handles all intuitive processing. It has been argued that different kinds of heuristics, with a different processing nature, need to be differentiated (e.g., De Neys, 2006a; Gigerenzer & Regier, 1996; Moshman, 2000; Newton & Roberts, 2003). De Neys and Verschueren's (2006) study pointed to an MHD trend that is specifically interesting in this respect. Note that one can distinguish different erroneous MHD responses. Whereas the vast majority of reasoners is biased by the number-of-cases heuristic and beliefs that switching or sticking does not matter, a small group of reasoners is convinced that they should stick to the initially selected door to win the prize. These people are biased by the general belief that when making a decision one should always stick to one's first choice. Such a bias has long been noted in responses to multiple-choice exams (e.g., Geiger, 1997). Gilovich, Medvec, and Chen (1995) clarified that this "stick with your pick" intuition would be based on an anticipation of regret.

De Neys and Verschueren (2006) found that reasoners in the group of erroneous responders who selected the "equal chances" response tended to have a slightly higher working memory span than those who believed that "sticking" was advantageous. Moreover, the secondary task load specifically boosted the rate of "sticking" responses whereas the selection of "chances equal" responses was hardly affected. Although the trends were not significant, De Neys and Verschueren noted that the two types of heuristic beliefs might indeed have a different processing nature. The number-of-cases heuristic would be based on a cognitive probability estimation (albeit a simple one) whereas the "stick with your pick" heuristic would have a more elementary, affective basis. Hence, the "chances are even" heuristic would be computationally more complex than the "stick with your pick" heuristic. Therefore, the more elementary, least demanding "stick with your pick" response would be the preferred answer under conditions of cognitive load.

De Neys and Verschueren (2006) suggested that in their sample of university students the trends presumably failed to reach significance because the basic number-of-cases computation would be completely automatic for educated adults. Consequently, the distinction with the alleged less demanding "sticking" responses would be blurred. The present study adopts a developmental approach to clarify the issue. The MHD was presented to twelve to seventeen year old adolescents. A first prediction concerned the selection rates of the different MHD responses in the different age groups. Younger reasoners have smaller cognitive resource pools and still lack an important part of the mathematical training that familiarized university students with fractions and probabilities. Therefore, one can expect that computation of the number-of-cases heuristic will be less automated and more demanding in the younger age groups. This should result in a less frequent selection of "equal chances" responses by younger reasoners. Under the assumption that the "stick with your pick" heuristic is more basic one predicts that younger reasoners will show a stronger preference for the "stick" responses. The alleged differential demands of the "stick" and "equal" heuristics should thus result in a specific developmental trend: The rate of "chances equal" responses should increase with age whereas the "sticking" responses should decrease. Given the high computational demands of the correct switching response for adult university students, correct MHD reasoning in the younger age groups was not expected.

A second prediction concerns the overall relation between young adolescents' responses and their cognitive capacity. After the students had solved the MHD they were also presented a specific syllogistic reasoning task where they had to inhibit automated responses. Previous studies established that this task is a good marker of children's general cognitive ability (e.g., Kokis, Macpherson, Toplak, West, & Stanovich, 2004). De Neys and Verschueren (2006) argued that the completely automated computation of the "equal chances" response in their sample of university students blurred the distinction with the alleged undemanding "sticking" responses. The less automated and more demanding nature of the number-of-cases heuristic for the younger reasoners (vs. adults) should show a clearer distinction. Therefore, it is predicted that youngsters who manage to give the "chances are equal" response will score better on the syllogisms than those who believe that mere sticking is the best strategy.

The developmental MHD trends will help clarifying possible differences in the nature of different heuristics. In addition, examining children's MHD performance will also have interesting implications for a fundamental controversy concerning the development of reasoning and decision making itself. The dual process framework and many developmental theories (e.g., Case, 1985; Inhelder & Piaget, 1985) share the assumption that children's reasoning becomes less heuristic and more logical across the lifespan. Hence, traditionally it has been assumed that analytic thinking simply replaces heuristic thinking with cognitive maturation. Recent developmental reasoning studies have argued against this so-called "illusion of replacement" (e.g., Brainerd & Reyna, 2001; Reyna & Ellis, 1994). Klaczynski (2001), for example, showed that whereas in some tasks (e.g., reasoning about sunk costs) the heuristic appeal indeed decreased with age, other tasks showed the opposite pattern and indicated that heuristic reasoning remained constant or increased with age (e.g., denominator neglect in statistical reasoning). Such findings are already hard to reconcile with the traditional view. The present MHD study allows a direct validation of the replacement claim within one and the same task. Based on the traditional view one would simply expect that both types of erroneous MHD responses will decrease with age and will be replaced by a higer number of correct responses. Evidence for the predicted differential developmental "equal chances" and "sticking" trends will cut the ground under the replacement view.

METHOD

Participants

A total of 132 high school students in grades 8 to 12 participated in the study. Forty-two students attended eighth grade (mean age = 12.9, SD = .91), 25 attended ninth grade (mean age = 14.64, SD = .64), 20 students were in grade 10 (mean age = 15.75, SD = 1.02), 16 were in grade 11 (mean age = 16.56, SD = .63), and 29 in grade 12 (mean age = 17.66, SD = .69). Students in grades 9/10 and grades 11/12 were collapsed in two age groups for the analyses. All participants were recruited from the same suburban school with socially mixed catchments areas. All spoke Dutch as their first language and had no known behavioral problems or learning difficulties.

Material

Monty Hall Dilemma. Students were presented a version of the MHD based on Krauss and Wang (2003, see De Neys & Verschueren, 2006). The formulation tried to avoid possible ambiguities (e.g., the random placement of the prize and duds behind the doors and the knowledge of the host were explicitly mentioned). As in Tubau and Alonso (2003), participants could choose between three answer alternatives (a. Stick – b. Switch – c. Chances are even). The complete problem format is presented bellow:

Suppose you're on a game show and you're given the choice of three doors. Behind one door is the main prize (a car) and behind the other two doors there are dud prizes (a bunch of toilet paper). The car and the dud prizes are placed randomly behind the doors before the show. The rules of the game are as follows: After you have chosen a door, the door remains closed for the time being. The game show host, Monty Hall, who knows what is behind the doors, then opens one of the two remaining doors which always reveals a dud. After he has opened one of the doors with a dud, Monty Hall asks the participants whether they want to stay with their first choice or to switch to the last remaining door. Suppose that you chose door 1 and the host opens door 3, which has a dud.

The host now asks you whether you want to switch to door 2. What should you do to have most chance of winning the main prize?

    a.   Stick with your first choice, door 1.
    b.   Switch to door 2.
    c.   It does not matter. Chances are even.

The MHD was presented on computer. Participants were instructed to carefully read the basic problem information first. When they were finished reading they pressed the ENTER-key and then the question and answer-alternatives (underscored text) appeared on the screen (other text remained on the screen). Participants typed their response (a, b, or c) on the keyboard. Instructions stated there were no time limits.

Syllogistic Reasoning Task. The syllogistic reasoning task was based on Sá, West, and Stanovich (1999). Participants evaluated four syllogisms taken from the work of Markovits and Nantel (1989) whereby the logical status of the conclusion conflicted with its believability (e.g., a valid but unbelievable conclusion like 'All mammals can walk. Whales are mammals. Therefore, whales can walk'). Thus, in order to give a correct response the reasoner has to override the tendency to judge the conclusion based on its believabilty. Individual differences studies (e.g., De Neys, 2006b; Stanovich & West, 2000; Newstead, Handley, Harley, Wright, Farrelly, 2004) and developmental research (Kokis et al., 2004) suggest that performance on this task is a good marker of cognitive capacity as measured with classic intelligence or working memory tests[2].

Procedure

Participants were tested in groups during a course break. The MHD was presented before the syllogistic reasoning task.

RESULTS

Figure 1 shows the selection rates of the three possible MHD responses in the different age groups. For completeness, rates are shown for every grade separately. Performance of university students in De Neys and Verschueren's (2006) study is also plotted for comparison.

As Figure 1 shows, twelve year old eighth graders have no clear preference for the "chances are equal" or "stick with your pick" response. Both are selected by about 45% of the eighth graders. As expected, however, the number-of-cases heuristic is becoming more and more dominant in the older age groups. The preference for the "stick" response, on the other hand, decreases with age. To test these trends statistically students in grades 9/10 and 11/12 were collapsed in two age groups. Selection rates in these two groups were compared with selection rates in grade 8. This resulted in an approximately equal n in the three age groups. Cochran's Q test showed that the increase in the proportion of "chances are equal" responses from grade 8, over grade 9/10, to grade 11/12 was significant, $Q(2)= 21.44$, $p < .0001$. The decrease in "sticking" responses over the three age groups also reached significance, $Q(2)= 16.91$, $p < .001$. These findings are consistent with the claim that the "stick with your pick" belief is based on a more basic and computationally less complex heuristic than the "chances are equal" belief. Cognitive maturation and mathematical training during the high school years seem to be especially boosting the number-of-cases heuristic.

---

[2] Time-constraints and school policy prevented the administration of more classic ability tests.

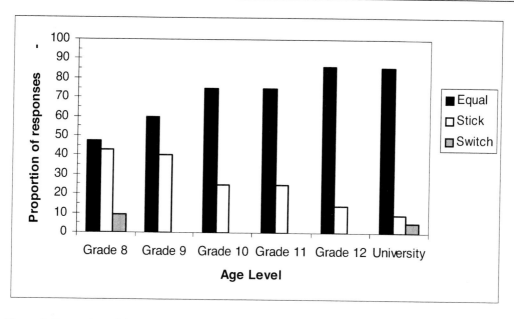

Figure 1. Proportion of the three possible Monty Hall Dilemma responses in different age groups.

None of the students in grades 9 to 12 managed to give the correct switching response on the standard MHD. However, the youngest participants in our study, the twelve to thirteen year old eighth graders, showed about 10% switching responses. The decrease in switching responses over the three high school age levels also reached significance, Cochran $Q(2) = 10$, $p < .01$. The finding that twelve year olds outperform senior high school (and even university) students might seem surprising at first sight. However, we believe that the higher rate of correct responding for the eighth graders can be described as a "Less Is More Effect". Adults' reasoning is impeded precisely because of the automated nature of the "50%" response. For adults the "equal chance" heuristic is so self-evident that it literally dominates their reasoning. For a twelve year old the conclusion that since two doors remain both will have a 50% chance of hiding the prize will be less evident and will require active, resource demanding computation. Bluntly put, for younger reasoners the switching response will be less counter-intuitive than for adults. In this sense children thus actually benefit from a lack of knowledge. This issue is further addressed in the General Discussion.

Students' performance on the syllogistic reasoning task was taken as a measure of their general cognitive ability. It was predicted that for less mature reasoners computation of the "chances are equal" response would be less automated than for adult, university students. Therefore, in the present younger age group the two response types should show a better differentiation in terms of cognitive capacity. The "chances are equal" heuristic is assumed to be more demanding than the "stick with your pick" intuition. Consequently it was predicted that children with a larger resource pool would be more likely to arrive at the "equal" response. This hypothesis was confirmed. Overall, students who selected the "equal" response solved 43% of the syllogisms correctly (mean score = 1.70, SD = 1.27) whereas students who believed that sticking was beneficial only solved 28% correctly (mean score = 1.12, SD = 1.08), $t(125) = 2.50$, n1 = 86, n2 = 41, $p < .015$, d = .48.

The eighth graders were the only students who gave switching responses. For completeness we compared the syllogistic reasoning performance of eighth graders who gave correct and incorrect responses. There were no significant differences between the two groups. Interestingly, contrary to the university students in De Neys and Verschueren's (2006) study, eighth graders who selected the switching response actually tended to score lower on the measure of executive capacities (19% correct conclusions) than the eighth graders who erroneously selected the "sticking" or "chances equal" responses (28% correct conclusions). This is consistent with the idea that selecting the switching response for eighth graders is based on an intuitive rather than an executive resource demanding reasoning process.

GENERAL DISCUSSION

The present study explored developmental trends in children's reasoning about the Monty Hall Dilemma (MHD). By comparing the MHD performance in different age groups, possible differences in the nature of erroneous intuitions were examined. Previous MHD studies distinguished at least two types of erroneous MHD reasoning (e.g., De Neys & Verschueren, 2006; Gilovich et al., 1995; Tubau & Alonso, 2003). Participants could indicate they believed that switching and sticking had both a 50% chance of winning or they could indicate they believed that sticking to the first chosen door was advantageous. Based on trends in the work of De Neys and Verschueren it was hypothesized that the "stick with your pick" response would be more elementary and computationally less demanding than the "chances are equal" response. Consistent with this claim results showed that maturation over the high school years boosted the dominance of the "chances are equal" heuristic. Children who selected this response also scored higher on an indirect measure of cognitive capacity than those who preferred the "sticking" response. These findings support the idea that the two heuristic responses differ in computational complexity. For educated adults, however, the computation of the "50%" heuristic would become fully automated. Indeed, it is precisely the automated, self-evident, and intuitive nature of this heuristic that is supposed to be impeding university students' reasoning.

Results further showed that the youngest reasoners in the study outperformed senior high school or university students. Twelve and thirteen year old eighth graders showed about 10% correct responses. It is interesting to note that such apparently counter-intuitive developmental findings have also been observed with other classic reasoning tasks. Jacobs and Potenza (1991), for example, studied children's performance on the notorious base-rate neglect problems (e.g., the lawyer-engineer problem, Kahneman & Tversky, 1973). In these tasks, salient, stereotypical information is pitted against more reliable statistical base rate information. When a person is described as an engineer, adults will conclude it is an engineer although they were told that the person was drawn from a sample were there were twice as many lawyers than engineers. The vast majority of educated adults typically neglect the statistical base rate information. Jacobs and Potenza observed that the base rate neglect decreased with decreasing age. As Kokis et al. (2004) argued, the finding that younger children err less frequently on these problems is not surprising because stereotype knowledge is typically less developed for children. Since children lack knowledge of many social stereotypes, they may seem to be using base-rate information more, simply because the potentially biasing information is unavailable to them. As with the present findings, the point is not that twelve year olds are actively computing the correct base rate or switching response but rather that twelve year olds are less tempted by the heuristics that are impeding adults' reasoning.

The present MHD trends support the rejection of the "illusion of replacement" in the developmental literature (e.g., Brainerd & Reyna, 2001). Traditionally, reasoning and decision making researchers have characterized cognitive development as a process whereby children's reasoning becomes less heuristic and more in line with logical standards. Recent developmental studies started cutting the ground under this view (e.g., Klaczynski, 2001). The present study strengthens this critique by showing that different heuristics can follow a different developmental path. This further dismisses the "illusion of replacement" as a simplistic idealization.

The work of De Neys and Verschueren (2006) stipulated that limitations in working memory resources cannot be neglected as cause of erroneous MHD reasoning. For educated adults, sidestepping salient intuitions and selecting the correct switching response will be compromised by a lack of cognitive resources. These findings fitted well with dual process theories' characterization of the *analytic* reasoning system. The present study clarifies that at the same time one must bear in mind that more extreme resource shortages for less mature or gifted reasoners might also compromise the automated cueing of erroneous heuristics itself. Moreover, the developmental findings seriously question the framework's characterization of the *heuristic* system as a unitary system that handles all intuitive processing uniformly (e.g., De Neys, Schaeken, & d'Ydewalle, 2005). The present MHD results stress that different kinds of heuristics, with a different processing nature, need to be differentiated. One and the same heuristic might be differentially computed by different groups of participants: A heuristic that is automatically triggered for one group of participants might require active cognitive resource demanding computations for a younger and/or less gifted group of reasoners. In line with recent critiques, dual process theories need to take this diversity into account in order to fully characterize the processing specifications of the two reasoning systems.

ACKNOWLEDGEMENTS

Wim De Neys is post doctoral fellow of the Fund for Scientific Research-Flanders (FWO-Vlaanderen). I would like to thank Ellen Gillard and Deborah Everaerts for their help testing the high school students. Parts of this study were presented at the 27th Annual Conference of the Cognitive Science Society, Stresa, Italy.

REFERENCES

Brainerd, C. J., & Reyna, V. F. (2001). Fuzzy-trace theory : Dual processes in memory, reasoning, and cognitive neuroscience. In H. W. Reese & R. Kail (Eds.), *Advances in child development and behavi*or (Vol. 28, pp. 41-100). San Diego: Academic Press.

Burns, B. D., & Wieth, M. (2004). The collider principle in causal reasoning: Why the monty hall dilemma is so hard. *Journal of Experimental Psychology: General, 133,* 434-449.

Case, R. (1985). *Intellectual development: Birth to adulthood.* New York: Academic Press.

De Neys, W. (2006a). Automatic-heuristic and executive-analytic processing in reasoning: Chronometric and dual task considerations. *Quarterly Journal of Experimental Psychology, 59,* 1070-1100.

De Neys, W. (2006b). Dual processing in reasoning: Two systems but one reasoner. *Psychological Science, 17,* 428-433.

De Neys, W., & Verschueren, N. (2006). Working memory capacity and a notorious brain teaser: The case of the Monty Hall Dilemma. *Experimental Psychology, 53,* 123-131

De Neys, W., Schaeken, W., & d'Ydewalle, G. (2005). Working memory and counterexample retrieval for causal conditionals. *Thinking & Reasoning, 11,* 123-150.

Epstein, S. (1994). Integration of the cognitive and psychodynamic unconscious. *American Psychologist, 49,* 709-724.

Evans, J. St. B. T. (2003). In two minds: Dual-process accounts of reasoning. *Trends in Cognitive Sciences, 7,* 454-459.

Evans, J. St. B. T., & Over, D. E. (1996). *Rationality and reasoning.* Hove, UK: Psychology Press.

Evans, J. St. B. T., & Over, D. E. (1997). Rationality in reasoning: The problem of deductive competence. *Current Psychology of Cognition, 16,* 3-38.

Falk, R. (1992). A closer look at the probabilities of the notorious three prisoners. *Cognition, 77,* 197-213.

Friedman, D. (1998). Monty Hall's three doors: Construction and deconstruction of a choice anomaly. *American Economic Review, 88,* 933-946.

Geiger, M. A. (1997). Educators' warnings about changing examination answers: Effects on students perceptions and performance. *College Student Journal, 31,* 429-432.

Gigerenzer, G., & Regier, T. (1996). How do we tell an association from a rule?: Comment on Sloman (1996). *Psychological Bulletin, 119,* 23-26.

Gilovich, T., Medvec, V. H., & Chen, S. (1995). Commission, omission, and dissonance reduction: Coping with regret in the "Monty Hall" problem. *Personality and Social Psychology Bulletin, 21,* 185-190.

Granberg, D., & Brown, T. A. (1995). The Monty Hall dilemma. *Personality and Social Psychology Bulletin, 21,* 182-190.

Inhelder, B., & Piaget, J. (1958). *The growth of logical thinking from childhood to adolescence.* New York: Basic books.

Jacobs, J. E., & Potenza, M. (1991). The use of judgment heuristics to make social and object decisions: A developmental perspective. *Child Development, 62,* 166-178.

Kahneman, D., Slovic, P., & Tversky, A. (1982). *Judgement under uncertainty: Heuristics and biases.* Cambridge, MA: Cambridge University Press.

Kahneman, D., & Tversky, A. (1973). On the psychology of prediction. *Psychological Review, 80,* 237-251.

Klaczynski, P. A. (2001). Framing effects on adolescent task representation, analytic and heuristic processing, and decision making: Implications for the normative/descriptive gap. *Applied Developmental Psychology, 22,* 289-309.

Kokis, J. V., Macpherson, R., Toplak, M. E., West, R. F., & Stanovich, K. E. (2002). Heuristic and analytic processing: Age trends and associations with cognitive ability and cognitive styles. *Journal of Experimental Child Psychology, 83,* 26-52.

Krauss, S., & Wang, X. T. (2003). The psychology of the Monty Hall Problem: Discovering psychological mechanisms for solving a tenacious brain teaser. *Journal of Experimental Psychology: General, 132*, 3-22.

Markovits, H., & Nantel, G. (1989). The belief bias effect in the production and evaluation of logical conclusions. *Memory and Cognition, 17*, 11-17.

Moshman, D. (2000). Diversity in reasoning and rationality: Metacognitive and developmental considerations. *Behavioral and Brain Sciences, 23*, 689-690.

Newstead, S. E., Handley, S. J., Harley, C., Wright, H., Farrelly, D. (2004). Individual differences in deductive reasoning. *Quarterly Journal of Experimental Psychology, 57A*, 33-60.

Newton, E. J., & Roberts, M. J. (2003). Individual differences transcend the rationality debate. *Behavioral and Brain Sciences, 26*, 530-531.

Reyna, V. F., & Ellis, S. (1994). Fuzzy-trace theory and framing effects in children's risky decision making. *Psychological Science, 5*, 275-279.

Sá, W., West, R. F., & Stanovich, K. E. (1999). The domain specificity and generality of belief bias: Searching for a generalizable critical thinking skill. *Journal of Educational Psychology, 91*, 497-510.

Shimojo, S., & Ichikawa, S. (1989). Intuitive reasoning about probability: Theoretical and experimental analysis of the "problem of three prisoners". *Cognition, 32*, 1-24.

Sloman, S. A. (1996). The empirical case for two systems of reasoning. *Psychological Bulletin, 119*, 3-22.

Stanovich, K. E., & West, R. F. (2000). Individual differences in reasoning: Implications for the rationality debate. *Behavioral and Brain Sciences, 23*, 645-726.

Tubau, E., & Alonso, D. (2003). Overcoming illusory inferences in a probabilistic counterintuitive problem : The role of explicit representations. *Memory & Cognition, 31*, 596-607.

Tversky, A., & Kahneman, D. (1983). Extensional versus intuitive reasoning: The conjunction fallacy in probability judgment. *Psychological Review, 90*, 293-315.

Vos Savant, M. (1997). *The power of logical thinking*. New York: St. Martin's Press.

INDEX

H

habitat, 147
hands, 50, 173, 177, 179, 181, 197
happiness, 38, 39
harmful effects, 255
harvesting, 144, 152
hazards, 79, 80, 97, 169, 172, 200
head trauma, 172
health, 8, 9, 126, 130, 131, 135, 137, 138, 139, 142, 176, 192, 196, 197, 201
health care, 131, 135, 138
health services, 131, 135
heart disease, 167
height, 15
hepatitis, 140
heterogeneity, 130
heterozygote, 219
heuristic processing, 280
high school, xii, 17, 41, 53, 70, 126, 127, 128, 130, 131, 132, 133, 134, 135, 136, 137, 138, 141, 142, 254, 271, 275, 276, 277, 278, 279
high scores, 53, 78, 83
higher education, xi, 243
histogram, 29
HIV, 138, 140
homozygote, 219
honesty, 10, 233
honey bees, 122
Hong Kong, 7, 243, 253, 255
hormone, 226
hospitals, 131
host, 157, 272, 275
hotels, 166
House, 69, 70, 71, 138
housing, 262, 263
human animal, x, 106, 107, 207, 222
human behavior, 8
human brain, 3, 223
human development, 137
human motivation, 2
human subjects, 107
human welfare, 8
hunting, 222
hypothesis, 38, 53, 61, 95, 109, 111, 114, 115, 118, 122, 136, 155, 161, 190, 212, 214, 219, 222, 226, 228, 237, 250, 251, 277

I

idealization, 279
identification, 76, 92, 93, 131, 205
identity, 3, 230, 252, 254
illusion, 239, 274, 279
illusions, 181
images, 39, 93
imagination, 187
imaging, 225
Immanuel Kant, 50
implementation, vii, 7, 9, 41, 58, 59, 130, 131, 153, 244, 245
imprinting, 267, 268, 269
impulsive, 113, 115, 119, 120, 123, 210
impulsiveness, 76, 118, 122
impulsivity, 75, 76, 119, 120
incidence, 76
inclusion, 34, 79, 236
income, 2, 15, 22, 31, 32, 38, 78, 83, 89, 100, 102, 127
indecisiveness, 252
independence, 84, 89, 102, 103, 104, 117, 121, 126, 189, 245, 246
independent variable, 236, 237, 249
indication, 135
indicators, 81, 82, 84
indices, 83, 84, 89, 244, 245, 246
indigenous, 250
indirect effect, 251
indirect measure, 278
individual development, 246
individual differences, 115, 211, 244, 245
induced bias, 12, 26, 27, 28
industrialized countries, 74
inferences, 159, 228, 229, 231, 240, 241, 281
inferiority, 64
inflation, 122
information processing, 1, 2, 3, 62
informational access, 233, 237, 241
informed consent, 249
ingestion, 178
inheritance, xii, 257, 267, 268
inhibition, 225, 273
inhibitor, 224
injuries, 74, 95, 139, 172
innovation, 59, 61, 194
input, xi, 9, 65, 181, 227
insects, 115, 145, 153
insight, 8, 28, 37, 93, 229, 231, 234, 236
inspiration, 9
instability, 76, 179
institutions, 129
instruction, 49, 52, 54, 59, 60, 69, 70, 127, 129, 142, 204, 217
instructional activities, 60
instructors, 63, 64

Q

R

S

U

V

W

Y

BF448 .P97 2007

Psychology of decision
making in education,
c2007.

2008 11 20

0 1341 1133952 6

Due Date		
Oct 12/09	JUN TYPE	OCT 0 8 2010
	OCT 0 7 2010	

www.library.humber.ca

RECEIVED

JAN 1 4 2009

GUELPH HUMBER LIBRARY
205 Humber College Blvd
Toronto, ON   M9W 5L7